A Special Issue of
The Quarterly Journal of Experimental Psychology

Neurocognitive Approaches to Developmental Disorders: A Festschrift for Uta Frith

Edited by

Dorothy V. M. Bishop
University of Oxford, Oxford, UK

Margaret J. Snowling
University of York, York, UK

and

Sarah-Jayne Blakemore
University College London, London, UK

 Psychology Press
Taylor & Francis Group
HOVE AND NEW YORK

First published 2008 by Psychology Press
27 Church Road, Hove, East Sussex BN3 2FA

www.psypress.com

Simultaneously published in the USA and Canada
by Psychology Press
270 Madison Avenue, New York NY 10016

Psychology Press is an imprint of the Taylor & Francis Group, an Informa business

British Library Cataloguing in Publication Data
A catalogue record for this book is available from the British Library

ISBN: 978–1–84169–839–7
ISSN: 1747–0218

Cover design by Anú Design, Tara, Co. Meath, Ireland.
Typeset in the UK by Techset Composition Ltd, Salisbury, Wiltshire.
Printed in the UK by Hobbs the Printers Ltd, Totton, Hampshire.
Bound in the UK by TJ International Ltd, Padstow, Cornwall.

The publication has been produced with paper manufactured to strict
environmental standards and with pulp derived from sustainable forests.

CONTENTS*

---

*This book is also a special issue of the *Quarterly Journal of Experimental Psychology*, and forms issue 1 of Volume 61 (2008).

Photographer: George Kaim, UCL Institute of Neurology

THE QUARTERLY JOURNAL OF EXPERIMENTAL PSYCHOLOGY
2008, 61 (1), 3–10

Ψ Psychology Press
Taylor & Francis Group

Uta Frith Bibliography

Aurnhammer-Frith, U. (1969). Emphasis and meaning in recall in normal and autistic children. *Language and Speech, 12*, 29–38.

Frith, U., & Hermelin, B. (1969). The role of visual and motor cures for normal, subnormal and autistic children. *Journal of Child Psychology and Psychiatry, 10*, 153–163.

Frith, U. (1970). Memory coding for binary sequences in children. *Quarterly Journal of Experimental Psychology, 22*, 618–630.

Frith, U. (1970). Studies in pattern detection: II. Reproduction and production of color sequences. *Journal of Experimental Child Psychology, 10*, 120–135.

Frith, U. (1970). Studies in pattern detection in normal and autistic children: I. Immediate recall of auditory sequences. *Journal of Abnormal Psychology, 76*, 413–420.

Frith, U. (1971). Spontaneous patterns produced by autistic, normal and subnormal children. In M. Rutter (Ed.), *Infantile autism: Concepts, characteristics and treatment* (pp. 113–135). London: Churchill Livingstone.

Frith, U. (1971). Why do children reverse letters? *British Journal of Psychology, 62*, 459–468.

Hermelin, B., & Frith, U. (1971). Psychological studies of childhood autism. Can autistic children make sense of what they see and hear? *Journal of Special Education, 5*, 107–117.

Frith, C. D., & Frith, U. (1972). The Solitaire Illusion: An illusion of numerosity. *Perceptions and Psychophysics, 11*, 409–410.

Frith, U. (1972). Cognitive mechanisms in autism: Experiments with color and tone sequence production. *Journal of Autism and Childhood Schizophrenia, 2*, 160–173.

Frith, U. (1972). The Georgian school of psychology: Impressions from a visit to Tbilisi. *Bulletin of the British Psychological Society, 25*, 197–201.

Frith, U. (1973). The application of experimental techniques to assessment. A discussion of A. D. B. Clarke & A. M. Clarke: "Assessment and Prediction". In P. Mittler (Ed.), *Assessment and planning learning for the mentally handicapped* (pp. 39–43). Edinburgh and London: Churchill Livingstone.

O'Connor, N., & Frith, U. (1973). Cognitive development and the concept of set. In A. S. Prangishvili (Ed.), *Psychological investigations dedicated to the 85th anniversary of the birth of D. N. Uznadze* (pp. 296–300). Tbilisi: Metsniereba.

Frith, C. D., & Frith, U. (1974). Sorting complex objects: A developmental study. *Bulletin of the British Psychological Society, 27*, 143–143.

Frith, U. (1974). A curious effect of reversed letters explained by a theory of schema. *Perceptions and Psychophysics, 16*, 113–116.

Frith, U. (1974). Internal schemata for letters in good and bad readers. *British Journal of Psychology, 65*, 233–241.

Frith, U. (1974). Scanning for reversed and rotated targets. *Acta Psychologica, 38*, 343–349.

Frith, U., & Frith, C. D. (1974). Specific motor disabilities in Down's Syndrome. *Journal of Child Psychology and Psychiatry, 15*, 293–301.

Frith, U. (1975). Are language problems in autistic and aphasic children different? A commentary on L. Bartak & M. L. Rutter: "Language and cognition in autistic and aphasic subjects." In N. O'Connor (Ed.), *Language, cognitive deficits and retardation* (pp. 203–208). London: Butterworths.

Frith, U. (1975). Emergency society [short story]. In P. Strick (Ed.), *Antigrav* (pp. 78–80). London: Arrow Books.

Frith, U. (1975). Lines that affect speed of visual scanning. *Perception, 4*, 407–409.

Frith, U., & Robson, J. (1975). Perceiving the language of films. *Perception, 4*, 97–103.

Frith, U. (1977). Sprache und Denken bei autistischen Kindern. In H. Kehrer (Ed.), *Der frühkindliche Autismus* (pp. 55–65). Basel: Karger.

Newman, S. E., & Frith, U. (1977). Encoding specificity versus associative continuity. *Bulletin of the Psychonomic Society, 10*, 73–75.

Frith, C. D., & Frith, U. (1978). Feature selection and classification: A developmental study. *Journal of Experimental Child Psychology*, *25*, 413–428.

Frith, U. (1978). From print to meaning and from print to sound. *Visible Language*, *12*, 43–54.

Frith, U. (1978). Spelling difficulties. *Journal of Child Psychology and Psychiatry*, *19*, 279–285.

Frith, U. (1979). Reading by eye and writing by ear. In R. A. Kolers, M. E. Wrolstad, & H. Bouma (Eds.), *Processing of visible language* (pp. 379–390). New York: Plenum Press.

Frith, U. (Ed.). (1980). *Cognitive processes in spelling*. London: Academic Press.

Frith, U. (1980). Reading and spelling skills. In M. Rutter (Ed.), *Scientific foundations of developmental psychiatry* (pp. 220–229). London: Heinemann.

Frith, U. (1980). Unexpected spelling problems. In U. Frith (Ed.), *Cognitive processes in spelling* (pp. 495–515). London: Academic Press.

Frith, U. (1980). The world of two dimensional space. In F. B. Murray (Ed.), *The development of the reading process* (pp. 1–19). Newark, DE: International Reading Association.

Frith, U., & Frith, C. D. (1980). Relationships between reading and spelling. In J. F. C. Kavanagh & R. L. Venezky (Eds.), *Orthography, reading and dyslexia* (pp. 287–295). Baltimore, MD: University Park Press.

Frith, U. (1981). Experimental approaches to developmental dyslexia: An introduction. *Psychological Research*, *43*, 97–109.

Henderson, D., Morris, J., & Frith, U. (1981). The motor deficit in Down's Syndrome children: A problem of timing. *Journal of Child Psychology and Psychiatry*, *22*, 233–245.

Snowling, M., & Frith, U. (1981). The role of sound, shape and orthographic cues in early reading. *British Journal of Psychology*, *72*, 83–87.

Frith, U. (1982). Cognitive processes in spelling and their relevance to spelling reform. *Spelling Progress Bulletin*, *22*, 6–9.

Frith, U. (1982). Psychological abnormalities in childhood psychoses. In J. Wing & L. Wing (Eds.), *Psychoses of uncertain aetiology* (pp. 215–221). Cambridge: Cambridge University Press.

Frith, U. (1983). Introduction to "Reading and Spelling". In D. R. Rogers & J. A. Sloboda (Eds.), *The acquisition of symbolic skills* (pp. 105–107). New York: Plenum Press.

Frith, U. (1983). Psychologische Studien zur Rolle der Orthographie beim Lesen und Schreiben. In K. B. Günther & H. Günther (Eds.), *Schrift, Schreiben, Schriftlichkeit* (pp. 119–131). Tübingen: Max Niemeyer Verlag.

Frith, U. (1983). Review of *Dyslexia. The pattern of difficulties*, by T. R. Miles, London: Granada. *Bulletin of the British Psychological Society*, *36*, 291–292.

Frith, U. (1983). The similarities and differences between reading and spelling problems. In M. Rutter (Ed.), *Developmental neuropsychiatry* (pp. 453–472). New York: Guilford Press.

Frith, U. (1983). Spelling. In E. Harré & R. Lamb (Eds.), *The encyclopaedic dictionary of psychology* (pp. 238–240). Oxford: Basil Blackwell.

Frith, U., & Snowling, M. (1983). Reading for meaning and reading for sound in autistic and dyslexic children. *British Journal of Developmental Psychology*, *1*, 329–342.

Shah, A., & Frith, U. (1983). An islet of ability in autistic children: A research note. *Journal of Child Psychology and Psychiatry*, *24*, 613–620.

Snowling, M., & Frith, U. (1983). Hyperlexia: Reading by autistic children. *Working Papers of the London Psycholinguistics Research Group*, *5*, 62–70.

Frith, U. (1984). Review of *"Autistic" Children: New hope for a cure*, by N. Tinbergen & E. G. Tinbergen, London: Allen & Unwin. *Psychological Medicine*, *14*, 461–483.

Frith, U. (1984). Specific spelling problems. In R. N. Malatesha & H. A. Whitaker (Eds.), *Dyslexia: A global issue* (pp. 83–103). The Hague: Martinus Nijhoff.

Baron-Cohen, S., Leslie, A. M., & Frith, U. (1985). Does the autistic child have a "theory of mind"? *Cognition*, *21*, 37–46.

Frith, U. (1985). Beneath the surface of developmental dyslexia. In K. Patterson, J. Marshall, & M. Coltheart (Eds.), *Surface dyslexia: Neuropsychological and cognitive studies of phonological reading* (pp. 301–330). Hove, UK: Erlbaum.

Frith, U. (1985). Cognitive processes in spelling and their relevance to spelling reform. In M. Clark (Ed.), *New directions in the study of reading* (pp. 95–102). London: Falmer Press.

Frith, U. (1985). Review of *Learning to Read. Literate Behaviour and Orthographic Knowledge*, by H. Francis, Hemel Hempstead, UK: Allen & Unwin. *Journal of Child Psychology and Psychiatry*, *26*, 171.

Baron-Cohen, S., Leslie, A. M., & Frith, U. (1986). Mechanical, behavioural and intentional understanding of picture stories in autistic children. *British Journal of Developmental Psychology*, *4*, 113–125.

Frith, U. (1986). A developmental framework for developmental dyslexia. *Annals of Dyslexia, 36*, 69–81.

Frith, U. (1986). Psychologische Aspekte des orthographischen Wissens: Entwicklung und Entwicklungsstörung. In G. Augst (Ed.), *New Trends and Graphemics in Orthography Research* (pp. 218–233). Berlin: De Gruyter.

Frith, U. (1986). Spelling. In E. Harré & R. Lamb (Eds.), *Dictionary of Developmental and Educational Psychology*. Oxford: Blackwell.

Snowling, M., & Frith, U. (1986). Comprehension in "hyperlexic" readers. *Journal of Experimental Child Psychology, 42*, 392–415.

Frith, U., & Baron-Cohen, S. (1987). Perception in autistic children. In D. Cohen, A. Donnellan, & R. Paul (Eds.), *Handbook of autism and disorders of atypical development* (pp. 85–102). New York: Wiley.

Frith, U., & Jackson, A. (1987). Review of *Children's creative spelling*, by C. Read, London: Routledge and Kegan Paul. *Journal of Child Psychology and Psychiatry, 28*, 951.

Leslie, A. M., & Frith, U. (1987). Metarepresentation and autism: How not to lose one's marbles. *Cognition, 27*, 291–294.

Attwood, A., Frith, U., & Hermelin, B. (1988). The understanding and use of interpersonal gestures by autistic and Down's Syndrome children. *Journal of Autism and Developmental Disorders, 18*, 241–157.

Frith, U. (1988). Autism: Possible clues to the underlying pathology: Psychological facts. In L. Wing (Ed.), *Aspects of autism: Biological research* (pp. 19–30). London: Gaskell, National Autistic Society and Royal College of Psychiatrists.

Leslie, A. M., & Frith, U. (1988). Autistic children's understanding of seeing, knowing and believing. *British Journal of Developmental Psychology, 6*, 315–324.

Frith, U. (1989). *Autism: Explaining the enigma.* Oxford: Blackwell.

Frith, U. (1989). Autism and "Theory of Mind". In C. Gillberg (Ed.), *Diagnosis and treatment of autism* (pp. 33–52). New York: Plenum Press.

Frith, U. (1989). A new look at language and communication in autism. *British Journal of Disorders of Communication, 24*, 123–150.

Perner, J., Frith, U., Leslie, A. M., & Leekam, S. (1989). Explorations of the autistic child's theory of mind: Knowledge, belief and communication. *Child Development, 60*, 689–700.

Frith, U. (1990). Autism. *MRC Annual Report, April 1989–March 1990*, 41–48.

Leslie, A. M., & Frith, U. (1990). Prospects for a cognitive neuropsychology of autism: Hobson's choice. *Psychological Review, 97*, 122–131.

Frith, C. D., & Frith, U. (1991). Elective affinities in schizophrenia and childhood autism. In P. Bebbington (Ed.), *Social psychiatry: Theory, methodology and practice* (pp. 65–88). Brunswick, NJ: Transactions.

Frith, U. (1991). Asperger and his syndrome. In U. Frith (Ed.), *Autism and Asperger Syndrome* (pp. 1–36). Cambridge: Cambridge University Press.

Frith, U. (1991). *Autism and Asperger Syndrome.* Cambridge: Cambridge University Press.

Frith, U. (1991). Dyslexia as a developmental disorder of language. In Bundesverband für Legasthenie (Ed.), *Legasthenie* (pp. 26–34). Aachen, Germany.

Frith, U. (1991). Translation and annotation of *"Autistic psychopathy" in childhood* by Hans Asperger. In U. Frith (Ed.), *Autism and Asperger Syndrome* (pp. 36–92). Cambridge: Cambridge University Press.

Frith, U., Morton, J., & Leslie, A. M. (1991). The cognitive basis of a biological disorder: Autism. *Trends in Neurosciences, 14*, 433–438.

Happé, F., & Frith, U. (1991). Is autism a pervasive developmental disorder? Debate and argument: How useful is the "PDD" label? *Journal of Child Psychology and Psychiatry, 32*, 1167–1168.

Frith, U. (1992). Cognitive development and cognitive deficit. The President's Award Lecture. *The Psychologist, 5*, 13–19.

Frith, U. (1992). Holes in the mind: Cognitive development and cognitive deficit. In L. Richards (Ed.), *Set research information for teachers, No2, Item 4* (pp. 6–6). Wellington, New Zealand: NZCER.

Happé, F., & Frith, U. (1992). How autistics see the world (Commentary on Cheney & Seyforth: How monkeys see the world). *Behavioural and Brain Sciences, 15*, 159–160.

Johnson, M. H., Siddons, F., Frith, U., & Morton, J. (1992). Can autism be predicted on the basis of infant screening tests? *Developmental and Child Neurology, 34*, 316–320.

Sodian, B., & Frith, U. (1992). Deception and sabotage in autistic, retarded and normal children. *Journal of Child Psychology and Psychiatry, 33*, 591–605.

Frith, U. (1993). Autism. *Scientific American, 268*, 108–114.

Frith, U. (1993). Autismus. *Spektrum der Wissenschaft, 8*, 48–55.

Frith, U. (1993). Den cognitive forklaring pa autisme. *Nordisk Tidsskrift for Spesialpedagogikk, 3*, 134–138.

Frith, U. (1993). Kinder, die lesen, ohne zu verstehen. Oder verstehen wir nicht, wie sie lesen? In H. Balhorn & H. Brügelmann (Eds.), *Bedeutungen erfinden—im Kopf, mit Schrift und miteinander* (pp. 338–347). Konstanz: Faude Verlag.

Frith, U., Soares, I., & Wing, L. (1993). Research into earliest detectable signs of autism: What the parents say. *Communication, 27,* 17–18.

Morton, J., & Frith, U. (1993). Approche de la dyslexie dévelopementale par la modélisation causale. In J.-P. Jaffré (Ed.), *Les Actes de la Villette* (pp. 38–56). Paris: Nathan.

Morton, J., & Frith, U. (1993). What lesson for dyslexia from Down's Syndrome? Comments on Cossu, Rossini & Marshall. *Cognition, 48,* 289–296.

Shah, A., & Frith, U. (1993). Why do autistic individuals show superior performance on the block design task? *Journal of Child Psychology and Psychiatry, 34,* 1351–1364.

Sodian, B., & Frith, U. (1993). The theory of mind deficit in autism: Consequences for deception. In S. Baron-Cohen, H. Tager-Flusberg, & D. Cohen (Eds.), *Understanding other minds and perspectives from autism* (pp. 158–177). Oxford: Oxford University Press.

Surian, L., & Frith, U. (1993). Prospettive della ricerca di neuropsicologia cognitive sull'autismo infantile. *Eta Evolutiva, 45,* 73–83.

Wimmer, H., Klampfer, B., & Frith, U. (1993). Lesenlernen bei englischen und deutschen Kindern. In H. Balhorn & H. Brügelmann (Eds.), *Bedeutungen erfinden—im Kopf, mit Schrift und miteinander* (pp. 324–329). Konstanz: Faude Verlag.

Fombonne, E., Siddons, F., Achard, S., Frith, U., & Happé, F. (1994). Adaptive behaviour and theory of mind in autism. *European Child and Adolescent Psychiatry, 3,* 176–186.

Frith, U. (1994). Das autistische Kind, oder: Eine Triade con Beeinträchtigungen. In R. Winkel (Ed.), *Schwierige Kinder—Problematische Schüler* (pp. 221–243). Baltmannsweiler: Schneider-Verlag Hohengehren.

Frith, U. (1994). Preface. In G. Brown & N. Ellis (Eds.), *Handbook of spelling: Theory, process and intervention* (pp. xi–xiv). Chichester, UK: Wiley.

Frith, U., & Happé, F. (1994). Autism: Beyond "theory of mind". *Cognition, 50,* 115–132.

Frith, U., & Happé, F. (1994). Language and communication in autistic disorders. *Philosophical Transactions of the Royal Society of London, Series B, 346,* 97–104.

Frith, U., & Lüdi, G. (1994). Introduction: Towards a three-dimensional view of literacy. In U. Frith, G. Lüdi, M. Egli, & C.-A. Zuber (Eds.), *Proceedings of the ESF workshop on the contexts of literacy* (pp. 5–8). Strasbourg: European Science Foundation. Network on Written Language and Literacy.

Frith, U., Happé, F., & Siddons, F. (1994). Autism and theory of mind in everyday life. *Social Development, 2,* 108–124.

Happé, F., & Frith, U. (1994). Theory of mind in autism. In E. Schopler & G. B. Mesibov (Eds.), *Learning and cognition in autism* (pp. 177–197). New York: Plenum Press.

Hurlburt, R., Happé, F., & Frith, U. (1994). Sampling the form of inner experience in three adults with Asperger syndrome. *Psychological Medicine, 24,* 385–395.

Fletcher, P., Happé, F., Frith, U., Baker, S., Dolan, R., Frackowiak, R., & Frith, C. D. (1995). Other minds in the brain: A functional imaging study of "theory of mind" in story comprehension. *Cognition, 57,* 109–128.

Frith, U. (1995). Dyslexia: Can we have a shared theoretical framework. *Educational and Child Psychology, 12,* 6–17.

Frith, U., Landerl, K., & Frith, C. D. (1995). Dyslexia and verbal fluency: More evidence for a phonological deficit. Generating words from sound is hard for dyslexics—generating words from meaning is easy. *Dyslexia: An International Journal of Research and Practice, 1,* 2–11.

Morton, J., & Frith, U. (1995). Causal modeling: Structural approaches to developmental psychopathology. In D. Cicchetti & D. Cohen (Eds.), *Developmental psychopathology* (pp. 357–390). New York: Wiley.

Paulesu, E., Frith, U., Snowling, M., Gallagher, A., Morris, J., Frackowiak, R., & Frith, C. D. (1995). Is developmental dyslexia a disconnection syndrome? Evidence from PET scanning. *Brain, 119,* 143–158.

Frith, C. D., & Frith, U. (1996). A biological marker for dyslexia. *Nature, 382,* 20–21.

Frith, U. (1996). Cognitive explanations of autism. *Acta Paediactrica, Supplement, 415,* 63–68.

Frith, U. (1996). Social communication and its disorder in autism and Asperger Syndrome. *Journal of Psychopharmacology, 10,* 48–53.

Frith, U., & Gallagher, A. (1996). Spelling disorders. In J. G. Beaumont & J. Sergeant (Eds.), *Dictionary of neuropsychology*. Oxford: Blackwell.

Frith, U., & Happé, F. (1996). Mary has more: Sex difference, autism, coherence, and theory of mind. Commentary on D. C. Geary: Sexual Selection and sex differences in mathematical abilities. *Behavioural and Brain Sciences*, *19*, 253–254.

Frith, U., & Morton, J. (1996). Why dyslexics are different. Commentary on Ellis, A. W., McDougall, S. J. P., & Monk, A. F.: Are dyslexics different? A comparison between dyslexics, reading age control, poor readers and precocious readers. *Dyslexia: An International Journal of Research and Practice*, *2*, 81–83.

Gallagher, A., Laxon, V., Armstrong, E., & Frith, U. (1996). Phonological difficulties in high-functioning dyslexics. *Reading and Writing*, *8*, 499–509.

Happé, F., Ehlers, S., Fletcher, P., Frith, U., Johansson, M., Gillberg, C., Dolan, R., Frackowiak, R., & Frith, C. D. (1996). "Theory of mind" in the brain. Evidence from a PET scan study of Asperger syndrome. *NeuroReport*, *8*, 197–201.

Happé, F., & Frith, U. (1996). The neuropsychology of autism. *Brain*, *19*, 1377–1400.

Happé, F., & Frith, U. (1996). Theory of mind and social impairment in children with conduct disorder. *British Journal of Developmental Psychology*, *14*, 385–398.

Landerl, K., Frith, U., & Wimmer, H. (1996). Intrusion of orthographic knowledge on phoneme awareness: Strong in normal, weak in dyslexic readers. *Journal of Applied Psycholinguistics*, *17*, 1–14.

Frederickson, N., Frith, U., & Reason, R. (1997). *Phonological Assessment Battery. Manual and Test Materials*. Windsor, UK: NFER-Nelson.

Frith, U. (1997). Brain, mind and behaviour in dyslexia. In C. Hulme & M. Snowling (Eds.), *Dyslexia: Biology, identification and intervention* (pp. 1–19). London: Whurr Publishers.

Frith, U. (1997). The neurocognitive basis of autism. *Trends in Cognitive Sciences*, *1*, 73–77.

Hughes, C., Soares-Boucaud, I., Hochmann, J., & Frith, U. (1997). Social behaviour in pervasive developmental disorders: Effects of group, informant and "theory of mind". *European Journal of Child and Adolescent Psychiatry*, *6*, 1–8.

Landerl, K., Wimmer, H., & Frith, U. (1997). The impact of orthographic consistency on dyslexia: A German–English comparison. *Cognition*, *63*, 315–334.

Snowling, M., Nation, K., Moxham, P., Gallagher, A., & Frith, U. (1997). Phonological processing skills of dyslexic students in higher education: A preliminary report. *Journal of Research in Reading*, *20*, 31–41.

Wimmer, H., & Frith, U. (1997). Reading difficulties among English and German children: Same cause–different manifestation. In C. Pontecorvo (Ed.), *Writing development: An interdisciplinary view* (pp. 259–271). Amsterdam: John Benjamins.

Frederickson, N., & Frith, U. (1998). Identifying dyslexia in bilingual children: A phonological approach with Inner London Sylheti speakers. *Dyslexia: An International Journal of Research and Practice*, *4*, 119–131.

Frith, U. (1998). Cognitive deficits in developmental disorders. *Scandinavian Journal of Psychology*, *39*, 191–195.

Frith, U. (1998). Editorial: Literally changing the brain. *Brain*, *121*, 1011–1112.

Frith, U. (1998). What autism teaches us about communication. *Logopedics, Phoniatrics and Vocology*, *23*, 51–58.

Frith, U., & Blair, J. (1998). Editorial: Does antisocial personality disorder have a neurological basis and can it be treated? *Criminal Behaviour and Mental Health*, *8*, 247–250.

Frith, U., & Frith, C. (1998). Modularity of mind and phonological deficit. In C. Von Euler, I. Lundberg, & R. Llinas (Eds.), *Basic mechanisms in cognition and language* (pp. 3–17). Elsevier Science.

Frith, U., & Happé, F. (1998). Why specific developmental disorders are not specific: On-line and developmental effect in autism and dyslexia. *Developmental Science*, *1*, 267–272.

Frith, U., Wimmer, H., & Landerl, K. (1998). Differences in phonological recoding in German- and English-speaking children. *Scientific Study of Reading*, *2*, 31–54.

Frith, U., Wimmer, H., & Landerl, K. (1998). Learning to read and phonological recoding in English and German. *Scientific Study of Reading*, *2*, 31–54.

Abell, F., Krams, M., Ashburner, J., Passingham, R., Friston, K. J., Frackowiak, R., Happé, F., Frith, C. D., & Frith, U. (1999). The neuroanatomy of autism: A voxel based whole brain analysis of structural MRI scans in high functioning individuals. *NeuroReport*, *10*, 1647–1651.

Brunswick, N., McCrory, E., Price, C., Frith, C. D., & Frith, U. (1999). Explicit and implicit processing of words and pseudowords by adult developmental dyslexics: A search for Wernicke's Wortschatz? *Brain*, *122*, 1901–1917.

Cipolotti, L., Robinson, G., Blair, J., & Frith, U. (1999). Fractionation of visual memory: Evidence from a case with multiple neurodevelopmental impairments. *Neuropsychologia, 37,* 455–465.

Frith, U. (1999). Autism. *The MIT Encyclopaedia of the Cognitive Sciences.*

Frith, U. (1999). Paradoxes in the definition of dyslexia. *Dyslexia: An International Journal of Research and Practice, 5,* 192–214.

Frith, U., & Frith, C. (1999). Interacting minds: A biological basis. *Science, 286,* 1692–1695.

Frith, U., & Happé, F. (1999). Theory of mind and self consciousness: What is it like to be autistic? *Mind and Language, 14,* 1–22.

Frith, U., & Kelly, S. W. (1999). Editorial: Neuropsychological case studies of developmental disorders. *Neurocase—Special Developmental Issue, 5,* 471–473.

Happé, F., & Frith, U. (1999). How the brain reads the mind. *Neuroscience News, 2,* 16–25.

Wimmer, H., Landerl, K., & Frith, U. (1999). Learning to read German: Normal and impaired acquisition. In M. Harris & G. Hatano (Eds.), *Learning to read and write: A cross-linguistic perspective* (pp. 34–50). Cambridge: Cambridge University Press.

Abell, F., Happé, F., & Frith, U. (2000). Do triangles play tricks? Attribution of mental states to animated shapes in normal and abnormal development. *Journal of Cognitive Development, 15,* 1–20.

Blair, R. J. R., & Frith, U. (2000). Neurocognitive explanations of the Antisocial Personality Disorders. *Criminal Behaviour and Mental Health, 10,* 66–81.

Castelli, F., Happé, F., Frith, U., & Frith, C. (2000). Movement and mind: A functional imaging study of perception and interpretation of complex intentional movement patterns. *NeuroImage, 12,* 314–325.

Frith, C. D., & Frith, U. (2000). The physiological basis of theory of mind. In S. Baron-Cohen, H. Tager-Flusberg, & D. Cohen (Eds.), *Understanding other minds* (pp. 334–356). Oxford: Oxford University Press.

Gallagher, A., Frith, U., & Snowling, M. (2000). Precursors of literacy delay among children at genetic risk of dyslexia. *Journal of Child Psychology and Psychiatry, 41,* 203–213.

Gallagher, H. L., Happé, F., Brunswick, N., Fletcher, P., Frith, C. D., & Frith, U. (2000). Reading the mind in cartoons and stories: An fMRI study of "theory of mind" in verbal and non-verbal tasks. *Neuropsychologia, 38,* 11–21.

Houston, R., & Frith, U. (2000). *Autism in history: The case of Hugh Blair of Borgue.* Oxford: Blackwell.

McCrory, E., Frith, U., Brunswick, N., & Price, C. (2000). Abnormal functional activation during a simple word repetition task: A PET study of adult dyslexics. *Journal of Cognitive Neuroscience, 12,* 753–762.

Paulesu, E., McCrory, E., Fazio, F., Menoncello, L., Brunswick, N., Cappa, S. F., Cotelli, M., Cossu, G., Corte, F., Lorusso, M., Pesenti, S., Gallagher, A., Perani, D., Price, C., Frith, C. D., & Frith, U. (2000). A cultural effect on brain function. *Nature Neuroscience, 3,* 91–96.

Scheuffgen, K., Happé, F., Anderson, M., & Frith, U. (2000). High "intelligence", low "IQ"? Speed of processing and measured IQ in children with autism. *Development and Psychopathology, 12,* 83–90.

Briskman, J., Happé, F., & Frith, U. (2001). Exploring the cognitive phenotype of autism: Weak "central coherence" in parents and siblings of children with autism. II. Real-life skills and preferences. *Journal of Child Psychology and Psychiatry, 42,* 309–316.

Cardoso-Martins, C., & Frith, U. (2001). Can individuals with Down syndrome acquire alphabetic literacy skills in the absence of phoneme awareness? *Reading and Writing, 14,* 361–375.

Frith, U. (2001). Mindblindness and the brain in Autism. *Neuron, 32,* 969–979.

Frith, U. (2001). Theory of mind. In C. Blakemore (Ed.), *The Oxford companion to the body.* Oxford: Oxford University Press.

Frith, U. (2001). What framework should we use for understanding developmental disorders? *Developmental Neuropsychology, 20,* 555–563.

Frith, U., & Frith, C. (2001). The biological basis of social interaction. *Current Directions in Psychological Science, 10,* 151–155.

Frith, U., & Vargha-Khadem, F. (2001). Are there sex differences in the brain basis of literacy related skills? Evidence from reading and spelling impairments after early unilateral brain damage. *Neuropsychologia, 39,* 1485–1488.

Happé, F., Briskman, J., & Frith, U. (2001). Exploring the cognitive phenotype of autism: Weak "central coherence" in parents and siblings of children with autism. I. Experimental tests. *Journal of Child Psychology and Psychiatry, 42,* 299–307.

Kampe, K., Frith, C. D., Dolan, R. J., & Frith, U. (2001). Attraction and gaze—the reward value of social stimuli. *Nature, 413,* 589.

Morton, J., & Frith, U. (2001). Why we need cognition: Cause and developmental disorder. In E. Dupoux (Ed.), *Language, brain, and cognitive development: Festschrift for Jacques Mehler* (pp. 263–278). Cambridge: MIT Press.

Paulesu, E., Démonet, J., Fazio, F., McCrory, E., Chanoine, V., Brunswick, N., Cappa, S., Cossu, G., Habib, M., Frith, C., & Frith, U. (2001). Dyslexia: Cultural diversity and biological unity. *Science, 291,* 2165–2167.

Blair, R. J. R., Frith, U., Smith, N., Abell, F., & Cipolotti, L. (2002). Fractionation of visual memory: Agency detection and its impairment in autism. *Neuropsychologia, 40,* 108–118.

Castelli, F., Frith, C. D., Happé, F., & Frith, U. (2002). Autism, Asperger syndrome and brain mechanisms for the attribution of mental states to animated shapes. *Brain, 125,* 1839–1849.

Frith, U. (2002). Autism—the quest continues. *Neuroreport, 13,* 1703–1705.

Frith, U. (2002). The cognitive phenotype of autism: Implications for treatment. *Developmental Medicine and Child Neurology, 44* (Suppl. No. 92), 7–8.

Frith, U. (2002). Culture, brain and dyslexia. In E. Hjelmquist & C. von Euler (Eds.), *Literacy in the new millennium* (pp. 179–191). London: Whurr.

Frith, U. (2002). Resolving the paradoxes of dyslexia. In J. Reid & J. Wearmouth (Eds.), *Dyslexia and literacy: Theory and practice* (pp. 45–68). Chichester: Wiley.

Griffiths, S., & Frith, U. (2002). Evidence for an articulatory awareness deficit in adult dyslexics. *Dyslexia, 8,* 14–21.

Kelly, S. W., Griffiths, S., & Frith, U. (2002). Evidence for implicit sequence learning in dyslexia. *Dyslexia, 8,* 43–52.

Lang, G., & Frith, U. (2002). Imago Cerebri I. Collaboration with the artist described in Albano, C., Arnold, K., & Wallace, M. (Eds.), *Catalogue of head on: Art with the brain in mind: A Wellcome Trust exhibition at the Science Museum* (pp. 50–52). London, March–July.

Backhouse, G., Bishop-Liebler, P., Frith, U., & Stewart, L. (2003). Music, dyslexia and the brain. *PATOSS (Professional Association of Teachers of Students with Specific Learning Difficulties), 16,* 9–14.

Frith, U. (2003). *Autism: Explaining the enigma* (2nd ed.). Oxford: Blackwell.

Frith, U., & Blakemore, S.-J. (2003). Social cognition. *Foresight Cognitive Systems Project Research Review.* Department of Trade and Industry UK, available at www.foresight.gov.uk

Frith, U., & Frith, C. D. (2003). Development and neurophysiology of mentalising. *Philosophical Transactions Series B, 1431,* 459–474.

Frith, U., & Hill, E. (2003). Introduction to Special Issue on Autism. *Philosophical Transactions of the Royal Society London B, 358,* 277–280.

Hill, E., & Frith, U. (2003). Understanding autism: Insights from mind and brain, *Philosophical Transactions of the Royal Society London B, 358,* 281–289.

Kampe, K., Frith, C. D., & Frith, U. (2003). "Hey John": Signals conveying communicative intention towards the self activate brain regions associated with mentalizing regardless of modality. *Journal of Neuroscience, 23,* 5258–5263.

Ramus, F., Pidgeon, L., & Frith, U. (2003). The relationship between motor control and phonology in dyslexic children. *Journal of Child Psychology and Psychiatry, 44,* 712–722.

Ramus, F., Rosen, S, Dakin, S., Day, B. L., Castellote, J. M., White, S., & Frith, U. (2003). Theories of developmental dyslexia: Insights from a multiple case study. *Brain, 126,* 841–865.

Snowling, M., Gallagher, A., & Frith, U. (2003). Genetic risk of dyslexia is continuous: Individual differences in the precursors of orthographic skill. *Child Development, 74,* 358–373.

Stewart, L., Henson, R., Kampe, K., Walsh, V., Turner, R., & Frith, U. (2003). Becoming a pianist. Brain changes associated with learning to read music. *Neuroimage, 20,* 71–83.

Stewart, L., Henson, R., Kampe, K., Walsh, V., Turner, R., & Frith, U. (2003). Becoming a pianist. An fMRI study of musical literacy acquisition. *Annals of the New York Academy of Sciences, 999,* 204–208.

Blakemore, S.-J., & Frith, U. (2004). How does the brain deal with the social world? *Neuroreport, 15,* 119–128.

Blakemore, S.-J., Winston, J., & Frith, U. (2004). Social cognitive neuroscience: Where are we heading? *Trends in Cognitive Neuroscience, 8,* 216–222.

Frith, U. (2004). Emmanuel Miller lecture: Confusions and controversies about Asperger syndrome. *Journal of Child Psychology and Psychiatry, 45,* 672–686.

Hamilton, A., Wolpert, D., & Frith, U. (2004). Your own action influences how you perceive another person's action, *Current Biology, 14,* 493–498.

Hill, E. L., Berthoz, S., & Frith, U. (2004). Brief report: Cognitive processing of own emotions in individuals with autistic spectrum disorder and their relatives.

Journal of Autism and Developmental Disorders, 34, 229–235.

Hill, E. L., Sally, D., & Frith, U. (2004). Does mentalising ability influence cooperative decision making in a social dilemma? Introspective evidence from a study of adults with autism spectrum disorder. *Journal of Consciousness Studies, 11,* 1–18.

Stewart, L., Walsh, V., & Frith, U. (2004). Music reading shapes spatial representation in pianists. *Perception and Psychophysics, 66,* 183–195.

Blakemore, S.-J., & Frith, U. (2005). *The learning brain: Lessons for education.* Oxford: Blackwell.

Blakemore, S.-J., & Frith, U. (2005). The learning brain: Lessons for education: A precis target article with commentaries. *Developmental Science, 8,* 459–471.

Dakin, S., & Frith, U. (2005). Vagaries of visual perception in autism. *Neuron, 48,* 497–507.

Den Ouden, H. E. M., Frith, U., Frith, C., & Blakemore, S.-J. (2005 e-publication). Thinking about intentions. *Neuroimage, 28,* 787–796.

Frith, C. D., & Frith, U. (2005). Quick guide: Theory of mind. *Current Biology, 15,* 644–664.

Frith, U., & de Vignemont, F. (2005). Egocentrism, allocentrism and Asperger syndrome. *Consciousness and Cognition, 14,* 719–738.

Frith, U., & Happé, F. (2005). Primer: Autistic spectrum disorder. *Current Biology, 15,* 786–790.

McCrory, E. J., Mechelli, A., Frith, U., & Price, C. J. (2005). More than words: A common neural basis for reading and picture naming. *Brain 128* (Pt 2), 261–267.

Silani, G., Frith, U., Demonet, J.-F., Fazio, F., Perani, D. C., Price, C., Frith, C. D., & Paulesu, E. (2005). Brain abnormalities underlying altered activation in dyslexia: A voxel based morphometric study. *Brain, 128,* 2453–2461.

Bird, G., Catmur, C. Silani, G., Frith, C., & Frith, U. (2006). Attention does not modulate neural responses to social stimuli in autism spectrum disorders. *Neuroimage, 31,* 1614–1624.

Blakemore, S.-J., Tavassoli, T., Calo, S., Thomas, R. M., Catmur, C., Frith, U., & Haggard, P. (2006). Tactile sensitivity in Asperger Syndrome. *Brain and Cognition, 61,* 5–13.

Frith, C. D., & Frith, U. (2006). How we predict what other people are going to do. *Brain Research, 1079,* 26–46.

Frith, C. D., & Frith, U. (2006). The neural basis of mentalizing. *Neuron, 50,* 531–534.

Hamilton, A., Wolpert, D., Frith, U., & Grafton, S. (2006). Where does your own action influence the perception of another person's action in the brain? *Neuroimage, 29,* 524–535.

Happé, F., & Frith, U. (2006). The weak coherence account: Detail-focused cognitive style in autism spectrum disorders. *Journal of Autism and Developmental Disorders, 36,* 5–25.

Ramus, F., White, S., & Frith, U. (2006). Weighing the evidence between competing theories of dyslexia. Discussion of peer commentary. *Developmental Science, 9,* 265–269.

Rogers, J., Viding, E., Blair, J. R., Frith, U., & Happé, F. (2006). Autism spectrum disorder and psychopathy: Shared cognitive underpinnings or double hit? *Psychological Medicine, 36,* 1789–1798.

Viding, E., & Frith, U. (2006). Genes for susceptibility to violence lurk in the brain. *Proceedings of the National Academy of Sciences, USA, 103,* 6085–6086.

White, S., Frith, U., Milne, E., Rosen, S., Swettenham, J., Hansen, P., & Ramus, F., (2006). A double dissociation between sensorimotor impairments and reading disability: A comparison of autistic and dyslexic children. *Cognitive Neuropsychology, 23,* 748–761.

White, S., Hill, E., Winston, J., & Frith, U. (2006). An islet of social ability in Asperger syndrome: Stereotypic attribution to faces. *Brain and Cognition, 61,* 69–77.

White, S., Milne, E., Rosen, S. Hansen, P., Swettenham, J., Frith, U., & Ramus, F. (2006). The role of sensorimotor impairments in dyslexia: A multiple case study of dyslexic children. *Developmental Science, 9,* 237–255.

Hamilton, A. F. d. C., Brindley, R. M., & Frith, U. (2007). How valid is the mirror neuron hypothesis for autism? *Neuropsychologia, 45,* 1859–1868.

Saldana, D., & Frith, U. (2007). Do readers with autism make bridging inferences from world knowledge? *Journal of Experimental Child Psychology, 96,* 310–319.

THE QUARTERLY JOURNAL OF EXPERIMENTAL PSYCHOLOGY
2008, 61 (1), 11

Contributors

Mike Anderson, School of Psychology, The University of Western Australia, Crawley, Perth, Western Australia, Australia.

Simon Baron-Cohen, Autism Research Centre, Department of Psychiatry, University of Cambridge, Cambridge, UK.

Dorothy V. M. Bishop, Department of Experimental Psychology, University of Oxford, Oxford, UK.

R. James R. Blair, Mood and Anxiety Program, National Institute of Mental Health, Bethesda, MD, USA.

Sarah-Jayne Blakemore, Institute of Cognitive Neuroscience, University College London, London, UK.

Rhonda D. L. Booth, Social, Genetic, and Developmental Psychiatry Centre, Institute of Psychiatry, King's College London, London, UK.

Frédérique de Vignemont, Institut Jean-Nicod, CNRS-EHESS-ENS, Paris, France.

Antonia F. de C. Hamilton, Department of Psychological and Brain Sciences, Dartmouth College, Hanover, NH, USA.

Francesca G. E. Happé, Social, Genetic, and Developmental Psychiatry Centre, Institute of Psychiatry, King's College London, London, UK.

Alice P. Jones, Social, Genetic, and Developmental Psychiatry Centre, Institute of Psychiatry, King's College London, London, UK.

Susan Leekam, Department of Psychology, University of Durham, Durham, UK.

Josef Perner, Department of Psychology, University of Salzburg, Salzburg, Austria.

Franck Ramus, Laboratoire de Sciences Cognitives et Psycholinguistique, Ecole Normale Supérieure, Paris, France.

Margaret J. Snowling, Department of Psychology, University of York, York, UK.

Beate Sodian, Department of Psychology, Ludwig-Maximilians-Universität München, Munich, Germany.

Gayaneh Szenkovits, Laboratoire de Sciences Cognitives et Psycholinguistique, Ecole Normale Supérieure, Paris, France.

Claudia Thoermer, Department of Psychology, Ludwig-Maximilians-Universität München, Munich, Germany.

Essi Viding, Department of Psychology, University College London, London, UK.

Contributors

THE QUARTERLY JOURNAL OF EXPERIMENTAL PSYCHOLOGY
2008, 61 (1), 13–15

Editorial

This Festschrift is based on the programme of talks during a stimulating and enjoyable two-day event held at the Royal Society, London, on 2–3 January 2007, to mark the occasion of Uta Frith's retirement. We are most grateful to the sponsors of the meeting, who included the Experimental Psychology Society, the British Psychological Society, The British Academy, University College London, and Blackwell and Jessica Kingsley publishers. We take this opportunity to thank the anonymous band of reviewers who worked so efficiently to make it possible to bring out this volume in a timely fashion.

Uta Frith is internationally renowned for her work on developmental cognitive disorders. Her scholarly influence has defined contemporary research on atypical development, notably in the fields of autism and dyslexia. This Festschrift brings together former graduate students, postdoctoral scientists, and collaborators of Uta in a series of papers that provide reflections on current theory and research. The volume bears the hallmark of Uta's mentoring by including critical "state-of-the-art" reviews, empirical research challenging mainstream views, and consideration of alternative hypotheses that set the stage for future research.

As the opening paper by Bishop makes clear, the landscape of developmental disorders is quite different now from that which Uta entered some forty years ago. In the field of autism in particular, the categorical boundary around classic Kanner's syndrome has been replaced by the notion of a spectrum of autistic disorders sharing the core feature of social impairment. Similarly, in the field of dyslexia, the notion of a specific discrepancy-defined reading disorder has been replaced by a view of dyslexia as a dimensional disorder with the core deficit in phonological processes. In addition, the advent of neuroimaging and advanced genetic methodologies has diversified the methods available for the investigation of developmental disorders of language and cognition. Nevertheless, the importance of clearly specifying the cognitive phenotype of different disorders remains as important as ever. As Uta has argued, cognition mediates the brain–behaviour relationships that developmental cognitive neuroscientists strive to understand, and a cognitive specification of a disorder is fundamental to advances in understanding of its neurobiological bases.

Uta's work has always been characterized by a strong commitment to the developmental perspective, recognizing not only the impact of deficient processes on behaviour but also the "downstream" effects of compensatory processes. Accordingly, it is important for research on developmental disorders to be cast within a developmental framework. Three papers in the present volume consider what is known about aspects of typical development, particularly in relation to autism. Sodian and Thoerner review work on the precursors of Theory of Mind in infancy and proceed to describe their own research on infant behaviour towards adults' intentional actions. Their plea for further research on the relationship between early aspects of social information processing and Theory of Mind is well taken. In a similar vein, Blakemore surveys brain development in adolescence and calls for more research on changes in social cognition during this critical life-phase. Happé and Booth turn to the weak central coherence (WCC) theory, which explains autistic assets (characterized by attention to local detail) as well as deficits (in global integrative processing). Following a comprehensive review of the precedence of global versus local processing across the life-span, they consider whether reduced global processing might be a secondary

http://www.psypress.com/qjep

DOI:10.1080/17470210701508624

effect of superior local processing. Their conclusion, that this is a false dichotomy, will undoubtedly have a significant impact on the direction of future research investigating the causes of WCC. Such research might also consider synergies between the attention to detail that characterizes WCC and the "hyper-systemizing" profile described by Baron-Cohen. If, as he suggests, this cognitive style is heritable, then such research could be productive for elucidating critical risk factors for autism, independent of those associated with deficits in social cognition that are part of the triad of autistic impairment.

Three papers present challenges to extant theories of autism and together show how current concepts can be refined in order to develop alternative hypotheses. Perner and Leekam argue persuasively that standard false-belief tasks are cognitively complex because they not only question a belief that is "invisible" (the mental state of the protagonist) but they also mis-represent the target's current state. Their basic argument is that as well as tapping domain-specific knowledge (Theory of Mind), the false-belief task also has high-level cognitive demands. Hence, failure is possible for more than one reason. From a philosophical stance, de Vignemont also encourages a refinement of the Theory of Mind account of autism. The nub of her argument is that different kinds of mind-reading are required for social observation and for social interaction. Specifically, it matters whether the other person is viewed from an "egocentric" (you in relation to me) or an allocentric (he, she, or they) frame of reference. An allocentric view of the world allows an understanding of social rules and social structure, whereas an egocentric view (in which the self is a referent) is important for social interaction. This dichotomy leads to a new hypothesis, that autism-spectrum disorders (e.g., Asperger's syndrome) are characterized by deficits in the mind-reading skills that are needed for social interaction but not in those required for social understanding.

A quite different theory of autism, the "broken mirror" hypothesis, posits that autism is caused by an impairment of the mirror neuron system, which leads to deficits in imitation. Hamilton's critical appraisal of the literature indicates that evidence does not support this hypothesis but, rather, suggests that purposeful imitation—which she defines as emulation—is intact, whereas automatic imitation of meaningless gestures (mimicry) is impaired. She argues that different brain regions subserve emulation and mimicry and proceeds to show how cognitive models of the mirror neuron system can be refined to accommodate these data. Speculatively, she suggests that the theory-of-mind network might exert a top-down influence on the mirror neuron system such that the use of mimicry to enhance social interaction is modulated to a non-optimal degree in autism.

As Anderson's paper highlights, Uta's influence has been pervasive not only in the field of autism but also in that of dyslexia. With respect to both disorders, his paper reacts against the tendency to regard IQ or "g" as a nuisance factor often dealt with as a matching variable. Instead he argues that it is important to represent explicitly "g" in the cognitive phenotype of a disorder. Although arguably an unpopular view, this argument finds support in work on autism where IQ scores are not a true reflection of general cognitive ability, and in dyslexia, where low "g" may lessen the resources available for compensation during development. Against this backdrop, two papers that address the cognitive deficit in dyslexia both present challenges to the dominant view that dyslexia is caused by a specific modular deficit in phonological representations. Ramus and Szenkovits describe a series of tightly controlled experiments on phonological grammar, speech perception, speech production, and short-term memory, comparing adults with dyslexia to normal readers. Contrary to the prevailing view, there was no evidence of qualitative differences in the phonological representations of the two groups, and the authors argue that phonological deficits only surface as a function of task requirements (e.g., conscious awareness and time constraints), suggestive of an access deficit. From the perspective of a longitudinal prospective study of children at family-risk of dyslexia, Snowling focuses on the adequacy of the phonological deficit hypothesis as an explanation of poor literacy outcome. Two sets of findings throw doubt on this simple view. First, children are more likely to succumb to dyslexia if they have a phonological deficit in the context of a more general oral language weakness, and, second, in dyslexic families it is common for unaffected children to show phonological deficits. Thus, a phonological deficit might be better conceptualized as an "endophenotype" of dyslexia (a process closer to the genotype than the disorder itself) that carries the risk of reading failure and, when observed in combination with other risk factors, will lead to the disorder.

The final two papers in the Festschrift consider a disorder, or more properly a set of disorders, that have only relatively recently been the subject of cognitive investigation. Blair begins his paper with a discussion of the definition of psychopathy, a disorder characterized by extreme anti-social behaviour that shows some (incomplete) overlap with conduct disorder. Blair proceeds to discuss the core features of psychopathy and to show how, although on the surface there may seem to be similarities with autism, careful scrutiny suggests differences in the nature of the impairments shown by the two groups in empathy and in amygdala dysfunction. Thus, although the literature is still murky (to use his term), the picture that emerges is that psychopathy is characterized by deficits in emotional empathy (the brain's response to rewarding and punishing stimuli) but not in cognitive empathy (Theory of Mind), whereas autism presents the contrasting case. In a similar vein, psychopathy is associated with deficits in stimulus-reward associations and in moral judgement, whereas autism is free of such impairments. Viding and Jones begin their paper by refining the behavioural concept of conduct disorder to differentiate between individuals who show antisocial behaviour in combination with callous–unemotional traits (CU+) and those who do not show such traits (CU−). They proceed to show that the two sub-types show different patterns of amygdala activation

to socio-emotional and non-social processing tasks and present findings of a behaviour-genetic analysis suggesting that the etiology of the two sub-types is different. Thus, CU+ traits are heritable, suggesting a genetic mediation of conduct disorder in such cases, whereas the genetic influence on anti-social behaviour in relation to CU− is more moderate, with a stronger environmental influence.

As the present volume makes clear, Uta Frith's work has provided an influential "road map" of neurodevelopmental disorders with implications for theory and practice. However, as hinted at by many of the contributors to this Festschrift, there is a growing need for more complex models of the relationships between brain and cognition that address variations in the behaviours observed within the same broad class of disorder, and that will also elucidate shared risk factors between different disorders. In addition, the field would benefit from more longitudinal studies and studies using genetically sensitive designs in order to tease apart issues of causality.

Together, the papers in this volume illustrate the breadth and extent of Uta's influence but cannot by themselves do justice to her distinctive approach to science, its theoretical rigour and ingenuity. The papers that are included also fail to acknowledge the important influence that her theorizing has had on education and clinical practice. All contributors to the volume have mentioned Uta's defining qualities, her kindness and generosity mixed with a critical yet encouraging style; to these we would add Uta's respect for those affected by neurodevelopmental disorders and her concern for the quality of their lives.

Margaret J. Snowling
Dorothy V. M. Bishop
Sarah-Jayne Blakemore

THE QUARTERLY JOURNAL OF EXPERIMENTAL PSYCHOLOGY
2008, 61 (1), 16−26

Forty years on:
Uta Frith's contribution to research on autism and dyslexia, 1966−2006

Dorothy V. M. Bishop
University of Oxford, Oxford, UK

Uta Frith has made a major contribution to our understanding of developmental disorders, especially autism and dyslexia. She has studied the cognitive and neurobiological bases of both disorders and demonstrated distinctive impairments in social cognition and central coherence in autism, and in phonological processing in dyslexia. In this enterprise she has encouraged psychologists to work in a theoretical framework that distinguishes between observed behaviour and the underlying cognitive and neurobiological processes that mediate that behaviour.

Early academic biography

Imagine a world without computers, printers, pocket calculators, or photocopiers. A world in which the dominant view was that autism was caused by "refrigerator parents", and the concept of developmental dyslexia was regarded as a self-serving invention of the middle classes. Into such a world came the young Uta Aurnhammer, fresh from the University of Saarbrücken in Germany, where she had been seduced away from her original plan to study art history by the discovery of psychology as an experimental science. Her interest was immediately engaged by the realization that the study of the mind need not rely on mere introspection or dictat, but could be researched using empirical methods, with hypotheses being tested using statistical procedures. Impressed by the spirited attacks by Hans Eysenck (1953,

1957) on psychoanalysis and other nonempirical schools of psychology, Uta decided that the place to go for further training was the Institute of Psychiatry (IOP) in London, and she came to do an internship there in 1964. It was only with hindsight that she became aware of just what a productive mix of influences was based at IOP at that time. Eysenck himself disappointed, being largely inaccessible, but the infant discipline of behaviour therapy was creating excitement, with Jack Rachman, Monty Shapiro, and Reg Beech all looking for applications of this new approach to a wide range of disorders. Uta offered her services as a "work experience" student and soon found herself doing statistical analyses for Reg Beech on a huge clanking calculator, while at the same time trying desperately to improve her English, a task that became a great deal easier

Correspondence should be addressed to Dorothy V. M. Bishop, Department of Experimental Psychology, University of Oxford, South Parks Road, Oxford, OX1 3UD, UK. E-mail: dorothy.bishop@psy.ox.ac.uk

Many thanks to Uta Frith herself for hosting me for the day during a most enjoyable interview about her academic history. Dorothy Bishop is supported by a Principal Research Fellowship from the Wellcome Trust.

DOI:10.1080/17470210701508665

when she found herself spending more and more time with Chris Frith. The internship came to an end, and Uta had packed up and sent her luggage off to Germany, but events rapidly took on a life of their own, and she unexpectedly found herself accepted on the clinical psychology course at IOP (then a 13-month diploma), and engaged to Chris Frith. During the clinical course she first encountered cases of "childhood psychosis" (which we would now term "autistic disorder") and was immediately fascinated at the contrast between the apparently intelligent and attractive appearance of such children and their profound level of handicap. She was convinced, despite the lack of hard evidence and in the teeth of contemporary psychogenic theories, that this must be a disorder with a biological basis, and she started to question the approach of the behaviour therapists, who would try to treat the symptoms, such as gaze avoidance, by conditioning, without any concern for underlying causes. Uta was strongly influenced by the clinical insights of Michael Rutter and Lorna Wing, and she started to hunt out literature that might throw light on the underlying causes of impairment in these strange children. She was drawn to experimental studies by Neil O'Connor and Beate (Ati) Hermelin, which were unique at that time in that they designed studies of developmental disorders from the perspective of experimental psychology. Having selected one of their papers for a journal club (O'Connor & Hermelin, 1959), she was amazed to find that they were based at IOP, in a research unit housed in Nissen huts in the grounds. Despite this insalubrious location, they were an undeniably glamorous pair, more like Hollywood celebrities than psychology researchers, and it took all of Uta's courage to approach them. Uta recounts that her recollection of their meeting was that she was overawed and reverential in their presence, but Ati's subsequent memory was of this challenging young woman who picked their study apart and discussed the flaws with them. Regardless of the reality, Uta clearly impressed and was subsequently offered the chance to study for a doctorate under their supervision, on

the topic of "childhood psychosis". She successfully applied for funding from the Deutscher Akademischer Austausch Dienst and embarked on her studies, only to find, three months into the doctorate, that she did not meet the University of London's eligibility criteria because she did not have a BA. Fortunately the powers that be had the good sense to find a solution by setting Uta a qualifying exam in psychology, and at last she was launched as a research psychologist.

Autism

In the 1960s, the predominant view of autistic disorder was that its origins were environmental rather than biological. It is all too easy to scoff at such views in the current climate, when genetic and neurobiological accounts of autism are commonplace and widely accepted, but in the light of the evidence they seemed reasonable. For a start, a genetic basis to autism did not seem plausible because the condition did not appear to run in families; there was no evidence of parent-to-child transmission, and it was unusual for more than one child in a family to be affected. Second, there was no indication of any gross neurological damage, and the children looked remarkably normal in physical appearance; unlike many other children of low IQ, their demeanour often suggested high intelligence, giving an impression that there were true abilities locked away beneath the surface. Furthermore, experienced clinicians noted certain deficiencies of social interaction in some parents of children with autism. Taken together, a logical conclusion was that autism was the result of a failure of the child to bond adequately with a parent, leading to a severe disturbance in social interaction. It has to be said that we are still a long way from understanding the neurobiological basis of autism: even with modern imaging techniques it is difficult to detect consistent abnormalities in the brains of children with autism, and the most plausible accounts, in terms of abnormal connectivity and/or deficient neurotransmitters, still lack strong evidence. Nevertheless, what has become clear is that this is a disorder with a genetic basis: The tide started to turn towards acceptance of this idea with a twin study by Folstein and Rutter (1977) and was strengthened by subsequent studies showing an increased incidence of milder "autistic-like" features in relatives of affected children (see Rutter, 2000, for a historical review). Nowadays it is accepted that social oddities do characterize a subset of parents of children with autism, but this is seen as evidence for a shared genetically determined trait in parent and child rather than as an indication of a psychogenic origin to autism. In the 1960s, however, when Uta started to work on autism, only a minority of experts were prepared to countenance the idea that it might be an "organic" condition, and she freely admits that her own conviction that we should look for brain bases rather than family origins was based more on hunch than on evidence. Fortunately, she found herself in an environment where there was sympathy for this hunch, and she was encouraged to do studies of basic perceptual and cognitive processes that might give a clue as to what distinguished these children from others. It is important to realize that autism research in the 1960s and 1970s was a very different enterprise from how it is today. The concept of "high-functioning autism" was not recognized, and the children who were the topic of study had severe cognitive limitations. Some lived in institutions, and others attended the handful of schools that specialized in educating such children, in particular the Sybil Elgar School in West London, which had been opened by the National Autistic Society in 1965. Doing experiments with such children required both stamina and ingenuity, and Uta addressed the difficult problem of devising tasks that would exploit the special interests and cognitive peaks of children with autism. Initially she learned by implementing studies devised by Ati Hermelin: these experiments, included in the classic text *Psychological experiments with austistic children* (Hermelin & O'Connor, 1970) were concerned with the extent to which children's ability to remember verbal or nonverbal material was influenced by meaning. The comparison group were younger children who were matched on memory span: the result,

seen for both verbal and nonverbal material, was that meaning improved recall for both groups, but its effect was far stronger in the typically developing controls than in the children with autism. This demonstration of a distinctive cognitive profile strengthened Uta's conviction that we were dealing with a neurological impairment rather than a social inhibition caused by poor parenting. She went on to devise her own experiment, which considered whether children with autism were able to take account of a stress pattern when remembering words. This could be investigated in two ways: first, did children remember more words when a sequence had prosodic structure; second, did they impose a natural prosodic structure on sequences that were presented with no stress? It was found that children with autism took less notice of prosody than did control children (Aurnhammer-Frith, 1969). This led on to work on pattern processing in language and in vision, including an ingenious study of pattern production that may be regarded as the first ever study demonstrating that children with autism had a deficit in generativity (the ability to generate ideas—the inverse of rigidity) (Frith, 1971a).

Throughout her doctoral studies, Uta benefited from the wholehearted support of Ati Hermelin and Neil O'Connor, and from them she learned the skill of designing elegantly simple experiments that illuminated the nature of underlying cognitive deficits. Once her PhD was completed, they offered her a post at their new Medical Research Council (MRC) Developmental Psychology Unit in central London; however, it was clear that she was now expected to develop a new line of research and so, rather than building on the work she had done on autism, she embarked on a series of studies of literacy development. It was only after Neil O'Connor's retirement, when John Morton took over as director of the re-named MRC Cognitive Development Unit in 1982, that Uta returned to studies of autism. Although by this time a more neuropsychological and biological approach to autism was gaining acceptance, in large part due to the influence of Uta's mentors at the IOP, Lorna Wing and Michael Rutter, there was still widespread resistance to the notion that there was a genetic component to the disorder. A remarkable development was the publication of a book entitled *Autistic children: New hope for a cure* by the Nobel laureate Niko Tinbergen and his wife Elisabeth (Tinbergen & Tinbergen, 1983). Tinbergen's reputation was founded on ethological work, and he had the highly original idea that the same observational methods that he had applied to the study of birds could throw light on the problems of children with autism. Unfortunately, his ingenious interpretations of autistic behaviour, and his consequent recommendation of "holding therapy" as a cure, were highly impressionistic and completely lacking in scientific rigour. This therapy involves parents in holding their child for prolonged periods, even if the child is resisting the embrace. The parent tries to establish eye contact and to share feeling with the child throughout the session. Uta wrote a scathing review of the book, but it continued to have a significant impact, with holding therapy continuing to be advocated as a treatment in Continental Europe as well as in the United Kingdom.

There followed a remarkably productive period of research on distinctive cognitive deficits in children with autism, fostered by the unique intellectual atmosphere of the Cognitive Development Unit, where John Morton encouraged his staff to question and debate both theory and experiments. During the early 1980s Uta's research students, Simon Baron-Cohen, Tony Attwood, and Amitta Shah, all made important new discoveries about autism.

Simon Baron-Cohen's influential doctoral studies (Baron-Cohen, Leslie, & Frith, 1985) were stimulated in part by Premack and Woodruff's (1978) work on chimpanzee cognition, in which the term "Theory of Mind" was first used to refer to the cognitive capacity to understand that others may have beliefs, desires, or intentions that differ from one's own. Uta recognized that this had potential relevance for studies of autism, and that Wimmer and Perner's (1983) studies of false belief in children provided an ideal paradigm for investigating Theory of Mind in this

population. The basic Sally-Anne task seemed so easy that Uta did not anticipate that children with autism would have any problem in responding correctly, and she was amazed when this task proved such a sensitive tool for revealing the underlying deficits in social cognition. Alan Leslie joined the collaboration working on this topic, providing a theoretical viewpoint that regarded Theory of Mind as a subset of more general metarepresentational knowledge. Throughout this period, the group benefited from John Morton's insistence that it was not enough just to describe what had been found: it was important to place it in a theoretical context that would allow for the development of new predictions that could be tested experimentally. It is not exaggerating to say that the Theory of Mind work transformed the conceptualization of autism by psychologists. Prior to this work, psychological studies on autism were not very coherent. The earlier studies on perceptual processes and pattern perception by Frith and others were clearly important, but it was difficult to relate these findings to the symptoms of the disorder, especially the core social impairments. In the United Kingdom, much theoretical debate had focused on the question of whether autism could be explained as a language disorder (e.g., Churchill, 1978), and new insights had been gained by explicit comparisons of children with autism and those with receptive language disorders (Bartak, Rutter, & Cox, 1975), but the core features of social impairment remained unexplained. In the United States, Marian Sigman, Peter Mundy and their collaborators were doing detailed observational studies of social interaction in children with autism, noting deficiencies in shared attention and nonverbal communication (Sigman, Mundy, Sherman, & Ungerer, 1986). The Theory of Mind work provided a way of conceptualizing social impairment as stemming from a cognitive failure in a system that computes representations of other minds and their contents. It not only made theoretical sense; it also provided new avenues for thinking about intervention, and many people working in special education found it helped them to understand why a child with autism might react in an unusual way to social situations. The fact that Theory of Mind could be assessed using a relatively simple experimental task must also have played a part in the enormous volume of research stimulated by the 1985 paper. This included fruitful collaborative studies with Josef Perner, who had hitherto worked solely on typical development, but who continued to develop new ways of looking at Theory of Mind, including the now-famous Smarties task (Perner, Frith, Leslie, & Leekam, 1989).

Tony Attwood was a part-time graduate student who also worked as a clinical psychologist. Previous studies had suggested that children with autism made deficient use of gestures: Attwood's studies showed that this was an oversimplification, and that the function of gestures was key. His findings related neatly to the Theory of Mind theorizing, showing that instrumental gestures, which do not require any interpersonal understanding, were intact, whereas expressive gestures, which serve a purely communicative function, were never observed in children with autism (Attwood, Frith, & Hermelin, 1988).

Amitta Shah's work was distinctively different. She focused on the unusually good performance on embedded figures and block design tasks in children with autism (Shah & Frith, 1983, 1993). Interest in strengths as well as weaknesses in the cognitive profile of autism was a distinctive aspect of work at the Cognitive Development Unit, and was key to the development of the theory of weak central coherence.

In parallel with these exciting developments on the cognitive front, there was a gradual broadening of the concept of autism. An epidemiological study by Lorna Wing and Judith Gould had already drawn attention to the existence of a large number of children with social abnormalities who did not have classic Kanner syndrome but nevertheless shared many features with these cases (Wing & Gould, 1979). A subsequent report noted that although most children with these characteristics were mentally retarded, this was not true for all (Wing, 1981a). At the same time, Asperger's report of a syndrome akin to autism but accompanied by relatively good language skills was summarized in English (Wing, 1981b), starting a lively debate as to whether this should be regarded as a subtype of autism or a distinct disorder. Meanwhile, as described above, genetic and family studies by Michael Rutter and associates were forcing researchers to the conclusion that there was a spectrum of autism, ranging from classic Kanner syndrome at one extreme to a broader phenotype at the other extreme, where the affected individual might function normally in society but have mild abnormalities of social interaction or communication. This was the start of a change in the nature of research on autism. Hitherto, cognitive studies had focused on children with intellectual retardation; gradually, as the concept of autism broadened, researchers turned more and more to the so-called high-functioning cases, who were far easier to work with and who, it was hoped, might throw autism-specific deficits into much sharper focus. Uta translated Asperger's text in 1991, and subsequently she became one of the world's experts in this syndrome.

One graduate student who took advantage of the broadened concept of autism to study cases of high-functioning autism and Asperger syndrome was Francesca Happé, who arrived at the Cognitive Development Unit in the late 1980s. Language in autism had always interested Uta, and she could see that investigation of the relationship between language and Theory of Mind would be a fruitful topic for study. Happé (1991) used Sperber and Wilson's (1986) Relevance Theory to generate predictions about how children with autism would interpret nonliteral language and found an impressive fit between theory and data. For Uta, the puzzle of language in autism made sense if one recognized that the core deficits were pragmatic failures in the appreciation of relevance, with other aspects of language impairment (e.g. in structural aspects such as grammar and phonology) being correlates of the condition rather than key features (Frith, 1989b).

In 1989 *Autism: Explaining the enigma*, Uta's synthesis of more than two decades of work on cognitive bases of this disorder (Frith, 1989a), appeared. She made a strong case for autism as a neurobiological disorder and presented compelling evidence for Theory of Mind as a core area of deficit, but she also drew attention to the a new idea concerning Weak Central Coherence as another aspect of the autistic mind. Unusually for an academic text, this was written in a clear, informal, and engaging style and accompanied by charming illustrations, and it immediately became a best-seller, with translations into numerous other languages.

Francesca Happé stayed on at the Cognitive Development Unit after completing her doctorate, and she and Uta worked together to consider how Weak Central Coherence related to other aspects of autistic cognition, including strengths in certain aspects of memory and perception as well as deficits in the ability to use context. This culminated in a detailed exposition of the Weak Central Coherence account by Frith and Happé in *Cognition* in 1994 (see also Happé & Frith, 2006, for an update of the theory).

The mid 1990s saw another major development that was to fundamentally change the course of Uta's research: the development of functional brain imaging. The earliest studies were done using the positon-emission tomography (PET) system at the MRC Cyclotron Unit at the Hammersmith Hospital, where Chris Frith was involved in developing activation paradigms using this new technology. Initially PET was used to probe the neural basis of Theory of Mind in normal adults (Fletcher et al., 1995); subsequently the same paradigm was applied to adults with Asperger syndrome, who showed a specific decrease of activation in the medial prefrontal cortex, which was the region activated by Theory of Mind tasks in control participants (Happé et al., 1996). Work on brain imaging gathered pace with the development of imaging facilities in central London at the Wellcome Department of Cognitive Neurology, where Chris Frith and his colleagues pioneered methods for analyzing brain activation in both PET and functional magnetic resonance imaging (fMRI) paradigms. Studies using fMRI provided yet more evidence for involvement of the medial frontal lobes in

Theory of Mind (Gallagher, Frith, & Snowling, 2000).

Chris Frith has always been a major influence in Uta's academic life, right from the earliest days at the IOP, when he helped her through her struggles with English language and culture. During 1970s and 1980s Uta and Chris would always discuss ideas and read one another's papers, but it was in the 1990s that their research collaboration really took off, as the new imaging techniques became increasingly important. In more recent years, their work has moved in a new and fruitful direction, with the integration of neuropsychological work on autism and schizophrenia. Both disorders involve abnormalities in social cognition as well as executive function impairments, but whereas people with autism under-utilize Theory of Mind, it appears that Theory of Mind is overactive in those with paranoid–schizophrenic symptoms, who see meaning and communication in situations where it is not intended. The cross-fertilization between research on these two disorders has led to innovative theoretical approaches to both autism and schizophrenia, engendering a line of work that promises to be enormously productive over the next few years.

Dyslexia

Uta's interest in causes of variation in children's reading goes right back to her undergraduate time in Saarbrücken, when she did a project on visuoperceptual skills and literacy development. Marianne Frostig's ideas on perceptuo-motor causes of learning disabilities were influential at the time (see: http://www.frostig-gesellschaft.de/M_Fro_EN.htm), and Uta's project involved training children to draw a line between two guidelines that got increasingly close together, to see how this related to literacy. The challenge of such a project in the pre-photocopier era should not be underestimated: To generate response forms, Uta needed to use a stylus to scratch out a template onto a special wax-impregnated paper, which could then be put through a special rotary printing press. She used this not only to make simple lines, but also drew pictures to create a "storyline" for what was otherwise a very boring task. The results were not conclusive, but Uta was interested to note that some children reversed letters, reading "b" as "d" and vice versa. She followed up this observation in her dissertation at IOP and subsequently picked it up again in her earliest papers on reading in the early 1970s (Frith, 1971b, 1974).

During the 1970s, three things happened that led Uta to radically rethink her views on dyslexia. First, during the summer of 1974, she made her first foray to the United States, spending a month at the University of Delaware, participating in an Institute on Reading and Child Development, sponsored by the Society for Research in Child Development. Around 30 postgrads and junior scientists took part, all living in a dorm on campus, and every few days new lecturers—including Lila Gleitman, Isabelle Liberman and Donald Shankweiler—would descend to give an intensive introduction to their own research. This experience led Uta to shift from regarding dyslexia as a disorder of visual perception to appreciate the important role of linguistic, especially phonological, processing.

The second factor was Uta's discovery of the extent to which reading and spelling could be dissociated in dyslexia. Particularly in older and brighter individuals, one could find cases where spelling problems persisted in a person who could read adequately. Uta became intrigued by this imbalance in skills, which led her to reflect on the different types of cognitive process involved in word recognition and written production. This led to her editing an influential book on this topic (Frith, 1980). This was very different from previous educational texts on spelling, because it brought together perspectives from cognitive neuropsychology, linguistics, and developmental psychology. The cognitive neuropsychology perspective was only just beginning to be applied to children, with the recognition that by studying cognitive development in atypical populations one could throw light on normal developmental processes. Chapters by Uta's colleagues Rick Cromer and Barbara Dodd, on spelling in

language-impaired and hearing-impaired children, respectively, exemplified this approach.

The third major influence on Uta's thinking was Maggie Snowling, who started her graduate studies at the Cognitive Development Unit in 1976. Maggie already had an intense interest in dyslexia, a problem that affected members of her immediate family, and she sought out Bevé Hornsby, who had founded the Hornsby International Dyslexia Centre in London and was developing pioneering new approaches to intervention (Hornsby & Miles, 1980). This gave Maggie experience of assessing and teaching children with severe and selective reading difficulties, who provided ample evidence of the importance of phonological processing problems in leading to literacy impairments. Her thesis studies built on the foundations set by the original Hermelin and O'Connor work: carefully designed small-scale studies in which performance of a disordered group was compared with that of younger children matched on performance on a key measure—in this case, reading level. This led to one of the earliest demonstrations that dyslexic children were poor even relative to reading-age matched controls on tasks involving phonological processing, even when no written language was involved (Snowling, 1981). Subsequently, Uta and Maggie carried out a study explicitly comparing reading skills in autism and dyslexia, showing that whereas processing of meaning was disrupted in the former group, processing of sounds was impaired in the latter (Frith & Snowling, 1983).

One of the things that made John Morton a remarkable director of the Cognitive Development Unit was the fact that he did not start out as a developmental psychologist: his background was in mainstream experimental psychology. The influence of this background, with its insistence on articulation of a clear theoretical framework, had a marked impact on his colleagues and students at the Unit. It also meant that John continued to move easily between the worlds of adult and child psychology, and encouraged interactions between the two domains. Thus it came to pass that Uta found herself participating in a meeting on Surface Dyslexia, a topic of considerable interest to neuropsychologists working on acquired dyslexias, which generated a book in which she was encouraged to lay out a theoretical position specifying how developmental dyslexia related to normal stages of reading development (Frith, 1985). This contrasted with models of reading development adapted from adult neuropsychology that attempted to describe possible processes causing change in behaviour. The model led to increasing international recognition of her work on reading, with an invitation to participate in a meeting of the prestigious Orton Society (Frith, 1986).

For the next few years, work on dyslexia took a back seat, as Uta again turned to concentrate on autism, where such remarkable progress was being made. However, the advent of brain imaging led to an opportunity to work on one of the first PET studies of dyslexia, in collaboration with Eraldo Paulesu, an Italian neurologist who was working at the Wellcome Department of Cognitive Neurology with Chris Frith. The crucial insight that stimulated these studies was that dyslexia was not just a childhood disorder: it persisted into adulthood, with residual signs being detectable even in those who appeared to have compensated for their difficulties. Maggie Snowling's long-term follow-ups of cases she had seen in childhood emphasized this point, and with her help it was possible to recruit adults who had been studied as dyslexic children. They showed a distinctive pattern of brain activation during phonological tasks, in which the normal connectivity between posterior and anterior areas appeared to be abolished (Paulesu et al., 1996).

Two other lines of work were started in the late 1990s: high-risk and crosslinguistic studies. The high-risk study, done in collaboration with Alison Gallagher and Maggie Snowling, capitalized on the evidence that dyslexia was a strongly genetic disorder, by selecting 3-year-olds whose parents had dyslexia, so that they could be studied before they were introduced to reading. Literacy impairment at 6 years was substantially more frequent in the at-risk than the control group and was associated with early language deficits, confirming the view that the problems of children with dyslexia encompass oral as well as written language (Gallagher, Frith, & Snowling, 2000). Maggie Snowling tells us more about the later phases of this study in her chapter in this volume (Snowling, 2008).

Cross-linguistic studies provide a particularly rich testbed for theories of reading disability, because they enable one to test predictions about the manifestations of dyslexia in languages that have different relationships between orthography and phonology. One set of studies arose from Uta's collaborations with Heinz Wimmer. Originally, they had worked together on Theory of Mind, but Wimmer was looking for something new, and comparisons of reading development in German and English was a topic that had not previously been adequately addressed. There followed a series of studies by Wimmer and his colleague Karin Landerl that emphasized the dangers of relying solely on one language, English, when developing a theory of dyslexia. Although there were many similarities between profiles of dyslexia in the two languages (Landerl, Wimmer, & Frith, 1997), the German-speaking children also posed problems for the theory that dyslexia was primarily a disorder of phoneme awareness (Landerl & Wimmer, 2000).

The other opportunity for cross-linguistic study arose from the collaboration with Eraldo Paulesu. Uta was able to obtain EU funds for a PET study of dyslexia in English, French, and Italian, three languages that contrasted considerably in the regularity of their orthography. This showed that, despite different levels of behavioural impairment, reduced activity in the same region of the left hemisphere was seen in dyslexics from all three countries. As the title of the paper aptly put it, there appeared to be a biological unity underlying the cultural diversity due to different orthographies (Paulesu et al., 2001). These same participants continue to be studied using new methods of imaging, with a recent voxel-based morphometry, finding altered density of grey and white matter of specific left hemisphere regions, and altered connectivity between regions (Silani et al., 2005).

The work on dyslexia nicely illustrates how Uta has succeeded in integrating different levels of explanation—neurobiological, cognitive, and behavioural—in her model of this disorder. Her theoretical approach has sharpened our thinking about causal pathways, and to recognize that we will only gain a full understanding if we take a cognitive neurobiological perspective (Frith, 1997).

Conclusion

Uta describes herself as someone whose early academic career was characterized by enormous good fortune: first, the fact that, by chance, she found herself at one of the few universities in Germany that taught experimental psychology and provided her with the opportunity to attend lectures in a subject far removed from her major discipline; second, her arrival at the IOP at a time when it was alive with iconoclastic young scientists who favoured empiricism and neurobiology over traditional psychoanalytic approaches; third, the chance drop-out of a potential student that allowed her to obtain a diploma in clinical psychology; and, fourth, the sequence of events that led her to be taken on as a PhD student by Hermelin and O'Connor, whose unique experimental approach was combined with a remarkable generosity of spirit towards their new student. The marital and academic partnership with Chris Frith has been the strongest formative influence on Uta's career and would never have happened had she not crept away from her art history lectures to find out what this psychology stuff was all about. It is intriguing to wonder what Uta would be doing now had any one of these events not occurred. One thing that is certain, however, is that Uta's success is not due simply to serendipity. She benefited from the opportunities provided because she matched them with her keen scientific interest and a talent for social communication that made her an excellent student, supervisor, and collaborator. For Uta, a theory was an important step in the process of hypothesis formation, and the goal was to test it rigorously rather than to shore it up at all costs. Her talent for devising simple, child-friendly experiments that cut to the heart of a question remains unsurpassed. Uta was indeed fortunate to have regular contact with so many talented and original academic influences, but she must also be credited for being someone who could extract the maximum from these, being ready to listen, debate, and learn wherever new ideas were being discussed. As well as the many distinguished academics whom she credits with influencing her work, she also pays tribute to the parents of children with autism and dyslexia, whose insights into their children's cognition have provided a rich source of ideas.

This chapter has barely been able to scratch the surface concerning Uta's own work and the formative influences on it. In the remainder of this book we will hear from her students and collaborators, who will amply demonstrate the important influence she has had on subsequent generations of researchers.

REFERENCES

Attwood, A., Frith, U., & Hermelin, B. (1988). The understanding and use of interpersonal gestures by autistic and Down's syndrome children. *Journal of Autism and Developmental Disorders, 18*, 241–257.

Aurnhammer-Frith, U. (1969). Emphasis and meaning in recall in normal and autistic children. *Language and Speech, 12*, 29–38.

Baron-Cohen, S., Leslie, A. M., & Frith, U. (1985). Does the autistic child have a "theory of mind"? *Cognition, 21*, 37–46.

Bartak, L., Rutter, M., & Cox, A. (1975). A comparative study of infantile autism and specific developmental receptive language disorder: I. The children. *British Journal of Psychiatry, 126*, 127–145.

Churchill, D. W. (1978). Language of autistic children: The problem beyond conditioning. In M. Rutter (Ed.), *Autism: A reappraisal of concepts and treatment*. New York: Plenum Press.

Eysenck, H. J. (1953). *Uses and abuses of psychology*. Harmondsworth: Penguin.

Eysenck, H. J. (1957). *Sense and nonsense in psychology*. Harmondsworth: Penguin.

Fletcher, P. C., Happé, F., Frith, U., Baker, S. C., Dolan, R. J., Frackowiak, R. S. J., & Frith, C. D. (1995). Other minds in the brain: A functional imaging study of "theory of mind" in story comprehension. *Cognition, 57*, 109–128.

Folstein, S., & Rutter, M. (1977). Infantile autism: A genetic study of 21 twin pairs. *Journal of Child Psychology and Psychiatry, 18*, 297–321.

Frith, U. (1971a). Spontaneous patterns produced by autistic, normal and subnormal children. In M. Rutter (Ed.), *Infantile autism: Concepts, characteristics and treatment* (pp. 113–135). London: Churchill Livingstone.

Frith, U. (1971b). Why do children reverse letters? *British Journal of Psychology, 62*, 459–468.

Frith, U. (1974). Internal schemata for letters in good and bad readers. *British Journal of Psychology, 65*, 233–241.

Frith, U. (Ed.). (1980). *Cognitive processes in spelling*. London: Academic Press.

Frith, U. (1985). Beneath the surface of developmental dyslexia. In K. E. Patterson, J. C. Marshall, & M. Coltheart (Eds.), *Surface dyslexia* (pp. 301–330). Hove, UK: Lawrence Erlbaum Associates Ltd.

Frith, U. (1986). A developmental framework for developmental dyslexia. *Annals of Dyslexia, 36*, 69–81.

Frith, U. (1989a). *Autism: Explaining the enigma*. Oxford: Blackwell.

Frith, U. (1989b). A new look at language and communication in autism. *British Journal of Disorders of Communication, 24*, 123–150.

Frith, U. (1991). Translation and annotation of "Autistic psychopathy in childhood" by Hans Asperger. In U. Frith (Ed.), *Autism and Asperger syndrome* (pp. 36–92). Cambridge: Cambridge University Press.

Frith, U. (1997). Brain, mind and behaviour in dyslexia. In C. Hulme & M. Snowling (Eds.), *Dyslexia: Biology, cognition and intervention* (pp. 1–19). London: Whurr Publishers Ltd.

Frith, U., & Happé F. (1994). Autism: Beyond "theory of mind". *Cognition, 50*, 115–132.

Frith, U., & Snowling, M. (1983). Reading for meaning and reading for sound in autistic and dyslexic children. *British Journal of Developmental Psychology, 1*, 329–342.

Gallagher, A., Frith, U., & Snowling, M. (2000). Precursors of literacy delay among children at genetic risk of dyslexia. *Journal of Child Psychology and Psychiatry, 41*, 202–213.

Happé, F. G. E. (1991). Communicative competence and theory of mind in autism: A test of relevance theory. *Cognition, 48*, 101–119.

Happé, F., Ehlers, S., Fletcher, P., Frith, U., Johansson, M., Gillberg, C., Dolan, R., Frackowiak, R., & Frith, C. (1996). Theory of mind in the brain: Evidence from a PET scan study of Asperger syndrome. *Neuroreport, 8*, 197–201.

Happé, F., & Frith, U. (2006). The weak coherence account: Detail-focused cognitive style in autism spectrum disorders. *Journal of Autism and Developmental Disorders, 36*, 5–25.

Hermelin, B., & O'Connor, N. (1970). *Psychological experiments with autistic children*. Oxford: Pergamon Press.

Hornsby, B., & Miles, T. R. (1980). The effects of a dyslexia-centred teaching programme. *British Journal of Educational Psychology, 50*, 236–242.

Landerl, K., Wimmer, H., & Frith, U. (1997). The impact of orthographic consistency on dyslexia: A German–English comparison. *Cognition, 63*, 315–334.

Landerl, K., & Wimmer, H. (2000). Deficits in phoneme segmentation are not the core problem of dyslexia: Evidence from German and English children. *Applied Psycholinguistics, 21*, 243–262.

O'Connor, N., & Hermelin, B. (1959). Discrimination and reversal learning in imbeciles. *Journal of Abnormal and Social Psychology, 59*, 409–413.

Paulesu, E., Demonet, J. F., Fazio, F., McCrory, E., Chanoine, V., Brunswick, N., Cappa, S. F., Cossu, G., Habib, M., Frith, C. D., & Frith, U. (2001). Dyslexia: Cultural diversity and biological unity. *Science, 291*, 2165–2167.

Paulesu, E., Frith, U., Snowling, M. J., Gallagher, A., Morton, J., Frackowiak, R. S. J., & Frith, C. D. (1996). Is developmental dyslexia a disconnection syndrome? Evidence from PET scanning. *Brain, 119*, 143–157.

Perner, J., Frith, U., Leslie, A. M., & Leekam, S. R. (1989). Exploration of the autistic child's theory of mind: Knowledge, belief, and communication. *Child Development, 60*, 688–700.

Premack, D., & Woodruff, G. (1978). Does the chimpanzee have a theory of mind? *Behavioral and Brain Sciences, 4*, 515–526.

Rutter, M. (2000). Genetic studies of autism: From the 1970s into the millennium. *Journal of Abnormal Child Psychology, 28*, 3–14.

Shah, A., & Frith, U. (1983). An islet of ability in autistic children: A research note. *Journal of Child Psychology and Psychiatry, 24*, 613–620.

Shah, A., & Frith, U. (1993). Why do autistic individuals show superior performance on the block design task? *Journal of Child Psychology and Psychiatry, 34*, 1351–1364.

Sigman, M., Mundy, P., Sherman, T., & Ungerer, J. (1986). Social interactions of autistic, mentally retarded and normal children and their caregivers. *Journal of Child Psychology and Psychiatry, 27*, 647–656.

Silani, G., Frith, U., Demonet, J. F., Fazio, F., Perani, D., Price, C., Frith, C. D., & Paulesu, E. (2005). Brain abnormalities underlying altered activation in dyslexia: A voxel based morphometry study. *Brain*, *128*, 2453–2461.

Snowling, M. (1981). Phonemic deficits in developmental dyslexia. *Psychological Research*, *43*, 219–234.

Sperber, D., & Wilson, D. (1986). *Relevance: Communication and cognition*. Oxford: Blackwell.

Tinbergen, N., & Tinbergen, E. A. (1983). *Autistic children: New hope for a cure*. Allen & Unwin: London.

Wimmer, H., & Perner, J. (1983). Beliefs about beliefs: Representation and constraining function of wrong beliefs in young children's understanding of deception. *Cognition*, *13*, 103–128.

Wing, L. (1981a). Language, social, and cognitive impairments in autism and severe mental retardation. *Journal of Autism and Developmental Disorders*, *11*, 31–44.

Wing, L. (1981b). Asperger's syndrome: A clinical account. *Psychological Medicine*, *11*, 115–129.

Wing, L., & Gould, J. (1979). Severe impairments of social interaction and associated abnormalities in children: Epidemiology and classification. *Journal of Autism and Developmental Disorders*, *9*, 11–29.

THE QUARTERLY JOURNAL OF EXPERIMENTAL PSYCHOLOGY
2008, 61 (1), 27–39

Precursors to a Theory of Mind in infancy: Perspectives for research on autism

Beate Sodian and Claudia Thoermer

Ludwig-Maximilians-Universität München, Munich, Germany

There is ample evidence for a conceptual deficit in normally developing 3-year-olds' and autistic children's understanding of the mind. Recent research using nonverbal tasks has challenged this view since even 15-month-old infants appear to base their action predictions on a representation of the agent's beliefs (Onishi & Baillargeon, 2005). Our own findings from looking-time experiments indicate, however, that 16-month-olds' action predictions depend on behavioural and situational cues, rather than on a person's access to information. Further research is reviewed that indicates that 14-month-olds understand what another person can and cannot see, and that 18-month-olds predict a person's action from what she previously saw, when supported by behavioural cues. These findings support a constructivist view of a gradual understanding of conditions for knowing during the second year. The relevance of such findings for research on autism is discussed.

Children's acquisition of a Theory of Mind proceeds in two steps: While even two-year-olds possess an understanding of desires and intentions, children acquire an understanding of knowledge and belief only around the age of three to four years (see Wellman, Cross, & Watson, 2001, for a meta-analysis; Sodian, 2005; Wellman, 2002, for reviews). This traditional view has been challenged, however, by more recent findings on the early development of social understanding in infancy. Towards the end of the first year of life, infants conceptualize humans as intentional agents, pursuing action goals in a rational way (see Gergely, 2002; Tomasello, Carpenter, Call, Behne, & Moll, 2005, for reviews). In the second year, they begin to understand people as *mental* agents in the sense that they construe the other's inner experience in terms of their own equivalent mental states (see Poulin-Dubois, 1999, for a review). Based on findings of a looking-time study, Onishi and Baillargeon (2005) even claim that 15-month-old infants have an understanding of belief and thus possess a Theory of Mind.

How do recent findings on infant social understanding bear on the traditional view of Theory of Mind development? We begin by arguing that the case for a conceptual deficit in 3-year-olds' and younger children's understanding of the mind cannot easily be dismissed. We then review recent research on early competencies in the third and second years of life and ask for their significance for Theory of Mind development in normal children and in children with autism.

Correspondence should be addressed to Beate Sodian, Department of Psychology, Ludwig-Maximilians-Universität München, Leopoldstr.13, D-80802 Munich, Germany. E-mail: sodian@edupsy.uni-muenchen.de

http://www.psypress.com/qjep
DOI:10.1080/17470210701508681

UNDERSTANDING KNOWLEDGE AND BELIEF: THE CASE FOR A CONCEPTUAL DEFICIT IN NORMALLY DEVELOPING THREE-YEAR-OLDS AND IN AUTISTIC CHILDREN

Theory of Mind research, since its beginnings, has demonstrated a conceptual deficit in normal 3-year-olds and in autistic children. From the start, however, the claim that young children and children with developmental disorders fail to understand the formation of knowledge and beliefs in the human mind has been under attack from proponents of a conceptual continuity view who argued that the deficit was due to the information-processing demands of the tasks. Research on mind reading in autism has proved to be extremely fruitful in developing methodological standards for providing evidence for the specificity of the deficit.

In their seminal paper, Baron-Cohen, Leslie, and Frith (1985) showed that autistic children with a verbal mental age above 4 years failed the false-belief task, but passed parallel tasks that required behavioural or mechanical inferences of similar complexity, but not mental-state attribution (Baron-Cohen, Leslie, & Frith, 1986). This research strategy was refined in subsequent studies, to provide more stringent controls. One example is work by Sodian and Frith (1992) on deception in autistic children (see also Frith, 2003). We showed that autistic children, like typically developing 3-year-olds (but unlike children with mental retardation), were extremely poor in acquiring a simple deceptive strategy in a competitive game, but passed a control task that required them to hinder an opponent from attaining a goal by physical obstruction ("sabotage"), rather than by inducing a false belief. Thus, the deficit could not be attributed to a failure to understand the competitive game or to a lack of motivation, but appeared to be specific to the representation of mental states. Similarly, Leslie and Thaiss (1992) compared the false-belief task to the "false-photos" task and found that autistic persons' difficulty was specific to understanding mental representation and not to understanding representation in general.

It is sometimes overlooked that studies of Theory of Mind in normally developing children have also controlled for the specificity of the conceptual deficit (Perner, Leekam, & Wimmer, 1987). In a recent study, Sodian, Thoermer, and Dietrich (2006) used an interactive nonstory task, similar to a paradigm used by Povinelli, Nelson, and Boysen (1990) in research on chimpanzees to test whether children before their third birthday have some understanding of the relation between seeing and knowing. Children aged 30 to 36 months observed that one person saw a hiding event (a sticker being hidden in one of four cups) while the other person turned her back towards the scene. They were then asked to choose the person who could help them find the sticker. Children below the age of 35 months performed at chance level, while all children at or above the age of 36 months were above chance (choosing the correct person in at least three out of four trials). Both the younger and the older children did, however, pass a nonepistemic control task, in which they had to decide which one of two persons could help them unlock a treasure box, where one person had a key, and the other one did not. Thus, the findings from the interactive task are remarkably consistent with earlier research on children's understanding of knowledge formation in indicating that the age of three years is the earliest age at which an ability to consistently judge another's epistemic state based on his access to information can be observed (e.g., Pratt & Bryant, 1990).

However, over the past 10 years a growing body of research has addressed two-year-olds' and even infants' ability for mental state attribution, with findings indicating that an implicit understanding of mental states precedes a full or explicit one. We briefly review research on Theory of Mind precursors in infants and young children, starting with the third year of life.

AN IMPLICIT THEORY OF MIND IN TWO-YEAR-OLDS?

Two sources of evidence indicate an implicit understanding of knowledge and belief in children below the age of three years: children's ability to take their own and others' epistemic states into account in communication, and their looking behaviours in false-belief tasks. Call and Carpenter (2001) presented 27- and 32-month-olds with the task of finding a reward in one of three possible hiding locations (tubes) and found that they checked (i.e., looked into) locations more if they had not seen the hiding than if they had witnessed the hiding event; some children also did not continue to check when only one possible location for the reward was left (because they had already found two to be empty). These findings indicate an ability to monitor their own knowledge state in 2-year-olds. With regard to other people's epistemic states, O'Neill (1996) found that 2-year-olds (27- and 31-month-olds) were aware of their mother's knowledge or ignorance of a critical fact (an object's displacement). They tended to name the object and indicate its location more frequently when the mother did not witness the critical (hiding) event than when she was present. Similarly, Shwe and Markman (1997) found that 30-month-olds were sensitive to an adult's misunderstanding of their verbal request. However, a recent study by Dunham, Dunham, and O'Keefe (2000) highlights the importance of control conditions: Both 28- and 33-month-old children employed the pointing gesture more often to convey information to a parent who had not witnessed the hiding event than to a parent who had. However, only the older group monitored the parent's ability to see the actual hiding event in a control (sham) condition in which the parent first covered her eyes but reopened them during the placement of the sticker and appropriately gestured less in the sham condition than in the parent-ignorant condition. Carpenter, Call, and Tomasello (2003) even found that 33- and 38-month-old children were able to take an adult's false belief into account when complying with a request ("can you get it for me?", "it" being the desired object that had been transferred unbeknownst to the adult). Thus, it appears that a representation of another person's epistemic state in communicative exchanges precedes the ability to make an action prediction or explanation based on an attribution

of knowledge or belief. Note, however, that such an implicit representation of belief appears to precede a full or explicit one by just a few months.

Interestingly, an implicit understanding of false belief, as indicated by visual orienting responses, has also been shown in children just below the age of three years: Children between the ages of 2;11 and 3;6 looked towards the location where a story figure would search for an object based on her false belief when anticipating the return of the story figure, but pointed towards the location where the object really was, when asked for an explicit action prediction (Clements & Perner, 1994; Garnham & Ruffman, 2001). Recent findings of an eye-tracking study by Southgate, Senju, and Csibra (2007) even indicate an implicit awareness of false belief in 25-month-olds. Ruffman, Garnham, and Rideout (2001) tested a group of children with autism on implicit (eye gaze) and explicit (verbal) false-belief understanding and found that the children with autism failed the implicit false-belief task while they passed a nonsocial control task. Verbal ability was correlated with performance on the explicit false-belief task whereas eye gaze was not. Thus, eye gaze may be better than verbal measures at differentiating children with autism from clinical controls (e.g., children with mental retardation), and may tap core knowledge in the social domain.

BEHAVIOUR RULES OR THEORY OF MIND IN THE SECOND YEAR OF LIFE?

Onishi and Baillargeon (2005) used a nonverbal unexpected-transfer false-belief task as a looking-time paradigm and found that 15.5-month-old infants looked longer at events that were inconsistent with the actress's belief than at events that were consistent with her belief. For example, infants who watched a sequence of events in which the actress initially placed an object in Location A, then disappeared behind a screen, and was unable to see that the object was moved from Location A to Location B, looked longer at the actress searching in Location B than in Location A. The looking-time patterns obtained in the experiment are consistent with the interpretation that 15.5-month-old infants represent a person's false belief and base their action expectations on their understanding of the person's true or false belief about reality. Perner and Ruffman (2005) pointed out, however, that a number of lower level interpretations of these findings are also possible: For example, infants may form action expectations by applying behaviour rules, such as "people look for objects where they last saw them". Moreover, the findings are also consistent with a teleological explanation, interpreting behaviour in terms of goals and external circumstances. A debate has arisen about these interpretations (Csibra & Southgate, 2006; Leslie, 2005; Ruffman & Perner, 2006), in which proponents of an innate Theory of Mind module argue that it is plausible that a specialized neurocognitive mechanism that matures during the second year of life produces early belief (as well as pretend and desire) representations. In contrast, Ruffman and Perner (2006) argue that a more constructivist view of Theory of Mind development as a result of an interaction between a genetic endowment and the environment is equally consistent with the empirical data. In particular, Ruffman and Perner (2006) point out that it is plausible that infants would evolve behaviour rules, possibly constrained by core principles, and that their statistical learning abilities provide them with the means to acquire and refine such rules over the course of the first years of life.

A STUDY OF 16-MONTH-OLDS' UNDERSTANDING OF KNOWLEDGE FORMATION

If infants' action predictions are based on behaviour rules, rather than an informational-representational understanding of the mind, then we would expect them to first acquire gross rules of thumb that are based on salient situational cues. Such early rules sometimes lead to wrong action predictions and are refined as a result of experience. For example, infants may expect an association between a person's presence at a certain sequence of events (such as a hiding event) and her subsequent successful action, based on the experience that a person's successful action is normally associated with her presence at a sequence of events preceding the action and that mistakes often happen if people were absent at events preceding the critical action. If such an expectation is based on an understanding of knowledge formation—that is, an understanding of the relation between access to information and knowledge or beliefs—then we would expect infants to closely monitor a person's access to information as a basis for action predictions. If, on the other hand, the action expectation is based on situational or behavioural contingencies, then we would expect infants to overgeneralize the rule that people who were present normally act correctly, and people who were absent normally do not.

We[1] carried out a series of studies of 16-month-old infants' understanding of the seeing–knowing relation in a habituation paradigm. In all studies, during the habituation phase, infants saw a person sitting behind a small stage watching a toy disappear in one of two locations, a blue box or a red box, located at the opposite ends of the stage while an off-voice said "*Look, the bunny is hiding in here*". (The toy was being moved surreptitiously from underneath the stage.) Subsequently, while saying "*I think the bunny is here*", the person reached into the box where the toy was hidden, but did not retrieve it (see Figure 1). Looking-time measurement started when the person reached into the hiding location and then remained still, and a trial ended when the infant looked away for at least two seconds. In the test phase, infants were presented with alternating test trials. In correct test trials, the person searched in the correct location (i.e., where the toy was hidden); in incorrect test trials the person searched in the empty location.

---

[1] The authors would like to acknowledge the collaboration of Carmen Krempel, who ran Experiment 2 for her Diploma thesis at the University of Würzburg.

Figure 1. *Basic procedure of the habituation phase: (a) toy in full view; (b) toy disappears in box in full view of person; (c) person searches for toy.*

In a preliminary study (Sodian, Thoermer, Metz, & Schöppner, 2002), we sought to establish that infants distinguished between correct and incorrect test trials when the person was present and had visual access to the hiding event during the test phase. A total of 15 infants (10 boys, 5 girls) with a mean age of 16 months and 24 days ($SD = 25$ days) looked reliably longer at incorrect ($M = 6.66$ s; $SD = 3.80$ s) than correct test trials ($M = 4.36$ s, $SD = 2.37$ s); $t(14) = 2.918$, $p = .011$; 13 out of 15 infants, indicating that they expected the person to search for the toy in the correct location (see Figure 2).

Experiment 1

In Experiment 1 we explored whether infants' expectations about the person's search behaviour

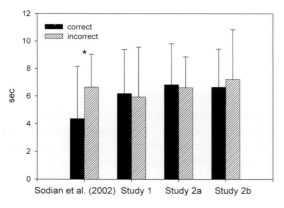

Figure 2. *Mean looking times at correct and incorrect search trials for the preliminary study by Sodian et al. (2002) and Experiments 1, 2a, and 2b.*

were influenced by the person's absence during the hiding event. If infants encoded the person's absence as a condition preventing her from successful action, then they should not expect her to search in the correct location—that is, they should not look longer at incorrect than at correct test trials.

Method

The study followed a 2 (order of test trials) × 2 (colour of hiding box during habituation) × 2 (side of hiding box during habituation) design.

The final sample comprised 32 children (17 girls and 15 boys), with a mean age of 16 months and 10 days ($SD = 16$ days). The procedure for each habituation trial was the same as that described above. Habituation trials were repeated until infants' total looking time over three consecutive trials had decreased to half the sum of looking times over the first three trials of habituation. Infants were spread approximately evenly across habituation conditions, and half the children saw incorrect test trials first, the other half correct test trials.

In the test phase, three correct and three incorrect test trials were presented in alternating order. In both trial types, the person first looked at the toy on the stage and then disappeared behind an occluder (see Figure 3a). While the occluder blocked her view, the toy was moved to one of the two hiding locations. The person then returned and reached into the correct box in correct trials and into the incorrect box in incorrect trials.

a

b

c

Figure 3. *Test procedures with correct search for Experiment 1 (a), Experiment 2a (b), and Experiment 2b (c).*
Fig 3a:
1) Bunny and person facing front
2) Screen closed, bunny facing front center
3) Screen closed, bunny moving into box
4) Person searching for bunny
Fig 3b:
1) Bunny and person facing front
2) Bunny moving into box, person watching
3) Screen closed, bunny hidden in box
4) Person searching for bunny
Fig 3c:
1) Bunny and person facing front
2) Screen closed, bunny facing front center
3) Bunny moving into box, person watching
4) Person searching for bunny

Results and discussion

Children needed a minimum of 6 and a maximum of 11 ($M = 7.22$, $SD = 1.62$) habituation trials.

A 2 (trial type) × 2 (order) × 2 (habituation box) × 2 (habituation side) × 2 (gender) analysis of variance (ANOVA) with repeated measures on the first factor revealed no main effects or interactions apart from a triple interaction of trial type, order, and gender. Separate planned t tests for independent groups showed that only girls looked significantly longer at correct trials if presented with correct trials first, $t(15) = 2.25$, $p = .04$. There were no effects of trial type on looking times in the test phase. Infants looked equally long at correct ($M = 6.2$ s, $SD = 3.2$ s) and at incorrect ($M = 5.95$ s, $SD = 3.63$ s) trials, $t(31) = 0.41$, *ns*; 50% of the children looking longer at one or the other trial type (see Figure 2).

This result is consistent with the interpretation that infants were aware of the significance of informational access. When the actress had no access to information, there was no reason to expect that she would search at the correct location. Thus, infants looked equally long at correct and incorrect search. The present findings indicate that infants encoded the actress's access to information.

However, it is possible that infants did not encode the person's access to information, but simply reacted to a salient situational cue—that is, the fact that the person was not present at some point in the sequence of events. We tested this interpretation in two subsequent studies in which we varied the point in time when an occluder was moved in, blocking the person's visual access from the hiding events. In these two studies, the person was always present during the critical hiding event (i.e., she watched the toy disappear in Location A or B), but an occluder was pushed in before or after the hiding event.

Experiment 2A

In Studies 2a and 2b we tested whether 16-month-olds encoded the person's access to information about the critical hiding event, irrespective of the fact that she was absent at some point before or after the hiding event.

Method

A total of 24 infants (11 girls and 13 boys), with a mean age of 16 months and 12 days ($SD = 12$ days) were in the final sample of Experiment 2a. Design and procedure for the habituation phase were the same as those in Experiment 1, with infants spread approximately evenly across habituation conditions and half the children seeing correct and the other half incorrect test trials first.

Test trials also proceeded as described for Experiment 1 except that the actress watched the toy being hidden in one of the two locations, and immediately after the toy had disappeared, an occluder was pushed in for the same amount of time as in Experiment 1. Then the occluder was removed, and the actress reached into the

correct box in correct trials and into the incorrect box in incorrect trials (see Figure 3b).

Results and discussion

Infants needed between 6 and 12 ($M = 7.63$, $SD = 2.1$) habituation trials.

An ANOVA parallel to that described for Experiment 1 showed no effects whatsoever.

Thus, even if the searcher was briefly absent after having watched the hiding event infants showed no differentiation between correct ($M = 6.84$ s, $SD = 2.99$ s) and incorrect ($M = 6.62$ s, $SD = 2.25$ s) test trials, with half of the participants looking longer at either kind of test trial.

This pattern of findings is consistent with the interpretation that infants' action expectations were influenced by a salient situational or behavioural cue (the person's absence) rather than an encoding of informational access. However, it is possible that memory problems accounted for the present findings, since the temporal contiguity between hiding event and search was disrupted.

Experiment 2B

In Experiment 2b we therefore changed the order of events such that the person was absent immediately before the hiding event.

Method

The final sample consisted of 20 infants (9 girls and 11 boys), with a mean age of 16 months and 8 days ($SD = 10$ days). Design and procedure for the habituation phase were the same as those described above, with infants spread approximately evenly across habituation conditions and half the infants being presented with correct and incorrect test trials first.

Test trials proceeded as described above except for the sequence of events: The actress established eye contact with the infant and then disappeared behind the occluder for the same length of time as in Experiment 2a. Then the occluder was removed, and the person watched the toy disappear in one of the two hiding locations. Immediately after the toy had disappeared, she searched in either the correct or the incorrect location, in correct and incorrect trials, respectively (see Figure 3c).

Results and discussion

Infants needed a minimum of 6 and a maximum of 14 ($M = 7.8$, $SD = 2.42$) habituation trials.

Again, the ANOVA as described for the previous studies showed no significant main or interaction effects.

Mean looking times at correct ($M = 6.66$ s, $SD = 2.78$ s) and incorrect ($M = 7.23$ s, $SD = 3.62$ s) test events did not differ significantly, $t(19) = 0.61$, ns; 11 out of 20 infants looking longer at incorrect trials. Infants failed to differentiate between the two trial types.

Qualitative coding did, however, reveal that in Experiment 2b infants looked more often back and forth between the two locations when the actress searched in the wrong location ($M = 1.0$, $SD = .725$) than when she searched in the correct location ($M = .45$, $SD = .51$); $t(19) = 3.24$, $p = .004$.

Taken together, the present findings indicate that at the age of 16 months infants do not understand the link between informational access and knowledge formation. Rather, they appear to base their action expectations on salient situational cues such as a person's presence or absence regardless of whether the person was present or absent during a critical event. Do infants fail to distinguish between informationally relevant and irrelevant disruptions because they fail to represent informational access? When do infants begin to represent what another person sees independently of what they themselves can see?

LEVEL 1 VISUAL PERSPECTIVE TAKING IN 14-MONTH-OLD INFANTS

The 16-month-olds' failure in the paradigm described above made us wonder whether infants at this age possess the prerequisites for encoding other persons' visual access to information: Do they represent what another person does and does not see? Earlier research on visual perspective taking showed that children pass simple verbal perspective-taking tasks at about $2\frac{1}{2}$ years (Flavell, Everett, Croft, & Flavell, 1981). Recent research on infants' understanding of seeing showed a basic understanding of the function of the eyes in 12-month-olds: Infants follow an experimenter's gaze direction and head turns more when the experimenter's eyes are open than when they are shut (Brooks & Meltzoff, 2002). Moreover, 14-month-olds follow an experimenter's gaze towards a target more when the experimenter's line of sight is clear than when it is obstructed by a barrier (or when the barrier is opaque rather than transparent; Butler, Caron, & Brooks, 2000; Dunphy-Lelii & Wellman, 2004). Moll and Tomasello (2004) found that even 12-month-olds followed an adult's gaze to an object behind a barrier and crawled or walked towards the barrier to see what the adult was looking at. This does not, however, necessarily imply that the infant understands that the adult sees something behind the barrier.

To investigate whether infants around their first birthday understand what others do and do not see, we developed a violation-of-expectation paradigm for the study of Level 1 visual perspective taking in infants (Sodian, Thoermer, & Metz, 2007). Infants were habituated to a goal-directed action, an actress reaching for and grasping one of two toys on a small stage—for example, the duck (and not the fish). When the habituation criterion was reached, the positions of the two toys were reversed. In the test phase, the actress always reached for the new, previously undesired, toy (e.g., the fish). We tested whether 12- and 14-month-olds were able to distinguish between two kinds of test events that differed in terms of whether the actress could or could not see her old goal object. In "rational" test events the actress reached for the new goal object without being able to see the old goal object (which was hidden behind an opaque screen), whereas in "irrational" test events the actress reached for the new goal object while the old goal object was fully visible for her (because it was placed next to the opaque screen). In both types of test trials the old goal object was always fully visible to the infant. Thus, if infants look longer at "irrational" than at "rational" test trials, they appeared to demonstrate Level 1 visual perspective-taking abilities, since the old goal object was visible to the infant in both conditions, and the distinction had to be made on the basis of the other person's ability to see the old goal object. We found that 14-month-olds, but not 12-month-olds, showed this looking-time pattern. In a control condition with a transparent screen neither age group showed a distinction between the two types of test events. Thus, 14-month-olds appeared to "rationalize" the actress's reach for a new object when the old goal object was out of sight and thereby demonstrated the ability to keep track of what another person could or could not see, independently of what they themselves could see. Note that 14-month-olds, to pass the present task, had to interpret a person's goal-directed action based on this person's visual access to information. Thus, it appears that 14-month-olds have some understanding of the epistemic consequences of seeing. It does not, however, follow that 14-month-olds understand the relation between seeing and knowing. While Level 1 perspective taking requires the infant to encode what another person sees at the moment, an understanding of knowledge formation implies that the infant understands how what another saw previously influences his or her current behaviour (e.g., her correct or incorrect search). The findings reported above indicate that at the age of 16 months infants do not make this connection between a person's previous access to information and her current search behaviour. Does this understanding develop during the second year of life? Since it is difficult to test infants above the age of about 16 months in habituation paradigms, we used a preferential-looking paradigm to address the development of infants' understanding of visual perception over a wider age range.

UNDERSTANDING OF VISUAL PERCEPTION DURING THE SECOND YEAR

Diane Poulin-Dubois has successfully used preferential looking techniques for the study of mental-state attribution in infancy (Poulin-Dubois, 1999). Collaboratively with her, we conducted a series of studies on infants' expectations about a person's search for a hidden object as a function of the person's prior visual experience (Poulin-Dubois, Sodian, Metz, Tilden, & Schnöppner, in press). Infants viewed films in which a protagonist either witnessed or was blindfolded when the location of an object was revealed. At the end of the film, infants were shown two still frames, one in which the protagonist pointed at the correct location and the other in which she pointed at the incorrect location. Looking times at each of these still frames were measured to determine whether infants formed an expectation about the looker's behaviour based on her visual experience. We found no differentiation between visual access and no visual access conditions in 14-month-olds in two experiments, one of which included gaze direction and body orientation as additional cues. The only interpretation that was consistent with the looking patterns in the 14-month-olds was that they remembered the location of the toy and therefore always looked at the screen where the actress pointed to the correct location, regardless of whether or not the actress had had visual access. At 18 months we found a differentiation between visual access and no visual access conditions, when head turn and body orientation were available as cues to the visual experience: Infants looked longer at the screen where the actress pointed to the incorrect location in the visual access condition and longer at her pointing to the correct location in the no visual access condition. When search behaviour had to be inferred from gaze alone, only 24-month-olds succeeded.

These findings indicate that the ability to predict future behaviour based on a person's previous visual contact with an event develops gradually during the second year of life. While

14-month-olds represent what another person currently sees, they do not appear to relate what a person previously saw to her current behaviour. At the age of 18 months, infants appear to understand that a connection between a person and an object or event can be used to infer a person's future behaviour—at least they can do so if helped by behavioural cues. At the end of the second year, infants appear to have a firm understanding of the importance of seeing for future action: They expect correct or incorrect search as a function of prior visual access, even if no additional cues are available.

Like Onishi and Baillargeon's (2005) findings, the present set of findings raises the question of how deep infants' insight into the mind really is. A rich interpretation of our pattern of results would grant 18-month-old infants with an implicit, nonverbal understanding of the relation between seeing and knowing. A lean interpretation would simply grant infants with the ability to predict that a person will act towards an object after orienting her gaze and head towards it. Infants could simply compute the co-occurrence of the person's body posture and the object in the visual access condition, without having any understanding of the perceptual experience of seeing. Given that it has been independently shown that 12- and 14-month-olds understand something about the perceptual experience of seeing (Brooks & Meltzoff, 2002; Moll & Tomasello, 2004; Sodian, Thoermer, & Metz, 2007), it appears unlikely that a simple association of person, object, and location can account for the present findings. Rather, we argue that the ability to predict search behaviour from a previous looker–object connection indicates some understanding of psychological states. Note that 18- and 24-month-olds represented a psychological relation between a person and an object that was hidden from view independently of their own knowledge of the object's location. Our finding that 18-month-olds' success depended on the kinds of situational cues that were provided is quite consistent with one of Perner and Ruffman's (2005) lower level accounts of Onishi and Baillargeon's findings: Infants in the second year of life gradually develop an understanding of knowledge formation by relying on an increasingly larger set of behavioural cues.

RELEVANCE OF INFANT SOCIAL UNDERSTANDING TO THE STUDY OF AUTISM

It would be extremely interesting to test autistic children in nonverbal Theory of Mind tasks such as the paradigms used in the studies reported above. Given the deficit in joint attentional skills in children with autism, it is likely that autistic children will fail to encode the behavioural cues that typically developing children use to predict another person's search behaviour. Moreover, if the account of a gradual development of an understanding of knowledge formation that we proposed is correct, then we should see some encoding of behavioural cues before we see an implicit or even an explicit understanding of knowledge and belief even in children with a gross delay in Theory of Mind development. Can the use of such behavioural cues for action prediction be trained, and if so, does such training eventually lead to an understanding of mental states?

One way to assess how children with autism encode social information is eye tracking. Several studies on eye movements in individuals with autism when observing social stimuli have reported abnormal gaze behaviour. Klin, Jones, Schultz, Volkmar, and Cohen (2002) found that young adult participants with autism tended to look at mouths and objects twice as often and at eyes half as often as normal controls did when watching a movie. Swettenham et al. (1998) report that young children with autism shifted attention less between an object and a person or a person and another person than did typically developing infants and developmentally delayed controls, and they shifted more between an object and another object. Van der Geest, Kemner, Verbaten, and van Engeland (2002) did not, however, find an abnormality of autistic children in processing cartoon-like scenes that included human figures. The processing of goal-directed social interaction has not, however, been specifically addressed in these studies. It appears that systematic studies of autistic persons' encoding of intentional action would be an extremely valuable source of information on abnormalities in social information processing and Theory of Mind development.

One example for a suitable paradigm from our own research is a study of action role encoding in meaningful social interaction. In a series of experiments on infants' encoding of action roles in a give-and-take interaction, Schöppner, Sodian, and Pauen (2006) found that by the age of 10.5 months infants selectively encode the change of action role (agent−recipient) over a change in the spatiotemporal properties (direction reversal) of the interaction. Thus, towards the end of the first year, infants appear to be capable of encoding subtle cues that are indicative of psychological causality.

In a follow-up study with this paradigm, Neumann, Thoermer, and Sodian (2007) used eye tracking to determine how infants differed from adults and how competent infants (i.e., infants who looked longer at role reversal than at direction reversal) differed from incompetent infants in encoding the social interaction. Preliminary findings indicate that adults looked longer at the agent (the giver) than any other element of the scene from the start, and that infants as a group did not show this clear focus on the agent, but looked longer at the object (the flower) than did the adults. Competent infants, however, differed from incompetent infants in showing a more adult-like gaze pattern. We plan to study children with autism in this paradigm to explore whether (and how) they deviate from typically developing infants and children in their encoding of cues to social causality.

To interpret findings on social information processing in children with autism, we need to know how early social information processing relates to later Theory of Mind in typical development. In what sense are infants' competencies in interpreting goal-directed human action precursors to a Theory of Mind?

Charman et al. (2000, 2003) have longitudinally assessed social-cognitive abilities in the second year of life as precursors to language and Theory of Mind development in the fourth year of life in normally developing and autistic children and found joint attentional and imitative competencies to be predictive of the outcome measures. However, little is known about the developmental relation between the competencies assessed in looking-time paradigms and later Theory of Mind development. Wellman, Phillips, Dunphy-Lelii, and LaLonde (2004) found that individual differences in social information processing in infancy were in fact predictive of individual differences in Theory of Mind development at the age of four years, independently of language abilities, but to date, the generality of this developmental relation is unclear. More longitudinal data are needed to determine the relation between social responsiveness and social understanding in the first two years of life and later developments in Theory of Mind.

CONCLUSIONS

The study of the Theory of Mind deficit in autism has been a highly relevant and productive source of progress in understanding normal development—and vice versa. It appears that recent findings on social understanding and precursors to a Theory of Mind in infancy provide the basis for an equally productive mutual interchange between research on autism and on normal development.

REFERENCES

Baron-Cohen, S., Leslie, A. M., & Frith, U. (1985). Does the autistic child have a "theory of mind"? *Cognition, 21,* 37−46.

Baron-Cohen, S., Leslie, A. M., & Frith, U. (1986). Mechanical, behavioural and intentional understanding of picture stories in autistic children. *British Journal of Developmental Psychology, 4,* 113−125.

Brooks, R., & Meltzoff, A. N. (2002). The importance of eyes: How infants interpret adult looking behavior. *Developmental Psychology, 38*, 958–966.

Butler, S. C., Caron, A. J., & Brooks, R. (2000). Infant understanding of the referential nature of looking. *Journal of Cognition and Development, 1*, 359–377.

Call, J., & Carpenter, M. (2001). Do apes and children know what they have seen? *Animal Cognition, 4*, 207–220.

Carpenter, M., Call, J., & Tomasello, M. (2003). A new false belief test for 36-month-olds. *British Journal of Developmental Psychology, 20*, 393–420.

Charman, T., Baron-Cohen, S., Swettenham, J., Baird, G., Cox, A., & Drew, A. (2000). Testing joint attention, imitation, and play as infancy precursors to language and theory of mind. *Cognitive Development, 15*, 481–498.

Charman, T., Baron-Cohen, S., Swettenham, J., Baird, G., Drew, A., & Cox, A. (2003). Predicting language outcome in infants with autism and pervasive developmental disorder. *International Journal of Language and Communication Disorders, 38*, 265–285.

Clements, W. A., & Perner, J. (1994). Implicit understanding of belief. *Cognitive Development, 9*, 377–395.

Csibra, G., & Southgate, V. (2006). Evidence for infants' understanding of false beliefs should not be dismissed. *Trends in Cognitive Sciences, 10*, 4–5.

Dunham, P., Dunham, F., & O'Keefe, C. (2000). Two-year-olds' sensitivity to a parent's knowledge state: Mind reading or contextual cues? *British Journal of Developmental Psychology, 18*, 519–532.

Dunphy-Lelii, S., & Wellman, H. M. (2004). Infants' understanding of occlusion of others' line-of-sight: Implications for an emerging theory of mind. *European Journal of Developmental Psychology, 1*, 49–66.

Flavell, J. H., Everett, B. A., Croft, K., & Flavell, E. R. (1981). Young children's knowledge about visual perception: Further evidence for the Level 1–Level 2 distinction. *Developmental Psychology, 17*, 95–120.

Frith, U. (2003). *Autism: Explaining the enigma* (2nd ed.). Malden, MA: Blackwell Publishers.

Garnham, W. A., & Ruffman, T. (2001). Doesn't see, doesn't know: Is anticipatory looking really related to understanding of belief? *Developmental Science, 4*, 94–100.

Gergely, G. (2002). The development of understanding self and agency. In U. Goswami (Ed.), *The Blackwell handbook of childhood cognitive development* (pp. 26–46). Oxford, UK: Blackwell Publishers.

Klin, A., Jones, W., Schultz, R., Volkmar, F., & Cohen, D. (2002). Visual fixation patterns during viewing of naturalistic social situations as predictors of social competence in individuals with autism. *Archives of General Psychiatry, 59*, 809–816.

Leslie, A. M. (2005). Developmental parallels in understanding minds and bodies. *Trends in Cognitive Sciences, 9*, 459–462.

Leslie, A. M., & Thaiss, L. (1992). Domain specificity in conceptual development: Evidence from autism. *Cognition, 43*, 225–251.

Moll, H., & Tomasello, M. (2004). 12- and 18-month-olds follow gaze to spaces behind barriers. *Developmental Science, 7*, F1–F9.

Neumann, A., Thoermer, C., & Sodian, B. (2007, March). *Action-role encoding in 10-month-old infants. An eye-tracking study.* Poster presented at SRCD, Boston.

O'Neill, D. (1996). Two-year-olds' sensitivity to a parent's knowledge state when making requests. *Child Development, 67*, 659–677.

Onishi, K., & Baillargeon, R. (2005). Do 15-month-old infants understand false beliefs? *Science, 308*, 255–258.

Perner, J., Leekam, S. R., & Wimmer, H. (1987). Three-year olds' difficulty with false belief: The case for a conceptual deficit. *British Journal of Developmental Psychology, 5*, 125–137.

Perner, J., & Ruffman, T. (2005). Infants' insight into the mind: How deep? *Science, 308*, 214–216.

Poulin-Dubois, D. (1999). Infants' distinction between animate and inanimate objects: The origins of naive psychology. In P. Rochat (Ed.), *Early social cognition. Understanding others in the first months of life* (pp. 281–297). Mahwah, NJ: Lawrence Erlbaum Associates.

Poulin-Dubois, D., Sodian, B., Metz, U., Tilden, J., & Schöppner, B. (in press). Out of sight is not out of mind: Developmental changes in infants' understanding of visual perception during the second year. *Journal of Cognition and Development.*

Povinelli, D. J., Nelson, K. E., & Boysen, S. T. (1990). Inferences about guessing and knowing by chimpanzees. *Journal of Comparative Psychology, 104*, 203–210.

Pratt, C., & Bryant, P. (1990). Young children understand that looking leads to knowing (so long as they are looking into a single barrel). *Child Development, 61*, 973–982.

Ruffman, T., Garnham, W., & Rideout, P. (2001). Social understanding in autism: Eye gaze as a measure of core insights. *Journal of Child Psychology and Psychiatry, 41*, 1083–1094.

Ruffman, T., & Perner, J. (2006). Do infants really understand false belief? *Trends in Cognitive Sciences*, *10*, 462–463.

Schöppner, B., Sodian, B., & Pauen, S. (2006). Encoding action roles in meaningful social interaction in the first year of life. *Infancy*, *9*, 289–311.

Shwe, H. J., & Markman, E. M. (1997).Young children's appreciation of the mental impact of their communicative signals. *Developmental Psychology*, *33*, 630–636.

Sodian, B. (2005). Theory of mind. The case for conceptual development. In W. Schneider, R. Schumann-Hengsteler, & B. Sodian (Eds.), *Young children's cognitive development. Interrelationships among working memory, theory of mind, and executive functions* (pp. 95–130). Hillsdale, NJ: Lawrence Erlbaum Associates.

Sodian, B., & Frith, U. (1992). Deception and sabotage in autistic, retarded, and normal children. *Journal of Child Psychology and Psychiatry*, *33*, 591–606.

Sodian, B., Thoermer, C., & Dietrich, N. (2006). Two- to four-year-old children's differentiation of knowing and guessing in a non-verbal task. *European Journal of Developmental Psychology*, *3*, 222–237.

Sodian, B., Thoermer, C., & Metz, U. (2007). Level-1 visual perspective taking in 14-month-old infants. *Developmental Science*, *10*, 199–204.

Sodian, B., Thoermer, C., Metz, U., & Schöppner, B. (2002, April). *16-month-olds' understanding of seeing*. Poster presented at the XIIIth International Conference on Infant Studies, Toronto, Canada.

Southgate, V., Senju, A., & Csibra, G. (2007). Action anticipation through attribution of false beliefs by two-year-olds. *Psychological Science*, *18*, 587–592.

Swettenham, J., Baron-Cohen, S., Cox, A., Baird, G., Drew, A., Charman, T., et al. (1998). The frequency and distribution of spontaneous attention shifts between social and non-social stimuli in autistic, typically developing, and nonautistic developmentally delayed infants. *Journal of Child Psychology and Psychiatry*, *39*, 747–753.

Tomasello, M., Carpenter, M., Call, J., Behne, T., & Moll, H. (2005). Understanding and sharing intentions: The origins of cultural cognition. *Behavioral and Brain Sciences*, *28*, 675–691.

Van der Geest, J. N., Kemner, C., Verbaten, M. N., & van Engeland, H. (2002). Gaze behavior in children with pervasive developmental disorder toward human faces: A fixation time study. *Journal of Child Psychology and Psychiatry*, *43*, 669–678.

Wellman, H. M. (2002). Understanding the psychological world: Developing a theory of mind. In U. Goswami (Ed.), *The Blackwell handbook of childhood cognitive development* (pp. 167–187). Oxford, UK: Blackwell.

Wellman, H. M., Cross, D., & Watson, J. (2001). A meta-analysis of theory of mind development: The truth about false belief. *Child Development*, *72*, 655–684.

Wellman, H. M., Phillips, A. T., Dunphy Lelii, S., & LaLonde, N. (2004). Infant social attention predicts preschool social cognition. *Developmental Science*, *7*, 283–288.

THE QUARTERLY JOURNAL OF EXPERIMENTAL PSYCHOLOGY
2008, 61 (1), 40–49

Ψ Psychology Press
Taylor & Francis Group

Development of the social brain during adolescence

Sarah-Jayne Blakemore

Institute of Cognitive Neuroscience, University College London, London, UK

Adolescence is usually defined as the period of psychological and social transition between childhood and adulthood. The beginning of adolescence, around the onset of puberty, is characterized by large hormonal and physical changes. The transition from childhood to adulthood is also characterized by psychological changes in terms of identity, self-consciousness, and cognitive flexibility. In the past decade, it has been demonstrated that various regions of the human brain undergo development during adolescence and beyond. Some of the brain regions that undergo particularly protracted development are involved in social cognitive function in adults. In the first section of this paper, I briefly describe evidence for a circumscribed network of brain regions involved in understanding other people. Next, I describe evidence that some of these brain regions undergo structural development during adolescence. Finally, I discuss recent studies that have investigated social cognitive development during adolescence.

The first time Uta Frith made an impression on me was when I was 15. That year I was given a copy of her book *Autism: Explaining the Enigma* (U. Frith, 1989), which had recently been published. I knew nothing about autism and found Uta's book captivating. It inspired me to write to its author and ask if I could do a week's work experience in her lab. With characteristic generosity, Uta agreed. So in the summer of 1990, I spent a week in the Medical Research Council (MRC) Cognitive Development Unit, where I observed children with autism being tested on the Sally Anne task, and joined in when Uta's group were generating spoonerisms like Dob Bylan and Himi Jendrix. At the time, I didn't quite realise that this research had revolutionized what is known about autism and dyslexia. Together with Simon Baron-Cohen and Alan Leslie, Uta had

just a few years earlier published the first paper to show that children with autism have problems passing Theory of Mind tasks. If you search for [Theory of Mind in autism] on the web today you get over one million entries! Uta's work on autism and dyslexia is not just renowned amongst scientists, but has also made a significant impact on teachers, clinicians, carers, and parents. Doing work experience with Uta all those years ago was truly inspirational.

I met Uta again when I was doing a PhD with Chris Frith. In 2000, Uta asked me to help her write a report for the Economic and Social Research Council (ESRC) on the implications of brain research for education. Uta had the vision to realise that this would soon become an important area of science. Indeed, brain and education research is now a flourishing discipline in itself,

Correspondence should be addressed to Sarah-Jayne Blakemore, Institute of Cognitive Neuroscience, University College London, 17 Queen Square, London WC1N 3AR, UK. E-mail: s.blakemore@ucl.ac.uk

I am grateful to the Royal Society, UK, which funds my research.

DOI:10.1080/17470210701508715

with ring-fenced funding, dedicated international conferences, books, and a new journal. While writing the ESRC report, Uta and I were struck by the scarcity of literature on brain research that was aimed at educators. This seemed curious since some areas of brain research are very relevant to education (and in other areas the implications are far from clear). In addition, we came across the substantial market of educational tools that make claims about the brain. Our experience was that there is real interest amongst educators about these claims and the research they are based on. As a consequence, Uta and I decided to write a book on the subject (Blakemore & Frith, 2005). On the basis of Uta's previous well-received and successful books (e.g., U. Frith, 1989, 2003; Houston & Frith, 2000), her long-time publisher, Blackwell, agreed to publish our book.

One of the areas of brain research that was just starting to take off at the time we wrote our book was development during adolescence. Much is known (mostly from animal research) about brain changes in the early years. In comparison, at the time of writing our book, there was a large gap in knowledge about brain development after early childhood, possibly because the extant research was carried out on animal brain tissue, and, unlike humans, animals do not go through extended periods of adolescent maturity. There were a handful of new magnetic resonance imaging (MRI) studies looking at development of the human adolescent brain, and these were pointing to significant waves of change in several areas of cortex. This was fascinating, not least because several developmental disorders develop during or just after adolescence. For example, schizophrenia is a disorder that usually develops at the end of adolescence. Was it possible that postpubescent cortical sculpting does not proceed normally in people who develop schizophrenia? While there are indications that neuropathology occurs in early development in schizophrenia (e.g., Weinberger, 1987), recently it has been suggested that aberrations in neurodevelopmental processes might also take place during the adolescent years (McGlashan & Hoffman, 2000). When

Uta and I were researching our book, there was relatively little research on brain development in typically developing adolescents and even less on adolescents who later develop schizophrenia.

Another field in which Uta's research has been influential from the start is social neuroscience. Together with Chris Frith and other colleagues, Uta published some of the first papers in this new area. In the next section, I describe evidence for a network of brain regions dedicated to understanding others.

The social brain

It is only in the past decade or two that the search for the biological basis of social behaviour began (Cacioppo & Berntson, 1992). Uta Frith was among the first to study the brain basis of social cognitive processes, in particular Theory of Mind (ToM; or what Uta termed "mentalizing"). Mentalizing is defined as the ability to attribute mental states to other people in order to predict their behaviour (e.g., U. Frith & Frith, 2003; see also Perner & Leekham, 2008 this issue; Sodian, 2008 this issue).

Uta and colleagues published one of the first neuroimaging studies of mentalizing in 1995 (Fletcher et al., 1995). In this positron emission tomography (PET) experiment, subjects read stories that required mental state attribution (ToM stories), stories about physical, natural events that did not require any attribution of mental states (physical stories), and paragraphs made up of unlinked sentences that were unconnected with each other and did not constitute a story. The Theory of Mind (ToM) stories, relative to unlinked sentences, activated the superior temporal sulcus (STS), medial prefrontal cortex (mPFC), precuneus/posterior cingulate cortex, and temporal poles (see Figure 1). Compared with the physical stories, the ToM stories activated the mPFC and precuneus, as well as the right inferior parietal cortex adjacent to the temporo-parietal junction (TPJ).

Since this ground-breaking paper, there have been dozens of neuroimaging studies investigating the neural basis of mentalizing, each showing

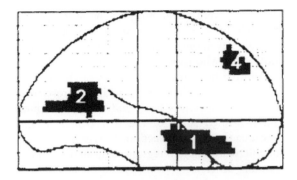

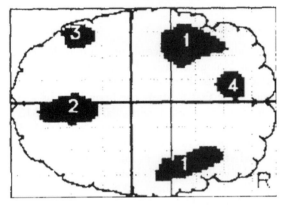

Figure 1. *Activity during reading stories that involve mental state attribution relative to unlinked sentences (from Fletcher et al., 1995), in (1) the temporal poles bilaterally, (2) the precuneus/ posterior cingulate, (3) left superior temporal sulcus (STS), and (4) medial prefrontal cortex (mPFC).*

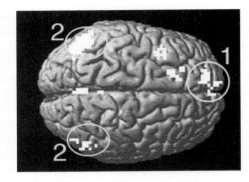

Figure 2. *Activity when subjects think about intentions compared with thinking about physical events (from den Ouden et al., 2005) in (1) the medial prefrontal cortex (mPFC) and (2) superior temporal sulcus/temporo-parietal junction (STS/TPJ).*

remarkable agreement with this first study. Here, I briefly review the evidence that mentalizing is associated with activation of the same circumscribed neural network. Recent neuroimaging studies, some by Uta Frith's group, others by labs all over the world, have used a wide range of stimuli including verbal stories (Gallagher et al., 2000; Saxe & Kanwisher, 2003), sentences (den Ouden, Frith, Frith, & Blakemore, 2005; see Figure 2), words (Mitchell, Heatherton, & Macrae, 2002), cartoons (Brunet, Sarfati, Hardy-Bayle, & Decety, 2000; Gallagher et al., 2000), and animations (Castelli, Happé, Frith, & Frith, 2000; see Figure 3). These studies have replicated the original finding by Fletcher and colleagues (Fletcher et al., 1995) of activation in mPFC, STS/TPJ, and the temporal poles when subjects

think about mental states (see C. D. Frith & Frith, 2006; U. Frith & Frith, 2003, for review).

The same brain regions have been implicated in mentalizing from lesion studies. In particular, lesions to the frontal cortex (Channon & Crawford, 2000; Gregory et al., 2002; Happé, Malhi, & Checkley, 2001; Rowe, Bullock, Polkey, & Morris, 2001; Stone, Baron-Cohen, & Knight, 1998; Stuss, Gallup, & Alexander, 2001) and STS/TPJ (Apperly, Samson, & Humphreys, 2005; Samson, Apperly, Chiavarino, & Humphreys, 2004) impair mentalizing performance. One exception is a study that Uta Frith was involved with (Bird, Castelli, Malik, Frith, & Husain, 2004). The researchers studied a patient with damage to much of her frontal cortex, including the whole of mPFC.

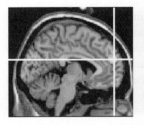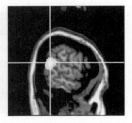

Figure 3. *Activity when subjects watch animations that involve mental state attribution to triangles relative to animations that show triangles moving randomly (from Castelli et al., 2000) in the medial prefrontal cortex (mPFC; left panel) and superior temporal sulcus/temporo-parietal junction (STS/TPJ; right panel).*

Surprisingly (given the neuroimaging literature), the patient showed normal performance on mentalizing tasks. Whether this rules out mPFC as being necessary for mentalizing, or whether this patient's good performance was because of neuronal reorganization, is unclear. Uta often says that surprising results, results that one would never predict, can be more important than predicted results. This is a clear example of a surprising result, which needs to be considered in theories of mPFC function.

The roles of the different regions in mentalizing are the subject of much debate. The mPFC is activated when subjects think about psychological states even if those states are applied to animals (Mitchell, Banaji, & Macrae, 2005). The mPFC is also activated by tasks that involve thinking about mental states in relation to the self (Johnson et al., 2002; Lou et al., 2004; Ochsner et al., 2004; Vogeley et al., 2001). Games that involve surmising an opponent's mental states also activate the mPFC (e.g., Gallagher, Jack, Roepstorff, & Frith, 2002; McCabe, Houser, Ryan, Smith, & Trouard, 2001). All of these tasks involve thinking about mental states. One prominent theory of mPFC function is that it is activated whenever subjects reflect on mental states (e.g., Amodio & Frith, 2006). Frith (C. D. Frith, 2007) has proposed that the mPFC is involved in the necessary decoupling of mental states from reality. Activity in mPFC is often observed during rest conditions in comparison with higher demand tasks (including mentalizing; Gusnard & Raichle, 2001). It has been suggested that, during rest or low-demand tasks, participants might indulge in spontaneous mentalizing (Amodio & Frith, 2006).

The STS has been proposed to play a role in the prediction of observed patterns of behaviour in order to surmise the mental states underlying this behaviour (C. D. Frith, 2007; C. D. Frith & Frith, 2006; U. Frith & Frith, 2003). This region is activated during the perception of biological motion (e.g., Allison, Puce, & McCarthy, 2000; Grezes et al., 2001; Grossman et al., 2000), faces and body parts (e.g., Campbell et al., 2001; Chao, Haxby, & Martin, 1999; Puce, Allison, Bentin, Gore, & McCarthy, 1998)

and eye movements (e.g., Pelphrey, Morris, Michelich, Allison, & McCarthy, 2005). One possibility is that this region is involved in predicting observed movements (C. D. Frith, 2007).

In summary, a network of brain regions including mPFC and STS/TPJ seems to be involved in many aspects of social cognition. In the next section I review evidence that these brain regions develop over several decades in humans.

Development of social cognition

There is a rich literature on the development of social cognition in infancy and childhood, and here I will not go into any detail (this literature is reviewed in papers by Perner & Leekham, 2008; Sodian, 2008). Signs of social competence develop during early infancy, such that by around 12 months of age infants can ascribe agency to a system or entity (Johnson, 2003; Spelke, Phillips, & Woodward, 1995). The understanding of intention emerges at around 18 months, when infants acquire joint attention skills—for example, they are able to follow an adult's gaze towards a goal (Carpenter, Nagell, & Tomasello, 1998). These early social abilities precede more explicit mentalizing, such as false-belief understanding, which usually emerges by about four or five years (Barresi & Moore, 1996). While normally developing children begin to pass Theory of Mind tasks by age five, the brain structures that underlie mentalizing (mPFC and STS/TPJ) undergo substantial development well beyond early childhood. These studies are reviewed in the next section.

Cellular development in the brain during adolescence

The notion that the brain continues to develop after childhood is relatively new. Experiments on animals, starting in the 1950s, showed that sensory regions of the brain go through sensitive periods soon after birth, during which time environmental stimulation appears to be crucial for normal brain development and for normal perceptual development to occur (Hubel & Wiesel, 1962). These experiments suggested that the human brain might be susceptible to the same sensitive periods in early development. Research on postmortem human brains carried out in the 1970s revealed that some brain areas, in particular the PFC, continue to develop well beyond early childhood (Huttenlocher, 1979; Huttenlocher, De Courten, Garey, & Van Der Loos, 1983; Yakovlev & Lecours, 1967).

Two main changes were found in the brain before and after puberty. As neurons develop, a layer of myelin is formed around their axon. Myelin acts as an insulator and significantly increases the speed of transmission of electrical impulses from neuron to neuron. While sensory and motor brain regions become fully myelinated in the first few years of life, axons in the frontal cortex continue to be myelinated well into adolescence (Yakovlev & Lecours, 1967). The implication of this research is that the transmission speed of neural information in the frontal cortex might increase throughout childhood and adolescence.

The second difference in the brains of prepubescent children and adolescents pertains to changes in synaptic density in PFC. Early in postnatal development, the brain begins to form new synapses, so that the synaptic density (the number of synapses per unit volume of brain tissue) greatly exceeds adult levels. This process of synaptogenesis lasts up to several months, depending on the species of animal and the brain region. These early peaks in synaptic density are followed by a period of synaptic elimination (pruning) in which frequently used connections are strengthened and infrequently used connections are eliminated. This process, which occurs over a period of years, reduces the overall synaptic density to adult levels. In sensory regions of the monkey brain, synaptic densities gradually decline to adult levels at around three years, around the time monkeys reach sexual maturity (Rakic, 1995).

In contrast to sensory brain regions, histological studies of monkey and human PFC have shown that there is a proliferation of synapses in the subgranular layers of the PFC during childhood and again at puberty, followed by a plateau phase and a subsequent elimination and reorganization of prefrontal synaptic connections after puberty (Bourgeois, Goldman-Rakic, & Rakic, 1994; Huttenlocher, 1979; Woo, Pucak, Kye, Matus, & Lewis, 1997; Zecevic & Rakic, 2001). According to these data, synaptic pruning occurs throughout adolescence and results in a net decrease in synaptic density in the PFC during this time.

MRI studies of adolescent brain development

Until recently, the structure of the human brain could be studied only after death. The scarcity of postmortem brains in research meant that knowledge of human brain development was limited. Since the advent of magnetic resonance imaging (MRI), a number of brain-imaging studies have provided further evidence of the ongoing maturation of the frontal cortex and other regions, into adolescence and even into adulthood. A consistent finding from both cross-sectional and longitudinal MRI studies is that there is a steady increase in white matter (WM) in certain brain regions, particularly PFC and parietal cortex, during childhood and adolescence (e.g., Giedd et al., 1999; Giedd et al., 1996; Paus et al., 1999b; Pfefferbaum et al., 1994; Reiss, Abrams, Singer, Ross, & Denckla, 1996; Sowell et al., 2003; Sowell et al., 1999). Most studies point to a linear increase in white matter with age (Barnea-Goraly et al., 2005; Giedd et al., 1999; Paus et al., 1999a, 1999b; Pfefferbaum et al., 1994; Reiss et al., 1996; Sowell et al., 1999). In light of histological studies, this has been interpreted as reflecting continued axonal myelination during childhood and adolescence.

While the increase in white matter in certain brain regions seems to be linear, changes in grey matter (GM) density appear to follow a region-specific, nonlinear pattern. Several studies have shown that GM development in certain brain regions follows an inverted-U shape. In one of the first developmental MRI studies, Giedd et al., (1999) performed a longitudinal MRI study on 145 healthy boys and girls ranging in age from about 4 to 22 years. The volume of GM in the frontal lobe increased during preadolescence with a peak occurring at around 12 years for males and 11 years for females. This was followed by a decline during postadolescence. Similarly, parietal lobe GM volume increased during the preadolescent stage to a peak at around 12 years for males and 10 years for females, and this was followed by decline during postadolescence. GM development in the temporal lobes was also nonlinear, and the peak was reached later at about 17 years. A similar inverted-U shaped developmental trajectory of GM in various cortical regions has been found in several subsequent MRI studies (e.g., Gogtay et al., 2004; Thompson et al., 2000). Most studies show that sensory and motor regions mature first, while PFC and parietal and temporal cortices continue to develop during adolescence and beyond.

In summary, several recent MRI studies have suggested that a perturbation in GM density more or less coincides with the onset of puberty in some cortical regions. This has been interpreted as reflecting the synaptic reorganization that occurs at the onset of puberty (Bourgeois et al., 1994; Huttenlocher, 1979). Thus, the increase in GM apparent at the onset of puberty (Giedd et al., 1999) might reflect a wave of synapse proliferation at this time, while the gradual decrease in GM density that occurs after puberty has been attributed to postpubescent synaptic pruning.

The brain regions that undergo protracted development include PFC, parietal cortex and superior temporal cortex (in some studies this has included STS). As discussed above, these are regions that are implicated in social cognition in adults. The effect of continued neural development in brain regions associated with social cognition is largely unknown. Only a relatively small number of studies have investigated social cognitive function during adolescence.

Development of social cognition during adolescence

While there is a wealth of social psychology research on socio-emotional processing in adolescence, there is surprisingly little empirical research

on social cognitive development during this period. One area of social processing that has been studied in the context of adolescence is face processing, perhaps because early behavioural studies of face processing found evidence for an interruption at puberty in the developmental course of face recognition (Carey, Diamond, & Woods, 1980; Diamond, Carey, & Back, 1983). In one study the percentage of correct responses in a behavioural face recognition task improved by over 20% between the ages of 6 and 10 and declined by about 10% around the age of puberty (Carey et al., 1980). Performance on the task recovered again during adolescence. In another study, face encoding was found to be worse in pubescent girls than in pre- and postpubescent girls matched for age (Diamond et al., 1983).

Recently, several groups have investigated the neural processing of facial expressions of emotion in adolescents. Thomas et al. (2001) investigated amygdala activation to fearful facial expressions in a group of children (mean age 11 years) and adults. Adults demonstrated greater amygdala activation to fearful facial expressions, whereas children showed greater amygdala activation to neutral faces. Slightly different results were obtained by Killgore, Oki, and Yurgelun-Todd (2001). Results indicated sex differences in amygdala development: Although the left amygdala responded to fearful facial expressions in all children, left amygdala activity decreased over the adolescent period in females but not in males. Females also demonstrated greater activation of the dorsolateral PFC over this period, whereas males demonstrated the opposite pattern. In a recent study, bilateral PFC activity increased with age (from 8 to 15 years) for girls, whereas only activity in right PEC was correlated with age in boys (Yurgelun-Todd & Killgore, 2006).

In a recent study, a group of adolescents (aged 7 to 17) and a group of adults (aged 25–36) viewed faces showing emotional expressions. While viewing faces with fearful emotional expressions, adolescents exhibited greater activation than adults of the amygdala, orbitofrontal cortex, and anterior cingulate cortex (Monk et al., 2003). When subjects were asked to switch their attention between a salient emotional property of the face (thinking about how afraid it makes them feel) and a nonemotional property (how wide is the nose), adults, but not adolescents, selectively engaged and disengaged the orbitofrontal cortex. These functional MRI (fMRI) results suggest that both emotion processing and cognitive appraisal systems develop during adolescence.

A recent fMRI study investigated the development during adolescence of the neural network underlying thinking about intentions (Blakemore, den Ouden, Choudhury, & Frith, 2007). In this study, 19 adolescent participants (aged 12.1 to 18.1 years), and 11 adults (aged 22.4 to 37.8 years), were scanned using fMRI. A factorial design was employed with between-subjects factor *age group* and within-subjects factor *causality* (intentional or physical). In both adults and adolescents, answering questions about intentional causality versus physical causality activated the mentalizing network, including medial PFC, STS and temporal poles. In addition, there was a significant interaction between group and task in the medial PFC. During intentional relative to physical causality, adolescents activated part of the medial PFC more than did adults and adults activated part of the right STS more than did adolescents. These results suggest that the neural strategy for thinking about intentions changes between adolescence and adulthood. Although the same neural network is active, the relative roles of the different areas change, with activity moving from anterior (medial prefrontal) regions to posterior (temporal) regions with age.

While face processing is an example of an area of social cognitive development during adolescence that has received attention in recent years, very little is known about how other aspects of social cognition change during the teenage years. It appears paradoxical that the some of the brain regions involved in social cognition undergo such dramatic development into adolescence, when the functions mediated by these regions (e.g., ToM) appear to mature much earlier. If an ability (such as passing a ToM task) is accomplished by early to mid childhood, it is unlikely that it will undergo dramatic

changes beyond that time. One possibility is that neural development during adolescence influences more subtle abilities, such as the capacity to modulate social cognitive processes in the context of everyday life. Another possibility is that tasks that tap into implicit social cognitive processes might be more likely to undergo change during adolescence. We have recently found some evidence for this in the domain of action imagery (Choudhury, Bird, Charman, & Blakemore, 2007, in press). However, in the realm of development of social cognition during adolescence, there is a large gap in knowledge waiting to be filled.

CONCLUSION

After Uta Frith and colleagues' seminal paper on the neural processing of Theory of Mind (Fletcher et al., 1995), much has been learned about the social brain. There is a general consensus about brain regions activated when subjects think about mental states, though the exact role each region plays in Theory of Mind processing is still debated. Some of these brain regions undergo substantial development during adolescence, which has implications for the development of social cognition, in particular understanding other people. Social cognitive development during adolescence is a new and rapidly expanding field. Many questions remain unanswered. The role of hormones, culture and the social environment on the development of the social brain are unknown. It is possible that changes in hormones and social environment (for example, changing school) interact with neural development at the onset of puberty. Future research is needed to disentangle the contributions of biological and environmental factors to the developing social brain.

REFERENCES

Allison, T., Puce, A., & McCarthy, G. (2000). Social perception from visual cues: Role of the STS region. *Trends in Cognitive Science, 4,* 267–278.

Amodio, D. M., & Frith, C. D. (2006). Meeting of minds: The medial frontal cortex and social cognition. *Nature Reviews Neuroscience*, 7, 268–277.

Apperly, I. A., Samson, D., & Humphreys, G. W. (2005). Domain-specificity and theory of mind: Evaluating neuropsychological evidence. *Trends in Cognitive Sciences*, 9, 572–577.

Barnea-Goraly, N., Menon, V., Eckert, M., Tamm, L., Bammer, R., Karchemskiy, A., et al. (2005). White matter development during childhood and adolescence: A cross-sectional diffusion tensor imaging study. *Cerebral Cortex*, 15, 1848–1954.

Barresi, J., & Moore, C. (1996). Intentional relations and social understanding. *Behavioral and Brain Sciences*, 19, 107–154.

Bird, C. M., Castelli, F., Malik, O., Frith, U., & Husain, M. (2004). The impact of extensive medial frontal lobe damage on "Theory of Mind" and cognition. *Brain*, 127, 914–928.

Blakemore, S. J., den Ouden, H., Choudhury, S., & Frith, C. (2007). Adolescent development of the neural circuitry for thinking about intentions. *Social Cognitive and Affective Neuroscience*, 2, 130–139.

Blakemore, S. J., & Frith, U. (2005). *The learning brain: The lessons for education*. Oxford, UK: Blackwell.

Bourgeois, J. P., Goldman-Rakic, P. S., & Rakic, P. (1994). Synaptogenesis in the prefrontal cortex of rhesus monkeys. *Cerebral Cortex*, 4, 78–96.

Brunet, E., Sarfati, Y., Hardy-Bayle, M. C., & Decety, J. (2000). A PET investigation of the attribution of intentions with a nonverbal task. *Neuroimage*, 11, 157–166.

Cacioppo, J. T., & Berntson, G. G. (1992). Social psychological contributions to the decade of the brain. Doctrine of multilevel analysis. *American Psychologist*, 47, 1019–1028.

Campbell, R., MacSweeney, M., Surguladze, S., Calvert, G., McGuire, P., Suckling, J., et al. (2001). Cortical substrates for the perception of face actions: An fMRI study of the specificity of activation for seen speech and for meaningless lower-face acts (gurning). *Cognitive Brain Research*, 12, 2330–2343.

Carey, S., Diamond, R., & Woods, B. (1980). The development of face recognition—a maturational component. *Developmental Psychology*, 16, 257–269.

Carpenter, M., Nagell, K., & Tomasello, M. (1998). Social cognition, joint attention, and communicative competence from 9 to 15 months of age. *Monographs of the Society for Research in Child Development*, 63(1–6), 1–143.

Castelli, F., Happé, F., Frith, U., & Frith, C. D. (2000). Movement and mind: A functional imaging study of perception and interpretation of complex intentional movement pattern. *Neuroimage*, 12, 314–325.

Channon, S., & Crawford, S. (2000). The effects of anterior lesions on performance on a story comprehension test: Left anterior impairment on a theory of mind-type task. *Neuropsychologia*, 38, 1006–1017.

Chao, L. L., Haxby, J. V., & Martin, A. (1999). Attribute-based neural substrates in temporal cortex for perceiving and knowing about objects. *Nature Neuroscience*, 2, 913–919.

Choudhury, S., Bird, V., Charman, T., & Blakemore, S.-J. (2007). Development of action representation during adolescence. *Neuropsychologia*, 45, 255–262.

Choudhury, S., Bird, V., Charman, T., & Blakemore, S.-J. (in press). Adolescent development of motor imagery in a visually guided pointing task. *Consciousness and Cognition*.

den Ouden, H. E., Frith, U., Frith, C., & Blakemore, S. J. (2005). Thinking about intentions. *Neuroimage*, 28, 787–796.

Diamond, R., Carey, S., & Back, K. (1983). Genetic influences on the development of spatial skills during early adolescence. *Cognition*, 13, 167–185.

Fletcher, P. C., Happé, F., Frith, U., Baker, S. C., Dolan, R. J., Frackowiak, R. S., et al. (1995). Other minds in the brain: A functional imaging study of "theory of mind" in story comprehension. *Cognition*, 57, 109–128.

Frith, C. D. (2007). The social brain? *Philosophical Transactions of the Royal Society of London. Series B: Biological Sciences*, 362(1480), 671–678.

Frith, C. D., & Frith, U. (2006). The neural basis of mentalizing. *Neuron*, 50, 531–534.

Frith, U. (1989). *Autism: Explaining the enigma* (1st ed.). Oxford, UK: Blackwell.

Frith, U. (2003). *Autism: Explaining the enigma* (2nd ed.). Oxford, UK: Blackwell.

Frith, U., & Frith, C. D. (2003). Development and neurophysiology of mentalizing. *Philosophical Transactions of the Royal Society of London. Series B: Biological Sciences*, 358, 459–473.

Gallagher, H. L., Happe, F., Brunswick, N., Fletcher, P. C, Frith, U., & Frith, C. D. (2000). Reading the mind in cartoons and stories: An fMRI study of "theory of mind" in verbal and nonverbal tasks. *Neuropsychologia*, 38, 11–21.

Gallagher, H. L., Jack, A. I., Roepstorff, A., & Frith, C. D. (2002). Imaging the intentional stance in a competitive game. *Neuroimage, 16*, 814–821.

Giedd, J. N., Blumenthal, J., Jeffries, N. O., Castellanos, F. X., Liu, H., Zijdenbos, A., et al. (1999). Brain development during childhood and adolescence: A longitudinal MRI study. *Nature Neuroscience, 2*, 861–863.

Giedd, J. N., Snell, J. W., Lange, N., Rajapakse, J. C., Kaysen, D., Vaituzis, A. C., et al. (1996). Quantitative magnetic resonance imaging of human brain development: Ages 4–18. *Cerebral Cortex, 6*, 551–560.

Gogtay, N., Giedd, J. N., Lusk, L., Hayashi, K. M., Greenstein, D., Vaituzis, A. C., et al. (2004). Dynamic mapping of human cortical development during childhood through early adulthood. *Proceedings of the National Academy of Sciences, USA, 101*, 8174–8179.

Gregory, C., Lough, S., Stone, V., Erzinclioglu, S., Martin, L., Baron-Cohen, S., et al. (2002). Theory of mind in patients with frontal variant fronto-temporal dementia and Alzheimer's disease: Theoretical and practical implications. *Brain, 125*, 752–764.

Grezes, J., Fonlupt, P., Bertenthal, B., Delon-Martin, C., Segebarth, C., & Decety, J., (2001). Does perception of biological motion rely on specific brain regions? *Neuroimage, 13*, 775–785.

Grossman, E., Donnelly, M., Price, R., Pickens, D., Morgan, V., Neighbor, G., et al. (2000). Brain areas involved in perception of biological motion. *Journal of Cognitive Neuroscience, 12*, 711–720.

Gusnard, D. A., & Raichle, M. E. (2001). Searching for a baseline: Functional imaging and the resting human brain. *Nature Reviews Neuroscience, 2*, 685–694.

Happé, F., Malhi, G. S., & Checkley, S. (2001). Acquired mind-blindness following frontal lobe surgery? A single case study of impaired "theory of mind" in a patient treated with stereotactic anterior capsulotomy. *Neuropsychologia, 39*, 83–90.

Houston, R., & Frith, U. (2000). *Autism in history: The case of Hugh Blair of Borgue.* Oxford, UK: Blackwell.

Hubel, D. N., & Wiesel, T. N. (1962). Receptive fields, binocular interactions and functional architecture in the cat's visual cortex. *Journal of Physiology, 160*, 106–154.

Huttenlocher, P. R. (1979). Synaptic density in human frontal cortex—developmental changes and effects of aging. *Brain Research, 163*, 195–205.

Huttenlocher, P. R., De Courten, C., Garey, L. J., & Van Der Loos, H. (1983). Synaptic development in human cerebral cortex. *International Journal of Neurology, 16–17*, 144–154.

Johnson, S. C. (2003). Detecting agents. *Philosophical Transactions of the Royal Society of London. Series B: Biological Sciences, 358*, 549–559.

Johnson, S. C., Baxter, L. C., Wilder, L. S., Pipe, J. G., Heiserman, J. E., & Prigatano, G. P. (2002). Neural correlates of self-reflection. *Brain, 125*, 1808–1814.

Killgore, W. D. S., Oki, M., & Yurgelun-Todd, D. A. (2001). Sex-specific developmental changes in amygdala responses to affective faces. *Neuroreport, 12*, 427–433.

Lou, H. C., Luber, B., Crupain, M., Keenan, J. P., Nowak, M., Kjaer, T. W., et al. (2004). Parietal cortex and representation of the mental self. *Proceedings of the National Academy of Sciences, USA, 101*, 6827–6832.

McCabe, K., Houser, D., Ryan, L., Smith, V., & Trouard, T. (2001). A functional imaging study of cooperation in two-person reciprocal exchange. *Proceedings of the National Academy of Sciences, USA, 98*, 11832–11835.

McGlashan, T. H., & Hoffman, R. E. (2000). Schizophrenia as a disorder of developmentally reduced synaptic connectivity. *Archives of General Psychiatry, 57*, 637–648.

Mitchell, J. P., Banaji, M. R., & Macrae, C. N. (2005). General and specific contributions of the medial prefrontal cortex to knowledge about mental states. *Neuroimage, 28*, 757–762.

Mitchell, J. P., Heatherton, T. F., & Macrae, C. N. (2002). Distinct neural systems subserve person and object knowledge. *Proceedings of the National Academy of Sciences, USA, 99*, 15238–15243.

Monk, C. S., McClure, E. B., Nelson, E. E., Zarahn, E., Bilder, R. M., Leibenluft, E., et al. (2003). Adolescent immaturity in attention-related brain engagement to emotional facial expressions. *Neuroimage, 20*, 420–428.

Ochsner, K. N., Knierim, K., Ludlow, D. H., Hanelin, J., Ramachandran, T., Glover, G., et al. (2004). Reflecting upon feelings: An fMRI study of neural systems supporting the attribution of emotion to self and other. *Journal of Cognitive Neuroscience, 16*, 1746–1772.

Paus, T., Evans, A. C., & Rapoport, J. L. (1999a). Brain development during childhood and adolescence: A longitudinal MRI study. *Nature Neuroscience, 2*, 861–863.

Paus, T., Zijdenbos, A., Worsley, K., Collins, D. L., Blumenthal, J., Giedd, J. N., et al. (1999b). Structural maturation of neural pathways in children and adolescents: In vivo study. *Science*, *283*, 1908–1911.

Pelphrey, K. A., Morris, J. P., Michelich, C. R., Allison, T., & McCarthy, G. (2005). Functional anatomy of biological motion perception in posterior temporal cortex: An fMRI study of eye, mouth and hand movements. *Cerebral Cortex*, *15*, 1866–1876.

Perner, J., & Leekam, S. (2008). The curious incident of the photo that was accused of being false: Issues of domain specificity in development, autism, and brain imaging. *Quarterly Journal of Experimental Psychology*, *61*, 76–89.

Pfefferbaum, A., Mathalon, D. H., Sullivan, E. V., Rawles, J. M., Zipursky, R. B., & Lim, K. O. (1994). A quantitative magnetic resonance imaging study of changes in brain morphology from infancy to late adulthood. *Archives of Neurology*, *51*, 874–887.

Puce, A., Allison, T., Bentin, S., Gore, J. C., & McCarthy, G. (1998). Temporal cortex activation in humans viewing eye and mouth movements. *Journal of Neuroscience*, *18*, 2188–2199.

Rakic, P. (1995). Corticogenesis in human and nonhuman primates. In M. S. Gazzaniga (Ed.), *The cognitive neurosciences* (pp. 127–145). Cambridge, MA: MIT Press.

Reiss, A. L., Abrams, M. T., Singer, H. S., Ross, J. L., & Denckla, M. B. (1996). Brain development, gender and IQ in children. A volumetric imaging study. *Brain*, *119*, 1763–1774.

Rowe, A. D., Bullock, P. R., Polkey, C. E., & Morris, R. G. (2001). "Theory of mind" impairments and their relationship to executive functioning following frontal lobe excisions. *Brain*, *124*, 600–616.

Samson, D., Apperly, I. A., Chiavarino, C., & Humphreys, G. W. (2004). Left temporoparietal junction is necessary for representing someone else's belief. *Nature Neuroscience*, *7*, 499–500.

Saxe, R., & Kanwisher, N. (2003). People thinking about thinking people. The role of the temporo-parietal junction in "theory of mind". *Neuroimage*, *19*, 1835–1842.

Sodian, B., & Thoermer, C. (2008). Precursors to a theory of mind in infancy: Perspectives for research on autism. *Quarterly Journal of Experimental Psychology*, *61*, 27–39.

Sowell, E. R., Peterson, B. S., Thompson, P. M., Welcome, S. E., Henkenius, A. L., & Toga, A. W. (2003). Mapping cortical change across the life span. *Nature Neuroscience*, *6*, 309–315.

Sowell, E. R., Thompson, P. M., Holmes, C. J., Batth, R., Jernigan, T. L., & Toga, A. W. (1999). Localizing age-related changes in brain structure between childhood and adolescence using statistical parametric mapping. *Neuroimage*, *6*, 587–597.

Spelke, E. S., Phillips, A. T., & Woodward, A. L. (1995). Infants' knowledge of object motion and human action. In D. Sperber, D. Premack, & A. Premack (Eds.), *Causal cognition: A multidisciplinary debate*. Oxford, UK: Oxford University Press.

Stone, V. E., Baron-Cohen, S., & Knight, R. T. (1998). Frontal lobe contributions to theory of mind. *Journal of Cognitive Neuroscience*, *10*, 640–656.

Stuss, D. T., Gallup, G. G., Jr., & Alexander, M. P. (2001). The frontal lobes are necessary for "theory of mind". *Brain*, *124*, 279–286.

Thomas, K. M., Drevets, W. C., Whalen, P. J., Eccard, C. H., Dahl, R. E., Ryan, N. D., et al. (2001). Amygdala response to facial expressions in children and adults. *Biological Psychiatry*, *49*, 309–316.

Thompson, P. M., Giedd, J. N., Woods, R. P., MacDonald, D., Evans, A. C., & Toga, A. W. (2000). Growth patterns in the developing brain detected by using continuum mechanical tensor maps. *Nature*, *404*, 190–193.

Vogeley, K., Bussfeld, P., Newen, A., Herrmann, S., Happe, F., Falkai, P., et al. (2001). Mind reading: Neural mechanisms of theory of mind and self-perspective. *Neuroimage*, *14*, 170–181.

Weinberger, D. R. (1987). Implications of normal brain development for the pathogenesis of schizophrenia. *Archives of General Psychiatry*, *44*, 660–669.

Woo, T. U., Pucak, M. L., Kye, C. H., Matus, C. V., & Lewis, D. A. (1997). Peripubertal refinement of the intrinsic and associational circuitry in monkey prefrontal cortex. *Neuroscience*, *80*, 1149–1158.

Yakovlev, P. A., & Lecours, I. R. (1967). The myelogenetic cycles of regional maturation of the brain. In A. Minkowski (Ed.), *Regional development of the brain in early life* (pp. 3–70). Oxford, UK: Blackwell.

Yurgelun-Todd, D. A., & Killgore, W. D. (2006). Fear-related activity in the prefrontal cortex increases with age during adolescence: A preliminary fMRI study. *Neuroscience Letters*, *406*, 194–199.

Zecevic, N., & Rakic, P. (2001). Development of layer I neurons in the primate cerebral cortex. *Journal of Neuroscience*, *21*, 5607–5619.

THE QUARTERLY JOURNAL OF EXPERIMENTAL PSYCHOLOGY
2008, 61 (1), 50–63

The power of the positive: Revisiting weak coherence in autism spectrum disorders

Francesca G. E. Happé and Rhonda D. L. Booth

Social, Genetic and Developmental Psychiatry Centre, Institute of Psychiatry, King's College London, London, UK

This paper reexamines Frith's original concept of weak coherence, its historical origins, recent reformulations, and alternative accounts. We suggest that the key notion of reduced global integration of information, which Frith proposed to underlie the assets in local processing, has been neglected in recent accounts of autism spectrum disorders (ASD). In fact, most paradigms used to test weak coherence conflate global and local processing, often placing them in direct trade-off, so that it is not possible to tell whether patterns of performance in ASD reflect reduced global processing, increased local processing, or both. We review the literature from typical development and ASD that may be pertinent to this distinction and examine some data from our own studies. Only once tasks are devised that measure separately the effects of reduced global processing and increased local processing will it be possible to test the on-line and developmental relations between these two aspects of "weak coherence". Some preliminary ideas about these relationships are discussed, and suggestions are made for why disentangling two possibly independent dimensions of weak coherence may be timely and productive.

This paper revisits Uta Frith's original concept of weak central coherence and asks whether the notion of reduced integrative processing has been prematurely abandoned in the recent focus on superior local processing in autism. Given the origin of this special issue in a celebration of Uta's contribution to the science of developmental disorders, perhaps a few words about Uta are not out of place in introducing the present theme.

Uta is a magnificently generous and kind mentor, with a steely ruthlessness in scientific matters matched only by her personal gentleness and warmth. A key aspect of her work on autism has been the notion that more can be learnt through a focus on assets in performance than through demonstration of task failure. This notion surely grew in part from Uta's tangible respect for those affected by developmental disorders, notably autism spectrum disorders (ASD): respect for individuals with ASD and also for their families and carers. Her suggestion was that task failure may have many sources (since no task is process pure) while task success, or superior performance, is likely to be more revealing regarding underlying cognitive processes. In the case of understanding ASD, then, a good theory must explain assets as well as deficits. The introduction of the concept of weak "central coherence" was an attempt to meet this challenge.

Correspondence should be addressed to Francesca G. E. Happé, Social, Genetic, and Developmental Psychiatry Centre, Institute of Psychiatry, King's College London, London SE5 8AF, UK. E-mail: f.happe@iop.kcl.ac.uk

DOI:10.1080/17470210701508731

Frith's original concept of "central coherence" and later developments

In "Autism: Explaining the Enigma" (1989) Frith described the "neurotypical" drive for coherence, which "pulls together large amounts of information" (p. 97) like the tributaries of a river; "without this type of high-level cohesion, pieces of information would just remain pieces, be they small pieces or large pieces" (p. 98). In the second edition and revision of the book Frith (2003) states that, "In the normal cognitive system there is a built-in propensity to form coherence over as wide a range of stimuli as possible, and to generalize over as wide a range of contexts as possible" (pp. 159–160). In ASD, by contrast, the suggestion was that this drive for global coherence is weak, reflected in a relative inability to integrate pieces of information into coherent wholes. Instead, a drive towards local detail, at the expense of global meaning, was suggested to be characteristic of individuals with ASD. Weak coherence is reflected in superior task performance in ASD when there is normally a disadvantageous "capture" by gestalt, and/or when ability to process featural information and parts is advantageous. Now-classic examples include superior performance by ASD groups versus matched control groups on the Embedded Figures Test (shown in Figure 1), which requires identification of a simple part within a complex and camouflaging

whole (Shah & Frith, 1983), and on the Block Design Test (Shah & Frith, 1993), which benefits from an ability to see the whole design in terms of its constituent parts. The latter task was particularly elegantly manipulated by Shah and Frith (see Figure 2), who showed that presegmenting the design to be copied helped control groups significantly more than it aided participants with ASD. This examination of condition effects allowed assessment of weak coherence independent of general visuo-spatial ability—a confound that dogs much of the research in this area (e.g., examining sex differences in global/local processing on visuo-spatial tasks).

Frith's notion of central coherence fairly quickly had a powerful impact on the autism field at grass roots level, with immediate recognition by parents and individuals with ASD themselves of the idea of "not seeing the wood for the trees" in ASD. Indeed, the notion chimes in with Kanner's own observations. Kanner, who first described and named autism in 1943, believed that the condition had two defining features: "autistic aloneness" and "obsessive desire for the preservation of sameness" (Kanner & Eisenberg, 1956). The latter he related to fragmented processing;

Inability to experience wholes without full attention to the constituent parts. . . . A situation, a performance, a sentence is not regarded as complete if it is not made up of exactly the same elements that were present at the time the child was first confronted with it. If the slightest ingredient is altered or

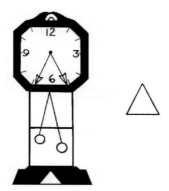

Figure 1. *Example of a test item adapted from the Children's Embedded Figures Test (Witkin et al., 1971), showing the target simple shape to be found within the complex form.*

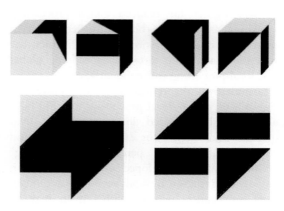

Figure 2. *Materials and sample designs for the Un/Segmented Block Design Task (after Shah & Frith, 1993).*

removed, the total situation is no longer the same and therefore is not accepted as such. (Kanner, 1943, p. 246)

Kanner's original observation is maintained in the current DSM-IV (*Diagnostic and Statistical Manual of Mental Disorders–Fourth Edition*; American Psychiatric Association, 1994) diagnostic criterion of "persistent preoccupation with parts of objects", very much in keeping with Frith's suggestion of weak central coherence.

However, certain elements from Frith's original idea of weak central coherence have been lost, perhaps, in most subsequent discussions. There is, for example, the notion of "local coherence", versus central coherence, as a process that is probably intact in ASD (see Happé & Frith, 2006). More generally, the emphasis on the inability to cohere information has, in recent years, been somewhat neglected in favour of the ability to focus on parts, features, and small details that others miss. Indeed, in a recent review of research on central coherence, Happé and Frith (2006) suggested three modifications to Frith's original account: independence of weak coherence and social-cognitive deficits in ASD; weak coherence as a processing *bias* (versus deficit) that can be overcome; and relegating reduced global processing to, possibly, a secondary effect of superior local processing. This last, which we aim to question here, was in part a response to the apparent weight of research evidence, which is relatively great for superior performance on local tasks and perhaps lighter for reduced global processing. However, as we argue below, further reflection might lead one to question whether, in fact, the necessary data, from tests clearly tapping global and local processing independently, exist.

Alternative theoretical accounts addressing research on global/local processing in ASD have also strongly favoured local superiority over global weakness. So, for example, Mottron and colleagues' "enhanced perceptual functioning" account posits overdeveloped low-level perception and atypical relationships between low- and high-level processing; "persons with autism may be over-dependent on specific aspects of perceptual functioning that are excessively developed and, as

a consequence, more difficult to control and more disruptive to the development of other behaviours and abilities" (Mottron & Burack, 2001, p. 137). In Baron-Cohen's "hypersystemizing" account (Baron-Cohen, 2006), too, the emphasis is on the ability to isolate parts, here in order to figure out the rules of a regular system. Indeed, Baron-Cohen has suggested that the ability of people with ASD to master "systems" such as mathematics, astronomy, and physics argues against the notion of weak coherence or poor integration of information, because such systems are themselves coherent and by extrapolation can only be understood through integrative processing (but see Heavey, Pring, & Hermelin, 1999, for an account of piecemeal solution of the day–date system in calendar calculation). Plaisted (2001) has suggested that the mechanism underlying weak coherence effects involves enhanced discrimination and reduced generalization. Plaisted hypothesizes that people with autism process features held in common between objects relatively poorly and process features unique to an object— that is, those that discriminate items—relatively well. While this account recognizes explicitly both local and global processing atypicalities in ASD, the key research findings from this group involve superior processing without clear indications of reduced integrative functions (e.g., superior visual search, O'Riordan, Plaisted, Driver, & Baron-Cohen, 2001; Plaisted, O'Riordan, & Baron-Cohen, 1998b; superior discrimination learning of highly confusable patterns, Plaisted, O'Riordan, & Baron-Cohen, 1998a).

Our aim here is to revisit the original notion of reduced integrative processing in ASD, beginning with a brief word about the historical roots of coherence and parallel work on local–global processing in typical development.

Historical perspectives on central coherence

The notion that human perception has a natural drive for coherence has a long history. The early concepts from which central coherence emerged included, most notably, those of the Gestalt movement. With a focus on universals in information processing, Gestalt psychologists took the view that perceptual organization is a top-down configuration of the whole, rather than a bottom-up sum of parts. Wertheimer (1924/1938) provided a classic example of this phenomenon in describing how melody is perceived:

What I hear of each individual note, what I experience at each place in the melody is a *part* which is itself determined by the character of the whole. What is given me by the melody does not arise (through the agency of any auxiliary factor) as a *secondary* process from the sum of the pieces as such. Instead, what takes place in each single part already depends upon what the whole is. (p. 5)

The view that the quality of a part is determined by the whole gave rise to the main tenet of the Gestalt movement: "The whole is more than the sum of the parts." Wertheimer (1924/1938) maintained that the initial perception of spatial patterns were as unanalysed and undifferentiated wholes, dominated by grouping principles, and only later analysed into constituent parts. This perspective was in direct opposition to the structuralists (e.g., Titchener, 1909; Wundt, 1902) who held the view that the sensory whole must be built up from a conglomerate of elementary sensations. The Gestalt school of thought was also in contrast to the associationists (e.g., Hebb, 1949) who asserted that repeated viewings or connections between parts led to integration and formation of the conceptual whole.

The study of wholistic or global processing was not, of course, limited to visual perception. Bartlett (1932), notably, referred to the "drive for meaning" to describe the tendency of adults to recall the gist, rather than verbatim form, of verbal material. He observed the tendency to introduce slight distortions during recall in order to make unfamiliar material more meaningful. In concluding his classic work on remembering images and stories, Bartlett stated:

An individual does not normally take such a situation detail by detail and meticulously build up the whole. In all ordinary instances he has an overmastering tendency simply to get a general impression of the whole; and, on the basis of this, he constructs the probable detail. (p. 206)

Very much in the tradition of the Gestaltists, Navon (1977) put forward the global precedence hypothesis, proposing that, in adults, the global properties of visual arrays are processed before local properties. Using hierarchical figures (e.g., an H composed of Ss), Navon found faster reaction times for identifying global letters than local letters and greater interference from global level to local level (global interference) than vice versa. Navon concluded that "global processing is a necessary stage of perception prior to more fine-grained analysis" (p. 371). Navon's paradigm has been used extensively in the study of local–global processing across a range of psychological fields (see Navon, 2003, for a review). Despite the experimental control gained by the use of hierarchical figures, the perceptual relation between the global and local levels is sensitive to variations such as number and relative size of the local elements (see Kimchi, 1992, for a review). Kimchi claims that this finding weakens the underlying assumption that global form and the local elements map directly onto distinct perceptual units, differing only in level of globality. She proposes that the study of wholistic properties of stimuli—that is, properties that depend on the configuration of component parts—may be more informative when exploring precedence effects in perceptual processing.

Independence of local and global processing in typical development

Recent work into the developmental trajectory of local–global processing has led researchers to the premise that independent mechanisms may exist in processing local and global level information (Burack, Enns, Iarocci, & Randolph, 2000; Dukette & Stiles, 1996, 2001; Porporino, Shore, Iarocci, & Burack, 2004). It is perhaps useful, then, to briefly review here what is known about local and global processing in typical development (TD) and the possible separability of these two types of processing.

One of the most enduring questions in developmental psychology is whether the primacy of processing parts versus wholes changes systematically with age. The study of part–whole perception in typical development has received great scrutiny across a number of diverse research fields such as featural and configural visual-perceptual processing (e.g., Kimchi, 1992), visuo-spatial construction (e.g., Akshoomoff & Stiles, 1995), coherence and comprehension in language (e.g., Gernsbacher, 1993), and music perception (e.g., Takeuchi & Hulse, 1993).

From infancy studies there is evidence of a developmental change in the perception of parts and wholes in the first few months of life (see Colombo, 2001, for a review). Several studies report a developmental sequence from local to global processing during infancy, with some suggesting that global processing may predominate in infants as young as 3 months (Bhatt, Rovee-Collier, & Shyi, 1994; Ghim & Eimas, 1988; van Giffen & Haith, 1984; Younger & Cohen, 1986). Cohen and Younger (1984) suggest that a shift in the perception of form occurs some time after 6 weeks of age. Prior to this age infants can remember (i.e., habituate to) the specific orientations of line segments, but not the angular relations that line segments make. Consistent with the constructivist view, Cohen and Younger propose, "only later through experience and/or development are [infants] able to integrate those line segments into entire angles and shapes" (p. 46). However, under certain experimental conditions newborn infants have been shown be sensitive to the emergent properties of line elements rather than component lines. Slater, Mattock, Brown, and Bremner (1991) demonstrated that repeated exposure of the same angle in different orientations led to habituation to that angle in newborns. Slater et al. propose the possibility that "form perception may not be dependent upon a lengthy period of learning and/or maturation for its development" (p. 405).

Developmental studies have traditionally focused on universals in local–global processing, although interest in individual variation can also be found. In infant research, individual variations have been found in the amount of time that infants tend to fixate visual stimuli, which may reflect differences in visual information processing. "Short-duration" infants are suggested to take in information in a global to local sequence, whereas "long-duration" infants may process information immediately at a local level and perform a feature-by-feature analysis (Colombo, Mitchell, Coldren, & Freeseman, 1991; Freeseman, Colombo, & Coldren, 1993; Stoecker, Colombo, Frick, & Allen, 1998). As a follow-up to this finding, Frick, Colombo and Allen (2000) examined whether individual differences in look duration were related to differences in processing hierarchical patterns. Short-duration infants showed global precedence effects after viewing a hierarchical pattern for 20 seconds (i.e., displayed a novelty preference to global, but not local, properties of the familiarized pattern). Global precedence effects were also present in the long-duration infants, but only after they were familiarized with the hierarchical pattern for 30 seconds. Stoecker et al. (1998) discuss whether prolonged looking could be related to an inability to disengage or "inhibit" looking at features. In their study long-duration infants were found to show no benefit from the symmetry of stimuli (typically processed faster than asymmetrical stimuli), possibly perseverating on a part of the stimulus in preference to the whole form. Fixation duration in infancy is also associated with later general cognitive abilities, with longer durations associated with lower intellect (Colombo & Mitchell, 1990).

Reviewing the literature on global–local processing in childhood, there appears to be little consensus on the nature of developmental changes. Early studies that questioned whether parts or wholes dominate children's perception generally provided mixed results. Some studies suggested that young children are best described as "piecemeal" processors, attending only to the parts of a configuration (e.g., Carey & Diamond, 1977; Corah & Gospodinoff, 1966; Elkind, Koegler, & Go, 1964); other studies suggested that young children are "wholistic" processors, perceiving patterns as undifferentiated wholes, without awareness of constituent parts (e.g., Gibson, 1969; Meili-Dworetzki, 1956). In the study of face perception, for example, Carey and Diamond (1977) reported that children below the age of 10 years showed a reduced face inversion effect, possibly reflecting an increased reliance on feature-based processing. Since then, however, several studies have suggested that young children use qualitatively similar (i.e., wholistic) face-coding strategies to those used by adults (Carey & Diamond, 1994; Gilchrist & McKone, 2003; Pellicano & Rhodes, 2003; Tanaka, Kay, Grinnell, Stansfield, & Szechter, 1998). However, Mondloch, Le Grand, and Maurer (2002) concluded that younger children's relatively poor performance in identifying faces is due largely to poor configural processing, which develops more slowly than the processing of individual features, suggesting that the two processes may develop independently.

The emphasis across the plethora of developmental studies appears to be on the proficiency with which information (visual or verbal) can be integrated into a coherent whole with age—for example, to extract gist (Brainerd & Gordon, 1994; Reyna & Kiernan, 1994), demonstrate global precedence (Kimchi, 1990; Kramer, Ellenberg, Leonard, & Share, 1996), or to show coherence in copying tasks (Akshoomoff & Stiles, 1995; Tada & Stiles, 1996). However, tasks that require detail-focused processing and an ability to ignore gestalt (e.g., EFT, Block Design) also show greater proficiency with age (e.g., Enns & Girgus, 1985; Pennings, 1988; Witkin, Oltman, Raskin, & Karp, 1971). It appears, then, that the reciprocal processes of integration and segmentation show developmental progression.

Using evidence from similarity judgement tasks and drawing tests using hierarchical figures, Dukette and Stiles (2001) concluded that "integration and segmentation processes of spatial analysis develop along somewhat different time courses, with segmentation abilities becoming more elaborated earlier than integration skills" (p. 247). Developmental studies by Burack and colleagues (based on visual search paradigms by Enns & Kingstone, 1995) contrasting long-range and short-range grouping processes in visual search led Burack et al. (2000) to suggest that developmental effects may operate on sensitivity to global structure in a pattern, independently

from local-level perception. Furthermore, adult-like efficiency may be attained earlier for local than for global processing. Porporino et al. (2004) also suggest that the developmental trajectories for local and global processing involve independent mechanisms, based on studies of selective attention to target shapes at either the local or the global level of a hierarchical figure; efficient local processing appears to be attained early, while global processing continues to improve at least until 8 years of age.

Evidence for independent mechanisms for local and global processing has also been found in the verbal-semantic modality. Memory studies by Reyna and Kiernan (1994) and Brainerd and Gordon (1994) suggested that memory for gist (global) was not dependent on verbatim (local) recall, particularly when participants were directed to remember information word for word. Instead, memory appears both to be constructive and to hold the ability to preserve details (Reyna & Kiernan, 1994). Consistent with the finding of Burack and colleagues that local processing may be attained earlier than global processing (Burack et al., 2000; Porporino et al., 2004), Brainerd and Gordon reported that gist was relatively higher than verbatim recall in 8-year-olds, with the opposite pattern of verbatim better than gist recall in 5-year-olds. Furthermore, the two age groups did not differ in absolute level of verbatim recall.

Dukette and Stiles (1996) point out that the historical emphasis on parts versus wholes may have produced a false dichotomy. Depending on task and stimulus conditions, young children have demonstrated an ability to attend to the parts, the whole pattern, or both (Dukette & Stiles, 1996, 2001; Tada & Stiles-Davis, 1989). Rather than an isolated ability to perceive parts or wholes during different development stages, Aslin and Smith (1988) stress that what changes is the "quality of the representation and the available operations that can be performed on it" (p. 458). This has directed research to consider the role of executive control when attending to local–global information: Age-related changes may not be due solely to a tendency to perceive either the larger global form or the local details, but also to an increased ability to adapt attentional strategies to the demands of the task (Enns & Girgus, 1985; Tada & Stiles, 1996). Such strategies may include the ability to shift from a feature to the whole, switch between processes of analysis and synthesis, and ignore an irrelevant level. It is well documented that many facets of executive functioning, such as the efficiency of working-memory capacity, planning, and problem-solving, develop with age (De Luca et al., 2003), as does the ability to ignore distractors (Goldberg, Maurer, & Lewis, 2001; Ridderinkhof & van der Molen, 1995). The role of executive skill in local–global processing, and the possible interaction between these processes across development, warrants further examination.

In sum, there is growing consensus that local and global processing should be considered independent constructs with different trajectories in typical development. However, it remains unclear whether tasks used to date can sufficiently discriminate the specific contributions of each process (see below), whether general statements can be made about the priority of global or local processing in development, and what role executive processes play in selecting optimal task strategies at the local or global level.

Local superiority or global weakness in ASD?

When one turns to the study of global and local processing biases in ASD, it becomes clear that most tasks conflate demands such that characteristic patterns of task performance in ASD may reflect weak integrative processing, strong local processing, or both. In the EFT, for example, quick and successful search for the hidden part, which has been demonstrated in ASD groups versus age and IQ-matched controls, might result from lack of distraction by the camouflaging gestalt due to reduced integration, or greater ability to focus in on the salient part (superior local processing). It is worth noting that Frith was quite aware of this; in their study using the children's EFT, Shah and Frith (1983) asked the participants to name the large pictures, to check

that information could be cohered at least when prompted (see also Jarrold, Gilchrist, & Bender, 2005, for an interesting analysis of possible contributory processes in EFT). The same conflation of demands holds true for success on the Block Design task (but see Caron, Mottron, Berthiaume, & Dawson, 2006, for a recent sophisticated exploration of cognitive and neural underpinnings of this task). Most hierarchical figures tasks, too, place local and global in competition such that good local processing necessarily implies poor global processing or vice versa.

Most tests relevant to weak coherence have the same shortcoming. The sentence completion task that we have designed (Happé, Briskman, & Frith, 2001), for example, asks participants to finish off sentence stems such as "You can go hunting with a knife and...", "fork" being a local completion taken as evidence of weak coherence, in contrast to globally coherent completions such as "and catch a bear". Local completions, characteristic of participants with ASD, may reflect failure to integrate the whole sentence stem or overfocus on the local stem ending. The same could be argued regarding the homograph reading test (Frith & Snowling, 1983; Happé, 1997; Snowling & Frith, 1986)—probably the best replicated verbal test of weak coherence; the characteristic lack of effect of preceding sentence context on homograph pronunciation ("in her dress there was a big *tear*") might reflect reduced integration or increased local processing.

Reviewing empirical studies of coherence in ASD, Happé and Frith (2006) concluded that the evidence for superior local processing was strong while that for impaired global processing was more mixed. Indeed, this reflects the stance taken by most authors reviewing this field. However, given that most tasks in that literature confound local and global processing, there appears to be something of an imbalance in the interpretation of negative findings. When an ASD group perform indistinguishably from their control group on a global–local task (e.g., hierarchical figures), the usual conclusion appears to be that global processing is therefore intact, rather than that local processing is not superior.

On reflection, therefore, it appears that sufficient data from tasks able to distinguish the contribution of global impairment and of local enhancement are not yet available.

It is quite possible, of course, to tap local processing and global integration separately. For example, in a study of drawing style and planning in which we tested weak coherence in ASD and attention-deficit/hyperactivity disorder (ADHD), we were able to rate local drawing style (starting drawings with a local element, or drawing fragment to fragment) distinct from violation of configuration in drawings (Booth, Charlton, Hughes, & Happé, 2003), as shown by the examples in Figure 3 and Figure 4. Both types of drawings were more common in the ASD than the TD or ADHD groups, but did not necessarily occur together in the same drawing or participant across drawings.

Mottron and his colleagues are notable for attempting to test global and local processes separately in order to isolate the abnormality in ASD. Mottron, Burack, Iarocci, Belleville, and Enns (2003) used a battery of tasks, comprising hierarchical figures, fragmented letter and silhouette identification, long-and short-range grouping, and disembedding. They found that their 12 high-functioning ASD participants differed from the matched TD controls only on the disembedding task, and they concluded that participants with ASD may be better able than TD participants to ignore global information when it is irrelevant to the task in hand. The lack of group difference on the other tasks was interpreted as showing

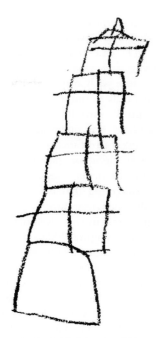

Figure 4. *Example of a finished drawing demonstrating impaired configuration without obvious evidence of heightened local processing.*

that global processing per se is intact in ASD, although the authors note that at least two of their tasks (silhouette and segmentation tasks) may have been insufficiently sensitive to find group differences among conditions.

Iarocci, Burack, Shore, Mottron, and Enns (2006) gave 12 young people with high-functioning ASD the same test of short- and long-range grouping as that used by Burack and colleagues with TD children (see above). This task neatly allowed separate manipulation of task difficulty for the relatively local and global targets. ASD and control groups performed indistinguishably on all conditions, suggesting intact global processing and no superiority in local processing. In a second experiment, the authors found the ASD group to be more sensitive than controls to the implicit task bias established through different probabilities of targets appearing at local versus global levels in a hierarchical figure. They conclude overall that global–local processing in ASD may

Figure 3. *Example of a drawing (four frames showing drawing sequence) by a boy with autism spectrum disorders (ASD), demonstrating local focus without problems in global integration.*

be unusually "piecemeal and data driven", versus processing that was "parsimonious and theory driven" in TD, and that this style leads to enhanced processing when global biases would normally interfere with task performance, as on the EFT. This calls to mind the idea of "reduced top-down control" introduced by Frith in her revised book (2003) and opens again the question of the role of executive functions in selecting the appropriate level (local or global) of attentional focus on any particular task. Indeed, some authors have suggested that many findings from the weak coherence literature can be recast as demonstrating executive dysfunction (Hala, Pexman, & Glenwright, 2007; but see Booth et al., 2003, for a counterargument).

Booth (2006) included tests designed to tap global integration unconfounded with local processing bias, among her battery of 16 coherence tasks, administered to over 200 TD individuals from 8 to 25 years and age- and IQ-matched groups of ASD and control participants. For example, a modified fragmented figures task (see Figure 5) required participants to identify a picture from fragments (from which identifying details were removed, as in Jolliffe & Baron-Cohen's, 2001a, modified Hooper test). Participants with ASD required more frames (i.e., more completed fragments) in order to identify the image. Another test of global integration

required a "possible/impossible" judgement of figures (see Figure 6), some of which were globally impossible (rather like M. C. Escher paintings); again poor integrative processing was seen in the ASD participants' lower sensitivity to impossibility.

Tasks that measure independently the ability to integrate information (see, for example, Jolliffe & Baron-Cohen, 2001a, 2001b) and the ability to focus on details are essential if we are to address key questions. These include: Is there a necessary trade-off between local and global processing, in stable individual differences? What is the on-line relation between local and global processing?

From Booth's (2006) large battery of tasks, it was possible to extract composites interpretable as reflecting segmentation ability on the one hand and integration ability on the other. Interestingly, segmentation and integration indices were positively correlated in the TD sample (particularly females) and the age- and IQ-matched control group; those who were good at segmenting were also good at integrating, even though effects of age and IQ had been partialled out. In the ASD group only, these processes appeared to be in trade-off, with good segmentation going with poor integration and vice versa.

One implication of separating out the (good) segmentation and (poor) integration processes that may contribute to weak coherence in ASD

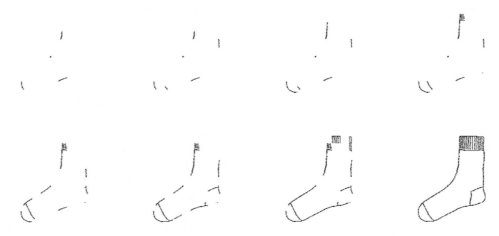

Figure 5. *Example of consecutive frames from the Fragmented Figures Test (Snodgrass, Smith, Feenan, & Corwin, 1987).*

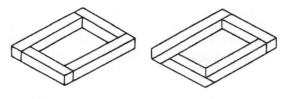

Figure 6. *Example of possible and impossible figures (Booth, 2006).*

is that analysis of ASD and control group data needs to consider individual profiles of task performance. Group comparisons alone will leave us unclear whether, in fact, some ASD participants show only poor integration while others, or a partly overlapping subgroup, show only superior segmentation. Caron et al. (2006) have recently demonstrated the power of subgrouping ASD participants, in this case by especially good Block Design relative to other IQ subtest scores, in their thorough analysis of component processes in the Block Design task. They found diminished sensitivity to perceptual coherence in ASD but no evidence of local bias/global impairment on tasks that necessitated global processing. Recent versions of the weak coherence account have emphasized that this is a cognitive style best considered as a bias toward local processing, rather than a cognitive deficit: Explicit instructions to focus on the global level/extract meaning result in reduction or obliteration of group differences (Happé & Frith, 2006). If global and local contributions to this cognitive style are to be distinguished, maybe the effect of explicit instruction can be hypothesized to act on (up-regulate) global processing, but perhaps have little or no effect on superior local processing in ASD?

Considering separately these two components of weak coherence will also allow us to revisit important questions for which the current evidence is unclear and contradictory. For example, what is the relationship between good local or poor global processing and social cognition deficits? To date, some studies show an apparent inverse relationship between, for example, EFT and Theory of Mind performance (Jarrold, Butler, Cottington, & Jimenez, 2000), while others show no relationship between measures of the two domains in ASD (Morgan, Maybery, & Durkin, 2003) or TD (Pellicano, Maybery, & Durkin, 2005). Might poor integration be inversely related to social cognition, but superior local processing be unrelated to social deficits?

A key question for future research concerns the developmental relationship between integrative processing and local featural bias in ASD. Does an early eye for detail lead to lack of practice with wholes and a resultant difficulty or reluctance to integrate information for meaning and gestalt? Or does early difficulty in integrative processing force a compensatory attention to parts, with over-development of this skill over time? With the right tasks, and longitudinal studies, it should be possible to find out.

Other sources of evidence on this question might include other clinical groups such as Williams syndrome, in which it has been suggested global processing is impaired (Bellugi, Lichtenberger, Jones, Lai, & St. George, 2000; but see Pani, Mervis, & Robinson, 1999, for evidence of intact global processing), without perhaps very much evidence of superior local processing. Babies born with cataracts, typically removed at or after 6 months of age, have been reported to show persistent impairments in global processing of faces (Le Grand, Mondloch, Maurer, & Brent, 2003)—do they show any local processing enhancements?

Individual differences within the autism spectrum will also be of special interest. Of course, not every person with ASD shows excellent Block Design performance or an eye for detail. What has not been systematically examined is whether the two parts of weak coherence—integrative weakness and local enhancement—might characterize rather different parts of the spectrum, or different age groups. Does poor integration mainly characterize lower functioning individuals with ASD? Does the increased ability to "zoom out" and take in more of the big picture, which some adults on the autism spectrum report with increasing age, have any costs for their eye for detail?

Conclusions

We have suggested that Frith's original notion of reduced integrative processing in ASD warrants a renewal of interest. Tasks need to be devised that can test integrative failure independently of superior local processing. Considering weak coherence to be the result of two separable dimensions—reduced tendency to integrate information and increased tendency to featural processing—could open a new series of research questions for the field. For example, what is the developmental relationship between these two processes? Is one or the other more characteristic of the broader autism phenotype, or is the relation (e.g., trade-off) between them the key indicator? How malleable is each dimension to task manipulations, instruction, or teaching? If integration and local bias are independent, at least in early stages of development, might it be possible to ameliorate the poor global processing without robbing people with ASD of their superior eye for detail? These and many more questions are the legacy of just one small part of Uta Frith's thinking about autism; we are all lucky that she has turned the light of her intellect on this most fascinating of enigmas.

REFERENCES

Akshoomoff, N. A., & Stiles, J. (1995). Developmental trends in visuospatial analysis and planning: I. Copying a complex figure. *Neuropsychology*, *9*, 364–377.

American Psychiatric Association. (1994). *Diagnostic and statistical manual of mental disorders* (4th ed.). Washington, DC: Author.

Aslin, R. N., & Smith, L. B. (1988). Perceptual development. *Annual Review of Psychology*, *39*, 435–473.

Baron-Cohen, S. (2006). Two new theories of autism: Hyper-systemising and assortative mating. *Archives of Disease in Childhood*, *91*, 2–5.

Bartlett, F. (1932). *Remembering*. Cambridge, UK: Cambridge University Press.

Bellugi, U., Lichtenberger, L., Jones, W., Lai, Z., & St. George, M. (2000). The neurocognitive profile of Williams syndrome: A complex pattern of strengths and weaknesses. *Journal of Cognitive Neuroscience*, *12*(Suppl. 1), 7–29.

Bhatt, R. S., Rovee-Collier, C., & Shyi, G. C. (1994). Global and local processing of incidental information and memory retrieval at 6 months. *Journal of Experimental Child Psychology*, *57*, 141–162.

Booth, R. (2006). *Local–global processing and cognitive style in autism spectrum disorder and typical development*. Unpublished PhD thesis, King's College London, London, UK.

Booth, R., Charlton, R., Hughes, C., & Happé, F. (2003). Disentangling weak coherence and executive dysfunction: Planning drawing in autism and attention-deficit/hyperactivity disorder. *Philosophical Transactions of the Royal Society of London. Series B: Biological Sciences*, *358*, 387–392.

Brainerd, C. J., & Gordon, L. L. (1994). Development of verbatim and gist memory for numbers. *Developmental Psychology*, *30*, 163–177.

Burack, J. A., Enns, J. T., Iarocci, G., & Randolph, B. (2000). Age differences in visual search for compound patterns: Long- versus short-range grouping. *Developmental Psychology*, *36*, 731–740.

Carey, S., & Diamond, R. (1977). From piecemeal to configurational representation of faces. *Science*, *195*, 312–314.

Carey, S., & Diamond, R. (1994). Are faces perceived as configurations more by adults than by children? *Visual Cognition*, *1*, 253–274.

Caron, M. J., Mottron, L., Berthiaume, C., & Dawson, M. (2006). Cognitive mechanisms, specificity and neural underpinnings of visuospatial peaks in autism. *Brain*, *129*, 1789–1802.

Cohen, L. B., & Younger, B. A. (1984). Infant perception of angular relations. *Infant Behavior and Development*, *7*, 37–47.

Colombo, J. (2001). The development of visual attention in infancy. *Annual Review of Psychology*, *52*, 337–367.

Colombo, J., & Mitchell, D. W. (1990). Individual differences in early visual attention: Fixation time and information processing. In J. W. Fagen (Ed.), *Individual differences in infancy: Reliability, stability, prediction* (pp. 193–227). Hillsdale, NJ: Lawrence Erlbaum Associates.

Colombo, J., Mitchell, D., Coldren, J. T., & Freeseman, L. J. (1991). Individual differences in infant visual attention: Are short lookers faster processors or feature processors? *Child Development*, *62*, 1247–1257.

Corah, N. L., & Gospodinoff, E. J. (1966). Color-form and whole-part perception in children. *Child Development*, *37*, 837–842.

De Luca, C. R., Wood, S. J., Anderson, V., Buchanan, J.-A., Proffitt, T. M., Mahony, K., et al. (2003). Normative data from the Cantab. I: Development of executive function over the lifespan. *Journal of Clinical and Experimental Neuropsychology*, 25, 242–254.

Dukette, D., & Stiles, J. (1996). Children's analysis of hierarchical patterns: Evidence from a similarity judgment task. *Journal of Experimental Child Psychology*, 63, 103–140.

Dukette, D., & Stiles, J. (2001). The effects of stimulus density on children's analysis of hierarchical patterns. *Developmental Science*, 4, 233–251.

Elkind, D., Koegler, R., & Go, E. (1964). Studies in perceptual development: II. Part-whole perception. *Child Development*, 35, 81–90.

Enns, J. T., & Girgus, J. S. (1985). Developmental changes in selective and integrative visual attention. *Journal of Experimental Child Psychology*, 40, 319–337.

Enns, J. T., & Kingstone, A. (1995). Access to global and local properties in visual search for compound stimuli. *Psychological Science*, 6, 283–291.

Freeseman, L. J., Colombo, J., & Coldren, J. T. (1993). Individual differences in infant visual attention: Four-month-olds' discrimination and generalization of global and local stimulus properties. *Child Development*, 64, 1191–1203.

Frick, J. E., Colombo, J., & Allen, J. R. (2000). Temporal sequence of global–local processing in 3-month-old infants. *Infancy*, 1, 375–386.

Frith, U. (1989). *Autism: Explaining the enigma*. Oxford, UK: Blackwell Publishing.

Frith, U. (2003). *Autism: Explaining the enigma* (2nd ed.). Oxford, UK: Blackwell Publishing.

Frith, U., & Snowling, M. (1983). Reading for meaning and reading for sound in autistic and dyslexic children. *British Journal of Developmental Psychology*, 1, 329–342.

Gernsbacher, M. A. (1993). Less skilled readers have less efficient suppression mechanisms. *Psychological Science*, 4, 294–298.

Ghim, H.-R., & Eimas, P. D. (1988). Global and local processing by 3- and 4-month-old infants. *Perception and Psychophysics*, 43, 165–171.

Gibson, E. J. (1969). *Principles of perceptual learning and development*. East Norwalk, CT: Appleton-Century-Crofts.

Gilchrist, A., & McKone, E. (2003). Early maturity of face processing in children: Local and relational distinctiveness effects in 7-year-olds. *Visual Cognition*, 10, 769–793.

Goldberg, M. C., Maurer, D., & Lewis, T. L. (2001). Developmental changes in attention: The effects of endogenous cueing and of distractors. *Developmental Science*, 4, 209–219.

Hala, S., Pexman, P. M., & Glenwright, M. (2007). Priming the meaning of homographs in typically developing children and children with autism. *Journal of Autism and Developmental Disorders*, 37, 329–340.

Happé, F. (1997). Central coherence and theory of mind in autism: Reading homographs in context. *British Journal of Developmental Psychology*, 15, 1–12.

Happé, F., Briskman, J., & Frith, U. (2001). Exploring the cognitive phenotype of autism: Weak "central coherence" in parents and siblings of children with autism: I. Experimental tests. *Journal of Child Psychology and Psychiatry*, 42, 299–307.

Happé, F., & Frith, U. (2006). The weak coherence account: Detail-focused cognitive style in autism spectrum disorders. *Journal of Autism and Developmental Disorders*, 36, 5–25.

Heavey, L., Pring, L., & Hermelin, B. (1999). A date to remember: The nature of memory in savant calendrical calculators. *Psychological Medicine*, 29, 145–160.

Hebb, D. O. (1949). *The organization of behavior: A neuropsychological theory*. Oxford, UK: Wiley.

Iarocci, G., Burack, J. A., Shore, D. I., Mottron, L., & Enns, J. T. (2006). Global–local visual processing in high functioning children with autism: Structural vs. implicit task biases. *Journal of Autism and Developmental Disorders*, 36, 117–129.

Jarrold, C., Butler, D. W., Cottington, E. M., & Jimenez, F. (2000). Linking theory of mind and central coherence bias in autism and in the general population. *Developmental Psychology*, 36, 126–138.

Jarrold, C., Gilchrist, I. D., & Bender, A. (2005). Embedded figures detection in autism and typical development: Preliminary evidence of a double dissociation in relationships with visual search. *Developmental Science*, 8, 344–351.

Jolliffe, T., & Baron-Cohen, S. (2001a). A test of central coherence theory: Can adults with high-functioning autism or Asperger syndrome integrate fragments of an object? *Cognitive Neuropsychiatry*, 6, 193–216.

Jolliffe, T., & Baron-Cohen, S. (2001b). A test of central coherence theory: Can adults with high-functioning autism or Asperger syndrome integrate objects in context? *Visual Cognition*, 8, 67–101.

Kanner, L. (1943). Autistic disturbances of affective contact. *Nervous Child*, 2, 217–250.

Kanner, L., & Eisenberg, L. (1956). Early infantile autism 1943–1955. *American Journal of Orthopsychiatry*, *26*, 55–65.

Kimchi, R. (1990). Children's perceptual organisation of hierarchical visual patterns. *European Journal of Cognitive Psychology*, *2*, 133–149.

Kimchi, R. (1992). Primacy of wholistic processing and global/local paradigm: A critical review. *Psychological Bulletin*, *112*, 24–38.

Kramer, J. H., Ellenberg, L., Leonard, J., & Share, L. J. (1996). Developmental sex differences in global-local perceptual bias. *Neuropsychology*, *10*, 402–407.

Le Grand, R., Mondloch, C. J., Maurer, D., & Brent, H. P. (2003). Expert face processing requires visual input to the right hemisphere during infancy. *Nature Neuroscience*, *6*, 1108–1112.

Meili-Dworetzki, G. (1956). The development of perception in the Rorschach. In B. Klopfer (Ed.), *Development in the Rorschach technique*. New York: Harcourt, Brace and World.

Mondloch, C. J., Le Grand, R., & Maurer, D. (2002). Configural face processing develops more slowly than featural face processing. *Perception*, *31*, 553–566.

Morgan, B., Maybery, M., & Durkin, K. (2003). Weak central coherence, poor joint attention, and low verbal ability: Independent deficits in early autism. *Developmental Psychology*, *39*, 646–656.

Mottron, L., & Burack, J. A. (2001). Enhanced perceptual functioning in the development of autism. In P. R. Zelazo (Ed.), *The development of autism: Perspectives from theory and research* (pp. 131–148). Mahwah, NJ: Lawrence Erlbaum Associates.

Mottron, L., Burack, J. A., Iarocci, G., Belleville, S., & Enns, J. T. (2003). Locally oriented perception with intact global processing among adolescents with high-functioning autism: Evidence from multiple paradigms. *Journal of Child Psychology and Psychiatry*, *44*, 904–913.

Navon, D. (1977). Forest before trees: The precedence of global features in visual perception. *Cognitive Psychology*, *9*, 353–383.

Navon, D. (2003). What does a compound letter tell the psychologist's mind? *Acta Psychologia*, *114*, 273–309.

O'Riordan, M., Plaisted, K. C., Driver, J., & Baron-Cohen, S. (2001). Superior visual search in autism. *Journal of Experimental Psychology: Human Perception and Performance*, *27*, 719–730.

Pani, J. R., Mervis, C. B., & Robinson, B. F. (1999). Global spatial organization by individuals with Williams syndrome. *Psychological Science*, *10*, 453–458.

Pellicano, E., Maybery, M., & Durkin, K. (2005). Central coherence in typically developing preschoolers: Does it cohere and does it relate to mindreading and executive control? *Journal of Child Psychology and Psychiatry*, *46*, 533–547.

Pellicano, E., & Rhodes, G. (2003). Holistic processing of faces in preschool children and adults. *Psychological Science*, *14*, 618–622.

Pennings, A. (1988). The development of strategies in embedded figures tasks. *International Journal of Psychology*, *23*, 65–78.

Plaisted, K. C. (2001). Reduced generalization in autism: An alternative to weak central coherence. In J. A. Burack, T. Charman, N. Yirmiya, & P. R. Zelazo (Eds.), *The development of autism: Perspectives from theory and research* (pp. 149–169). Mahwah, NJ: Lawrence Erlbaum Associates.

Plaisted, K. C., O'Riordan, M., & Baron-Cohen, S. (1998a). Enhanced discrimination of novel, highly similar stimuli by adults with autism during a perceptual learning task. *Journal of Child Psychology and Psychiatry*, *39*, 765–775.

Plaisted, K. C., O'Riordan, M., & Baron-Cohen, S. (1998b). Enhanced visual search for a conjunctive target in autism: A research note. *Journal of Child Psychology and Psychiatry*, *39*, 777–783.

Porporino, M., Shore, D. I., Iarocci, G., & Burack, J. A. (2004). A developmental change in selective attention and global form perception. *International Journal of Behavioral Development*, *28*, 358–364.

Reyna, V. F., & Kiernan, B. (1994). Development of gist versus verbatim memory in sentence recognition: Effects of lexical familiarity, semantic content, encoding instructions, and retention interval. *Developmental Psychology*, *30*, 178–191.

Ridderinkhof, K., & van der Molen, M. W. (1995). A psychophysiological analysis of developmental differences in the ability to resist interference. *Child Development*, *66*, 1040–1056.

Shah, A., & Frith, U. (1983). An islet of ability in autistic children: A research note. *Journal of Child Psychology and Psychiatry*, *24*, 613–620.

Shah, A., & Frith, U. (1993). Why do autistic individuals show superior performance on the block design task? *Journal of Child Psychology and Psychiatry*, *34*, 1351–1364.

Slater, A., Mattock, A., Brown, E., & Bremner, J. (1991). Form perception at birth: Cohen and Younger (1984) revisited. *Journal of Experimental Child Psychology*, *51*, 395–406.

Snodgrass, J. G., Smith, B., Feenan, K., & Corwin, J. (1987). Fragmenting pictures on the Apple Macintosh computer for experimental and clinical applications. *Behavior Research Methods, Instruments and Computers, 19*, 270–274.

Snowling, M., & Frith, U. (1986). Comprehension in "hyperlexic" readers. *Journal of Experimental Child Psychology, 42*, 392–415.

Stoecker, J. J., Colombo, J., Frick, J. E., & Allen, J. R. (1998). Long- and short-looking infants' recognition of symmetrical and asymmetrical forms. *Journal of Experimental Child Psychology, 71*, 63–78.

Tada, W. L., & Stiles, J. (1996). Developmental change in children's analysis of spatial patterns. *Developmental Psychology, 32*, 951–970.

Tada, W. L., & Stiles-Davis, J. (1989). Children's analysis of spatial patterns: An assessment of their "errors" in copying geometric forms. *Cognitive Development, 4*, 177–195.

Takeuchi, A. H., & Hulse, S. H. (1993). Absolute pitch. *Psychological Bulletin, 113*, 345–361.

Tanaka, J. W., Kay, J. B., Grinnell, E., Stansfield, B., & Szechter, L. (1998). Face recognition in young children: When the whole is greater than the sum of its parts. *Visual Cognition, 5*, 479–496.

Titchener, E. B. (1909). *Lectures on the experimental psychology of the thought-processes*. Oxford, UK: Macmillan.

van Giffen, K., & Haith, M. M. (1984). Infant visual response to Gestalt geometric forms. *Infant Behavior and Development, 7*, 335–346.

Wertheimer, M. (1938). About Gestalt theory [an address before the Kant Society, Berlin, 17th December, 1924]. In W. D. Ellis (Ed. & Trans.), *A source book of Gestalt psychology*. Oxford, UK: Harcourt, Brace. (Original work published 1924)

Witkin, H. A., Oltman, P. K., Raskin, E., & Karp, S. A. (1971). *A manual for the Embedded Figures Test*. Palo Alto, CA: Consulting Psychologists Press.

Wundt, W. (1902). *Outlines of psychology* (C. H. Judd, Trans., 2nd ed.). Oxford, UK: Engelmann.

Younger, B. A., & Cohen, L. B. (1986). Developmental change in infants' perception of correlations among attributes. *Child Development, 57*, 803–815.

THE QUARTERLY JOURNAL OF EXPERIMENTAL PSYCHOLOGY
2008, 61 (1), 64–75

Autism, hypersystemizing, and truth

Simon Baron-Cohen

Autism Research Centre, Department of Psychiatry, University of Cambridge, Cambridge, UK

Evidence is reviewed suggesting that, in the general population, empathizing and systemizing show strong sex differences. The function of systemizing is to predict lawful events, including lawful change, or patterns in data. Also reviewed is the evidence that individuals on the autistic spectrum have degrees of empathizing difficulties alongside hypersystemizing. The hypersystemizing theory of autism spectrum conditions (ASC) proposes that people with ASC have an unusually strong drive to systemize. This can explain their preference for systems that change in highly lawful or predictable ways; why they become disabled when faced with systems characterized by less lawful change; and their "need for sameness" or "resistance to change". If "truth" is defined as lawful patterns in data then, according to the hypersystemizing theory, people with ASC are strongly driven to discover the "truth".

It is a privilege, a pleasure, and an honour to contribute to a Special Issue of this journal celebrating the remarkable scientific career of Uta Frith. Like many in this anthology, I have known her over more than a quarter of a century and have enjoyed her elegant empirical and theoretical contributions to the field of autism; at the same time my own work has been deeply influenced by hers. It is said that science makes progress by each generation standing on the shoulders of giants in the preceding generation. She, more than any autism scientist in the UK, has supported and enabled a whole raft of research programmes.

I count myself as fortunate in being in an academic lineage that dates back to her doctoral supervisors, Neil O'Connor and Beate Hermelin, the codirectors of the MRC Developmental Psychology Unit in Gordon Square in London. Hermelin and O'Connor (1970) were one of the first to define a rigorous experimental cognitive method in this area and to employ the mental-age-matching strategy in the search for autism-specific deficits. Uta Frith in her own PhD in 1970 took this at least one step further in using this method to identify autism-specific assets as well as deficits. Her move in 1982 to the MRC Cognitive Development Unit, also in Gordon Square, continued the important tradition in autism studies. I was lucky enough to be supervised by her there in my own doctorate. Over the subsequent decades she has moved ever deeper, from cognition to functional magnetic resonance imaging (fMRI), in pursuit of a clearer understanding of the nature of autism.

In this paper, I discuss two cognitive processes, *empathizing* and *systemizing*, and their relevance not only to autism but also to the field of sex differences. I review some of the evidence that links sex

Correspondence should be addressed to Simon Baron-Cohen, Autism Research Centre, Department of Psychiatry, University of Cambridge, Douglas House, 18b Trumpington Road, Cambridge CB2 8AH, UK. E-mail: sb205@cam.ac.uk

I am grateful for the support of the MRC and the Nancy Lurie-Marks Family Foundation during this work.

http://www.psypress.com/qjep

DOI:10.1080/17470210701508749

differences and systemizing to foetal testosterone. I then discuss the new idea that the autistic cognitive style searches for *truth* (defined as precise, reliable, consistent, or lawful patterns or structure in data) that can lead people with autism to perceive patterns with remarkable accuracy but at the same time renders them challenged by fiction and by information that is ambiguous or unlawful.

Viewed in this light, their difficulties with empathy are the result of a mind that is seeks the truth in a domain (emotions) that is not very lawful. The truth of another's feelings is ultimately unknowable and requires representing multiple, different perspectives on reality, rather than a single truth. Equally, when viewed in this light, their hypersystemizing reflects the same kind of mind exquisitely adapted to identifying key details in how systems work. Such a view may help us make sense of the recent evidence of an association between autistic traits and scientific talent.

Empathizing and the female advantage

Empathizing is the drive to identify another person's emotions and thoughts and to respond to these with an appropriate emotion (Davis, 1994). This definition suggests there are (at least) two "fractions" to empathy: a cognitive component (overlapping with what is also called "Theory of Mind" or mind reading), and an affective component (responding emotionally to another's mental state). Uta and I worked together on what today we could think of as cognitive empathy (inferring another's mental state), but in recent years I have found it important to broaden the focus to consider affective empathy too.

Empathy is a skill (or a set of skills). As with any other skill, we vary in it. We can therefore think about individual differences in empathy. Many studies converge on the conclusion that there is a female superiority in empathizing. For example, girls show more turn-taking (Charlesworth & Dzur, 1987), and women are better at decoding nonverbal communication, picking up subtle nuances from tone of voice or facial expression, or judging a person's emotional

state (Hall, 1978). Questionnaires measuring empathy typically find that women score higher than men (Davis, 1994). Girls' speech is more cooperative, reciprocal, and collaborative. Girls are also more able to keep a conversational exchange with a partner going for longer. When they disagree, girls are more likely to express their different opinion sensitively, asking a question, rather than making an assertion. Boys' talk is described as more "single-voiced discourse" (the speaker presents their own perspective alone). The female speech style is described as more "double-voiced discourse" (girls spend more time negotiating, trying to take the other person's wishes into account; Smith, 1985). Women's conversation involves much more talk about feelings, whilst men's conversation with each other is more object or activity focused (Tannen, 1991). From birth, females look longer at faces, particularly at people's eyes, and males are more likely to look at inanimate objects (Connellan, Baron-Cohen, Wheelwright, Ba'tki, & Ahluwalia, 2001).

Why might this sex difference in empathy exist? One possibility is that it reflects natural selection of empathy among females over human evolution. Good empathizing would have led to better care giving, and since care giving can be assumed to have been primarily a female activity until very recent history, those mothers who had better empathy would have succeeded in reading their infant offspring's emotional and physical needs better, which may have led to a higher likelihood of the infant surviving to an age to reproduce. Hence, good empathy in the mother would have promoted her inclusive fitness. This is unlikely to have been the only factor, but it illustrates how empathy could have been shaped by natural selection. Having spent some time discussing empathizing, I want to now turn to a very different cognitive process, systemizing.

Systemizing and the male advantage

Systemizing is a new concept. By a "system" I mean something that takes inputs and deliver outputs. To systemize, one uses "if–then" (correlation) rules. The brain attends to a detail or parameter of the system and observes how this varies. That is, it treats a feature of a particular object or event as a variable. Some systemizing occurs purely as the result of passive observation, but in other cases a person actively, or systematically, manipulates a given variable. In such cases, the person notes the effect(s) of operating on one single input in terms of its effects elsewhere in the system (the output). If I do *x*, *a* changes to *b*. If *z* occurs, *p* changes to *q*. Systemizing thus requires an exact eye for detail.

Systemizing involves observation of *input–operation–output* relationships, leading to the identification of laws to predict that event *x* will occur with probability *p* (Baron-Cohen, 2002). Some systems are totally lawful (e.g., an electrical light switch, or a mathematical formula). Systems that are 100% lawful have zero variance, or only 1 degree of freedom, and can therefore be predicted (and controlled) 100%. A computer might be an example of a 90% lawful system: The variance is wider—there are more degrees of freedom. The weather might be only 70% lawful, whilst the social world may be only 10% lawful. This is why systemizing the social world is of little predictive value.

Systemizing involves five phases. Phase 1 is *Analysis*: Single observations of input and output are recorded in a standardized manner, at a low level of detail. Phase 2 is *Operation*: An operation is performed on the input, and the change to the output is noted. Phase 3 is *Repetition*: The same operation is repeated over and over again, to test whether the same pattern between input and output is obtained. Phase 4 is *Law derivation*: A law is formulated of the form "If X (operation) occurs, A (input) changes to B". Phase 5 is *Confirmation/disconfirmation:* If the same pattern of input–operation–output holds true for all instances, the law is retained. If a single instance does not fit the law, Phases 2–5 are repeated, leading to modification of the law, or a new law.

Systemizing nonagentive change is effective because these are *simple* changes: The systems are moderately lawful, with narrow variance (or limited degrees of freedom). Agentive change is less suited to systemizing because the changes in the system are *complex* (wide variance, or many degrees of freedom). Systemizing works for phenomena that are ultimately lawful, finite, and deterministic. The explanation is exact, and its truth-value is testable. Systemizing is of little use for predicting moment-to-moment changes in a person's behaviour. To predict human behaviour, empathizing is required. Systemizing and empathizing thus have different functions.

Just as there are sex differences in empathy, so too are there (different) sex differences in systemizing, pointing to a stronger drive to systemize in males. For example, boys are more interested in toy vehicles, building blocks, and mechanical toys, all of which are open to being systemized (Jennings, 1977). In adulthood, certain occupations are largely male. These include metalworking, weapon making, manufacture of musical instruments, and the construction industries, such as boat building. The focus of these occupations is on creating systems (Geary, 1998). Similarly, maths, physics, and engineering all require high systemizing and are largely male. The Scholastic Aptitude Math Test (SAT-M) is the mathematics part of the test administered nationally to college applicants in the United States. Males on average score 50 points higher than females on this test (Benbow, 1988). Considering only individuals who score above 700, the sex ratio is 13:1 (men to women; Geary, 1996). Men also score higher in an assembly task in which people are asked to put together a three-dimensional (3-D) mechanical apparatus. Boys are also better at constructing a 3-D structure from just an aerial view in a picture (Kimura, 1999). A general feature of systemizing is good attention to relevant detail, and this is superior in males. One measure of this is the Embedded Figures Test. On average, males are quicker and more accurate in locating a target object from a larger, complex pattern (Elliot, 1961). Males, on average, are also better at detecting a particular feature (static or moving) than are women (Voyer, Voyer, & Bryden, 1995).

The Mental Rotation Test provides another example of a test on which males are quicker and more accurate. This involves systemizing because it is necessary to treat each feature in a display as a variable that can be transformed and then predict how it will appear after transformation (Collins & Kimura, 1997). Reading maps is another everyday test of systemizing, because features from 3-D input must be transformed to a two-dimensional representation. In general, boys perform better than girls in map reading and are more likely to use directional than landmark cues. The directional strategy represents an approach to understanding space as a geometric system (Galea & Kimura, 1993). The Systemizing Quotient is a questionnaire that includes items that ask about a subject's level of interest in a range of different systems (e.g., technical, abstract, and natural systems). Males score higher on this measure (Baron-Cohen, Richler, Bisarya, Gurunathan, & Wheelwright, 2003). Finally, the Physical Prediction Questionnaire (PPQ) is based on a method for selecting applicants to study engineering. The task involves predicting which direction levers will move when an internal mechanism of cog wheels and pulleys is engaged. Men score significantly higher on this test (Lawson, Baron-Cohen, & Wheelwright, 2004). Evolutionary accounts of the male advantage in systemizing include the argument that males were primarily involved in hunting and tracking of prey, and that a male who was a good systemizer would have had greater success in both using and making tools for hunting, or navigating space to explore far afield. Both could have affected a male's reproductive success.

Biology plays a part in empathy and systemizing

Although evidence exists for differential socialization contributing to sex differences, this is unlikely to be a sufficient explanation. Connellan and colleagues showed that among 1-day-old babies, boys look longer at a mechanical mobile, which is a system with predictable laws of motion, than at a person's face, an object that is hard to systemize. One-day-old girls show the opposite profile (Connellan et al., 2001). These sex differences

are therefore present very early in life. This raises the possibility that, while culture and socialization may partly determine the development of a male brain with a stronger interest in systems or a female brain with a stronger interest in empathy, biology also partly determines this.

There is ample evidence to support both cultural and biological determinism (Eagly, 1987; Gouchie & Kimura, 1991). For example, the amount of time a 1-year-old child maintains eye contact is inversely correlated to the level of foetal testosterone (FT) (Lutchmaya, Baron-Cohen, & Raggatt, 2002). This inverse relationship to FT is also seen in relation to social skills at age 4 years (Knickmeyer, Baron-Cohen, Raggatt, & Taylor, 2005) and empathizing at age 8 years, as measured on the Reading the Mind in the Eyes Test and the Empathy Quotient (Chapman et al., 2006). In contrast, a positive correlation with FT is seen in relation to "narrow interests" (Knickmeyer et al., 2005), the Systemizing Quotient (Auyeung et al., 2006), and ability on the Embedded Figures Test (Auyeung et al., 2007). The evidence for the biological basis of sex differences in the mind is reviewed elsewhere (Baron-Cohen, 2003).

One can envisage five broad types of profile or "brain type", as Table 1 shows. The evidence reviewed here suggests that not all men have the "male brain", and not all women have the "female brain". That is, some women have the male brain, and some men have the female brain. Using the Systemizing Quotient (SQ) and Empathy Quotient (EQ), more males than females have a brain of type S, and more females than males have a brain of type E (Goldenfeld, Baron-Cohen, & Wheelwright, 2005).

Autism: Hypersystemizing alongside impaired empathizing?

The autistic spectrum comprises two major subgroups: Asperger syndrome (AS) (Asperger, 1944; U. Frith, 1991), and classic autism (Kanner, 1943). They share the phenotype of social difficulties and obsessional interests (American Psychiatric Association, 1994). In AS,

Table 1. *The main brain types*

Profile of individuals	Shorthand notation	Type of brain
Empathizing more developed than systemizing	E > S	"female" (or Type E)
Systemizing more developed than empathizing	S > E	"male" (or Type S)
Systemizing and empathizing both equally developed	S = E	"balanced" (or Type B)
Systemizing hyperdeveloped and empathizing hypodeveloped (the autistic end of the spectrum)—may be talented systemizers, but at the same time may be "mind blind"	S >> E	extreme male brain
Hyperdeveloped empathizing skills and systemizing hypodeveloped—may be "system blind"	E >> S	extreme female brain (postulated)

the individual has normal or above-average IQ and no language delay. In classic autism there is typically some degree of language delay, and level of functioning is indexed by overall IQ, with learning difficulties in those with below-average IQ. I use the term autism spectrum conditions (ASC) to refer to both of these subgroups.

The consensus is that ASC have a genetic aetiology (Bailey et al., 1995), leading to altered brain development (Courchesne, 2002), affecting social and communication skills, and leading to the presence of narrow interests and repetitive behaviour (American Psychiatric Association, 1994). There is considerable evidence for empathy impairments in ASC (Baron-Cohen, 1995) not just using child-level tests of false-belief understanding (Baron-Cohen, Leslie, & Frith, 1985) but also more subtle tests of complex emotion recognition (Baron-Cohen, Wheelwright, Hill, Raste, & Plumb, 2001a), recognition of faux pas (Baron-Cohen, O'Riordan, Jones, Stone, & Plaisted, 1999a), and spontaneous ascription of intentional states (Castelli, Happé, Frith, & Frith, 2000). In this sense, people with ASC can be said to show hypoempathizing. This is apparent using neuroimaging during empathy tasks, where there is reduced blood flow in key brain regions such as the amygdala and medial prefrontal cortex (Baron-Cohen et al., 1999b; Courchesne, 2002; C. Frith & Frith, 1999; Happé et al., 1996).

Alongside the hypoempathizing there is also evidence for hypersystemizing in autism. For example, people with ASC have an increased rate of savant skills, often in lawful systems such as calendars, calculation, or train timetables (Hermelin, 2002). People with ASC score higher than average on the SQ (Baron-Cohen et al., 2003), on tests of folk physics (Baron-Cohen, Wheelwright, Scahill, Lawson, & Spong, 2001b; Jolliffe & Baron-Cohen, 1997; Lawson et al., 2004; Shah & Frith, 1983) and on tests of attention to detail (O'Riordan, Plaisted, Driver, & Baron-Cohen, 2001; Plaisted, O'Riordan, & Baron-Cohen, 1998). People with AS can achieve high levels in domains such as mathematics, physics, or computer science (Baron-Cohen, Wheelwright, Stone, & Rutherford, 1999c) and may have an "exact mind" when it comes to art (Myers, Baron-Cohen, & Wheelwright, 2004). On the picture-sequencing task, they perform above average on sequences that contain temporal or physical-causal (i.e., systematic) information (Baron-Cohen, Leslie, & Frith, 1986). Their obsessions cluster in the domain of systems, such as watching electric fans go round (Baron-Cohen & Wheelwright, 1999). Given a set of coloured counters, they show extreme "pattern imposition" (U. Frith, 1970)—they hypersystemize.

The evidence for systemizing being part of the "broader autism phenotype" includes the finding that fathers—and even grandfathers—of children with ASC are twice as likely to work in the occupation of engineering (a clear example of a systemizing occupation) (Baron-Cohen, Wheelwright, Stott, Bolton, & Goodyer, 1997b). Students in the natural sciences (engineering, mathematics, physics) also have a higher number of relatives with autism (Baron-Cohen et al., 1998). Mathematicians have a higher rate of AS, and so do their siblings (Baron-Cohen, Wheelwright, Burtenshaw, & Hobson, in press). Both mothers and fathers of children with AS have been found to be strong in systemizing on the Embedded Figures Test (Baron-Cohen & Hammer, 1997a). Finally, there is some evidence that above-average systemizers have more autistic traits. Thus, scientists score higher than nonscientists on the Autism Spectrum Quotient (AQ). Mathematicians score highest of all scientists on the AQ (Baron-Cohen, Wheelwright, Skinner, Martin, & Clubley, 2001c). These findings suggest a link between systemizing talent and autistic traits, the link being likely to be genetic. We will need molecular genetic studies of both systemizing and ASC to understand the nature of this link.

Truth

In trying to understand both the assets and the deficits in ASC, it may be useful to consider the role of truth in what the brain is trying to do. The term "truth" is associated with religious beliefs or with those who claim to have privileged access to some absolute knowledge. I am not using the term "truth" in either of these senses. Rather, I am defining it (as in the Introduction) as precise, reliable, consistent, or lawful patterns or structure in data. If a wheel is spinning round and round, there are consistent, lawful patterns to be detected. Sometimes the pattern will occur with 100% predictability (this particular person's birthday always falls on April 4th), sometimes with relatively high predictability (daffodils typically bloom in the second week of March in England). Systemizing is the means by which we identify lawful patterns in data.

When we systemize, we make the implicit assumption that the pattern of data coming into our senses tells us about the nature of reality. The pattern in the data reveals the truth. If all we detected was random noise, we would have no clue about the nature of the outside world that our brain inhabits. But just as a spy listens

to the beeps and clicks and starts to discern pattern, such as Morse code, treating it as intentional communication by the enemy, so the brain processes data and treats the data as information not just from intentional agents, but from a physical reality. Data are our only route to the truth.

My contention is that the autistic brain is highly tuned to systemize: It is the ultimate pattern detector and truth detector (Baron-Cohen, 2006). The low-functioning child with autism who loves to spend hours bouncing repetitively on a trampoline, or swinging on a swing repetitively, or "twiddling" a piece of string repetitively, or spinning the wheel of a toy car repetitively, or watching the cycles of a washing machine repetitively is hypersystemizing. Such repetitive behaviour was traditionally described as "purposeless" and as a "symptom", suggesting it lacks purpose or value. In fact, within the hypersystemizing theory, it has a very clear purpose: to provide input for a neural mechanism whose sole function is to seek and find patterns in data.

In a high-functioning individual on the autistic spectrum, such pattern seeking can reveal scientific truths about the nature of reality, since their systemizing can help the individual understand how things work. These may be mechanical systems (like computers or car engines), abstract systems (like mathematics or syntax), natural systems (like a biological organ, or the weather), collectible systems (like a library or a lexicon), or even social systems (like a legal code or a historical chronology). What was previously dismissed as an "obsession" can be viewed more positively as a "strong, narrow interest" in a topic that, when harnessed, can lead the person with autism or AS to excel in a highly specific field.

Such a view of systemizing, which by definition requires massive repetition in order to check and recheck the consistency of patterns, to establish that the truth so discovered actually holds, is clearly at odds with the old view of "obsessions" and repetitive behaviour being the result of perseveration due to an executive dysfunction (Russell, 1997). An executive dysfunction sees repetitive behaviour as a routine that the person would like to interrupt but they cannot. The hypersystemizing view in contrast sees the same behaviours as driven by the need for patterned data. Just as hunger drive is attracted by a food source, and there is pleasure attached to the satiation of this drive, so the systemizing drive is attracted towards patterns, and there is pleasure (sometimes referred to as "stimming" by people on the autistic spectrum) in finding such patterns.

Consider an example of a system: a car engine that we might hypothetically say has 100 components. Systemizing requires an initial pass at the data using strong "local" processing. The local level of analysis allows one to see all 100 features as distinct and different to each other. It then requires a "global" level of analysis to allow one to see three relationships: (a) if Component 37 is "on", Component 84 may or may not be "on";

(b) if Component 84 is "on", Component 37 is always "on"; and (c) Component 37 always fires up just before Component 84. These three global or relational bits of data allow the inference that Component 84 is dependent on Component 37, but not vice versa.

Notice that such systemizing would benefit from the data being represented in a matrix of rows and columns, so that the relation between two data points can be tracked with ease. Figure 1 shows the notebook from a man with Asperger syndrome who collects meteorological data as his "obsession", going out at midnight every night into his garden to measure a set of variables (e.g., rainfall, wind speed, temperature, humidity, and wind direction) and recording these "systematically" against the day and month,

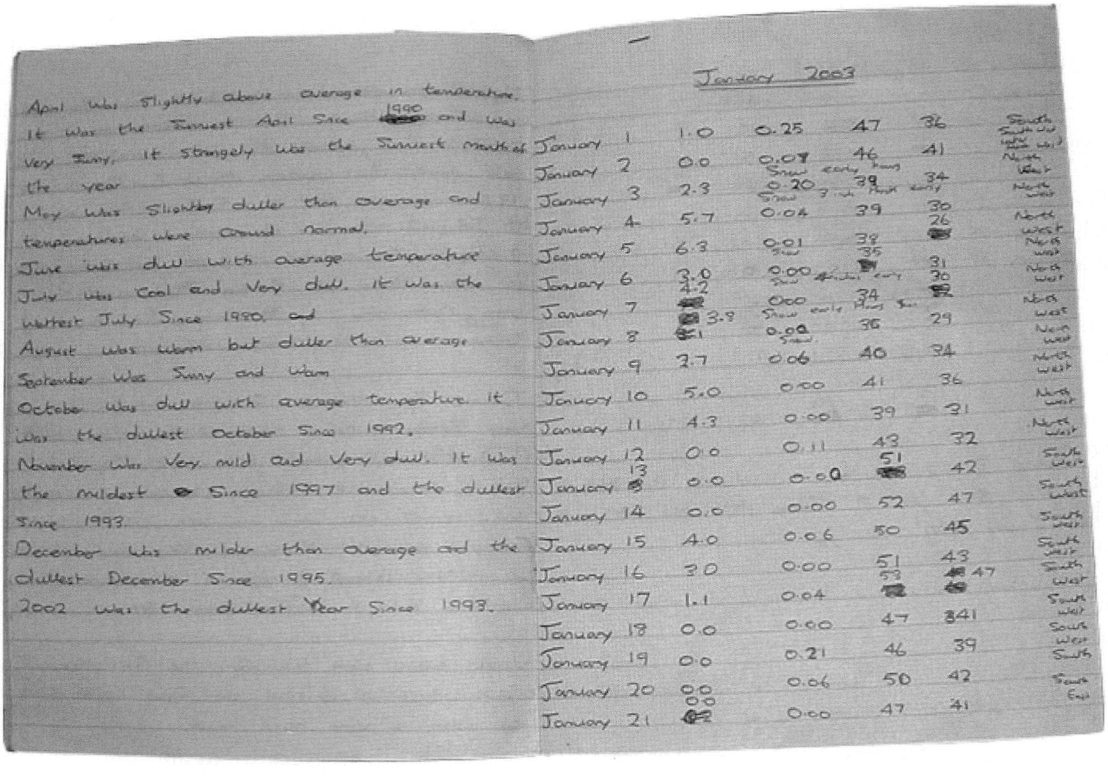

Figure 1. *An example of systemizing the weather, from the notebook of a man with Asperger syndrome. With kind permission. This figure was published as Figure 1 in* Progress in Neuro-Psychopharmacology and Biological Psychiatry, *30, Simon Baron-Cohen, The hyper-systemizing, assortative mating theory of autism, pp. 869. Copyright Elsevier (2006).*

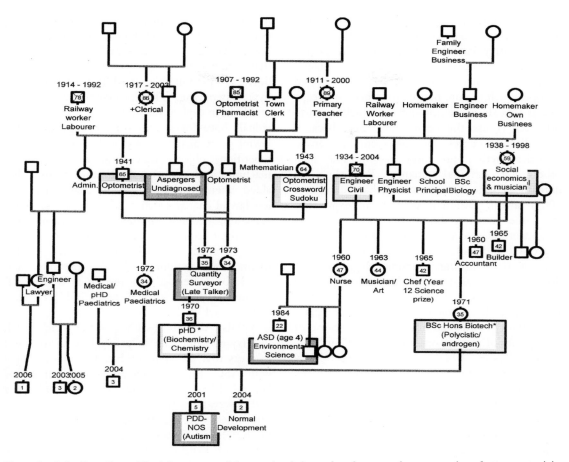

Figure 2. *A family pedigree. The informant recorded occupational data where known and any suggestion of strong systemizing interests, again where known. She also indicated definite diagnoses of autism spectrum conditions (ASC; shaded blue) and strongly suspected cases of ASC (shaded yellow). Also indicated is one case of polycystic ovary syndrome (PCOS), which is testosterone related. Such one-off pedigrees are not very informative, but are suggestive of a genetic association between strong systemizing and ASC liability. Current research is investigating whether the rate of ASC is higher in such families and whether this reflects assortative mating between two strong systemizers. To view the figure in colour, visit the Journal's website (http://www.psypress.com/qjep) and navigate to the online version of the paper.*

to identify patterns. What we see in a man with AS, who has no formal training as a scientist, is that his mind is naturally prone to representing information in a rows-by-columns matrix, which allows for inferences of the sort "If A and B, then X". If repetition of A and B always delivers X, then one has identified a truth. It may not be an earth-shattering one (if I push the light switch from up, A, to down, B, the light on the landing goes on, X), but it is nevertheless a truth

about the world. Seen in this light, hypersystemizing is truth oriented. Interestingly, in families where there are many strong systemizers (like the one depicted in Figure 2) it is anecdotally observed that one finds multiple cases of autism or Asperger syndrome. Research is underway to determine if the rates of ASC are higher in such families (especially when both parents are hypersystemizers), as a test of the assortative mating theory.

Whilst systemizing can deliver truths in the form of laws, it can only do so in domains that are ultimately lawful. One reason why people with ASC (postulated to be hypersystemizers) may struggle with empathy and be less interested in topics such as pure fiction, pretence, or deception is that these are not and never will be truth oriented. (I use the term "pure" here because some literary genres, such as science fiction or historical fiction, are more systemizable than others, e.g., fictional romance). Regarding the domain of emotions, human behaviour is not 100% lawful. Different people can expression the same emotion differently, or an emotion may even have no external expression. I can be depressed and look sad, or I can be depressed and act as if nothing is wrong. Regarding the domain of mental states, as Alan Leslie pointed out (when Uta and I worked with him now 25 years ago), the domain of mental states plays havoc with "truth relations". This is because of the opacity of mental states like "belief" or "pretence" (Leslie, 1987). The sentence "Mary believes that 'John is having an affair with his colleague'" is true if Mary believes it, irrespective of whether John really is having an affair. When we mind read, we have to keep track of what we believe to be true (John is not having an affair) whilst representing someone else's different (possibly false) belief—what they believe to be true (Mary believes he is).

Empathy is therefore arguably impossible without such an ability to play with and even suspend the truth. Recent efforts to teach people with ASC to mind read have succeeded only when taking the quite artificial approach of presenting mental states (such as emotional expressions) as if they are lawful and systemizable, even if they are not (Golan, Baron-Cohen, Wheelwright, & Hill, 2006). Such an approach tailors the information to the learning style of the learner so that at least they can begin to process it.

Conclusions

This article has reviewed evidence that empathizing and systemizing show strong sex differences in the general population. The function of systemizing is to predict lawful events, including lawful change. Also reviewed is the evidence that individuals on the autistic spectrum have degrees of empathizing difficulties alongside hypersystemizing. The hypersystemizing theory of ASC can explain the preference that such individuals have for systems that change in highly lawful or predictable ways (such as mathematics, repetition, objects that spin, routine, music, machines, collections) and why they become disabled when faced with systems characterized by less lawful change (such as social behaviour, conversation, people's emotions, or pure fiction), since these cannot be easily systemized and are not oriented towards discovering "truth" (defined as lawfulness). It also explains their "need for sameness" or "resistance to change" (Kanner, 1943) in such unsystemizable contexts as the social world.

Whilst ASC are disabling in the social world, hypersystemizing can in principle lead to talent in areas that are systemizable. For many people with ASC, their hypersystemizing never moves beyond Phase 1—massive collection of facts and observations (lists of trains and their departure times, watching the spin-cycle of a washing machine)—or Phases 2 and 3—massive repetition of behaviour (spinning a plate or the wheels of a toy car). But for those who go beyond Phase 3 to identify a law or a pattern in the data (Phases 4 and 5), this can constitute original insight. In this sense, it is likely that the genes for increased systemizing have made remarkable contributions to human history (Fitzgerald, 2000, 2002; James, 2003). Finally, the assortative mating theory (Baron-Cohen, 2006) proposes that the cause of ASC is the genetic combination of having two strong systemizers as parents. This theory remains to be fully tested, but if confirmed, may help explain why the genes that can cause social disability have also been maintained in the gene pool, as they confer all the fitness advantages that strong systemizing can bring on the first-degree relatives of people with such conditions.

REFERENCES

American Psychiatric Association. (1994). *Diagnostic and statistical manual of mental disorders* (4th ed.). Washington, DC: Author.

Asperger, H. (1944). Die "Autistischen Psychopathen" im Kindesalter [Autistic psychopathy in children]. *Archiv fur Psychiatrie und Nervenkrankheiten, 117,* 76–136.

Auyeung, B., Baron-Cohen, S., Chapman, E., Knickmeyer, R., Taylor, K., & Hackett, G. (2006). Foetal testosterone and the Child Systemizing Quotient (SQ-C). *European Journal of Endrocrinology, 155,* 123–130.

Auyeung, B., Baron-Cohen, S., Chapman, E., Knickmeyer, R., Taylor, K., & Hackett, G. (2007). *Is foetal testosterone positively correlated with number of autistic traits?* Manuscript submitted for publication.

Bailey, A., Le Couteur, A., Gottesman, I., Bolton, P., Simmonoff, E., Yuzda, E., et al. (1995). Autism as a strongly genetic disorder: Evidence from a British twin study. *Psychological Medicine, 25,* 63–77.

Baron-Cohen, S. (1995). *Mindblindness: An essay on autism and theory of mind.* Boston: MIT Press/ Bradford Books.

Baron-Cohen, S. (2002). The extreme male brain theory of autism. *Trends in Cognitive Science, 6,* 248–254.

Baron-Cohen, S. (2003). *The essential difference: Men, women and the extreme male brain.* London: Penguin.

Baron-Cohen, S. (2006). The hyper-systemizing, assortative mating theory of autism. *Progress in Neuro-Psychopharmacology and Biological Psychiatry, 30,* 865–872.

Baron-Cohen, S., Bolton, P., Wheelwright, S., Short, L., Mead, G., Smith, A., et al. (1998). Does autism occurs more often in families of physicists, engineers, and mathematicians? *Autism, 2,* 296–301.

Baron-Cohen, S., & Hammer, J. (1997a). Parents of children with Asperger syndrome: What is the cognitive phenotype? *Journal of Cognitive Neuroscience, 9,* 548–554.

Baron-Cohen, S., Leslie, A. M., & Frith, U. (1985). Does the autistic child have a "theory of mind"? *Cognition, 21,* 37–46.

Baron-Cohen, S., Leslie, A. M., & Frith, U. (1986). Mechanical, behavioural and intentional understanding of picture stories in autistic children. *British Journal of Developmental Psychology, 4,* 113–125.

Baron-Cohen, S., O'Riordan, M., Jones, R., Stone, V., & Plaisted, K. (1999a). A new test of social sensitivity: Detection of faux pas in normal children and children with Asperger syndrome. *Journal of Autism and Developmental Disorders, 29,* 407–418.

Baron-Cohen, S., Richler, J., Bisarya, D., Gurunathan, N., & Wheelwright, S. (2003). The Systemising Quotient (SQ): An investigation of adults with Asperger syndrome or high functioning autism and normal sex differences. *Philosophical Transactions of the Royal Society, 358,* 361–374.

Baron-Cohen, S., Ring, H., Wheelwright, S., Bullmore, E. T., Brammer, M. J., Simmons, A., et al. (1999b). Social intelligence in the normal and autistic brain: An fMRI study. *European Journal of Neuroscience, 11,* 1891–1898.

Baron-Cohen, S., & Wheelwright, S. (1999). Obsessions in children with autism or Asperger syndrome: A content analysis in terms of core domains of cognition. *British Journal of Psychiatry, 175,* 484–490.

Baron-Cohen, S., Wheelwright, S., Burtenshaw, A., & Hobson, E. (in press). Mathematical talent is genetically linked to autism. *Human Nature.*

Baron-Cohen, S., Wheelwright, S., Hill, J., Raste, Y., & Plumb, I. (2001a). The "Reading the Mind in the Eyes" test revised version: A study with normal adults, and adults with Asperger syndrome or high-functioning autism. *Journal of Child Psychology and Psychiatry, 42,* 241–252.

Baron-Cohen, S., Wheelwright, S., Scahill, V., Lawson, J., & Spong, A. (2001b). Are intuitive physics and intuitive psychology independent? *Journal of Developmental and Learning Disorders, 5,* 47–78.

Baron-Cohen, S., Wheelwright, S., Skinner, R., Martin, J., & Clubley, E. (2001c). The Autism Spectrum Quotient (AQ): Evidence from Asperger syndrome/high functioning autism, males and females, scientists and mathematicians. *Journal of Autism and Developmental Disorders, 31,* 5–17.

Baron-Cohen, S., Wheelwright, S., Stone, V., & Rutherford, M. (1999c). A mathematician, a physicist, and a computer scientist with Asperger syndrome: Performance on folk psychology and folk physics test. *Neurocase, 5,* 475–483.

Baron-Cohen, S., Wheelwright, S., Stott, C., Bolton, P., & Goodyer, I. (1997b). Is there a link between engineering and autism? *Autism: An International Journal of Research and Practice, 1,* 153–163.

Benbow, C. P. (1988). Sex differences in mathematical reasoning ability in intellectually talented preadolescents: Their nature, effects and possible causes. *Behavioural and Brain Sciences, 11,* 169–232.

Castelli, F., Happé, F., Frith, U., & Frith, C. (2000). Movement and mind: A functional imaging study of perception and interpretation of complex intentional movement patterns. *NeuroImage, 12,* 314–325.

Chapman, E., Baron-Cohen, S., Auyeung, B., Knickmeyer, R., Taylor, K., & Hackett, G. (2006). Foetal testosterone and empathy: Evidence from the Empathy Quotient (EQ) and the "Reading the Mind in the Eyes" test. *Social Neuroscience, 1,* 135–148.

Charlesworth, W. R., & Dzur, C. (1987). Gender comparisons of preschoolers' behavior and resource utilization in group problem-solving. *Child Development, 58,* 191–200.

Collins, D. W., & Kimura, D. (1997). A large sex difference on a two-dimensional mental rotation task. *Behavioral Neuroscience, 111,* 845–849.

Connellan, J., Baron-Cohen, S., Wheelwright, S., Ba'tki, A., & Ahluwalia, J. (2001). Sex differences in human neonatal social perception. *Infant Behavior and Development, 23,* 113–118.

Courchesne, E. (2002). Abnormal early brain development in autism. *Molecular Psychiatry, 7,* 21–23.

Davis, M. H. (1994). *Empathy: A social psychological approach.* Boulder, CO: Westview Press.

Eagly, A. H. (1987). *Sex differences in social behavior: A social-role interpretation.* Hillsdale, NJ: Lawrence Erlbaum Associates.

Elliot, R. (1961). Interrelationship among measures of field dependence, ability, and personality traits. *Journal of Abnormal and Social Psychology, 63,* 27–36.

Fitzgerald, M. (2000). Did Ludwig Wittgenstein have Asperger's syndrome. *European Child and Adolescent Psychiatry, 9,* 61–65.

Fitzgerald, M. (2002). Asperger's disorder and mathematicians of genius. *Journal of Autism and Developmental Disorders, 32,* 59–60.

Frith, C., & Frith, U. (1999). Interacting minds: A biological basis. *Science, 286,* 1692–1695.

Frith, U. (1970). Studies in pattern detection in normal and autistic children: II. Reproduction and production of color sequences. *Journal of Experimental Child Psychology, 10,* 120–135.

Frith, U. (1991). *Autism and Asperger's syndrome.* Cambridge, UK: Cambridge University Press.

Galea, L. A. M., & Kimura, D. (1993). Sex differences in route learning. *Personality & Individual Differences, 14,* 53–65.

Geary, D. (1996). Sexual selection and sex differences in mathematical abilities. *Behavioural and Brain Sciences, 19,* 229–284.

Geary, D. C. (1998). *Male, female: The evolution of human sex differences.* Washington, DC: American Psychological Association.

Golan, O., Baron-Cohen, S., Wheelwright, S., & Hill, J. J. (2006). Systemising empathy: Teaching adults with Asperger syndrome to recognise complex emotions using interactive multi-media. *Development and Psychopathology, 18,* 589–615.

Goldenfeld, N., Baron-Cohen, S., & Wheelwright, S. (2005). Empathizing and systemizing in males, females and autism. *Clinical Neuropsychiatry, 2,* 338–345.

Gouchie, C., & Kimura, D. (1991). The relationship between testosterone levels and cognitive ability patterns. *Psychoneuroendocrinology, 16,* 323–334.

Hall, J. A. (1978). Gender effects in decoding nonverbal cues. *Psychological Bulletin, 85,* 845–857.

Happé, F., Ehlers, S., Fletcher, P., Frith, U., Johansson, M., Gillberg, C., et al. (1996). Theory of mind in the brain. Evidence from a PET scan study of Asperger syndrome. *NeuroReport, 8,* 197–201.

Hermelin, B. (2002). *Bright splinters of the mind: A personal story of research with autistic savants.* London: Jessica Kingsley.

Hermelin, B., & O'Connor, N. (1970). *Psychological experiments with autism.* Oxford, UK: Pergamon Press.

James, I. (2003). Singular scientists. *Journal of the Royal Society of Medicine, 96,* 36–39.

Jennings, K. D. (1977). People versus object orientation in preschool children: Do sex differences really occur? *Journal of Genetic Psychology, 131,* 65–73.

Jolliffe, T., & Baron-Cohen, S. (1997). Are people with autism or Asperger's syndrome faster than normal on the Embedded Figures Task? *Journal of Child Psychology and Psychiatry, 38,* 527–534.

Kanner, L. (1943). Autistic disturbance of affective contact. *Nervous Child, 2,* 217–250.

Kimura, D. (1999). *Sex and cognition.* Cambridge, MA: MIT Press.

Knickmeyer, R., Baron-Cohen, S., Raggatt, P., & Taylor, K. (2005). Foetal testosterone, social cognition, and restricted interests in children. *Journal of Child Psychology and Psychiatry, 45,* 1–13.

Lawson, J., Baron-Cohen, S., & Wheelwright, S. (2004). Empathising and systemising in adults with and without Asperger syndrome. *Journal of Autism and Developmental Disorders, 34,* 301–310.

Leslie, A. M. (1987). Pretence and representation: The origins of "theory of mind". *Psychological Review, 94,* 412–426.

Lutchmaya, S., Baron-Cohen, S., & Raggatt, P. (2002). Foetal testosterone and eye contact in 12-month-old infants. *Infant Behavior and Development, 25*, 327–335.

Myers, P., Baron-Cohen, S., & Wheelwright, S. (2004). *An exact mind.* London: Jessica Kingsley.

O'Riordan, M., Plaisted, K., Driver, J., & Baron-Cohen, S. (2001). Superior visual search in autism. *Journal of Experimental Psychology: Human Perception and Performance, 27*, 719–730.

Plaisted, K., O'Riordan, M., & Baron-Cohen, S. (1998). Enhanced visual search for a conjunctive target in autism: A research note. *Journal of Child Psychology and Psychiatry, 39*, 777–783.

Russell, J. (Ed.). (1997). *Autism as an executive disorder.* Oxford, UK: Oxford University Press.

Shah, A., & Frith, U. (1983). An islet of ability in autism: A research note. *Journal of Child Psychology and Psychiatry, 24*, 613–620.

Smith, P. M. (1985). *Language, the sexes and society.* Oxford, UK: Basil Blackwell.

Tannen, D. (1991). *You just don't understand: Women and men in conversation.* London: Virago.

Voyer, D., Voyer, S., & Bryden, M. (1995). Magnitude of sex differences in spatial abilities: A meta-analysis and consideration of critical variables. *Psychological Bulletin, 117*, 250–270.

THE QUARTERLY JOURNAL OF EXPERIMENTAL PSYCHOLOGY
2008, 61 (1), 76–89

The curious incident of the photo that was accused of being false: Issues of domain specificity in development, autism, and brain imaging

Josef Perner
University of Salzburg, Salzburg, Austria

Susan Leekam
University of Durham, Durham, UK

We resume an exchange of ideas with Uta Frith that started before the turn of the century. The curious incident responsible for this exchange was the finding that children with autism fail tests of false belief, while they pass Zaitchik's (1990) photograph task (Leekam & Perner, 1991). This finding led to the conclusion that children with autism have a domain-specific impairment in Theory of Mind (mental representations), because the photograph task and the false-belief task are structurally equivalent except for the nonmental character of photographs. In this paper we argue that the false-belief task and the false-photograph task are not structurally equivalent and are not empirically associated. Instead a truly structurally equivalent task is the false-sign task. Performance on this task is strongly associated with the false-belief task. A version of this task, the misleading-signal task, also poses severe problems for children with autism (Bowler, Briskman, Gurvidi, & Fornells-Ambrojo, 2005). These new findings therefore challenge the earlier interpretation of a domain-specific difficulty in inferring mental states and suggest that children with autism also have difficulty understanding misleading nonmental objects. Brain imaging data using false-belief, "false"-photo, and false-sign scenarios provide further supporting evidence for our conclusions.

"Grau, teurer Freund, ist alle Theorie,
Doch grün durchlebte Empirie."
With gratitude to our Mephisto.

Research on Theory of Mind has travelled a long way in the last two and a half decades. Undoubtedly, the most important turning point in its history was the discovery that children with autism have impairments in understanding false beliefs (Baron-Cohen, Leslie, & Frith, 1985), a finding that changed people's thinking about the concept of "Theory of Mind" and had a profoundly positive impact on subsequent scientific progress in the field of autism. In the late 1980s, Uta Frith invited us to join her and Alan Leslie on their initial journey to explore the nature of the difficulty of Theory of Mind in children with autism (Perner, Frith, Leslie, & Leekam, 1989)—a step that enabled us to get away from mere theory to first-hand experience of what

Correspondence should be addressed to Josef Perner, Department of Psychology, University of Salzburg, Hellbrunnerstrasse 34, A-5020 Salzburg, Austria. E-mail: josef.perner@sbg.ac.at

http://www.psypress.com/qjep

DOI:10.1080/17470210701508756

these children are like, and which, ultimately, shaped our own future work. In this chapter we describe the path we took from early work on children's understanding of false belief and other mental states to research on their understanding of nonmental representations.

When we embarked on research aimed at investigating autistic children's understanding of nonmental representation, we believed that the evidence from this research could help shape the answer to the question about whether Theory of Mind is a domain-specific deficit in children with autism, independent of more general problems in understanding representations. The findings could also have a bearing on the question of whether there is a unitary body of knowledge that is innately impaired in autism or a conglomeration of different abilities that undergo significant development with particular features that are developmentally affected in autism. With hindsight, we now wonder whether the evidence we produced at this time unwittingly provided a false signpost for the interpretations of the theory-of-mind impairment in autism. Our early evaluation of the evidence and more recent studies now all point to a different, more plausible interpretation of the evidence. However, in the wisdom of advancing years we are aware that by testing out one path of interpretation it has helped to prepare the way for an alternative direction that might in turn be either right or wrong.

Zaitchik's photo task

The story starts with our research using Debbie Zaitchik's (1990) photograph task. Zaitchik designed a task called the "false"-photo task in order to provide a nonmental analogue of the false-belief task. In Wimmer and Perner's (1983) version of the false-belief story, the protagonist is Maxi. In Zaitchik's photo task, Maxi's role is taken by a Polaroid® camera. In the false-belief task, Maxi sees his piece of chocolate being put inside the blue cupboard in the kitchen, whereas in the photo task there is a parallel event: The camera takes a picture of Rubber Duckie on the bed. While in the false-belief task, Maxi is on

the playground when his chocolate is being transferred to the green cupboard, in the photo task the photo is in the process of being developed, and Rubber Duckie is put back into the bath tub. Then at the end of the false-belief story the chocolate is in the green cupboard but Maxi has it in his head that it is still in the blue cupboard. Correspondingly, at the end of the photo task, Rubber Duckie is in the bath tub but in the picture it is sitting on the bed. In other words, the transfer of the chocolate from the blue to the green cupboard leaves Maxi's belief unchanged; similarly the transfer of Rubber Duckie from the bed to the bath tub leaves the photo unchanged.

The photo story therefore proceeds in neat analogy to the belief story. The chocolate in Maxi's mind is in a different place to where it currently is, while Rubber Duckie in the photo is in a different place than where it currently is. Children's task in both cases is also similar: They have to answer the test questions, "Where does Maxi think the chocolate is?" and "Where is Rubber Duckie in the photo?" with the location that is different from the object's actual location at the time of the question. The result for these two tasks was also similar. Zaitchik found that 3-year-olds had as much difficulty with her photo task as with the false-belief story. In contrast, the majority of 4-year-olds and older children showed competence on both tasks with slightly more advanced performance on the false belief. This finding was widely interpreted as showing that children around 4 years become able to understand representation whether or not these representations are mental.

We replicated Zaitchik's study (Leekam & Perner, 1991) with the aim of discovering how children with autism would fare on the photograph task. Given our earlier research with Uta Frith and Alan Leslie on false-belief difficulties in children with autism (Perner et al., 1989), we expected poor performance on this mental-state task. But if the photograph task is a nonmental analogy of the false-belief task then it should help us to establish whether children with autism have a specific difficulty with the mental aspect of mental states or a more general difficulty with representations. The belief and photo sketches that we used feature an elegant lady by the name of Uta (lacking sufficient foresight, the lady was wrongly named *Judy* at the time) dressed in red who exchanged her dress for a green one while, in the belief condition, her friend Sue had gone to find a matching belt or, in the photo condition, the photo was developing. As in Zaitchik's study, children of 3 and 4 years found both tasks equally difficult. We gave the same tasks to children with autism. The result was striking. Children with autism only showed problems with the false-belief condition. Hardly any of them had a problem with the photo sketch, as shown in Figure 1a. Leslie and Thaiss (1992) using different materials replicated these results remarkably closely (Figure 1b). However, our interpretations were quite different.

Alan Leslie and Leila Thaiss (1992) interpreted their data to mean that children with autism have a

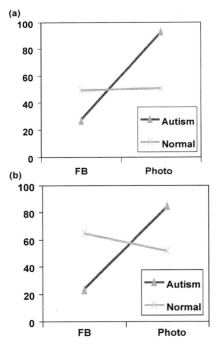

Figure 1. *(a) Data from Leekam and Perner (1991). (b) Data from Leslie and Thaiss (1992). To view the figure in colour, visit the Journal's website (http://www.psypress.com/qjep) and navigate to the online version of the paper.*

domain specific deficit in understanding mental states like belief. Their deficit must be highly specific to mental states—unobservable inner states—because they passed with flying colours on Zaitchik's photo task (Zaitchik, 1990), which, presumably, assesses understanding of the same representational processes as does the belief task except that the relevant entity is not a mental state but a photo, a tangible external object. Uta following this line of reasoning (U. Frith, 2003, p. 89) spoke of the photo and belief task being "formally identical" (C. D. Frith & Frith, 1999, p. 1693). Such an impression of "formal identity" was also preempted by Zaitchik calling her task a "false-photo task".

In fact, although like others we started out with the assumption that both tasks measured understanding of false representations, we changed our view after rethinking the content of these tasks and writing up the data (Leekam & Perner, 1991, p. 215; Perner, 1991, pp. 97–101). Instead we argued that there is a more substantial difference between beliefs and photos than just being observable versus unobservable, internal versus external, and mental versus nonmental. In some ways this difference is almost obvious: Maxi's belief about the chocolate is a *false* belief, but the photo of Rubber Duckie on the bed is not really a "false" photo. If it were then all our holiday pictures would be "false". Easy to see, but then, why did it take practically everybody concerned so many years to realise this?

Why the photos in Zaitchik's photo task are not false
Figure 2 may help us explain why Zaitchik's photos (Zaitchik, 1990) are not false and also why so many people thought they were. The left half captures four time points (t1,..., t4) of the false-belief story. The right half captures the corresponding points in time of the photograph story. At the last point (t4) the critical question is asked: that is, "What colour dress does Sue think Uta is wearing?" in the belief task and, "What colour dress is Uta wearing in the photo?" in the photo task, respectively. The answer to both questions is "red", which stands in contrast to what Uta is actually wearing at that point in

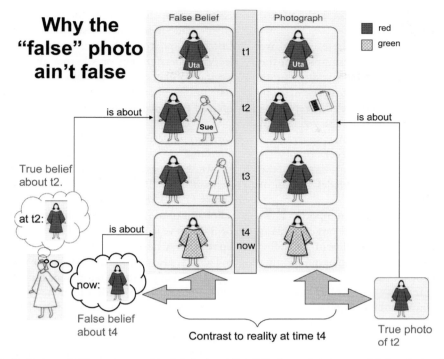

Figure 2. *Similarity and difference between false-belief task and Zaitchik's photo task (using materials from Leekam & Perner, 1991). To view the figure in colour, visit the Journal's website (http://www.psypress.com/qjep) and navigate to the online version of the paper.*

time—namely, green. This makes the belief and photo look practically identical in their essential feature—namely, how they relate to what they represent. This similarity is highlighted by the two large arrows at the bottom of the figure. But then, why is the belief false but not the photo, even though both of them show Uta in a different colour from the one she is actually wearing? The answer to this question comes from the realization that the truth of a belief or accuracy of a photo does not depend on how things are in the world at the time. Instead, truth or accuracy depends on whether the *content* of a *representation* (belief or photo) matches or mismatches the *target* of the representation. To get clear on what this means in case of belief and photo a short termino-logical clarification is useful.

In the case of the photo, the *representation* (representational vehicle) consists of the piece of paper with its shades, contours, and colours that typically make up a photo. The representational *target* of

the photo is that state in the world that the photo is supposed to represent. This is typically the state of the world when the photo was taken—that is, Uta in her red dress at time t2. The representational *content* of the photo consists in how the photo shows Uta as being dressed— that is, in red. Since this content (dressed in red) matches the target (Uta was dressed in red at time t2) the photo is quite accurate and not at all "false" (an unfortunate historical misnomer). One reason why the photo was originally labelled "false" may hinge on another useful distinction— namely, between *target* and *referent*. Photos have targets but no clear referent. For instance, we can describe the photo either as, "Uta is wearing a red dress," then Uta is the referent of this descrip-tion, or as, "the red dress is being worn by Uta," where now the red dress is the referent. It is only descriptions of the photo that can turn various aspects of it into referents; the photo as such has no referent, but it has a representational target or satisfaction conditions (the situation in the past of which it was taken).

Now, when talking about these issues we describe the photo verbally—for example, "In the photo Uta is dressed in red". In this description Uta is the referent of the linguistic representation. If we are not careful and equate the representational target of the photo with the referent of this description of the photo, it may appear as if the photo mismatches the target (hence is "false") because its content mismatches the current state of the referent of our description of the photo's content.

Beliefs are more versatile than photos as to what can be their representational target. This is indicated in Figure 2 by two different beliefs of Sue's. For instance, at time t4 (time of questioning the child) she has a belief about the colour of Uta's dress at that very time (t4). This belief (shown in the boldly drawn think bubble) is false because it shows Uta as wearing red when, in fact, she is wearing green at that time. Sue probably also has another belief about Uta's dress (shown in the faintly drawn think bubble), namely that Uta was wearing red when she last saw her (at t2). This belief is true because its target is the scene at t2, and, there, Uta was indeed wearing red. It is this belief that corresponds to the photo in terms of their representational target. They both are about what Uta was wearing at time t2. However, this true belief is not what is being assessed in the false-belief task.

For that reason the understanding assessed in the false-belief task and in Zaitchik's photo task (Zaitchik, 1990) differ not only with respect to the visibility of the representational entity (belief = invisible; photo = visible) but also in their representational relation to their target (belief misrepresents its target; photo shows its target correctly). Moreover, since falseness is a case in which the distinction between the target of a representation (what the representation represents) and its content (how the representation shows its target as being) needs to be clearly understood, the false-belief task requires a deeper understanding (of a particularly central aspect) of representation than does the photo task. Therefore it

remains an open question whether children with autism fail false-belief tasks and succeed on Zaitchik's photo task because they lack this deeper understanding or whether their deficit is specific to the narrow domain of mental states that, unlike photos, are invisible and need to be inferred from observable indicators.

Correlations between false-belief task and Zaitchik's photo task

As we have seen, Zaitchik (1990) as well as Leekam and Perner (1991) and Leslie and Thaiss (1992) report that performance on false-belief and photo tasks are of comparable difficulty for 3- to 5-year-old children. This has since been reported in a host of further studies summarized in Table 1, also including studies that used drawings instead of photos (Charman & Baron-Cohen, 1992; Pollack, 1990) with a tendency to be somewhat easier than the photo and false-belief tasks. In any case, if this similarity is to reflect the development of a common underlying ability we would also expect some positive correlation between false-belief and photo/drawing tasks. Curiously, no correlations were reported in the first studies with typically developing children, with the exception of Leekam and Perner (1991). They found a significant correlation but did not investigate whether this correlation persists when children's age and/or intelligence scores are partialled out. Most of the later studies listed in Table 1 report very weak and nonsignificant correlations, and none of them reports a correlation that stays significant after partialling out children's age. In sum, there is not even any good suggestive evidence that the false-belief task and the photo task capture the development of a common underlying ability. The fact that the false-belief and the photo task tend to be of similar difficulty at the particular ages that these tasks were studied seems to be a developmental coincidence.

To summarize, the long-held erroneous assumption that Zaitchik's photograph task (Zaitchik, 1990) measures an understanding of "falsity" in a representation has perpetuated the view that 3-year-old typically developing children have difficulty understanding representations

Table 1. *Comparison of children's performance in the false-belief and variations of Zaitchik's (1990) photo task*

Study	Expt.	n	Age[a]	% correct		r	Comments[b]
				PH	FB		
Zaitchik, 1990	E1&5	70	2;11–5;1	46	63	?	
Leekam & Perner, 1991		37	3;5–4;9	57	56	.43**	
Leslie & Thaiss, 1992	E1	20	3;8–4;5	53	65	?	
	E2	21	3;7–4;6	33	81	?	maps
Charman & Baron-Cohen, 1992		20	3;2–5;7	65	50	?	drawings
Lewis, Freeman, & Smith, 1992	E3	24	3;8	42	25	.09	
Perner, Leekam, Myers, Davis, & Odgers, 1993	E1	67	3;4–4;9	47	55	.15	
	E2	17	2;2–3;8	53	—	—	
				94	—	—	PH: point
	E3	36	3;2–4;10	36	28	.12	
				67	33	?	PH & FB: point
Davis & Pratt, 1995		64	3;4–5;4	66	65	.25	
Slaughter, 1998	E1	37	3;2–4;4	72	37	.12	PH: point
Peterson & Siegal, 1998	E1	35	3;0–4;11	68	44	.09	
	E2	47	3;5–4;10	82	68	?	
Müller, Zelazo, & Imrisek, 2005		69	3;1–5;5	69	51	.26*	PH: point, FB: self,
					54	.08	FB: other
Sabbagh, Moses, & Shiverick, 2006	E1	44	3;0–5;2	64	40	.32*	r_{age}=.11, ns.
	E2	54	3;1–4;10	58	42	.39*	r_{age}<.24, ns.
Leekam et al., 2006	E2	45	2;11–5;0	23	30	.38*	r_{age}=.18, ns. PH: point

Notes: Expt. = Experiment; PH = photo; FB = false belief; ? = data not reported; — = no data collected;
[a]in years and months.
[b]on variations of the photo and false belief task and on refinement of statistical analyses:
  PH: point = Experimenter points at back of photo when asking the test question;
  FB: point = Experimenter points at protagonist's head when asking the test question.
  FB: self = test question is asked about child's own false belief.
  FB: other = test question is asked about story character's false belief (default condition).
  r_{age} = partial correlation after variable *age* has been partialled out.
  *$p \leq .05$; **$p \leq .01$; ns = not significant.

while children with autism have difficulty understanding mental states. But in view of our conceptual analysis showing that belief and photo tasks do not assess the same kind of representational understanding, we do not actually know anything about children's understanding of false nonmental representation. Given that Zaitchik's task does not test what it purports to, we need another test.

The false-sign task

To return to Zaitchik's original agenda of assessing children's difficulty with the representational demands intrinsic to the false-belief task in a nonmental context (Zaitchik, 1990), Lindsey Parkin (1994), designed a "false-sign" task. In this task, a signpost in a story scenario indicates a state of affairs (e.g., object in Location 1). The object is then moved (to Location 2), but the signpost is not changed, and it therefore becomes a false sign. Children have to infer where the sign shows that the object is. A false sign is like a photograph in that it is a nonmental, observable object. Like the case of false belief, however, in order to understand what the false sign shows, one needs to understand that the signpost represents a situation (target) that is different from how the signpost shows it to be (content). In other words, like a false belief, the false sign misrepresents (as a belief misconceives) current reality.

False Direction Signs: Lindsey Parkin

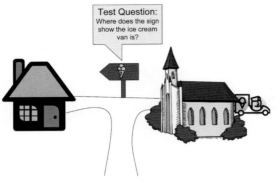

Test Question:
Where does the sign show the ice cream van is?

Figure 3. *Example scenario after Lindsey Parkin's (1994) false-sign study. To view the figure in colour, visit the Journal's website (http://www.psypress.com/qjep) and navigate to the online version of the paper.*

Before describing the false-sign task we should point out that photos, too, can misrepresent. In fact, Parkin (1994) first tried to develop Zaitchik's (1990) task into involving genuinely false photos by using, for example, a yellow colour filter so that blue objects came out looking green. This task, however, proved too confusing for 3- to 4-year-old children, which led to the development of the false-sign task.

For instance, in one scenario there was a branching road (see Figure 3). One branch goes behind a house and the other behind the church. In the sign condition a sign at the intersection indicates the way to the ice cream van. Children can use this to find the van behind the house. But then the van drives over to the church and the driver forgets to change the sign, which keeps pointing along the road to behind the house. When the van is stationed behind the church children are asked, "Where does the *sign show* the ice cream van is?" (correct answer: "behind the house"). In the false-belief story children know that the ice cream van is behind the church but when Jimmy comes along he is misinformed by a friend that the van is behind the house and children are asked, "Where does *Jimmy think* the ice cream van is?" (correct answer: "behind the house"). In two experiments Parkin obtained robust correlations between the belief tasks and

the sign tasks, and the sign tasks explained a significant amount of variance on the false-belief tasks even when age was introduced first in stepwise regression.

Sabbagh, Moses, and Shiverick (2006, Exp. 2) adopted the false-sign task and compared it to false-belief and "false"-photo tasks. The false-belief task was related to false photos and to false signs, but when age was partialled out, the latter fell to marginal significance, and the former became completely nonsignificant. Leekam, Perner, Healey, and Sewell (2006) also used all three tasks. False-belief and false-sign tasks were correlated even after age and performance on "false" photos was partialled out, whereas when age and performance on false signs were partialled out false belief and "false" photos were not significantly correlated. In a somewhat altered version of the false-sign task Bowler, Briskman, Gurvidi, and Fornells-Ambrojo (2005) had a signal determine the course of an automatic train to pick up cargo from a landing strip. When the plane changed location the signal sent the train to the wrong, original location. Children had to predict where the train would go. This prediction was as difficult as a standard false-belief task, and performance on the two tasks correlated highly for typically developing children, children with intellectual disabilities, and children with autism. The data from these studies are shown in Table 2.

In sum, there is strong evidence that the false-sign task and the false-belief task share a developmental factor not shared by Zaitchik's photo task . This common factor not only underlies normally developing children's problems in understanding false beliefs and false signs, but it also captures the difficulty that children with autism have with the false-belief task. Since this factor also affects the nonmental false-sign task it cannot be a specific problem with understanding mental states. There is also recent evidence from brain imaging supporting this conclusion.

Brain imaging

Uta Frith and Chris Frith (C. D. Frith & Frith, 1999; U. Frith & Frith, 2003) meta-analysed the

Table 2. *Summary data from studies comparing performance on false-belief and false-sign studies*

Study	Expt.	n	Age[a]	% correct FS	% correct FB	r	Partial out	Sample characteristics
Parkin, 1994 (Parkin &	E1	48	2;10–5;0	35	44	.66***	r_{age}***	
Perner, 1996)	E2	16	3;5–4;9	44	50	.88***	r_{age}***	
Bowler et al., 2005 (false signals)	E1&2	47	3;4–5;10	53	61	~.65***	r_{vma}***	Normal develop.
		42	4;10–17;9	48	41	~.67***		Autism
	E1	21	8;7–17;8	43	48	.72***		Intellect. disability
Sabbagh et al., 2006	E2	54	3;1–4;10	51	42	.53***	r_{age}=.24*	
Leekam et al., 2006	E1	80	3;0–4;11	42	29	between		
	E2	48	2;11–5;0	42	30	.50***	r_{age}=.35**	
							r_{PH}=.48***	

Notes: Expt. = Experiment. FB = false belief. FS = false sign. PH = Photo task. vma = verbal mental age. $r_{/x}$ = partial correlation after variable x has been partialled out.
[a]In years and months.
*$p \leq .05$; **$p \leq .01$; ***$p \leq .001$.

first 10 or so brain-imaging studies of Theory of Mind (ToM), most of which involved some false-belief scenario. They came to the conclusion that it is the medial prefrontal/paracingulate cortex bilaterally that is specifically responsible for processing Theory of Mind, helped by the posterior superior temporal sulcus (pSTS) for processing information on animated objects and the temporal poles responsible for social scripts. Rebecca Saxe and her colleagues have used the contrast between false-belief vignettes and photo vignettes for narrowing down the brain areas specifically involved in processing false beliefs (Saxe & Kanwisher, 2003; Saxe & Powell, 2006; Saxe & Wexler, 2005). Although the Frithian ToM-area in the paracingulate also shows up in these studies, the authors stress the importance of the temporo-parietal junction (TPJ), especially in the right hemisphere (TPJ-R). The importance of the TPJ region over the medial frontal areas was also underlined by findings on Patient G.T. (Bird, Castelli, Malik, Frith, & Husain, 2004), who has no demonstrable theory-of-mind deficit despite extensive damage to the medial frontal lobes bilaterally including the paracingulate area. Moreover, Apperly, Samson, Chiavarino, and Humphreys (2004) and Samson, Apperly, Chiavarino, and Humphreys (2004) report that a group of patients with lesions in the left TPJ (TPJ-L) show specific theory-of-mind deficits, while patients with medial frontal damage show a mixture of theory-of-mind and other cognitive and executive impairments.

One of us got involved in checking whether the areas detected by Saxe and colleagues for processing false-belief information over processing Zaitchik's photo vignettes are also employed for false signs (Perner, Aichhorn, Kronbichler, Staffen, & Ladurner, 2006). This study showed interpretable results for the left and right TPJ. As Saxe et al. also found, the right TPJ showed the strongest activation for false belief. The activation by the false-belief vignettes was also stronger than the activation caused by false-sign vignettes, which did not differ significantly from the photo vignettes. This is shown in the left side of Figure 4. The pattern suggests that TPJ-R is mostly responsible for processing specifically information about the mind—that is, about false beliefs but not about false signs or photos, as Saxe and Kanwisher (2003) originally claimed (N.B., this claim, of course, only applies within the limits of alternatives assessed in this study). However the pattern of activations found in TPJ-L is different, as shown on the right side of Figure 4.

In TPJ-L the region activated by false-belief vignettes over photo vignettes is much smaller

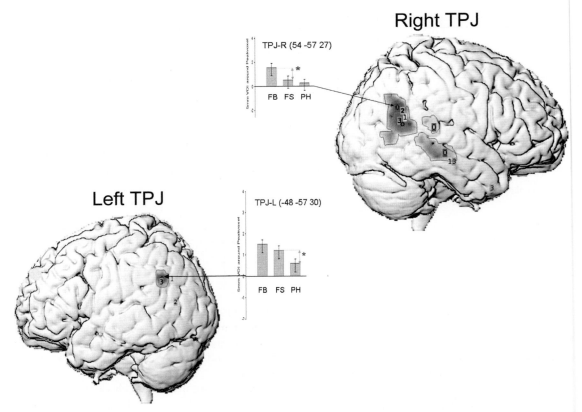

Figure 4. *Patterns of activation for false-belief (FB), false-sign (FS), and photo (PH) vignettes from Perner et al. (2006). The numbered rectangles refer to peak voxels in the three studies by Saxe and colleagues (Saxe & Kanwisher, 2003; Saxe & Powell, 2006; Saxe & Wexler, 2005). TCC was a temporal change control. *p < .05. To view the figure in colour, visit the Journal's website (http://www.psypress.com/qjep) and navigate to the online version of the paper.*

than that on the right side. But here also the false-sign vignettes activated the region more strongly than the photo vignettes, indicating that this region is not specifically responsible for mental-state information but also for processing matters of representation for nonmental signs. Another way of capturing what this region is responsible for is to say that it is concerned with the processing of alternative perspectives. In the case of false beliefs and false signs, two contrasting perspectives (two representations with different contents, e.g., "the van is behind the house" vs. "the van is behind the church") of one and the same target (*the van's current location*) are involved, which is not the case in the photo vignettes. Interestingly,

in a study on visual perspective contrasts (the cube being in front of the pole when seen from an avatar's vantage point but being behind the pole from participants' own perspective) activation was found only around TPJ-L but not TPJ-R or the medial frontal areas in the paracingulate (Aichhorn, Perner, Kronbichler, Staffen, & Ladurner, 2006).

Moreover, we looked at existing theory-of-mind studies and classified them as involving contrasting perspectives (e.g., false-belief studies) or not involving such a contrast (e.g., studies looking at understanding goal-oriented action, or pretend action). Figure 5 plots the peak voxels reported in these studies within the TPJ/pSTS

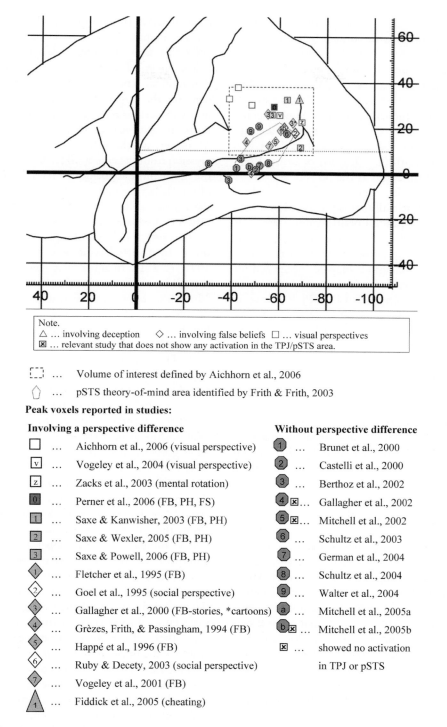

Note.
△ … involving deception   ◇ … involving false beliefs   □ … visual perspectives
☒ … relevant study that does not show any activation in the TPJ/pSTS area.

⌐⌐⌐ …   Volume of interest defined by Aichhorn et al., 2006

◯ …   pSTS theory-of-mind area identified by Frith & Frith, 2003

Peak voxels reported in studies:

Involving a perspective difference

□ …   Aichhorn et al., 2006 (visual perspective)

v …   Vogeley et al., 2004 (visual perspective)

z …   Zacks et al., 2003 (mental rotation)

0 …   Perner et al., 2006 (FB, PH, FS)

1 …   Saxe & Kanwisher, 2003 (FB, PH)

2 …   Saxe & Wexler, 2005 (FB, PH)

3 …   Saxe & Powell, 2006 (FB, PH)

◇1 …   Fletcher et al., 1995 (FB)

◇2 …   Goel et al., 1995 (social perspective)

◇3 …   Gallagher et al., 2000 (FB-stories, *cartoons)

◇4 …   Grèzes, Frith, & Passingham, 1994 (FB)

◇5 …   Happé et al., 1996 (FB)

◇6 …   Ruby & Decety, 2003 (social perspective)

◇7 …   Vogeley et al., 2001 (FB)

△1 …   Fiddick et al., 2005 (cheating)

Without perspective difference

① …   Brunet et al., 2000

② …   Castelli et al., 2000

③ …   Berthoz et al., 2002

④☒ …   Gallagher et al., 2002

⑤☒ …   Mitchell et al., 2002

⑥ …   Schultz et al., 2003

⑦ …   German et al., 2004

⑧ …   Schultz et al., 2004

⑨ …   Walter et al., 2004

ⓐ …   Mitchell et al., 2005a

ⓑ☒ …   Mitchell et al., 2005b

☒ …   showed no activation
         in TPJ or pSTS

Figure 5. *Peak activations of theory of mind studies with (△, ◇, □) and without involving a perspective contrast (◯).*

region. Studies involving a perspective contrast are marked by symbols with corners (triangles Δ for studies involving deception, diamonds $\Diamond$ for false belief, and squares $\Box$ for visual perspective studies), and their centres of activation tend to lie more dorsally—that is, within TPJ. In contrast, theory-of-mind studies that do not involve such a contrast (marked by circles $\bigcirc$) tend to activate more ventrally in the area described by Chris Frith and Uta Frith (C. D. Frith & Frith, 1999; U. Frith & Frith, 2003) as the pSTS.

To us these results suggest that Theory of Mind is not a monolithic skill that is processed by a narrowly circumscribed local brain region. Rather, as far as the processing of information about false beliefs, false signs, photos, and visual perspectives is concerned, some regions may be specialized for internal, unobservable mental states involved in belief-desire reasoning—that is, TPJ-R is associated with false beliefs and intentional action (the separation of these different tasks as involving TPJ and pSTS is not as clear in the right TPJ as in the left TPJ) but not false signs, photos, or visual perspectives. In contrast, other regions have the responsibility of dealing with mental and nonmental problems involving a contrast of perspectives—that is, TPJ-L is responsible for false beliefs, false signs, and visual perspectives but not for photos or mental states that do not involve a perspective problem (these are associated with the pSTS region on the left).

Different theoretical stances

Uta opened for us the pearly gates of theory-of-mind research on children with autism—arguably the most exciting area of Theory of Mind. Later we took off in somewhat different theoretical directions. Uta was attracted to the domain specificity of Theory of Mind. We found it more attractive to think of theory-of-mind development as a case of theory change, where the later developing theory does not supplant the earlier one, but both are used for different purposes. This view raises issues about what the domains of different theories actually are. In brief, in normal development we recognize an earlier emerging understanding of

rational action (Csibra & Gergely, 1998; situation theory: Perner, 1991; see Sodian & Thoermer, 2008 this issue, for recent developments in this field), which is later transformed by the realization that rational action is strictly speaking not dependent on the circumstances in the world but on how the world is represented by the actor. This we think is achieved around the age of 4 years. Moreover, we think that there is no simple progression from the earlier understanding to exclusive use of the more sophisticated level. Rather, in most of our daily reasoning as adults we still operate on the 1-year-old level and only use the extra sophistication that we are capable of when it is needed.

This switch in levels of explanation can be illustrated by the following example (after Perner, 1991, p. 211): Imagine that you and Uta go to the Chinese Tower in the English Garden in Munich to have some beer, which only comes in double pints. It's particularly fine beer you find, but Uta says: "dreadful stuff." Your immediate reaction is to ask what's wrong with Uta's double pint. That is, you think in terms of beer being objectively good or bad (situation theory). Only the discovery that Uta's stuff is as delicious as your own induces you to take the higher intentional stance and consider that it is Uta's aberrant relationship to beer (because she grew up in the wine-growing areas of Germany, which, by the way, may also be the reason for Uta's preserved sense of sarcasm and irony, which—she claims—the beer-drinking Germans often lack) that caused her derogatory remark, not the beer itself (from the "objective" point of view of *your* taste buds). Similarly, when cooperating on a joint enterprise we simply do what needs doing and assume that everybody else involved will do so too. Only when someone doesn't do what needs doing and doesn't fulfil their assigned role in the interaction do we start to think about whether the other *doesn't know* what needs doing or whether she or he *doesn't want* to do it.

This view raises questions about the domains of the different theories. In some sense they aim at explaining the same—namely, actions. But they make different ontological assumptions about the entities that drive action. The earlier teleology sees action as bridging between what is and what ought to be, while the later, representational view sees action driven by representations of what is (belief) and what ought to be (desires).

A perhaps helpful, but obviously imperfect analogy would be the relationship between Newtonian mechanics and modern particle physics. Both apply to physical objects, but the former is restricted to larger (macro level) objects and becomes seriously inaccurate at the atomic and subatomic level. The latter applies to subatomic particles, and since larger objects are made up of such particles it applies in principle to the macro level as well. However, physicists and engineers still use classical mechanics to deal with standard kinds of objects because quantum mechanics and the theory of relativity are practically impossible to use, and the loss of accuracy at the macro level is negligible. Similarly, a simple teleology (people do what is needed in given circumstances) is accurate enough for most everyday interaction. Although a theory of a representational mind has more general validity, it is unnecessarily cumbersome for normal interaction. It only pays off to consider the subjective representation of the world when something goes wrong—for example, when someone has a false belief.

Moreover, the data on false belief and false signs indicate that each theory creates a different domain. A false sign plays no role in teleology, because it does not act rationally, but it plays an obvious role in a representational Theory of Mind. We also tried to argue that these shifts in domains are reflected in the cerebral processes. Different brain areas seem to be responsible for different functional alliances. For instance, pSTS might be involved in understanding rational action, TPJ-R is a module for belief-desire reasoning (involved for understanding false beliefs but not involved in processing false signs or visual perspectives), and TPJ-L for perspectival thinking (involved in processing false beliefs, false signs, and visual perspectives, but not for rational action when no perspective difference arises). For a similar argument that different brain regions can be identified for different functional allegiances, see also Saxe (2006) and Blakemore (2008 this issue).

Despite our plea for a rather fractured view of domains we can see great historical value in assuming that our understanding of the mind and social cognition form a single, coherent domain. The technological advance that makes modern brain-imaging techniques possible needed to be harnessed in the service of the behavioural sciences (functional imaging). To get this process started the technology needed a theoretical background that made its success likely. Structuring all of our knowledge into distinct domains provided this back-up at the right time. A plausible strategy for determining these domains is to look at the sciences and how they partition the world. For knowledge about behaviour psychology is the obvious candidate, especially since there is an everyday naïve psychology about (i.e., Theory of Mind/folk psychology). And this approach has paid off. We now have a set of imaging studies on "Theory of Mind" with surprisingly coherent results. This effort would not have been made without theoretic commitment that naïve psychology is a natural coherent domain of knowledge. However, now that we have made a start, it is time to move on (away) from this commitment to the specificity of this domain and consider alternatives. One of our approaches is to glimpse likely alternatives from development and then see how they pan out in the brain.

REFERENCES

Aichhorn, M., Perner, J., Kronbichler, M., Staffen, W., & Ladurner, G. (2006). Do visual perspective tasks need theory of mind? *NeuroImage, 30*, 1059–1068.

Apperly, I. A., Samson, D., Chiavarino, C., & Humphreys, G. W. (2004). Frontal and temporo-parietal lobe contributions to theory of mind: Neuropsychological evidence from a false-belief task with reduced language and executive demands. *Journal of Cognitive Neuroscience, 16*, 1773–1784.

Baron-Cohen, S., Leslie, A. M., & Frith, U. (1985). Does the autistic child have a "theory of mind"? *Cognition, 21*, 37–46.

Berthoz, S., Armony, J. L., Blair, R. J. R., & Dolan, R. J. (2002). An fMRI study of intentional and unintentional (embarrassing) violations of social norms. *Brain*, *125*, 1696–1708.

Bird, C. M., Castelli, F., Malik, O., Frith, U., & Husain, M. (2004). The impact of extensive medial frontal lobe damage on "theory of mind" and cognition. *Brain*, *127*, 914–928.

Blakemore, S.-J. (2008). Development of the social brain during adolescence. *Quarterly Journal of Experimental Psychology*, *61*, 40–49.

Bowler, D. M., Briskman, J., Gurvidi, N., & Fornells-Ambrojo, M. (2005). Understanding the mind or predicting signal-dependent action? Performance of children with and without autism on analogues of the false-belief task. *Journal of Cognition and Development*, *6*, 259–283.

Brunet, E., Sarfati, Y., Hardy-Baylé, M.-C., & Decety, J. (2000). A PET investigation of the attribution of intentions with a nonverbal task. *NeuroImage*, *11*, 157–166.

Castelli, F., Happé, F., Frith, U., & Frith, C. (2000). Movement and mind: A functional imaging study of perception and interpretation of complex intentional movement patterns. *NeuroImage*, *12*, 314–325.

Charman, T., & Baron-Cohen, S. (1992). Understanding beliefs and drawings: A further test of the metarepresentation theory of autism. *Journal of Child Psychology and Psychiatry*, *33*, 1105–1112.

Csibra, G., & Gergely, G. (1998). The teleological origins of mentalistic action explanations: A developmental hypothesis. *Developmental Science*, *1*, 255–259.

Davis, H. L., & Pratt, C. (1995). The development of children's theory of mind: The working memory explanation: Cognitive development [Special issue]. *Australian Journal of Psychology*, *47*, 25–31.

Fiddick, L., Spampinato, M. V., & Grafman, J. (2005). Social contracts and precautions activate different neurological systems: An fMRI investigation of deontic reasoning. *NeuroImage*, *28*, 778–786.

Fletcher, P. C., Happé, F., Frith, U., Baker, S. C., Dolan, R. J., Frakowiak, R. S., et al. (1995). Other minds in the brain: A functional imaging study of "theory of mind" in story comprehension. *Cognition*, *57*, 109–128.

Frith, C. D., & Frith, U. (1999). Interacting minds—a biological basis. *Science*, *286*, 1692–1695.

Frith, U. (2003). *Autism: Explaining the enigma* (2nd ed.). Oxford, UK: Blackwell Publishing.

Frith, U., & Frith, C. D. (2003). Development and neurophysiology of mentalizing. *Philosophical Transactions of the Royal Society of London, Series B*, *358*, 685–694.

Gallagher, H. L., Happé, F., Brunswick, N., Fletcher, P. C., Frith, U., & Frith, C. D. (2000). Reading the mind in cartoons and stories: An fMRI study of "theory of mind" in verbal and nonverbal tasks. *Neuropsychologia*, *38*, 11–21.

Gallagher, H. L., Jack, A. I., Roepstorff, A., & Frith, C. D. (2002). Imaging the intentional stance in a competitive game. *NeuroImage*, *16*, 814–821.

German, T. P., Niehaus, J. L., Roarty, M. P., Giesbrecht, B., & Miller, M. B. (2004). Neural correlates of detecting pretense: Automatic engagement of the intentional stance under covert conditions. *Journal of Cognitive Neuroscience*, *16*, 1805–1817.

Goel, V., Grafman, J., Sadato, N., & Hallett, M. (1995). Modelling other minds. *NeuroReport*, *6*, 1741–1746.

Grèzes, J., Frith, C. D., & Passingham, R. E. (2004). Inferring false beliefs from the actions of oneself and others: An fMRI study. *NeuroImage*, *21*, 744–750.

Happé, F., Ehlers, S., Fletcher, P., Frith, U., Johansson, M., Gillberg, C., et al. (1996). "Theory of mind" in the brain: Evidence from a PET scan study of Asperger syndrome. *NeuroReport*, *8*, 197–201.

Leekam, S., & Perner, J. (1991). Does the autistic child have a metarepresentational deficit? *Cognition*, *40*, 203–218.

Leekam, S., Perner, J., Healey, L., & Sewell, C. (2006). *False signs and the non-specificity of theory of mind: Evidence that preschoolers have general difficulties in understanding representations*. Manuscript submitted for publication.

Leslie, A. M., & Thaiss, L. (1992). Domain specificity in conceptual development: Neuropsychological evidence from autism. *Cognition*, *43*, 225–251.

Lewis, C. N., Freeman, N. H., & Smith, C. (1992). *Dissociation of inferences about beliefs and pictures in preschoolers*. Unpublished manuscript, University of Lancaster, UK.

Mitchell, J. P., Banaji, M. R., & Macrae, C. N. (2005a). The link between social cognition and self-referential thought in the medial prefrontal cortex. *Journal of Cognitive Neuroscience*, *17*, 1306–1315.

Mitchell, J. P., Banaji, M. R., & Macraeb, C. N. (2005b). General and specific contributions of the medial prefrontal cortex to knowledge about mental states. *NeuroImage*, *28*, 757–762.

Mitchell, J. P., Heatherton, T. F., & Macrae, C. N. (2002). Distinct neural systems subserve person and object knowledge. *Proceedings of the National Academy of Sciences USA*, *99*, 15238–15243.

Müller, U., Zelazo, D. P., & Imrisek, S. (2005). Executive function and children's understanding of false belief: How specific is the relation? *Cognitive Development, 20*, 173–189.

Parkin, L. J. (1994). *Children's understanding of misrepresentation.* Unpublished doctoral thesis, University of Sussex, Brighton, UK.

Parkin, L. J., & Perner, J. (1996). *Wrong directions in children's theory of mind: What it means to understand belief as representation.* Unpublished manuscript, University of Sussex, UK.

Perner, J. (1991). *Understanding the representational mind.* Cambridge, MA: MIT Press.

Perner, J., Aichhorn, M., Kronbichler, M., Staffen, W., & Ladurner, G. (2006). Thinking of mental and other representations: The roles of left and right temporo-parietal junction. *Social Neuroscience, 1*, 245–258.

Perner, J., Frith, U., Leslie, A. M., & Leekam, S. R. (1989). Exploration of the autistic child's theory of mind: Knowledge, belief and communication. *Child Development, 60*, 689–700.

Perner, J., Leekam, S. R., Myers, D., Davis, S., & Odgers, N. (1993). *Misrepresentation and referential confusion: children's difficulty with false beliefs and outdated photographs.* Unpublished manuscript, Laboratory of Experimental Psychology, University of Sussex, UK.

Perner, J., Ruffman, T., Olson, D. R., & Doherty, M. (1993). *Misrepresentation and referential confusion: Children's difficulty with false beliefs and outdated photographs.* Unpublished manuscript, Laboratory of Experimental Psychology, University of Sussex, UK.

Peterson, C. C., & Siegal, M. (1998). Changing focus on the representational mind: Deaf, autistic and normal children's concepts of false photos, false drawings and false beliefs. *British Journal of Developmental Psychology, 16*, 301–320.

Pollack, J. (1990). *Children's understanding of "false" drawings.* Unpublished manuscript, St. John's College, University of Oxford, UK.

Ruby, P., & Decety, J. (2003). What do you believe vs. what do you think they believe: A neuroimaging study of conceptual perspective-taking. *European Journal of Neuroscience, 17*, 1–6.

Sabbagh, M. A., Moses, L. J., & Shiverick, S. (2006). Executive functioning and preschoolers' understanding of false beliefs, false photographs and false signs. *Child Development, 77*, 1034–1049.

Samson, D., Apperly, I. A., Chiavarino, C., & Humphreys, G. W. (2004). Left temporoparietal junction is necessary for representing someone else's belief. *Nature Neuroscience, 7*, 499–500.

Saxe, R. (2006). Uniquely human social cognition. *Current Opinion in Neurobiology, 16*, 235–239.

Saxe, R., & Kanwisher, N. (2003). People thinking about thinking people: The role of the temporo-parietal junction in "theory of mind". *NeuroImage, 19*, 1835–1842.

Saxe, R., & Powell, J. (2006). It's the thought that counts: Specific brain regions for one component of theory of mind. *Psychological Science, 17*, 692–699.

Saxe, R., & Wexler, A. (2005). Making sense of another mind: The role of the right temporo-parietal junction. *Neuropsychologia, 43*, 1391–1399.

Schultz, R. T., Grelotti, D. J., Klin, A., Kleinman, J., Van der Gaag, C., Marois, R., et al. (2003). The role of the fusiform face area in social cognition: Implications for the pathobiology of autism. *Philosophical Transactions of the Royal Society of London, Series B, 358*, 415–427.

Schultz, J., Kawato, H. M., & Frith, C. D. (2004). Activation of the human superior temporal gyrus during observation of goal attribution by intentional objects. *Journal of Cognitive Neuroscience, 16*, 1695–1705.

Slaughter, V. (1998). Children's understanding of pictorial and mental representations. *Child Development, 69*, 271–576.

Sodian, B., & Thoermer, C. (2008). Precursors to a theory of mind in infancy: Perspectives for research on autism. *Quarterly Journal of Experimental Psychology, 61*, 27–39.

Vogeley, K., Bussfeld, P., Newen, A., Herrmann, S., Happé, F., Falkai, P., et al. (2001). Mind reading: Neural mechanisms of theory of mind and self-perspective. *NeuroImage, 14*, 170–181.

Walter, H., Adenzato, M., Ciaramidaro, A., Enrici, I., Pia, L., & Bara, B. G. (2004). Understanding intentions in social interaction: The role of the anterior paracingulate cortex. *Journal of Cognitive Neuroscience, 16*, 1854–1863.

Wimmer, H., & Perner, J. (1983). Beliefs about beliefs: Representation and constraining function of wrong beliefs in young children's understanding of deception. *Cognition, 13*, 103–128.

Zacks, J. M., Vettel, J. M., & Michelon, P. (2003). Imagined viewer and object rotations dissociated with event-related fMRI. *Journal of Cognitive Neuroscience, 15*, 1002–1018.

Zaitchik, D. (1990). When representations conflict with reality: The preschooler's problem with false beliefs and "false" photographs. *Cognition, 35*, 41–68.

THE QUARTERLY JOURNAL OF EXPERIMENTAL PSYCHOLOGY
2008, 61 (1), 90–100

Frames of reference in social cognition

Frédérique de Vignemont

Institut Jean-Nicod, CNRS–EHESS–ENS, Paris, France

How is mindreading affected by social context? It is often implicitly assumed that there is one single way to understand others, whatever the situation or the identity of the person. In contrast, I emphasize the duality of functions of mindreading depending on the context (social interaction and social observation), as well as the duality of social frames of reference (egocentric and allocentric). I argue in favour of a functional distinction between knowledge-oriented mindreading and interaction-oriented mindreading. They both aim at understanding other people's behaviour. But they do so using different strategies. However, to say that mindreading has two functions does not suffice to show that there are two kinds of mindreading. One and the same ability could accomplish different functions. Unfortunately, there has been almost no experimental data on a possible dissociation between two kinds of mindreading abilities. Nonetheless, I discuss a few results that point towards a dual ability.

What would be more relevant to Uta Frith's work and personality than to focus on the social dimension of cognition? I do not detail here how she has been able to create a real family atmosphere within her group and within the Institute of Cognitive Neuroscience, or how enjoyable it is to work with her. I rather highlight some of the ideas that we had developed together in previous papers about social frames of reference (de Vignemont & Frith, 2007; Frith & de Vignemont, 2005). We suggested that there is more than one way to understand others and that it depends on the frame of reference of our social understanding. Here I develop and refine the hypothesis of a dual mindreading ability.

Social observation and social interaction

The problem of other minds—or how I can understand others—has often been understood in such a way that there seems to be only one unique valid answer. The context should not matter, nor should the identity of the person one tries to understand. You could be conversing with someone, or seeing her converse with someone else; it could be your mother or a stranger in the street: The problem would stay the same, and the solution too. The literature in cognitive psychology for more than twenty years now has indeed provided a rather unilateral view of mindreading and social cognition. It is often assumed that there is one single way to understand the other, although people disagree on its nature. It is also often assumed that it is accomplished by a unique brain structure dedicated to the representation of mental states, like the temporoparietal junction, for instance (Saxe, 2006). Although Saxe agrees that social cognition involves more than that, she views mindreading per se as a unique ability realized by a unique brain structure. I call this assumption the *single-perspective view*.

We can contrast the single-perspective view with what I call the *dual-perspective view*, which

Correspondence should be addressed to Frédérique de Vignemont, Institut Jean-Nicod, 1bis avenue de Lowendal 75007 Paris, France. E-mail: fvignemont@isc.cnrs.fr

DOI:10.1080/17470210701508764

has been first defended by the philosopher Alfred Schütz, who founded phenomenological sociology in the thirties. In the *Phenomenology of the Social World* (1937/1967), he made a distinction between two fundamental kinds of relationship with the other: social interaction and social observation. These two kinds of relationship are both oriented toward others. They both aim at understanding other people's behaviour. But they do so using different strategies. *Social interaction* is oriented toward persons that are considered as a "thou", as another agent that cannot be treated as an object. The interaction can consist of affecting the other's behaviour and experiences. The face-to-face relationship is characterized by immediacy and flexibility. We can adjust to each other, and I can test your reactions, to see how your assumed motives produce what you say. Furthermore, the environment can be guaranteed as a common one, shared in experience, which is useful in understanding the other. We can make unambiguous references to objects within our mutual reach and check our guesses by questions. On the other hand, *social observation* is oriented toward persons located outside the nexus of intimacy. People are no longer perceived and reckoned with as unique individuals, but as instances of classes. For example, one expects policemen to act in certain ways, and thus we can relate to them in a prototypical way without ever knowing them as individuals. Such people are only relevant to us insofar as they correspond with our prototype. In social observation, I cannot modify your behaviour. Nonetheless, I can still guess your mental states based on inferences from the behaviour that I observe, on memories of similar past situations where I was involved, on general knowledge of prototypes of people based on assumptions of generalizability (e.g., policemen). I validate my understanding according to my experience of the social world and my knowledge of the character of the observed persons, actual or typical. However, no testing is possible, since we can make no reference to objects and cannot ask questions to check observations.

In contrast to the single-perspective view, Schütz distinguished two modes of relationship with the other based on phenomenological and epistemological differences between the two modes. His view is actually quite modern, although it was proposed more than 70 years ago. It goes in the same direction as some recent theories about the architecture of the mind that emphasize the possibility of multiple coding of a same category. One of the main proponents of such trend is Jackendoff (1996, p. 1): "The general idea is that the mind/brain encodes information in many distinct formats or 'languages of the mind'." We can provide a series of examples of this principle in various domains of cognition.

- Language: dual route of language understanding through the phonological pathway and the semantic pathway (Forster, 1979).
- Number: dual route of counting through subitizing and serial counting (Dehaene & Sybesma, 1999).
- Body: dual representation of the body through the body schema dedicated to action and the body image dedicated to recognition (Paillard, 1999).
- Action: dual representations of action, either semantic or pragmatic (Jeannerod, 1997).
- Vision: dual representation of visual inputs through the dorsal pathway of sensorimotor transformation and through the ventral pathway of object recognition (Milner & Goodale, 1995).
- Space: dual representation of the location of objects relative to other objects within an allocentric frame of reference and relative to the agent within an egocentric frame of reference (Pick & Lockman, 1981).

Interestingly, one criterion of distinction is present in several of these examples. For the body, for action and for vision, the duality of coding results from a difference in functional role. On the one hand, there is a representation dedicated to the recognition and identification of the input. This semantic representation constitutes the basis for judgements about the input and about its properties (e.g., I believe that the ball is red). On the other hand, there is a representation dedicated to actions. This pragmatic representation is used to plan and control movements performed toward the input (e.g., the ball is big so I make a large grip aperture to grasp it). This distinction is founded on an impressive amount of evidence coming from physiology, psychophysics, neuropsychology, and neuroscience (for review, see Jacob & Jeannerod, 2003). It has been shown not only for vision, but also for other sensory modalities like audition (Belin & Zatorre, 2000) and proprioception (Dijkerman & de Haan, 2007). It seems to be widespread in the cognitive architecture, and one might even wonder whether we could not extend it further by applying it to social cognition.

Schütz's theory can indeed be reinterpreted in more cognitive terms using the perception–action model. If one takes seriously the parallel with the perception–action model, one would first have to describe the nature and the extent of the differences between social interaction and social observation. Putting it another way, one would have to show that social interaction and social observation rely on distinct cognitive mechanisms. To be exhaustive, the dual-perspective view would have to specify the properties of each of these mechanisms and to provide empirical evidence of this distinction based on neuropsychological dissociations and on developmental data. However, this paper is more exploratory and does not pretend to reach such level of achievement. I rather suggest a weaker version of the dual-perspective view. I show that it makes a difference whether I understand the other in the context of social interaction or social observation. This difference could be explained by assuming either that there are two distinct mindreading abilities (i.e., strong version of the dual-perspective view) or that there is one single ability, used differently given the context. I leave this latter question open, although I try to provide some suggestions that might be worth investigating experimentally.

Functions of mindreading

Mindreading is often characterized as the ability to understand and predict someone else's behaviour. This definition gives us what mindreading does, not what mindreading is for. We are supposed constantly to try to guess what others feel or think, but why do we do that? Is it just out of curiosity by a kind of voyeurism? Or is there anything beyond, that would be essential to our survival in society? Can the perception–action distinction also be applied to mindreading?

Let us start with the false-belief task, which is paradigmatic of the mindreading literature. The standard version presents the subject with a character, Sally, who puts a chocolate in her basket before leaving the room. In her absence, another character, Anne, removes the chocolate and places it in a box. Subjects are asked to predict, on Sally's return to the room, where Sally will look for the object. Subjects have to make a judgement about what Sally believes. Mindreading here is considered as a strategy to form beliefs about someone else's mental states. It is what I call *knowledge-oriented*. One uses mindreading in order to know what the other believes. Mindreading is a way to detect information about the other necessary to make judgements about mental properties. We can compare this function of mindreading with the function of the ventral pathway of vision, which is dedicated to the identification and recognition of the perceived object in order to make judgements about the properties of the object. In the same way that we have beliefs about the colour of the sofa, for example, we have beliefs about other people's mental states, although in both cases the information is not directly relevant to us (e.g., we are not thinking of buying the sofa, nor do we intend to interact with the individuals to whom we ascribe mental states).

However, one might suggest a different function of mindreading, as suggested by Rutherford (2004, p. 92): "One of the functions of ToM [Theory of Mind] reasoning is to assess another's knowledge, beliefs, intentions, etc. in order to manipulate their behaviour." Rutherford is interested in competitive situations. Fortunately, our social interactions are not limited to conflicts between individuals. As pointed out by Schütz (1937/1967), there are different ways of affecting the behaviour of others. For instance, teaching involves being understood and remembered and influencing the other's behaviour more positively. More generally, all situations of communication necessitate carrying a communicative intention in such a way that the other will understand it (Sperber & Wilson, 1986). Cooperation is another situation that involves mindreading. To cooperate, we must know that we have a shared intention (we both intend to do X). We are committed to mutual responsiveness and mutual support (Bratman, 1992). Each agent must understand the other's intention to react accordingly. In all these distinct social situations, mindreading is what I call *interaction-oriented*. One uses mindreading in order to be able to interact with others. The type of interaction can be very different. Yet, I would like to argue that all situations of interaction have something in common when mindreading is concerned. Mindreading is a way to detect information about other people's mental states to guide our behaviour with them. We can compare this function of mindreading with the function of the dorsal pathway of vision, which is dedicated to sensorimotor transformations to perform actions toward the perceived object. In the same way that we represent the width of a glass in order to adjust our grip aperture, we represent other people's mental states in order to adjust our own behaviour and to interact with them.

Consequently, there are two functions of mindreading. On the one hand, it can be knowledge-oriented. On the other hand, it can be interaction-oriented. But does it really make a difference?

Social frames of reference

Let us compare two everyday-life situations illustrating the distinction between knowledge-oriented and interaction-oriented mindreading (see Figure 1).

(a) In the metro, I listen to two other travellers who have an argument together. Let us call them Peter and Mary.
(b) At one point they start to pay attention to me, and Peter accuses me of spying on them. We have an argument together.

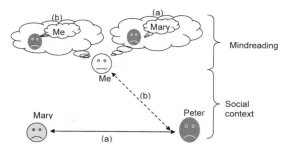

Figure 1. *Social frames of reference.*

The first stage (a) corresponds to what Schütz calls social observation. I try to guess the background of their argument: Peter does not like that Mary came back too late last night and believes that she is cheating on him; she thinks that he is being unfair. The second stage (b) is a case of social interaction, a rather conflictive one. I am directly involved in the argument and no longer an external witness. I try to understand why Peter is so angry with me in order to calm him down. At both stages, I ascribe mental states to Peter, although for different purposes. At the beginning, I just want to kill time and entertain myself; afterwards I just want to find a good way to react and to stop this argument. Do I use the same strategy in both situations? What are the differences between knowledge-oriented and interaction-oriented mindreading? I consider two ways to understand the difference: scope of interest and frame of reference. Although none of these differences exhausts the distinction between social observation and social interaction, they allow us to refine the contrast between the two kinds of mindreading.

At the core of the perception–action distinction, there is the idea that the visual system does not process the same type of information for action and for perception. For instance, if I want to grasp a glass, I need to encode the size of the glass to programme my grip aperture. But its colour might not be relevant for my motor system. Similarly, in interaction-oriented mindreading, I am interested only in the pieces of information that are relevant for interacting. For instance, it is important for me to detect whether

Peter has the intention to hit me, but I do not need to know what he thinks of the government. More generally, understanding the intentions of others plays a key role for social interaction and constitutes "a foundational skill", whether it is for communication, for competition, or for cooperation: "These two dimensions of human expertise—reading intentions and interacting with others culturally—are intimately related" (Tomasello, Carpenter, Call, Behne, & Moll, 2005, p. 675). In contrast, the scope of knowledge-oriented mindreading is broader. It includes all the mental properties, as diverse as food-related desires, religious beliefs, emotional states, and so on. However, based on this distinction, we cannot draw a sharp boundary between knowledge-oriented and interaction-oriented mindreading. What is relevant varies between each social interaction.

A different way to approach the distinction may be to look not at the information encoded, but at the way the information is encoded. In our example, at the beginning, Peter is considered from a third-person perspective. I refer to him with a "he". Later, while arguing with him, I refer to him with a "you". With Uta Frith, we have emphasized the importance of the distinction between the third person (the other unrelated to the self), and the second person (the other related to the self), this distinction between the latter two perspectives being often neglected (Frith & de Vignemont, 2005). Drawing further on the parallel with the perception–action distinction, we have suggested that one needs to take into account the frame of reference in which the other is encoded. We propose that it makes a difference to mindreading whether the other person is understood using an egocentric ("you") or an allocentric ("he/she/they") stance.

The distinction between egocentric and allocentric representations was first made in spatial cognition. A frame of reference was first defined as "a locus or set of loci with respect to which spatial position is defined" (Pick & Lockman, 1981, p. 40). The spatial location of an object can be encoded either in its perceptual relation to the agent (e.g., the apple is in front of me) or in terms of its surroundings independently of the

agent (e.g., the apple is on the table). The former frame of reference is egocentric, centred on the agent, whether the agent is me, you, or a third person. The latter frame of reference is allocentric, which does not depend on the presence of the agent, or on her location. Similarly, we have suggested that one can adopt either an egocentric or an allocentric stance toward the other. When one takes an egocentric stance, one understands the other person relative to oneself. When one takes an allocentric stance, one represents the other in her relationship with other individuals independently of oneself.

However, the notion of social frames of reference may seem obscure. In the case of spatial cognition, the relationship is spatial. But what is the nature of the relationship in social cognition? There are at least two components. The first component is external. It is the relationship between the individuals in the society (e.g., a relative, a colleague, a friend, etc.). Interestingly, Piaget pointed out that young children can easily understand the relationship between themselves and their mother but have more difficulties in understanding that their mother is also their father's wife. They understand the egocentric relationship with their mother, but not the allocentric relationship between their mother and their father. The second component is internal and concerns the content of the target's mental states. People have thoughts directed towards other people. The egocentric stance is interested in thoughts directed towards me. The allocentric stance is interested in thoughts directed towards others. Let us go back to Peter and Mary. At the beginning, I understand Peter and Mary in an allocentric frame of reference independently of myself: I understand that Mary is Peter's girlfriend (i.e., allocentric social relationship), and I mindread that Peter thinks that Mary is cheating on him (i.e., allocentric reference). Later, I understand Peter and Mary in an egocentric frame of reference centred on myself: I understand that Peter is a stranger that I will never meet again (i.e., egocentric social relationship), and I mindread that Peter is angry with me (i.e., egocentric reference).

I would like to argue that the egocentric frame of reference is necessary to interact with others. In spatial cognition, the egocentric representation of the location of the perceived object is directly linked to the actions that the agent can perform toward the object: It is only if I know where the apple is relative to my body that I can reach it. Similarly, in social cognition, one needs to understand the other relative to oneself if one wants to cooperate, compete or communicate. For example, to react properly to Peter, I need to know that it is with me and not with anybody else that he is angry. I also need to take into account the fact that I will never see him again, so I do not care too much if he leaves upset. Both egocentric types of information—self-reference and egocentric social relationship—are thus necessary for interacting with Peter. The situation is the same for cooperation. It relies on the mutual knowledge that we both have "the intention that we do X" (Bratman, 1992). To be able to form such an intention, I need to relate the other to myself, creating the first-person plural (e.g., I + you = we). I need to understand that the other intends to do the work with *me*, and not with anybody else. And when the other holds a paintbrush in my direction, I need to understand that it is to *me* that the other gives the paintbrush so that we paint the house together. In communication too, I need to understand that your communicative intentions are addressed to *me*. It is easy to see what happens when we fail to understand the egocentric reference. For instance, as long as you do not understand that the chairman of a conference is pointing at *you*, you cannot ask your question. Conversely, you might start speaking while it was not your turn. It is thus important to understand self-reference. Interestingly, it has been shown that for the same level of syntactical complexity, children understand more easily sentences that are referring to themselves than those referring to others and than impersonal sentences (Mood, 1979). Putting it another way, in the same way that one cannot reach a glass if one does not know where the glass is relative to oneself, one cannot talk and work with others if one does not know what the other thinks of oneself.

What is then the relationship between the egocentric stance and the classical notion of egocentrism, which has a long history in psychology? Egocentrism actually covers several distinct concepts. It can be tracked down to Piaget and the three-mountains problem (Piaget & Inhelder, 1948). A child is egocentric if he is unable to distinguish his own spatial perspective and someone else's perspective on the world. Egocentrism is characterized by the saliency of one's own perspective, leading to an inability to disregard one's own experiences and to imagine other people's experiences. The child therefore assumes that all people will react like him. A second type of egocentrism arises during adolescence. It is characterized by two main personality features: the imaginary audience and the personal fable (Elkind, 1967). First, adolescents believe that other people's thoughts centre on them. In this respect, they play to an imaginary audience perceiving that others share their own self concerns. Second, adolescents convince themselves that their emotions and experiences are entirely unique. Egocentrism in adolescence can be thus defined by self-concern with no concern for others. It is related to what is considered as egocentric speech, characterized by monologue, repetition, muttering, self-answered question, and frequent self-reference (Garvey & Hogan, 1973). For instance, children's discourse often mentions the other's behaviour toward themselves, or their own behaviour or affective attitude toward the other, or they compare themselves to others (Honess, 1980). Another aspect of egocentrism is imposing one's will. For instance, individuals with Asperger syndrome want other people to behave exactly as they want and get very frustrated if they are not obeyed (Moore, 2004). In summary, egocentrism can be defined according to three different axes: (a) lack of understanding of the other; (b) lack of interest towards the other; and (c) lack of respect for the other's will.

In all these cases, the egocentric frame of reference is pushed to its limits, so much that it becomes an obstacle to social interaction. Defining the other by her relationship to the self is not denying the other. Egocentrism results when the social world is not only centred on the self but is reduced to the self. We suggested, with Uta Frith, that egocentrism results from a lack of interaction between egocentric and allocentric representations of others (Frith & de Vignemont, 2005). In normal adults, the egocentric and allocentric stances interact constantly with each other. Allocentric and egocentric representations are complementary. In spatial cognition, an allocentric representation of an object allows one to link this object to other objects, independently of the agent. Objects have to be perceived in their mutual relationship in allocentric coordinates to be perceived in their own right. Similarly, the allocentric representation of others is detached from possible interactions with them. It secures the existence of the other person independently of the relationship one may have with her. A second role played by the allocentric frame of reference is that it allows one to understand the social world. By observing others and understanding their mutual relationships, one can learn about the social rules and the social structure. This knowledge can later be used during social interactions. Therefore, one needs both egocentric and allocentric representations of others to achieve satisfying interactions with others.

However, some people may doubt the possibility of non-egocentric frame of reference. They may argue that egocentrism is not something that happens only to young children or adolescents. It would be more pervasive than that. For example, social psychology has studied extensively what has been called the "contrast effect" (Dunning & Hayes, 1996). Contrast effects occur when people judge the behaviour and attitudes of others relative to their own. They use their own particular behaviours as norms when evaluating the performances of others. For instance, if you go swimming every day, you will judge that the person that goes swimming only once a week is not very sporty. Conversely, if you never go swimming, you will consider the weekly swimmer as sporty. The other is judged in a frame of reference centred on the self. Another well-known example is the "curse of knowledge". Even adults have difficulties in inhibiting what they themselves know to predict

someone else's behaviour. For instance, well-informed subjects had to predict what other less-informed people would forecast for the earning of a company. Despite the fact that they knew that they were less informed, still they predicted that they would say what they themselves forecasted (Camerer, Loewenstein, & Weber, 1989). Such egocentric biases happen not only for knowledge but also for values and feelings (for review, see Goldman, 2006). Does it mean that egocentric reference always invades mindreading? Can we really get rid of the self in understanding others?

My reply to this is twofold. First, although egocentric biases are indeed more frequent than one might think, fortunately they are not always the rule. Most of the time, we are able to "quarantine" our own feelings and beliefs from our understanding of others (Goldman, 2006). Mindreading is not necessarily contaminated by egocentric biases. The second point that I want to make is more theoretical. The fact that we use egocentric reference when making judgements about other people in situations of social observation is not self-contradictory. The egocentric/allocentric distinction is not equivalent to the distinction between interaction-oriented and knowledge-oriented mindreading. This is true of spatial cognition too. The fact that the glass is in front of me is necessary for action, but it can also constitute the content of a conscious perceptual belief. Egocentric representations can be used by both visual systems. The distinction between the two frames of reference does not perfectly overlap with the distinction between the two functions of mindreading. All I want to claim is that the egocentric frame of reference is necessary for social interaction, while it is not necessary for social observation. In this sense, it constitutes a difference between the two types of mindreading.

However, we have not yet provided any conclusive evidence that knowledge-oriented and interaction-oriented mindreading rely on two different abilities. This paper is prospective and exploratory. It does not pretend to provide a definite reply to this question. Nonetheless, as a conclusion I would like to review a few results that point towards a dual ability.

One or two?

At the beginning, I described the single-perspective view, according to which there is one single ability to understand others, independent of the context. I then emphasized the duality of functions of mindreading, as well as the duality of social frames of reference. However, to say that mindreading has two functions does not suffice to show that there are two kinds of mindreading. One and the same ability could accomplish different functions. According to a principle of cognitive economy, it would be even more parsimonious to defend the single-perspective view. To be able to argue in favour of the strong version of the dual-perspective view, one needs to leave armchair speculations and philosophical ruminations for experimental evidence. Unfortunately, this has not been really studied, and there are almost no data on the existence of a dissociation between two mindreading abilities.

Let me start first with a slightly different domain than mindreading—that is, action observation. It has been shown that brain activation differs relative to the aim of the observation of the action (Decety et al., 1997). If you observe the action in order to be able to recognize it later, you activate structures dedicated to memory encoding. In contrast, if you observe the action in order to be able to imitate it later, you activate the regions involved in the planning and in the generation of actions. Put another way, action observation differs whether it is knowledge-oriented or interaction-oriented. It shows that observation of other people can be affected by the role played by the observation.

Similarly, one might suggest comparing two versions of the false-belief task. I described the false-belief task as a typical example of knowledge-oriented mindreading. However, we could suggest a slightly modified version of the standard task to test interaction-oriented mindreading. Rather than being the external witness of a story involving two remote characters, the child could be directly involved in the story (Gallagher, 2005). For instance, the child in presence of two examiners puts a chocolate in a basket. One of the examiners leaves, and the other suggests to the child to put the chocolate somewhere else. The child removes the chocolate and puts it in a box. Then the examiner who has left comes back. In contrast to the standard version, the child would be directly in interaction with the target to whom he ascribes a belief about the location of the chocolate. He is the one who has tricked the target. Intentional deceptive behaviour involves the intention to induce a false belief in the other. Interestingly, it has been shown that children spontaneously deceive other children as early as three years old (Carlson, Moses, & Hix, 1998). However, they are able to understand deception only at four years old (Perner, 1991). Therefore, I would suggest that children would have greater ability in this task than in the standard false-belief task. If we could show that interaction-oriented mindreading has a different developmental story than knowledge-oriented mindreading, then it would be a good starting point to argue for the dual-perspective view.

As far as I know, a systematic comparison between the two versions of the false-belief task has never been done, and the literature about deceptive behaviour in children is not always consistent. Furthermore, even if we could show an improvement with the interactive false-belief task, it could be argued that the difference between the two versions is just a question of difficulty. The classical version of the false-belief task is indeed highly difficult and demanding (Bloom & German, 2000). When the task is made simpler by using more specific or more pragmatic questions or by giving memory aid, even 3-year-old children succeed (Freeman & Lacohée, 1995; Lewis & Osborne, 1990; Siegal & Beattie, 1991; Surian & Leslie, 1999). Similarly, the interactive task would just make the task simpler. The false-belief task requires more than just mindreading, and the additional processing capacities could be responsible for the failure in the classical version. Consequently, it will not be easy to provide conclusive evidence of a dual way of understanding others.

There are however some preliminary results that show the role of social relationships for mind-reading. It was noticed in the 1950s that people coming from an ethnic minority had a deeper understanding of the "white mentality" than vice versa (Dollard, 1957). The underlying assumption is that people in a weaker position need to know more about the others to be able to get what they want and to compensate for their lower social status:

Whereas a more powerful person might be able to manipulate another's behaviour using brute force alone, a less powerful person would not be able to change another's behaviour without tracking mental states. A person of average or below-average status is especially dependent on ToM [Theory of Mind] reasoning to control their social situations through negotiations, bargaining, threatening, appeasing, etc. (Rutherford, 2004, p. 92)

Putting it another way, you had better be aware of the feelings and thoughts of your boss if you want to gain his favour. But your boss does not care what you feel. Interestingly, when one is given the role of subordinate in an experimental situation, one becomes better in assessing the feeling of others, and, conversely, when the same person is attributed the role of leader, one becomes less good (Snodgrass, 1985). Rutherford (2004) used the classical false-belief task to evaluate whether social status can indeed affect mind-reading. Subjects first participated in a general quiz game, but unbeknownst to them some received an easy version and the others a difficult version, leading to two groups, the winners and the losers. In order to introduce a hierarchy between them even more, the losers were later taught and evaluated by the winners. They all then took a false-belief task. The results showed that the losers had a better performance than the winners (i.e., fewer errors and shorter reaction time). Rutherford concluded that people with a lower social status allocate more resources to mindreading. One might regret that the author used a classical false-belief task based on story telling. It would have been even more interesting if the losers had to judge the winners' false belief and vice versa. Furthermore, one may also suggest a slightly different interpretation of the results. The losers felt in competition with the others. They wanted to win at least at this task. In contrast, the winners had nothing to prove. They did not feel in competition with the others. They might not even pay attention to the others. Putting it another way, some took into account their social relationship with the others and felt themselves to be in a social situation of competition, while the others simply did the task as required. The difference in performance could then reflect a difference between interaction-oriented and knowledge-oriented mindreading. However, once again it does not tell us whether both rely on the same ability or not. It might be just a question of motivation and resource allocation.

The best way to argue for a conceptual distinction is to provide a case of double dissociation. If an individual is impaired in A and not in B, and if another individual is impaired in B and not in A, then we are entitled to conclude that A and B are two distinct abilities. The problem here is that we do not have such double dissociation. However, as a starting point, we might be interested in Asperger syndrome. Although people with Asperger syndrome sometimes succeed in the false-belief task, they still show strong social impairments characterized by the inability to interact with peers and a lack of desire to do so, a poor appreciation of social cues, and socially and emotionally inappropriate responses. I have argued with Uta Frith that their impairment can be explained in part by a disconnection between egocentric and allocentric representations of others (de Vignemont & Frith, 2007; Frith & de Vignemont, 2005). While we know—with some exceptions—when to use an egocentric or an allocentric frame of reference, they are unable to switch appropriately from one to the other. In social interaction, they display an extreme egocentrism, leading them to ignore that the others have their own existence independent of themselves. As for social observation, either they are not interested or they use a very abstract and detached view of the social world, completely disconnected from what they themselves would feel in such situations. However, there is no experimental data to support our hypothesis, merely autobiographical cues. It would be interesting to investigate in further detail mindreading abilities in Asperger syndrome.

This leads us to the core question. What could be the experiment to test the dual-perspective view? We would need to compare two situations: the subject in the presence of two persons interacting with each other and the subject interacting with one of the two. The type of interaction should be the same. In both conditions, the subject would be required to judge the mental state of the same person. One would have to make sure that in both conditions, the subject pays as much attention and is as motivated. If we could show differences of performance, then we would have an argument for the strong version of the dual-perspective view. This would be even stronger if we could find distinct neural networks activated in the two conditions. We could also expect the differences in performance to vary relative to the age. In addition, people with Asperger syndrome might display a different pattern of performance. However, as long as we do not have such type of evidence, we are limited to emphasize the importance of the conceptual distinction between knowledge-oriented and interaction-oriented mindreading. It makes a difference whether mindreading is used for social interaction or for social observation.

REFERENCES

Belin, P., & Zatorre, R. J. (2000). "What", "where" and "how" in auditory cortex. *Nature Neuroscience, 3,* 965–966.

Bloom, P., & German, T. P. (2000). Two reasons to abandon the false belief task as a test of theory of mind. *Cognition, 77,* B25–B31.

Bratman, M. E. (1992). Shared cooperative activity. *The Philosophical Review, 101,* 327–341.

Camerer, C. F., Loewenstein, G. F., & Weber, M. (1989). The curse of knowledge in economic settings: An experimental analysis. *Journal of Political Economy, 97,* 1232–1254.

Carlson, S. M., Moses, L. J., & Hix, H. R. (1998). The role of inhibitory processes in young children's difficulties with deception and false belief. *Child Development, 69,* 672–691.

Decety, J., Grezes, J., Costes, N., Perani, D., Jeannerod, M., Procyk, E., et al. (1997). Brain activity during observation of actions. Influence of action content and subject's strategy. *Brain, 120,* 1763–1777.

Dehaene, S., & Sybesma, R. (1999). *The number sense: How the mind creates mathematics.* New York: Oxford University Press.

de Vignemont, F., & Frith, U. (2007), Autism, morality and empathy. In W. Sinnott-Armstrong (Ed.), *Moral psychology: Vol. 3. The neuroscience of morality: Emotion, disease, and development.* Cambridge, MA: MIT Press.

Dijkerman, H. C., & de Haan, E. H. F. (2007). Somatosensory processes subserving perception and action. *Behavioral and Brain Sciences, 30,* 189–201.

Dollard, J. (1957). *Caste and class in a southern town.* Garden City, NY: Doubleday.

Dunning, D., & Hayes, A. F. (1996). Evidence for egocentric comparison in social judgment. *Journal of Personality and Social Psychology, 71,* 213–229.

Elkind, D. (1967). Egocentrism in adolescence. *Child Development, 38,* 1025–1034.

Forster, K. I. (1979). Levels of processing and the structure of the language processor. In W. E. Copper & E. C. T. Walker (Eds.), *Sentence processing: Psycholinguistic studies presented to Merrill Garrett.* Hillsdale, NJ: Lawrence Erlbaum Associates.

Freeman, N., & Lacohée, H. (1995). Making explicit 3-year-old's implicit competence with their own false beliefs. *Cognition, 56,* 31–60.

Frith, U., & de Vignemont, F. (2005). Egocentrism, allocentrism and Asperger syndrome. *Consciousness and Cognition, 14,* 719–738.

Gallagher, S. (2005). *How the body shapes the mind.* Oxford, UK: Oxford University Press.

Garvey, C., & Hogan, R. (1973). Social speech and social interaction: Egocentrism revisited. *Child Development, 44,* 562–568.

Goldman, A. (2006). *Simulating minds.* New York: Oxford University Press.

Honess, T. 1980. Self-reference in children's descriptions of peers: Egocentricity or collaboration? *Child Development, 51,* 467–480.

Jackendoff, R. (1996). The architecture of the linguistic-spatial interface. In P. Bloom, M. A. Peterson, L. Nadel, & M. F. Garrett (Eds.), *Language and space.* Tucson, AZ: University of Arizona Press.

Jacob, P., & Jeannerod, M. (2003). *Ways of seeing.* New York: Oxford University Press.

Jeannerod, M. (1997). *The cognitive neuroscience of action*. Oxford, UK: Blackwell.

Lewis, C., & Osborne, A. (1990). Three-year-olds' problems with false belief: Conceptual deficit or linguistic artifact? *Child Development, 61*, 1514–1519.

Milner, D., & Goodale, M. A. (1995). *The visual brain in action*. New York: Oxford University Press.

Mood, D. W. (1979). Sentence comprehension in preschool children: Testing an adaptive egocentrism hypothesis. *Child Development, 50*, 247–250.

Moore, C. (2004). *George and Sam*. London: Penguin Books.

Paillard, J. (1999). Body schema and body image—a double dissociation in deafferented patients. In G. N. Gantchev, S. Mori, & J. Massion (Eds.), *Motor control, today and tomorrow*. Sophia, Bulgaria: Academic Publishing House.

Perner, J. (1991). *Understanding the representational mind*. Cambridge, MA: MIT Press.

Piaget, J., & Inhelder, B. (1948). *The child's conception of space*. London: Routledge and Kegan Paul.

Pick, H. L., & Lockman, J. J. (1981). From frames of reference to spatial representation. In L. S. Liben, A. H. Patterson, & N. Newcombe (Eds.), *Spatial representation and behaviour across life span*. New York: Academic Press.

Rutherford, M. D. (2004). The effect of social role on theory of mind reasoning. *British Journal of Psychology, 95*, 91–103.

Saxe, R. (2006). Uniquely social cognition. *Current Opinion in Neurobiology, 16*, 235–239.

Schütz, A. (1967). *The phenomenology of the social world* (G. Walsh & F. Lenhert, Trans.). Evanston, IL: Northwestern University Press. (Original work published 1937)

Siegal, M., & Beattie, K. (1991). Where to look first for children's knowledge of false beliefs. *Cognition, 38*, 1–12.

Snodgrass, S. E. (1985). Women's intuition: The effect of subordinate role on interpersonal sensitivity. *Journal of Personality and Social Psychology, 49*, 146–155.

Sperber, D., & Wilson, D. (1986). *Relevance: Communication and cognition*. Oxford, UK: Blackwell.

Surian, L., & Leslie, A. M. (1999). Competence and performance in false belief understanding: A comparison of autistic and three-year-old children. *British Journal of Developmental Psychology, 17*, 141–155.

Tomasello, T., Carpenter, M., Call, J., Behne, T., & Moll, H. (2005). Understanding and sharing intentions: The origins of cultural cognition. *Behavioral and Brain Sciences, 28*, 675–735.

THE QUARTERLY JOURNAL OF EXPERIMENTAL PSYCHOLOGY
2008, 61 (1), 101–115

Emulation and mimicry for social interaction: A theoretical approach to imitation in autism

Antonia F. de C. Hamilton

Dartmouth College, Hanover, NH, USA

The "broken-mirror" theory of autism argues that dysfunction of the "mirror neuron system" is a root cause of social disability in autism. The present paper aims to scrutinize this theory and, when it breaks down, to provide an alternative. Current evidence suggests that children with autism are able to understand and emulate goal-directed actions, but may have specific impairments in automatic mimicry of actions without goals. These data are not compatible with the broken-mirror theory, but can be accounted for by a new model called EP-M. The EP-M model segments the mirror neuron system into an indirect, parietal route for goal emulation and planning (EP) and a direct occipital-frontal route for mimicry (M). This fractionation is consistent with neuroimaging and behavioural studies of the mirror neuron system in typical children and adults. I suggest that top-down modulation of the direct M route may be dysfunctional in individuals with autism, leading to abnormal behaviours on mimicry tasks as well as other social disabilities.

There exists a small population of children with dramatic impairments in social and communication abilities, in conjunction with normal or exceptional performance on a limited set of nonsocial tasks. These children were defined as autistic by Kanner and Asperger over 60 years ago (Frith, 2003). Extensive behavioural testing has now characterized more precisely the autistic profile in terms of poor performance on tasks requiring an understanding of mental states, abnormal imitation and emotion processing, and good performance on tasks requiring the perception of detail or local form.

A number of theoretical models have been proposed to account for some or all of these behaviours. Of particular importance are the ideas that a delay in the development of Theory of Mind may account for many of the social and communication disabilities seen in children with autism (Baron-Cohen, Leslie, & Frith, 1985; Frith, Morton, & Leslie, 1991; Happé, 1995), while differences in information-processing style, in particular weak central coherence, may account for many of the nonsocial features of autism (Frith & Happé, 1994). Other theories focusing on emotion (Baron-Cohen et al., 2000), perceptual processing (Behrmann, Thomas, & Humphreys, 2006), gender differences (Baron-Cohen, 2002), and self–other processing (Hobson, 1995) have been proposed.

Correspondence should be addressed to Antonia Hamilton, School of Psychology, University of Nottingham, University Park, Nottingham NG7 2RD, UK. E-mail: Antonia.Hamilton@nottingham.ac.uk

Many many thanks to Uta Frith for encouraging me to carry out the studies of autistic children described in this paper and for numerous essential discussions of the theories developed in this paper, always with a nice meal. Any errors and inconsistencies are entirely mine.

101

DOI:10.1080/17470210701508798

However, in the last five years, a bold new attempt to understand autism at both the cognitive and neural levels has attracted widespread attention. The provocatively named "broken-mirror" theory of autism (Iacoboni & Dapretto, 2006; Ramachandran & Oberman, 2006; Williams, Whiten, Suddendorf, & Perrett, 2001) has been hailed as a unifying explanation for the various social disabilities seen in autistic spectrum disorders. The aim of the current paper is to examine the broken-mirror hypothesis, in particular in relation to studies of the imitation and understanding of other people's actions. The data reviewed provide clear evidence against a simple "broken-mirror" account and demonstrate that a more sophisticated model of different types of imitation behaviour is required. I present a new candidate model, called EP-M because it proposes an indirect EP (emulation and planning) route for emulating actions and a direct M route for mimicking. This model details how different regions of the human mirror neuron system contribute to different types of imitation behaviour and may be differentially impaired in autism. Using EP-M, is it possible to account for data from wide range of developmental, psychophysical, and neuroimaging experiments and to make new predictions for future studies.

The "broken-mirror" hypothesis

At its simplest, the broken-mirror hypothesis claims that children with autism have a dysfunction of the mirror neuron system and that this is the primary cause of their social disability (Dapretto et al., 2006; Iacoboni & Dapretto, 2006; Ramachandran & Oberman, 2006; Williams et al., 2001). Thus, to understand and test the hypothesis, we must first examine the mirror neuron system (MNS). The core of the human mirror neuron system is the inferior parietal lobule (IPL) and inferior frontal gyrus (IFG; Rizzolatti & Craighero, 2004). Both of these regions respond robustly when hand actions are performed (Grafton, Mazziotta, Woods, & Phelps, 1992), imagined (Grafton, Arbib, Fadiga, & Rizzolatti, 1996), observed (Buccino et al., 2001), planned (Johnson et al., 2002), and imitated (Aziz-Zadeh, Koski, Zaidel, Mazziotta, & Iacoboni, 2006; Buccino et al., 2004b; Iacoboni et al., 1999) and are widely assumed to contain "mirror neurons" similar to those studied in equivalent regions of the macaque brain (Gallese, Fadiga, Fogassi, & Rizzolatti, 1996). Closely associated with the MNS is a region stretching from lateral occipital sulcus through middle temporal gyrus to the superior temporal sulcus (abbreviated to MTG for simplicity), which is robustly engaged in action observation tasks (Grossman & Blake, 2002) and is also modulated by motor performance (Astafiev, Stanley, Shulman, & Corbetta, 2004). Some definitions of the MNS also include more diverse regions showing "mirror" responses to pain (Singer et al., 2004), disgust (Wicker et al., 2003), and touch (Keysers et al., 2004), but the present paper focuses only on the core MNS in IFG, IPL, and MTG, which encodes human hand actions.

The mirror neuron regions of the human brain have several important functions. First, it is often forgotten that the MNS is part of the motor system, with an essential role in controlling our own actions (Grafton et al., 1992). The MNS is necessary for performing flexible, visually guided goal-directed hand actions, such as using a fork to eat or using a hammer to hit a nail. Damage to the MNS leads to apraxia, characterized by an inability to perform tool-use hand actions in daily life or to verbal or visual command (Buxbaum, Kyle, & Menon, 2005; Halsband et al., 2001; Heilman, Rothi, & Valenstein, 1982). Second, the MNS has attracted much attention in recent years because as well as its motor role, it has an important social function. In particular, the MNS is robustly activated by imitation tasks (Aziz-Zadeh et al., 2006; Buccino et al., 2004b; Iacoboni et al., 1999) and action observation tasks (Buccino et al., 2001). These activations are likely to reflect the role of the MNS in understanding the goal or meaning of an observed action (Buccino, Binkofski, & Riggio, 2004a; Hamilton & Grafton, 2006) and in predicting the future actions of another person (Kilner, Vargas, Duval, Blakemore, & Sirigu, 2004; Wilson & Knoblich, 2005). Based on these findings, we can make explicit the first prediction of the broken-mirror theory of autism. If children with autism have a dysfunctional mirror neuron system, we would expect them to be impaired in all the cognitive tasks that depend on the MNS—that is, performing goal-directed actions, imitating the actions of others, and understanding the goals of others. Evidence for and against the integrity of these cognitive abilities in autism are reviewed below.

However, the broken-mirror theory of autism claims to explain much more than just imitation behaviour. Researchers investigating the MNS have attempted to link this system to a wide variety of social functions, including language (Rizzolatti & Arbib, 1998), Theory of Mind (Gallese & Goldman, 1998), and empathy (Gallese, 2003). Despite the sparse evidence for some of these links, the broken-mirror theory makes the same claims, arguing that the lack of a functioning mirror neuron system could be the underlying cause of the disabilities in Theory of Mind and in emotion processing that have been observed in autism. The robustness of these more speculative claims are considered in the final section of the paper.

Testing the broken-mirror hypothesis

The first prediction of the broken-mirror hypothesis is that children with autism should perform poorly on tasks requiring the mirror neuron system, in particular tests of visuomotor control, imitation, and action understanding. Numerous studies have examined imitation abilities in children with autism (Hobson & Lee, 1999; Ohta, 1987; Rogers, Bennetto, McEvoy, & Pennington, 1996; Rogers, Hepburn, Stackhouse, & Wehner, 2003; Smith & Byrson, 1998), and a recent review concluded that children with autism are delayed in imitation skills relative to control children (Williams, Whiten, & Singh, 2004). This imitation data would seem to provide straightforward evidence in favour of the broken-mirror hypothesis.

However, some recent results cast doubt on this conclusion. I recently carried out a behavioural study of MNS function in autism, in collaboration with Rachel Brindley and Uta Frith (Hamilton, Brindley, & Frith, 2007). In order to assess goal emulation and goal understanding abilities in autism, we tested 25 autistic children with a verbal mental age around 4 years 6 months as well as 31 controls matched for verbal mental age. All the autistic children were substantially impaired on a battery of Theory of Mind tasks, as expected (Happé, 1995). However, when the children were tested on a goal-directed imitation task (Bekkering, Wohlschläger, & Gattis, 2000; Gattis, Bekkering, & Wohlschläger, 2002; Figure 1A), autistic children performed just the same as typically developing children. Both groups imitated the demonstrator's goal but failed to use the correct hand on contralateral trials, with good performance on all other trials (Figure 1C). In typical children, this systematic pattern of error has been taken as evidence that the children encode action goals rather than the means by which the goal is accomplished (Wohlschläger, Gattis, & Bekkering, 2003). Thus, the presence of hand errors on contralateral trials in the autistic group indicates that these children also understand the demonstrator's goal and emulate it.

We also examined motor planning and gesture understanding abilities in the same children. On a test of motor planning abilities (Rosenbaum et al., 1990), we found that both controls and the autistic group were better able to plan an action when the experimenter demonstrated the correct action first (Hamilton et al., 2007, Exp. 3). Finally, we tested children on gesture understanding, using stimuli developed for assessing patients with apraxia (Mozaz, Rothi, Anderson, Crucian, & Heilman, 2002; Figures 1B and 1D) and found that children with autism performed better than controls at this task (Hamilton et al., 2007, Exp. 4). That is, children with autism were better able to judge if a pictured gesture matched a cartoon, compared to their VMA-matched controls. Overall, we concluded that autistic children have no difficulties understanding the meaning of an action or imitating the goal of an action.

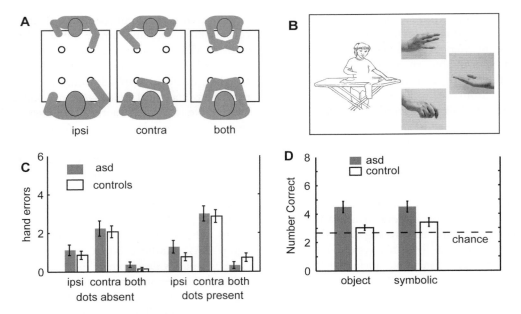

Figure 1. *Emulation in autism. (A) Goal-directed imitation task. Three possible trial types are illustrated, with the child as the upper figure and the adult demonstrator as the lower figure. On each trial, the child is required to copy the adult's action. The typical hand error is illustrated on the contralateral trial. (B) Gesture understanding task. One stimulus card is illustrated. The child was shown the cartoon and the pictures and was asked "which hands fill the gap?". Each child performed eight trials with object-use gestures and eight with symbolic gestures. (C) Performance on the goal-directed imitation task. Both control children and those with autism made substantially more errors on the contralateral trials when dots were present on the tabletop. (D) Performance on the gesture-understanding task. Autistic children gave significantly more correct responses than did control children.*

These results are not compatible with the broken-mirror theory of autism, but are congruent with several other studies. Two independent groups have used an incomplete intentions task (Meltzoff, 1995) with autistic children. In this task, the child sees an adult try and fail to perform a task and then has the chance to do the same task; Both groups report that children with autism emulate the adult's goal, just like typical children (Aldridge, Stone, Sweeney, & Bower, 2000; Carpenter, Pennington, & Rogers, 2001). Young children with autism are also able to imitate object-directed actions in order to receive nonsocial feedback in the form of lights and sounds (Ingersoll, Schreibman, & Tran, 2003). Other researchers have reported good imitation of object-use actions by children with autism (Stone, Ousley, & Littleford, 1997), good imitation of meaningful actions (Rogers et al., 1996),

and good performance on an explicit imitation task (Beadle-Brown & Whiten, 2004). Children with autism also have an intact ability to monitor their own actions and intentions (Russell & Hill, 2001). Two studies using neuroimaging methods in adults provide similar results. Adults with autism represent the goal of another person's action (Sebanz, Knoblich, Stumpf, & Prinz, 2005) and show normal brain responses during the observation of goal-directed actions (Avikainen, Kulomaki, & Hari, 1999).

To summarize, on a range of studies testing explicit, goal-directed imitation, both behaviour and neural activity were normal in the autistic population. These data are not compatible with a straightforward broken-mirror theory of autism in which the whole of the mirror neuron system is dysfunctional in these individuals.

Emulation and mimicry in autism

The data reviewed thus far present a challenge. If children with autism are passing a variety of tasks testing MNS function, what are we to make of the multitude of reports claiming profound imitation deficits in autism? For example, children with autism failed to mimic meaningless actions (Rogers et al., 1996; Stone et al., 1997) or gestures (Smith & Byrson, 1998). They make perspective errors on some meaningless imitation tasks (Ohta, 1987; Smith & Byrson, 1998) and have difficulties with common batteries of a mixture of imitation tasks (Charman et al., 1997; DeMeyer et al., 1972; Rogers et al., 2003). Work with adults suggests that mixed lists of meaningful and meaningless actions may all be treated as if they are meaningless (Tessari & Rumiati, 2004). Abnormal brain activity has also been reported in children with autism during tasks involving imitation of emotional facial expressions (Dapretto et al., 2006). Similarly, autistic children fail to show mu rhythm suppression (Oberman et al., 2005) or motor cortical facilitation (Theoret et al., 2005) during observation of meaningless actions.

Looking over these lists of tasks, we can see some similarities between those that the children with autism pass and those that they fail. Autistic children show normal performance and normal brain activity on imitation tasks that involve a goal or object. I classify these tasks as *emulation* tasks, using the word in the sense of goal emulation (Byrne & Russon, 2007). An individual who emulates an observed action must first obtain a teleological understanding of the goal or meaning of an action (Csibra, 2007) and may then, if she chooses, plan or reconstruct the action by her own means. Thus, emulation describes the process of goal-directed imitation (Bekkering et al., 2000; Wohlschläger et al., 2003), which I suggest is intact in children with autism (Hamilton et al., 2007).

In contrast, the tasks that children with autism fail can be broadly classified as *mimicry* tasks. That is, these tasks require the child to spontaneously copy the low-level, kinematic features of an action. The tested actions do not normally involve an object, but are either meaningless hand gestures or facial actions including emotional expressions. Typically developing children spontaneously mimic each other as a form of communication (Nadel, 2002), and typical adults unconsciously mimic each other's meaningless actions in order to facilitate social interaction (Chartrand & Bargh, 1999; Lakin & Chartrand, 2003). However, this spontaneous mimicry of meaningless actions appears to be lacking in children with autism. Some differences between emulation and mimicry are summarized in Table 1.

Further evidence for a distinction between emulation and mimicry in autism can be found in two studies that have examined both types of imitation. McIntosh and colleagues used electromyography to record from facial muscles and obtain an accurate, implicit measure of mimicry. They found that adults with autism did not show automatic mimicry of emotional facial expressions, but typical adults did. However, both groups showed the same responses when explicitly instructed to copy the expression they saw in the stimulus picture (McIntosh, Reichmann-Decker,

Table 1. *Characteristics of emulation and mimicry*

Emulation	Mimicry
Requires goal-oriented action representations	Uses low-level representations of kinematic features
Occurs in two stages: The E route involves understanding of the action goal while the P route involves planning a new action to achieve the goal	Occurs in a single stage, in the M route, which directly links visual and motor representations of kinematic features.
Relies particularly on inferior parietal lobule/anterior intraparietal sulcus	Relies on middle temporal gyrus/lateral occipital cortex and inferior frontal gyrus
Often explicit and controlled	Normally implicit and automatic
Intact in autism	Impaired in autism
Useful in practical situations such as gaining food or using tools	Useful in social situations such as building social affiliations

Winkielman, & Wilbarger, 2006). Thus, the adults with autism failed to spontaneously mimic but could emulate when the desired facial expression was explicitly set as a goal. A second behavioural study of children examined the imitation of both the style and goal of a novel action—for example, rattling two objects to make a sound either loudly or softly (Hobson & Lee, 1999). Hobson and Lee found that children with autism tended to imitate the goal of the action, they were able to hold the objects and make a sound, but did not spontaneously copy the style or manner in which the action was performed. That is, the children emulated the demonstrator, but did not mimic the precise style of the action.

Overall, these data demonstrate that the conclusion that children with autism show a global deficit in imitation is premature. Children with autism clearly have major difficulties with tasks requiring mimicry of style or of meaningless action. However, on a different subset of imitation tasks—those that involve using an object and those that require understanding the goal of an action—the autistic children are not impaired. These results mean that a global breakdown of the mirror neuron system is not found in autism, and therefore the broken-mirror hypothesis cannot be sustained. I now consider how our understanding of the mirror neuron system can be refined to accommodate these data.

Breaking up the mirror neuron system

If we are to understand the origins of the different types of imitation behaviour—emulation and mimicry—in typical individuals as well as those with autism, we must take a closer look at the mirror neuron system itself. Many previous neuroimaging studies of the human MNS (for example, Buccino et al., 2001; Buccino et al., 2004b) report activation in all three MNS nodes—that is, the inferior frontal gyrus (IFG) and inferior parietal lobule (IPL) and the middle temporal gyrus (MTG). Similarly, many theoretical approaches to the function of the MNS treat the system as a whole (Gallese, Keysers, & Rizzolatti, 2004; Keysers & Perrett, 2004;

Rizzolatti & Craighero, 2004) and do not systematically distinguish between the three different nodes. However, new work suggests that this idea of a unitary MNS is too simplistic. By examining the functions of the different components of the MNS, it is possible to obtain a new model of the cognitive and neural systems underlying human emulation and mimicry behaviour.

The first clue to the breakdown of the MNS comes from a neuroimaging study that I conducted to examine the representation of the goals of other people's actions in the brain. Several previous studies have attempted to localize goals or intentions in the human brain, reporting activity in IFG (Iacoboni et al., 2005) and in the superior temporal sulcus (Pelphrey, Morris, & McCarthy, 2004). However, both these studies used subtraction methods, which are not ideal for dealing with goals, because an action with the goal object or the goal context removed becomes a mime or a complex action, not a goal-less action. I have been able to bypass this problem by using a repetition suppression approach. Compared to observation of novel goals, observation of repeated goals results in suppression of activity in the anterior intraparietal sulcus (Hamilton & Grafton, 2006), part of the parietal node of the MNS. Because repetition suppression arises due to the population coding within a brain region (Grill-Spector, Henson, & Martin, 2006), this means that the anterior intraparietal sulcus contains populations of neurons that encode the object-goal of an observed action—for example, the goal of taking a cookie (Figure 2A).

A second study replicates and extends this finding. I used repetition suppression to differentiate between neural representations of the identity of a grasped object (wine-bottle or dumbbell) and the type of grasp used to take the object (a fingertip grasp on the neck of the wine bottle or a whole-hand grasp on the middle of the bottle; Hamilton & Grafton, 2007). As before, repetition suppression for the object-goal was found in the anterior intraparietal sulcus. In contrast, repetition suppression for the type of grasp was found in the other two MNS regions—IFG and MTG (Figure 2B).

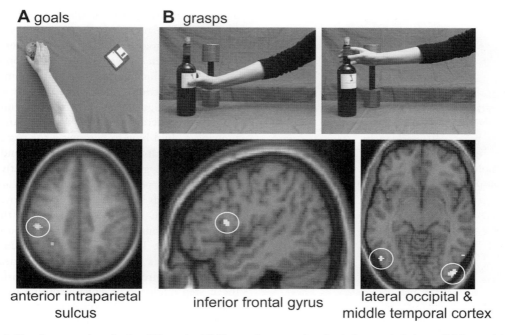

A goals **B** grasps

anterior intraparietal sulcus

inferior frontal gyrus

lateral occipital & middle temporal cortex

Figure 2. *Neural representations of goals and kinematics. (A) The neural representation of goals, for example, "take a cookie" (top row), is found in the left anterior intraparietal sulcus (bottom row). (B) The neural representation of grasps, for example, grasping a wine bottle with the whole hand compared to grasping it with the fingertips (top row) is found in the inferior frontal gyrus and lateral occipital cortex (bottom row).*

These results are consistent with several other studies that implicate the IPL in a more abstract, goal-oriented action representation than the IFG or MTG. Transcranial magnetic stimulation over the anterior intraparietal sulcus disrupts a person's ability to perform goal-directed hand actions (Tunik, Frey, & Grafton, 2005), and stroke damage to the IPL disrupts the ability to understand and imitate goal-directed actions (Buxbaum et al., 2005). Recordings from mirror neurons in the macaque parietal lobule reveals that these cells encode complex, goal-directed action sequences for both self and other (Fogassi et al., 2005). In contrast, studies of IFG suggest that this region is required for interpreting low-level action properties (Pobric & Hamilton, 2006; Urgesi, Candidi, Ionta, & Aglioti, 2007), and for performing grasping actions (Ehrsson et al., 2000; Rizzolatti et al., 1996).

Taking all these results together, it is now possible to build a cognitive model of visual-motor control and action understanding in the different components of the mirror neuron system (Figure 3). This model is described in detail elsewhere (Hamilton & Grafton, 2007), so only a brief summary is provided here. The key feature is that the three nodes of the MNS do not all perform the same function. Rather, the MTG node provides a visual representation of the low-level, kinematic parameters observed actions, the IPL node provides a more abstract representation of the goal of the observed action, and the IFG node provides a motor representation of the observed kinematic parameters, in preparation for imitating the action. These three nodes enable humans to plan and perform complex visually guided hand actions, to imitate another person's action, and to understand the meaning of that action.

Emulation and mimicry in the brain

Figure 3 illustrates the proposed localization of different visuo-motor representations of action in the brain. However, to understand imitation

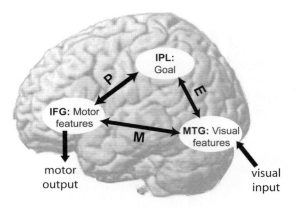

Figure 3. *The EP-M model. The EP-M model distinguishes three nodes for social-motor information processing within the mirror neuron system. The MTG (middle temporal gyrus) node provides a visual representation of kinematic features of observed actions; the IPL (inferior parietal lobule) node represents the goal of the action; and the IFG (inferior frontal gyrus) node contains a motor representation of the kinematic features of the action. There are three routes by which information can flow between these nodes. The E-route from MTG to IPL allows for emulation and understanding of the goal of an action, and the P-route from IPL to IFG allows for action planning. Together, these two form the indirect EP route, which supports goal-emulation behaviour. In contrast, the M-route from MTG to IFG allows the formation of direct associations from visual kinematic to motor kinematic representations and supports mimicry behaviours.*

behaviours, it is not enough to simply localize action representations; we must also understand how information flows between the different nodes. I now present a new model of cognitive information processing within the mirror neuron system, which provides an explanation for both emulation and mimicry behaviours and for the differential impairment of these behaviours in autism.

The primary route of information processing through the MNS is the EP route illustrated in Figure 3. There is clear anatomical evidence for this pathway in both humans (Catani, Jones, & ffytche, 2005) and macaques (Rozzi et al., 2006), and it is central to most models of MNS function (Keysers & Perrett, 2004). The important feature of the EP route is that imitation occurs in two stages. First, the visual representation of the observed action (in MTG) is used to infer the goal or meaning of the action (in IPL). The

process of inferring a goal, which is a key component of emulation behaviours, requires the E route. Once a goal representation is obtained, the P route can then be used to plan an action based on that goal, which may or may not be similar to the observed action. The planned action is represented in IFG, in terms of its motor parameters. To give a concrete example, consider an adult showing a child how to hammer a toy peg into a board. The adult takes the toy hammer and with an exaggerated gesture and sound, gently taps the top of one peg. The child watches carefully and understands that the aim of the toy is to sink the peg (E route). She then grabs the toy and with her thumbs forces the peg through the board (P route). The child has succeeded in emulating the adult's action, using her own means to achieve the desired goal. In other circumstances, the E step might occur alone, resulting in action understanding without copying. Or the child might form her own goal and use the P route to accomplish it, again without copying. But when the two steps occur together, the observed behaviour can be described as goal emulation. Previous theories have proposed that action understanding and skill learning depend on emulation abilities (Csibra, 2007; Wohlschläger et al., 2003), and the indirect EP route provides a route for emulation to occur.

However, increasing evidence suggests that the EP route is not the only way that information about actions is processed in the brain. Humans have a tendency to mimic the low-level kinematic features of observed actions (Chartrand & Bargh, 1999), and a series of studies demonstrate direct effects of a perceived action on the performance of a similar or different action (Brass, Bekkering, & Prinz, 2001; Heyes, 2001). Furthermore, observation of action interferes with performance of an incompatible action (Kilner, Paulignan, & Blakemore, 2003), and performance interferes with observation (Hamilton, Wolpert, & Frith, 2004). All of these effects are best explained by a direct M route (Figure 3), which allows immediate associations between visual representations of kinematic features and motor representations of the same kinematic features. For example, as two people watch each other dance across a nightclub, one might unconsciously copy the style and rhythm of the other, by representing the kinematic patterns of the observed dance in MTG and translating them by means of the M route directly to a motor representation in IFG. This behaviour might increase the social bond between the dancers, without either having an explicit goal in each dance move.

Though the behavioural evidence for the direct M route is powerful, there is an important reason to hesitate before allowing this route in the model. The majority of our data on neuro-anatomical connectivity comes from the macaque, but there is little anatomical evidence for a direct connection between middle temporal regions and inferior frontal gyrus in macaques. Thus, most reviews of the MNS in the macaque focus on the role of the EP route alone (Keysers & Perrett, 2004; Rizzolatti & Craighero, 2004). It is interesting to note here that the MNS regions in the macaque respond only to goal-directed actions (Fogassi et al., 2005; Gallese et al., 1996; Umiltà et al., 2001), consistent with the idea that the goal-mediated EP route is dominant in the monkey.

However, using anatomical studies of the macaque to draw conclusions about the function and structure of the human brain can be misleading. New studies using diffusion tensor imaging to track neural pathways suggest that a direct route between MTG and IFG may exist in humans (Catani et al., 2005; Rilling et al., 2006). These same studies also demonstrate dense interconnections between MTG and IPL (E route), and between IPL and IFG (P route). Overall, current anatomical data support the present proposal that imitation and action understanding can use both an indirect EP route via the IPL and an M route directly linking MTG to IFG. As a caveat, it is important to note that the human anatomical studies were conducted in the context of examining language processing, not the MNS. Further research will be needed to determine the exact termination of each neural path and their role in action processing.

Finally, the EP-M model presented in Figure 3 is a dual-route model of action processing. It is similar to previous dual-route schemes that have been proposed for the imitation of actions (Rothi, Ochipa, & Heilman, 1991; Tessari & Rumiati, 2004) and for language processing (Lichtheim, 1885). Drawing on this heritage, the EP-M model now maps the dual-route architecture to the brain in the context of the MNS. The EP route from MTG to IPL to IFG requires an understanding of the goal of an observed action in the IPL, which can then be planned and performed. The M route directly associates visual and motor kinematics, allowing automatic mimicry of actions without any abstract interpretation. In typical individuals, both routes may often be used together, but in neuropsychological populations, in individuals with autism or by using neuroimaging, it is now possible to distinguish between the two routes. Thus, the EP-M model makes new predictions for action representation in developmental and neuroimaging studies.

The EP-M model for autism

Of particular interest here is how the EP-M model can help us understand the pattern of performance in imitation tasks that we observed in children with autism. As summarized above, autistic children succeed on tasks requiring emulation of the goal of an action, but show abnormal performance on tasks requiring automatic mimicry. This behavioural distinction maps cleanly onto the EP-M model. In particular, I suggest that the indirect EP route is intact in children with autism, allowing the children to emulate an observed action if they understand the goal of the action. In contrast, the functioning of the direct M route may be compromised in autism, reducing the child's ability to spontaneously imitate a meaningless gesture or facial expression.

The EP and M pathways both start from the same visual representation of action, and both involve self−other processing, which means that purely perceptual theories (Behrmann et al., 2006) or self−other theories (Hobson, 1995) cannot account for the difference between the pathways. Furthermore, both the EP and M pathways involve the brain regions that make up the human MNS. Thus, the distinction between an intact EP route and a damaged M route in autism makes a radical reassessment of the broken-mirror hypothesis necessary. This hypothesis argued that the whole of the MNS is dysfunctional in autistic children (Ramachandran & Oberman, 2006; Williams et al., 2001). In contrast, the present data demonstrate that the MNS can be fractionated into two different pathways—the EP and M routes—while behavioural testing of children with autism indicates that the EP route is intact but the M route is compromised. Thus, we must reject the idea that a global MNS dysfunction—a single "broken-mirror"—is responsible for the disabilities in social interaction seen in autism. However, it is still possible that the MNS has some role in autism. In particular, the M route, which provides for direct associations between visual and motor kinematic representations, may be compromised in children with autism. Could a deficit in the M route alone be sufficient to cause the social impairments observed in autism and thus "rescue" part of the broken-mirror hypothesis?

There are several reasons to believe that mimicry behaviour has an important social function. Typical individuals do not mimic one another all the time, but must select who to mimic and when. Adults mimic when they want to enhance a social affiliation with another individual (Lakin & Chartrand, 2003), and being mimicked enhances prosocial behaviour (van Baaren, Holland, Kawakami, & van Knippenberg, 2004). However, too much mimicry is liable to be consciously detected and result in ridicule rather than friendship. Thus, mimicry behaviours must be carefully controlled to achieve a social bond. One possibility is that children with autism, with an impairment in the direct M route, fail to mimic and thus fail to gain the social advantages of mimicry. It is likely that the proponents of the broken-mirror theory would support this idea.

However, an alternative hypothesis is possible. Individuals with autism may have an intact M route, but might have difficulties modulating the route and deciding who and when to mimic. Thus, in some situations, children with autism might show excess mimicry (for example, echolalia or echopraxia), while in other situations they would fail to mimic at all. An intriguing recent experiment provides some support for this "top-down modulation hypothesis". When typical adults are required to inhibit their natural tendency to mimic observed actions, neural activation is found in the medial prefrontal cortex, precuneus, and bilateral temporal-parietal junction (Brass, Derrfuss, & von Cramon, 2005). This network of brain regions is commonly activated in tasks requiring inferences about other people's mental states—that is, Theory of Mind tasks (Frith & Frith, 2003). Impairments of Theory of Mind (Baron-Cohen et al., 1985; Happé, 1995) and abnormal activity in the Theory of Mind network (Castelli, Frith, Happé, & Frith, 2002; Happé et al., 1996) are characteristic of autism. The results of Brass and colleagues suggest that the Theory of Mind network may be responsible for controlling mimicry behaviour in typical adults. Thus, dysfunction of the "Theory of Mind network" could be a cause (not a consequence) of abnormalities of the direct M route and abnormal mimicry behaviour in autism.

Under this hypothesis, the mirror neuron system is not broken in autism. Rather, top-down modulation of the direct M route is abnormal, and this lack of modulation causes abnormal social behaviour. Such abnormalities in top-down modulation would have a devastating effect on mimicry but could also have a wider impact on other social and even nonsocial behaviours. For example, differences in top-down modulation of face processing (Bird, Catmur, Silani, Frith, & Frith, 2006) in autism might be able to account for some of the perceptual differences in autism (Behrmann et al., 2006). The top-down modulation hypothesis has much in common with the idea that weak central coherence is a defining characteristic of autism (Frith & Happé, 1994). In both cases, there is no single, low-level cognitive process that is impaired in autism; rather an imbalance in higher level processing can lead to a broad and varied array of impairments, in particular in social skills, as well as strengths in some nonsocial skills. Thus, we return to an appreciation of the complex mixture of cognitive abilities and disabilities seen in children with autism. And as so often in the past, Uta Frith's work gives an important insight into the cognitive systems underlying intact emulation behaviour and impaired mimicry behaviour in autism.

These last ideas are of course speculative and only hint at some ways in which we may be able to understand imitation behaviours in relation to autism. New experiments will be needed to determine whether a broken-mirror neuron system, a broken "M-route", a dysfunction of top-down modulation, or some other cause, can account for the varied profile of cognitive strengths and weaknesses seen in autism. The EP-M model provides one way in which to make sense of the varied performance of autistic children on imitation tasks and makes new predictions for future experiments in neuroimaging and developmental social neuroscience.

Conclusions

This paper aimed to examine and dissect the "broken-mirror" theory of autism, which argued that a dysfunction of the mirror neuron system is responsible for poor social skills in autism. I presented data demonstrating that children with autism are able to understand and emulate the goals of other people's actions, but may have difficulties with mimicry. This pattern of behaviour can be understood in terms of the EP-M model, in which there are two possible routes for imitation behaviour. The indirect EP route allows emulation and planning of goal-directed actions, while the direct M route associates low-level visual and motor representations. Current data suggest that the M route may be abnormal in autism, but the EP route intact. The EP-M model is compatible with the idea that individuals with autism have particular difficulties with top-down modulation of the M route, but further research will be needed to test this hypothesis.

REFERENCES

Aldridge, M. A., Stone, K. R., Sweeney, M. H., & Bower, T. G. R. (2000). Preverbal children with autism understand the intentions of others. *Developmental Science, 3,* 294.

Astafiev, S. V., Stanley, C. M., Shulman, G. L., & Corbetta, M. (2004). Extrastriate body area in human occipital cortex responds to the performance of motor actions. *Nature Neuroscience, 7,* 542–548.

Avikainen, S., Kulomaki, T., & Hari, R. (1999). Normal movement reading in Asperger subjects. *Neuroreport, 10,* 3467–3470.

Aziz-Zadeh, L., Koski, L., Zaidel, E., Mazziotta, J., & Iacoboni, M. (2006). Lateralization of the human mirror neuron system. *Journal of Neuroscience, 26,* 2964–2970.

Baron-Cohen, S. (2002). The extreme male brain theory of autism. *Trends in Cognitive Science, 6,* 248–254.

Baron-Cohen, S., Leslie, A. M., & Frith, U. (1985). Does the autistic child have a "theory of mind"? *Cognition, 21,* 37–46.

Baron-Cohen, S., Ring, H. A., Bullmore, E. T., Wheelwright, S., Ashwin, C., & Williams, S. C. (2000). The amygdala theory of autism. *Neuroscience and Biobehavioral Review, 24,* 355–364.

Beadle-Brown, J. D., & Whiten, A. (2004). Elicited imitation in children and adults with autism: Is there a deficit? *Journal of Intellectual & Developmental Disability, 29,* 147–163.

Behrmann, M., Thomas, C., & Humphreys, K. (2006). Seeing it differently: Visual processing in autism. *Trends in Cognitive Science, 10,* 258–264.

Bekkering, H., Wohlschläger, A., & Gattis, M. (2000). Imitation of gestures in children is goal-directed. *Quarterly Journal of Experimental Psychology, 53A,* 153–164.

Bird, G., Catmur, C., Silani, G., Frith, C., & Frith, U. (2006). Attention does not modulate neural responses to social stimuli in autism spectrum disorders. *Neuroimage, 31,* 1614–1624.

Brass, M., Bekkering, H., & Prinz, W. (2001). Movement observation affects movement execution in a simple response task. *Acta Psychologica, 106,* 3–22.

Brass, M., Derrfuss, J., & von Cramon, D. Y. (2005). The inhibition of imitative and overlearned responses: A functional double dissociation. *Neuropsychologia, 43,* 89–98.

Buccino, G., Binkofski, F., Fink, G. R., Fadiga, L., Fogassi, L., Gallese, V., et al. (2001). Action observation activates premotor and parietal areas in a somatotopic manner: An fMRI study. *European Journal of Neuroscience*, *13*, 400–404.

Buccino, G., Binkofski, F., & Riggio, L. (2004a). The mirror neuron system and action recognition. *Brain and Language*, *89*, 370–376.

Buccino, G., Vogt, S., Ritzl, A., Fink, G. R., Zilles, K., Freund, H. J., et al. (2004b). Neural circuits underlying imitation learning of hand actions: An event-related fMRI study. *Neuron*, *42*, 323–334.

Buxbaum, L. J., Kyle, K. M., & Menon, R. (2005). On beyond mirror neurons: Internal representations subserving imitation and recognition of skilled object-related actions in humans. *Brain Research: Cognitive Brain Research*, *25*, 226–239.

Byrne, R. W., & Russon, A. E. (1998). Learning by imitation: A hierarchical approach. *Behavioral and Brain Sciences*, *21*, 667–684; discussion 684–721.

Carpenter, M., Pennington, B. F., & Rogers, S. J. (2001). Understanding of others' intentions in children with autism. *Journal of Autism and Developmental Disorders*, *31*, 589–599.

Castelli, F., Frith, C., Happé, F., & Frith, U. (2002). Autism, Asperger syndrome and brain mechanisms for the attribution of mental states to animated shapes. *Brain*, *125*, 1839–1849.

Catani, M., Jones, D. K., & ffytche, D. H. (2005). Perisylvian language networks of the human brain. *Annals of Neurology*, *57*, 8–16.

Charman, T., Swettenham, J., Baron-Cohen, S., Cox, A., Baird, G., & Drew, A. (1997). Infants with autism: An investigation of empathy, pretend play, joint attention, and imitation. *Developmental Psychology*, *33*, 781–789.

Chartrand, T. L., & Bargh, J. A. (1999). The chameleon effect: The perception–behavior link and social interaction. *Journal of Personality and Social Psychology*, *76*, 893–910.

Csibra, G. (2007). Action mirroring and action understanding: An alternative account. In P. Haggard, Y. Rossetti, & M. Kawato (Eds.), *Attention and performance: XXII. Sensorimotor foundations of higher cognition*. Oxford: Oxford University Press.

Dapretto, M., Davies, M. S., Pfeifer, J. H., Scott, A. A., Sigman, M., Bookheimer, S. Y., et al. (2006). Understanding emotions in others: Mirror neuron dysfunction in children with autism spectrum disorders. *Nature Neuroscience*, *9*, 28–30.

DeMeyer, M. K., Alpern, G. D., Barton, S., DeMyer, W. E., Churchill, D. W., Hingtgen, J. N., et al. (1972). Imitation in autistic, early schizophrenic, and non-psychotic subnormal children. *Journal of Autism and Childhood Schizophrenia*, *2*, 264–287.

Ehrsson, H. H., Fagergren, A., Jonsson, T., Westling, G., Johansson, R. S., & Forssberg, H. (2000). Cortical activity in precision- versus power-grip tasks: An fMRI study. *Journal of Neurophysiology*, *83*, 528–536.

Fogassi, L., Ferrari, P. F., Gesierich, B., Rozzi, S., Chersi, F., & Rizzolatti, G. (2005). Parietal lobe: From action organization to intention understanding. *Science*, *308*, 662–667.

Frith, U. (2003). *Autism: Explaining the enigma*: Oxford, UK: Blackwell Publishing.

Frith, U., & Frith, C. D. (2003). Development and neurophysiology of mentalizing. *Philosophical Transactions of the Royal Society of London. Series B*, *358*, 459–473.

Frith, U., & Happé, F. (1994). Autism: Beyond "theory of mind". *Cognition*, *50*, 115–132.

Frith, U., Morton, J., & Leslie, A. M. (1991). The cognitive basis of a biological disorder: Autism. *Trends in Neuroscience*, *14*, 433–438.

Gallese, V. (2003). The manifold nature of interpersonal relations: The quest for a common mechanism. *Philosophical Transactions of the Royal Society of London. Series B*, *358*, 517–528.

Gallese, V., Fadiga, L., Fogassi, L., & Rizzolatti, G. (1996). Action recognition in the premotor cortex. *Brain*, *119*, 593–609.

Gallese, V., & Goldman, A. (1998). Mirror neurons and the simulation theory of mind-reading. *Trends in Cognitive Sciences*, *2*, 493–501.

Gallese, V., Keysers, C., & Rizzolatti, G. (2004). A unifying view of the basis of social cognition. *Trends in Cognitive Sciences*, *8*, 396–403.

Gattis, M., Bekkering, H., & Wohlschläger, A. (2002). Goal directed imitation. In A. Meltzoff & W. Prinz (Eds.), *The imitative mind: Development, evolution and brain bases*. Cambridge, UK: Cambridge University Press.

Grafton, S. T., Arbib, M. A., Fadiga, L., & Rizzolatti, G. (1996). Localization of grasp representations in humans by positron emission tomography. 2. Observation compared with imagination. *Experimental Brain Research*, *112*, 103–111.

Grafton, S. T., Mazziotta, J. C., Woods, R. P., & Phelps, M. E. (1992). Human functional anatomy of visually guided finger movements. *Brain*, *115*, 565–587.

Grill-Spector, K., Henson, R., & Martin, A. (2006). Repetition and the brain: Neural models of stimulus-specific effects. *Trends in Cognitive Sciences*, *10*, 14–23.

Grossman, E. D., & Blake, R. (2002). Brain areas active during visual perception of biological motion. *Neuron, 35*, 1167–1175.

Halsband, U., Schmitt, J., Weyers, M., Binkofski, F., Grutzner, G., & Freund, H. J. (2001). Recognition and imitation of pantomimed motor acts after unilateral parietal and premotor lesions: A perspective on apraxia. *Neuropsychologia, 39*, 200–216.

Hamilton, A., Brindley, R., & Frith, U. (2007). Imitation and action representation in autistic spectrum disorders: How valid is the hypothesis of a deficit in the mirror neuron system? *Neuropsychologia, 45*, 1859–1868.

Hamilton, A., & Grafton, S. T. (2006). Goal representation in human anterior intraparietal sulcus. *Journal of Neuroscience, 26*, 1133–1137.

Hamilton, A., & Grafton, S. T. (2007). The motor hierarchy: From kinematics to goals and intentions. In P. Haggard, Y. Rossetti, & M. Kawato (Eds.), *Attention and performance: XXII. Sensorimotor foundations of higher cognition*. Oxford: Oxford University Press.

Hamilton, A., Wolpert, D., & Frith, U. (2004). Your own action influences how you perceive another person's action. *Current Biology, 14*, 493–498.

Happé, F. (1995). The role of age and verbal ability in the theory of mind task performance of subjects with autism. *Child Development, 66*, 843–855.

Happé, F., Ehlers, S., Fletcher, P., Frith, U., Johansson, M., Gillberg, C., et al. (1996). "theory of mind" in the brain. Evidence from a PET scan study of Asperger syndrome. *Neuroreport, 8*, 197–201.

Heilman, K. M., Rothi, L. J., & Valenstein, E. (1982). Two forms of ideomotor apraxia. *Neurology, 32*, 342–346.

Heyes, C. (2001). Causes and consequences of imitation. *Trends in Cognitive Sciences, 5*, 253–261.

Hobson, R. P. (1995). *Autism and the development of mind*. Hove, UK: Psychology Press.

Hobson, R. P., & Lee, A. (1999). Imitation and identification in autism. *Journal of Child Psychology and Psychiatry, 40*, 649–659.

Iacoboni, M., & Dapretto, M. (2006). The mirror neuron system and the consequences of its dysfunction. *Nature Reviews Neuroscience, 7*, 942–951.

Iacoboni, M., Molnar-Szakacs, I., Gallese, V., Buccino, G., Mazziotta, J. C., & Rizzolatti, G. (2005). Grasping the intentions of others with one's own mirror neuron system. *PLoS Biology, 3*, e79.

Iacoboni, M., Woods, R. P., Brass, M., Bekkering, H., Mazziotta, J. C., & Rizzolatti, G. (1999). Cortical mechanisms of human imitation. *Science, 286*, 2526–2528.

Ingersoll, B., Schreibman, L., & Tran, Q. H. (2003). Effect of sensory feedback on immediate object imitation in children with autism. *Journal of Autism and Developmental Disorders, 33*, 673–683.

Johnson, S. H., Rotte, M., Grafton, S. T., Hinrichs, H., Gazzaniga, M. S., & Heinze, H. J. (2002). Selective activation of a parietofrontal circuit during implicitly imagined prehension. *Neuroimage, 17*, 1693–1704.

Keysers, C., & Perrett, D. I. (2004). Demystifying social cognition: A Hebbian perspective. *Trends in Cognitive Sciences, 8*, 501–507.

Keysers, C., Wicker, B., Gazzola, V., Anton, J. L., Fogassi, L., & Gallese, V. (2004). A touching sight: Sii/pv activation during the observation and experience of touch. *Neuron, 42*, 335–346.

Kilner, J. M., Paulignan, Y., & Blakemore, S. J. (2003). An interference effect of observed biological movement on action. *Current Biology, 13*, 522–525.

Kilner, J. M., Vargas, C., Duval, S., Blakemore, S. J., & Sirigu, A. (2004). Motor activation prior to observation of a predicted movement. *Nature Neuroscience, 7*, 1299–1301.

Lakin, J. L., & Chartrand, T. L. (2003). Using nonconscious behavioral mimicry to create affiliation and rapport. *Psychological Science, 14*, 334–339.

Lichtheim, L. (1885). On aphasia. *Brain, 7*, 433–484.

McIntosh, D. N., Reichmann-Decker, A., Winkielman, P., & Wilbarger, J. L. (2006). When the social mirror breaks: Deficits in automatic, but not voluntary, mimicry of emotional facial expressions in autism. *Developmental Science, 9*, 295–302.

Meltzoff, A. (1995). Understanding the intentions of others: Re-enactment of intended acts by 18-month-old children. *Developmental Psychology, 31*, 838–850.

Mozaz, M., Rothi, L. J., Anderson, J. M., Crucian, G. P., & Heilman, K. M. (2002). Postural knowledge of transitive pantomimes and intransitive gestures. *Journal of the International Neuropsychological Society, 8*, 958–962.

Nadel, J. (2002). Imitation and imitation recognition: Functional use in preverbal infants and nonverbal children with autism. In A. Meltzoff & W. Prinz (Eds.), *The imitative mind: Development, evolution and brain bases*. Cambridge, UK: Cambridge University Press.

Oberman, L. M., Hubbard, E. M., McCleery, J. P., Altschuler, E. L., Ramachandran, V. S., & Pineda, J. A. (2005). EEG evidence for mirror neuron dysfunction in autism spectrum disorders. *Brain Research: Cognitive Brain Research, 24*, 190–198.

Ohta, M. (1987). Cognitive disorders of infantile autism: A study employing the WISC, spatial relationship conceptualization, and gesture imitations. *Journal of Autism & Developmental Disorders, 17*, 45–62.

Pelphrey, K. A., Morris, J. P., & McCarthy, G. (2004). Grasping the intentions of others: The perceived intentionality of an action influences activity in the superior temporal sulcus during social perception. *Journal of Cognitive Neuroscience, 16*, 1706–1716.

Pobric, G., & Hamilton, A. F. (2006). Action understanding requires the left inferior frontal cortex. *Current Biology, 16*, 524–529.

Ramachandran, V. S., & Oberman, L. M. (2006). Broken mirrors: A theory of autism. *Scientific American*.

Rilling, J. K., Glasser, M. F., Preuss, T. M., Ma, X., Zhang, X., Zhao, T., et al. (2006). A comparative diffusion tensor imaging study of the arcuate fasiculus pathway in humans, chimpanzees and rhesus macaques. *Society of Neuroscience Abstracts*.

Rizzolatti, G., & Arbib, M. A. (1998). Language within our grasp. *Trends in Neuroscience, 21*, 188–194.

Rizzolatti, G., & Craighero, L. (2004). The mirror-neuron system. *Annual Review of Neuroscience, 27*, 169–192.

Rizzolatti, G., Fadiga, L., Matelli, M., Bettinardi, V., Paulesu, E., Perani, D., et al. (1996). Localization of grasp representations in humans by PET: 1. Observation versus execution. *Experimental Brain Research, 111*, 246–252.

Rogers, S. J., Bennetto, L., McEvoy, R., & Pennington, B. F. (1996). Imitation and pantomime in high-functioning adolescents with autism spectrum disorders. *Child Development, 67*, 2060–2073.

Rogers, S. J., Hepburn, S. L., Stackhouse, T., & Wehner, E. (2003). Imitation performance in toddlers with autism and those with other developmental disorders. *Journal of Child Psychology and Psychiatry, 44*, 763–781.

Rosenbaum, D. A., Marchak, F., Barnes, H. J., Jonathan Vaughan, James D. Slotta, & Jorgensen, M. J. (1990). Constraints for action selection: Overhand versus underhand grips. In M. Jeannerod (Ed.), *Attention and performance XIII: Motor representation and control* (pp. 321–342): Hillsdale, NJ: Lawrence Erlbaum Associates.

Rothi, L. J., Ochipa, C., & Heilman, K. M. (1991). A cognitive neuropsychological model of limb praxis. *Cognitive Neuropsychology, 8*, 443–458.

Rozzi, S., Calzavara, R., Belmalih, A., Borra, E., Gregoriou, G. G., Matelli, M., et al. (2006). Cortical connections of the inferior parietal cortical convexity of the macaque monkey. *Cerebral Cortex, 16*, 1389–1417.

Russell, J., & Hill, E. L. (2001). Action-monitoring and intention reporting in children with autism. *Journal of Child Psychology and Psychiatry, 42*, 317–328.

Sebanz, N., Knoblich, G., Stumpf, L., & Prinz, W. (2005). Far from action blind: Action representation in individuals with autism. *Cognitive Neuropsychology, 22*, 433–454.

Singer, T., Seymour, B., O'Doherty, J., Kaube, H., Dolan, R. J., & Frith, C. D. (2004). Empathy for pain involves the affective but not sensory components of pain. *Science, 303*, 1157–1162.

Smith, I. M., & Byrson, S. E. (1998). Gesture imitation in autism: 1. Nonsymbolic postures and sequences. *Cognitive Neuropsychology, 15*, 747–770.

Stone, W. L., Ousley, O. Y., & Littleford, C. D. (1997). Motor imitation in young children with autism: What's the object? *Journal of Abnormal Child Psychology, 25*, 475–485.

Tessari, A., & Rumiati, R. I. (2004). The strategic control of multiple routes in imitation of actions. *Journal of Experimental Psychology: Human Perception and Performance, 30*, 1107–1116.

Theoret, H., Halligan, E., Kobayashi, M., Fregni, F., Tager-Flusberg, H., & Pascual-Leone, A. (2005). Impaired motor facilitation during action observation in individuals with autism spectrum disorder. *Current Biology, 15*, R84–R85.

Tunik, E., Frey, S. H., & Grafton, S. T. (2005). Virtual lesions of the anterior intraparietal area disrupt goal-dependent on-line adjustments of grasp. *Nature Neuroscience, 8*, 505–511.

Umiltà, M. A., Kohler, E., Gallese, V., Fogassi, L., Fadiga, L., Keysers, C., et al. (2001). I know what you are doing. A neurophysiological study. *Neuron, 31*, 155–165.

Urgesi, C., Candidi, M., Ionta, S., & Aglioti, S. M. (2007). Representation of body identity and body actions in extrastriate body area and ventral premotor cortex. *Nature Neuroscience, 10*, 30–31.

van Baaren, R. B., Holland, R. W., Kawakami, K., & van Knippenberg, A. (2004). Mimicry and prosocial behavior. *Psychological Science, 15*, 71–74.

Wicker, B., Keysers, C., Plailly, J., Royet, J. P., Gallese, V., & Rizzolatti, G. (2003). Both of us disgusted in my insula: The common neural basis of seeing and feeling disgust. *Neuron, 40*, 655–664.

Williams, J. H., Whiten, A., & Singh, T. (2004). A systematic review of action imitation in autistic spectrum disorder. *Journal of Autism and Developmental Disorders, 34*, 285–299.

Williams, J. H., Whiten, A., Suddendorf, T., & Perrett, D. I. (2001). Imitation, mirror neurons and autism. *Neuroscience and Biobehavioral Reviews, 25*, 287–295.

Wilson, M., & Knoblich, G. (2005). The case for motor involvement in perceiving conspecifics. *Psychological Bulletin, 131*, 460–473.

Wohlschläger, A., Gattis, M., & Bekkering, H. (2003). Action generation and action perception in imitation: An instance of the ideomotor principle. *Philosophical Transactions of the Royal Society of London. Series B, 358*, 501–515.

THE QUARTERLY JOURNAL OF EXPERIMENTAL PSYCHOLOGY
2008, 61 (1), 116–128

What can autism and dyslexia tell us about intelligence?

Mike Anderson

The University of Western Australia, Perth, Australia

This paper argues that understanding developmental disorders requires developing theories and models that explicitly represent the role of general intelligence in the cognitive phenotype of the disorder. In the case of autism it is argued that the low-IQ scores of people with autism are not likely to be due to a deficit in the cognitive process that is arguably the major cause of mental retardation—namely, speed of processing—but rather low IQ reflects the pervasive and cascading effects of the deficit in the information-processing module that causes autism. In the case of dyslexia, two radically different models of reading disorder (ability = disability and a modular deficit model) are likely to be influenced by the effect of general intelligence on reading performance in ways that will remain unclear without an explicit model of how general intelligence influences reading.

I think it was Donald Broadbent who used the analogy of waves on a beach to describe progress in psychology. The idea is that particular waves push up the beach but inevitably fall back into the sea with the gains or advances made by individual waves largely unrecognized. Another set of waves then wash over the same territory as if anew, only in their turn to fall back again. And yet remorselessly the tide comes in. This captures a truth of science in general—namely, that what is truly novel rarely succeeds, and what succeeds is never truly novel. As Dorothy Bishop (2008 this issue) has pointed out, Uta Frith has been one of the major wave-makers in our field for over 40 years, particularly in our understanding of both autism and dyslexia. It is also clear that Uta's great contribution has been made against the backdrop of a number of

developments of that time, many of which still ebb and flow to this day.

The fact that Uta has made a contribution to not just one, but two, major developmental disorders is significant. This is because 40 years ago the context in which developmental disorders such as autism were studied was perhaps broader than the one that faces us currently. That context was one where studies of developmental disorders were conducted in concert with two other intellectual waves of the time—one was the application of new techniques and ideas from both experimental psychology and cognitive development, and the other was the attempt to understand intellectual development in the "subnormal". Both of those approaches were pioneered by two of Uta's mentors—Neil O'Connor and Beate Hermelin

Correspondence should be addressed to Professor Mike Anderson, School of Psychology, The University of Western Australia, 35 Stirling Highway, Crawley, Perth, Western Australia, 6009, Australia. E-mail: mike@psy.uwa.edu.au

The author would like to thank Uta Frith for the inspiration that her work and her personality have provided over many years. The Australian Research Council has supported this work through its discovery grant to the author (DP0665616) and colleagues, Allison Fox, Corinne Reid, and Dorothy Bishop. Thanks to members of the Neurocognitive Development Unit and the BigLab for feedback.

DOI:10.1080/17470210701508806

(see particularly, Hermelin & O'Connor, 1970; O'Connor & Hermelin, 1963). The significance of this is two-fold. First, at that time it was pretty much taken for granted that the purpose of studying developmental disorders was because of the light they cast on more general issues of child development. Second, at that time the relationship between specific developmental disorders and development in the face of general mental retardation was seen as the core issue. In my view both of those contexts no longer apply. Most research in developmental disorders has evolved to understand the disorder for its own sake, and the backdrop of both typical development and the role of general intelligence in understanding developmental disorders have receded over the past 30 years.

In the spirit in which I began this paper I attempt to surf a new wave—one that recognizes advances made both in our understanding of general intelligence and in our understanding of genetic influences on cognition. The principal aim is to argue that models of developmental disorders should explicitly accommodate general intelligence. I first give a pencil sketch of what we have learned in the last 40 years or so about intelligence and how it relates to the two developmental disorders that have been central to Uta's career—autism and dyslexia. I then use a theory of intelligence and development to demonstrate how explicitly representing general intelligence in our models of disorders illuminates our understanding of the cause of disorders and also, in turn, allows developmental disorders to inform our theories of intelligence. In this small way I hope to help bring issues that nurtured Uta in her early days into the foreground of current research.

Changing conceptions of intelligence

The 1960s was probably the nadir of Spearman's concept of general intelligence or g (Spearman, 1904). Leaving aside what seemed to be interminable disputes between alternative factor analytic solutions of the same set of data, there were two main reasons for this. The first was the rise of

cognitive psychology. One of the central goals of cognitive psychology is the specification of the means by which thought processes are instantiated. It became clear from very early on that this specification would vary enormously depending on the thinking task to be analysed and the kinds of processes hypothesized to be involved. In other words the very basis of cognitive psychology is largely antithetical to the notion of general intelligence. The second was the dominance of empiricist views of learning and development that were opposed to alternative nativist or genetic views of mind and its development. It didn't help that all things genetic had been tainted in no small part by associations with odious political philosophies such as eugenics or even Nazism. However, it is important to note that general intelligence is not in principle incompatible with cognitive psychology (as I hope to show), nor is it the case that genetic influence could not just as readily be found for specific abilities (indeed this is where much of the current activity lies). Yet, a concept of general intelligence that played no part in the theoretical structure of cognitive psychology but that was associated with genetics made it inevitable that a consideration of general intelligence would rapidly become a no-go area for cognitive psychologists, including developmentalists (see Anderson, 2000; Jensen, 2000, for a debate on this issue).

So what have we learned about general intelligence in the past 40 years that might make it intellectually respectable again? For the full story (not to say polemic) I would urge you to consult Jensen (1998) and Deary (2000), and for a more theoretical defence of the concept of g I would draw your attention to Anderson (1992, 2001), but the main reasons are as follows:

- The development of ever more sophisticated data analytic techniques, particularly structural equation modelling, tipped the balance in favour of models that posit a general factor as opposed to those that do not (Gustafson, 1984).
- A great deal of empirical research seemed to validate the concept of g as a property of speed of information processing. The impetus for the

speed of processing hypothesis is the finding that elementary cognitive tasks with little or no knowledge content, such as reaction time (Jensen, 1982) and inspection time (Nettelbeck, 1987) tasks, are nevertheless correlated with knowledge-rich intelligence test performance (Anderson, 1992). The rationale of the speed of processing hypothesis is that because these elementary cognitive tasks are so easy they leave no room for intelligent strategic variation, and differences in performance can only be attributed to differences in the speed with which stimuli are processed and simple decisions are made: hence the hypothesis that simple elementary cognitive tasks and knowledge-rich intelligence tests share common speed variance. This hypothesis found wide application in explaining not only differences in IQ but changing intellectual abilities in children and elderly adults.

- The rise of behaviour genetics has generated data that is most compatible with the idea that general intelligence is the major heritable component of individual differences in cognitive abilities.
- Cognitive and cognitive neuropsychologists have begun to take fluid intelligence (g by any other name) seriously: some sticking with the view that differences in fluid intelligence are based on differences in speed of processing (Salthouse, 2000), others arguing that working memory is the basis of g (Colom, Rebollo, Palacios, Juan-Espinosa, & Kyllonen, 2004), and others that it is goal maintenance (some might call this version executive functioning) that requires the involvement of the frontal lobes of the brain (Duncan, Emslie, & Williams, 1996), and yet others that there are two dimensions to g, one related to individual differences in IQ and speed of processing, and the other to developmental change and executive functioning (Anderson, 2001). The point is that g, or general intelligence, has became a respectable line of enquiry once again.

The theory of the minimal cognitive architecture of intelligence and development

There is one current cognitive theory of intelligence that places general intelligence at centre stage (Anderson, 1992). Of particular note in this context is that the goal of this theory was to not only explain individual differences in intelligence but also to explain the development of intelligence. Furthermore, while this theory places the notion of general intelligence in the centre of its research agenda, it also considers that exceptions to the rule of general intelligence were just as important for understanding intelligence. It is in this context that the theory is relevant to developmental disorders. The structure of the theory was motivated by what I consider to be the most important distinction made in cognitive science in the 1980s—Fodor's (1983) distinction between input modules and central processes of thought. In my view much of the current misunderstanding about whether the mind is or is not modular and whether, by extension, developmental disorders do or do not have a modular basis is based on a failure to appreciate both classes of process. Almost everyone since Fodor has focused on modularity, neglecting the point that a consideration of modularity took up only half of Fodor's seminal work and in many ways can only be appreciated in the light of nonmodularity. That the mind clearly has modular and nonmodular domains is a key feature of my own theory of intelligence and has major ramifications for the cause of developmental disorders and more specifically for the role of genes in that cause.

The theory of the minimal cognitive architecture was developed to explain a number of regularities and exceptions to those regularities that a psychological theory of intelligence and its development should be able to explain. The regularities are: (a) the phenomenon of general intelligence—marked most clearly by the observation that all thinking abilities are correlated; (b) a characteristic pattern of development where most abilities that typically end up on an omnibus test of intelligence such as the Wechsler scales undergo large developmental change in the years up to about late teens when most measured performance reaches a plateau—thenceforth there is a difference of view as to whether it then manifests a long but very slow decline or performance maintains itself till shortly before death; (c) there is a stability in general intelligence over a time-span from about 5 years onwards—this is despite the fact that the measures of intelligence can have almost no knowledge items in common across the span of child development, and indeed the stability is found until a very old age (Deary, Whiteman, Starr, Whalley, & Fox, 2004).

While explaining these regularities should be a central objective of any theory of intelligence and development, it is also the case that there are a number of exceptions to these regularities that are as important. The main exceptions are indicated as follows: (a) there are specific cognitive abilities that, while influenced by *g*, nevertheless show some independence of *g*—in psychometric terms they have usually been thought of as the major group abilities, primarily verbal and spatial ability; (b) savant syndrome, where individuals with IQs in the mentally retarded range can nevertheless perform a remarkable cognitive feat—for example, great musicianship or drawing artistry, or feats of calculation; (c) some individuals with high IQs have great difficulty in performing a task that is relatively easy even for someone of substantially lower IQ—for example, reading—and consequently it is claimed that they have a specific cognitive deficit; (d) there is a conundrum of "computational complexity", where people with mental retardation are capable of processing information that is massively computationally complex (as calculated by how difficult it is to have a computer do it), such as identifying faces or perceiving human movement or understanding the meaning of spoken sentences, but are often incapable of performing extremely computationally simple functions like adding numbers together. All these exceptions argue that there is more to intelligence than *g*. Fully justifying the claim that the theory of the minimal cognitive architecture can explain both the regularities and exceptions listed in the agenda required a whole book (Anderson, 1992). For present purposes it is enough to simply state the main tenets of the theory (see Figure 1), the most important of which is the agreement with Fodor that there are two routes to knowledge.

The first route to knowledge is through *thought* (central processes), and this is the route that is

related to differences in IQ. Thoughtful problem solving can be done either by "verbalizing" a problem (crudely put, using language-like propositions to think) or by "visualizing" it (using visuo-spatial representations to think). In the theory this is accomplished by having two different kinds of knowledge acquisition routines, each generated by one of two specific processors. The speed of a basic processing mechanism (BPM) constrains the complexity of these routines—slow speed can only support simple routines. It is this constraint that is the basis of individual differences in *g*. While estimates of the speed of the BPM can be derived from inspection time and reaction time tasks, arguably developmental change in these tasks, particularly reaction time, can be attributed to response selection components of performance and not speed of processing per se (Anderson, 1989; Anderson, Nettelbeck, & Barlow, 1997). Indeed, a specific proposal of the theory is that the speed of the BPM does not change through childhood, and consequently speed of processing cannot be the basis of a developmental *g*.

The second route for acquiring the knowledge that will influence intelligence test performance is through dedicated information processing *modules*, and it is this route that is related to cognitive development. In the theory there are three kinds of modules. Mark I modules have evolved to provide information about the environment that could not be provided by central processes of thought (Route 1 knowledge acquisition) in an ecologically useful time frame. For example, if we had to "think through" all the perceptual information presented to us in order to construct a three-dimensional view of the world we would be literally lost in thought. Because this activity is so important to us and requires great computational power and speed, evolution has created special modular devices to allow us to do this automatically. Other examples of likely Mark I modules are various language acquisition devices, face recognition systems, and perhaps some systems that provide us with important social information, such as "cheater detection". Mark II modules are the fetch and carry mechanisms of the information-processing system. They would

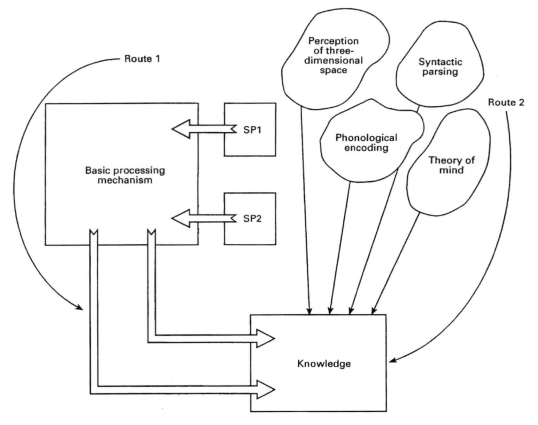

Figure 1. *The theory of the minimal cognitive architecture underlying intelligence and development. From* Intelligence and development: A cognitive theory *(p. 107), by M. Anderson, 1992, Oxford: Blackwell. Copyright 1992 by M. Anderson. Reprinted with permission.*

include devices for retrieving items from long-term memory, certain kinds of attentional and inhibitory processes related to what might be called executive functions, and, most importantly for the present discussion, the core computational procedures involved in acquiring a theory of mind. Mark III modules are specific processing systems that are acquired through extensive practice to master one task or one task domain. It is likely that the architecture of processing underlying these acquired modules would be connectionist, allowing the possibility of considerable cognitive skill in the absence of thought, as in the case, for example, of a savant calendrical calculator (Norris, 1990). The theory proposes that developmental *g* is based on the acquisition and

maturation of modules, particularly those Mark II modules underlying executive functions.

The role of intelligence and modularity in autism and dyslexia

Autism and dyslexia can be considered as classical developmental disorders within the theory of the minimal cognitive architecture. According to this theory they are caused by a deficit in a very specific information-processing module (say, a theory of mind, ToM, module in the case of autism and a phonological "processing" module in the case of dyslexia). In this case it might be argued that the role of intelligence is, by theoretical definition, irrelevant to a consideration of the disorder (because, simply put, modular functions are independent of speed of processing and therefore general intelligence). However, this gets to the heart of the matter for this paper. In the case of autism there are two different reasons why people with autism may in general have low IQs. One reason has little or no impact on our understanding of either autism or intelligence, and for the other the impact is theoretically very important. Consequently, it matters why people with autism have low IQs. In the case of dyslexia, even if the primary cause was a modular deficit, such is the influence of general intelligence that under any plausible diagnostic system a substantial proportion of individuals would be so diagnosed because of the influence of general intelligence and not because they have the requisite modular deficit. Moreover this is influenced by how intelligence is factored into diagnosis and in ways that are not altogether obvious. Building intelligence explicitly into our model of disorder allows this influence to be predictable and perhaps even law-like. My central point is that in both cases an explicit consideration of general intelligence provides key insights into the nature of the disorder.

Intelligence and autism

Hermelin and O'Connor (1970) were the first to systematically study the cognitive abilities of children with autism using experimental techniques and ideas from cognitive psychology, and they did so acknowledging that the children, despite having low IQs, were not classically "subnormal". Uta Frith fleshed out these early observations about the relationship between intelligence and cognition in autistic people in a number of crucial ways, and the basic data are relatively straightforward and well known.

First, autism is associated with mental retardation. Most children with autism have low IQs, and, importantly, their IQ is about as predictive of their functional capacity (the ability to live independently for example) as it is for nonautistic people—a point that Frith (1983) has stressed. Recently it has been emphasized that some autistic people display what look like normal or even superior levels of intelligence. That this might

represent something of a different case is evident in the formation of a different diagnostic category, Asperger's syndrome, motivated by this difference.

Second, children with autism with IQs in the mentally retarded range are nevertheless regarded as being cognitively distinct from those who have mental retardation without autism. They sometimes show enhanced skills related to perceptual and spatial tasks. However, Frith has argued that these apparent cognitive strengths are more a manifestation of another cognitive weakness—weak central coherence. Weak central coherence shows up in a number of ways where children with autism fail to benefit from context (e.g., sentence structure when remembering lists of words), but can be an aid to performance when context makes the task difficult (e.g., the embedded figures test).

Third, autism is very strongly associated with the presence of splinter skills (Hermelin, 2001) and less frequently (but with a greatly enhanced prevalence compared with the general population) with savant syndrome itself. Ever since Gardner (1983) popularized the notion of multiple intelligences, savant syndrome and the sometimes spectacular capabilities of low-IQ autistic people have led to a popular belief that there is no such thing as general intelligence. How wrong can you be? We shall see.

Fourth, and most importantly, there is very strong evidence that autism is caused by a set of mechanisms underlying the normal capacity for mentalizing or theory of mind. Establishing the domain specificity of this autistic deficit has been the crown jewel of Uta Frith's glittering career—though, as always, the precise nature of this specificity is subject to investigation and dispute (Russell & Hill, 2001).

So if, according to the minimal cognitive architecture, modules are independent of general intelligence, (a) why do children with autism have low IQ scores, (b) how is this relevant for understanding the disorder, and (c) how is this relevant for understanding intelligence?

In considering the first question the key point to consider is whether low-IQ scores in autistic individuals reflect low intelligence. At first blush we would say yes—because as mentioned above, the IQ-score of a person with autism is predictive of everyday functional capacity. But this does not constitute a theoretical conception of intelligence but a practical association, and we can ask in theory, must a low IQ score reflect low intelligence? Uta Frith and John Morton developed the causal modelling framework with autism as key exemplar (Morton, 2004; Morton & Frith, 1995). In the causal modelling framework it is crucial to distinguish between biological, cognitive, and behavioural levels of description. It is important to realize that an IQ-score is itself a piece of behaviour (or rather a summary of a number of test-taking behaviours). The concept of general intelligence is, on the other hand, either a cognitive or a biological construct depending on your particular theory of intelligence (but, importantly not when it is operationalized as the *g*-factor). Given this distinction there are at least two possible answers to the question of why, if autism reflects a modular deficit, should it result in lower IQ? One of these answers makes the relationship with intelligence an incidental and theoretically uninteresting one. This is where the biological cause of autism is comorbid with the biological cause of mental retardation. In such a case there is no functional overlap at the cognitive level between the disorders but rather a coincidence of genes and/or brain areas involved in both autism and mental retardation. So, for example, the same set of genes that might cause autism could lead to damage in two different brain systems—one specific to autism but also another one implicated in mental retardation. Or again the kind of insult that leads to damage of the brain system underlying autism is also likely to lead to damage of the brain system underlying mental retardation. The relationship between autism and low IQ in these cases would be due to a genetic or organic association and would not be functionally interesting for cognitive theories of autism or for cognitive theories of intelligence. However, another answer might say that the low IQ scores of autistic people are not caused in the same way as the low IQ scores of the nonautistic mentally retarded population. This answer

becomes much more interesting for both theories of the disorder and theories of intelligence because it forces us to say how the autistic deficit at the cognitive level can cause low intelligence and opens up the possibility for those interested in the disorder that in some sense people with autism are not unintelligent at all. There are good arguments for the former and evidence for the latter.

Frith and Happé (1998) pointed out how a modular deficit could have a global impact "downstream" in development. Their argument is that while the cause of a disorder could be a deficit in a specific mechanism it can have a cascading effect in development. In the case of a theory of mind deficit there are many plausible "knock-on" effects of having difficulties recognizing the intentions of others and not least for the acquisition of world knowledge. Much of the informal learning of world knowledge takes place around social interactions (and we can include teacher–pupil relations amongst these). A severe deficit in managing such interactions would lead to many lost opportunities to acquire the cultural knowledge embedded in many IQ tests (Frith, 2003). Consistent with this observation is the fact that people with autism typically do most poorly on intelligence test subtests that load most highly on social knowledge and require the most communicative interaction in their administration. Indeed poor performance on the Comprehension subtest of the Wechsler scales has been shown to be related to poor performance on the standard false-belief test of theory of mind (Happé, 1994). Even more obviously, the effect of the autistic deficit in mentalizing on the acquisition of vocabulary and language acquisition would obviously impact on verbal intelligence and crystallized knowledge, both of which are major determinants of both IQ and general intelligence. For the current purpose it is not important whether the core modular deficit in autism is in theory of mind or metarepresentation in general, or in executive functioning, as long as the core of these processes could be considered modular too. Certainly the defining feature of a module for the theory of the minimal cognitive architecture is that its function should be independent of speed of processing. In turn this leads to a prediction that if the core deficit is modular then speed of processing (the fount of general intelligence in typically developing children) should itself be unimpaired. And, intriguingly, this seems to be the case for people with autism.

Scheuffgen, Happé, Anderson, and Frith (2000) gave an inspection time task, believed to be one of the best current measures of speed of processing, to a group of children with autism, a group of age-matched typically developing children, and a group of learning-disabled children. The autistic groups had inspection times as short as the typically developing children and 50% lower (indicating faster speed of processing) than the learning-disabled group. In other words in this study children with autism had speed of processing typical of normal levels of intelligence despite having low IQ scores. A detailed case study of the mathematical abilities of an autistic prime number calculator by Anderson, O'Connor, and Hermelin (1998) is consistent with this picture. Anderson et al. argued that the computational method that the young man used to solve his prime number problems was most consistent with a thoughtful calculating strategy that belied his undoubted low IQ (cf. Norris, 1990). He too had a measured inspection time in the normal to above-average range. The conclusion is that while speed of processing may underpin individual differences in general intelligence (IQ) in a nonbrain-damaged population, fast speed of processing is not a sufficient condition for high intelligence.

What we can take from this very brief consideration of intelligence and autism is that the low IQs of children with autism is not caused by the process underlying general intelligence in typically developing children. In other words, low general ability at the cognitive level (determined by speed of processing in this particular theory) is not part of the causal chain necessary to explain the low IQ scores of children with autism. However, it would be a mistake to then conclude that intelligence per se might be regarded as an accidental or maybe even irrelevant feature of autism. Although as Morton (2004) has pointed

out "features that can be accounted for as part of a general condition need not be mentioned within the causal theory for the specific condition" (p. 99), the theory of how intelligence is affected by autism, and by extension what that tells us about intelligence, is one of the things that makes autism interesting for students of the mind. Moreover it may be that an explicit representation of the role of general intelligence in most if not all developmental disorders might be necessary because of the important role that general intelligence has in the link between biology and behaviour. In my view making this explicit might disentangle some of the current tangles over comorbidity. Perhaps of more long-term importance it will help us to properly interpret the burgeoning knowledge about genetic contributions to developmental disorders especially given that general intelligence is one of the most highly heritable psychological traits.

Intelligence and dyslexia

I would venture to propose that what makes dyslexia interesting for students of cognition is the possibility that a reading problem can be caused by a modular deficit. If it turns out, as some are now proposing, that dyslexia is simply the extreme end of a continuum of reading ability (see, for example, Plomin & Kovas, 2005), then it loses much of its power to excite. This is especially true if it turns out that the overlap between measures of reading and measures of general intelligence are large enough to consider that the only thing specific about reading is the task itself rather than the processes it invokes. Clearly then it is worth discussing the ways in which intelligence and dyslexia might be related.

It is easy enough to see why reading in typically developing children might be related to general intelligence. Comprehension typically aids reading as does understanding the meaning of words. Tests of comprehension and vocabulary are the staple fare of omnibus tests of intelligence. However, there are children of high intelligence who have a special problem with reading. Why should this be if their intelligence is intact? If the deficit is caused by damage to a module this presents no conundrum. The difficulty is how to determine when a case of reading failure (or any other developmental disorder for that matter) is a consequence of such a specific deficit in a modular function (presumably rarely) rather than a failure of general learning mechanisms underpinned by general intelligence.

Disputes over whether intelligence is a causal factor in reading disability (or at least one that needs to be controlled) or a red herring for reading researchers have also ebbed and flowed over the years (see, for example, Baldwin & Vaughn, 1989; Siegel, 1989; Stanovich, 1991). It is not that the potential relevance of intelligence to specific abilities is not recognized, it is how to accommodate it that is the subject of dispute. Up to now a kind of "lip service" has been paid to the relevance of intelligence, principally in the form of somehow "controlling" for intelligence in studies of reading disorder. This is because if a child is failing at reading but has a low IQ, the parsimonious conclusion is that the failure is a general failure of learning rather than something to do with reading per se. But as Max Coltheart has remarked—why could it not be that a low-IQ child could have a specific reading disorder?[1] The answer is surely that they could but that without making intelligence explicit in our models we would have no way of recognizing it even if we saw it. The compromise position has been to acknowledge the role of intelligence in reading by defining the disorder as a discrepancy in performance from that expected given a child's intelligence. But this causes a number of problems. Dyck et al. (2004) have shown that there are two unfortunate consequences of defining developmental disorders as a discrepancy from the level of performance predicted by their IQ. The first is that the probability of being identified with a deficit rises with the child's IQ. So children with specific deficits have higher IQs by definition. Secondly the probability of achieving a significantly lower score than that predicted by IQ varies with the correlation between IQ and the specific ability test. For example, this is much higher for language abilities than it is for attentional abilities, making it "easier" to be diagnosed with an attentional disorder than a language disorder for purely definitional reasons.

A theoretical model of intelligence and reading ability/disability

Arguments about whether intelligence should be factored into our consideration of reading disorder have so far been conducted in the dark. That is to say, these discussions have taken place without any consideration of a specific theory of intelligence, never mind one that might highlight different ways in which a child could come to be diagnosed with a reading disorder. In this section I show how the theory of the minimal cognitive architecture (MCA) could address the relationship between general intelligence and the cause of reading disorder.

A major current theoretical dispute concerns whether a reading deficit is best thought of as simply one end of a continuum of reading ability and is referred to as the "ability = disability" model (Plomin & Kovas, 2005). This contrasts with what is by now the more traditional specific-deficit model. In its most stark form, this model posits a failure of a cognitive module. While such a module would be considered necessary for "normal" reading, the module itself does not itself provide the locus of major individual differences in reading ability in a normal reading population. For the theory of the minimal cognitive architecture these two alternative models are easily characterized (see Figure 2).

Model 1 (ability = disability) says that reading ability is largely determined by the manifest variation in one of the specific processors—SP1, or the "verbal" processor. Thus a reading deficit will result from an individual being at the low end of functioning of this mechanism, just as very good reading will primarily be the result of high functioning. Note that because it is the manifest ability of SP1 that would determine reading

---

[1] Keynote address at the Australasian Human Development Association Conference, July, 2005, Perth, Western Australia.

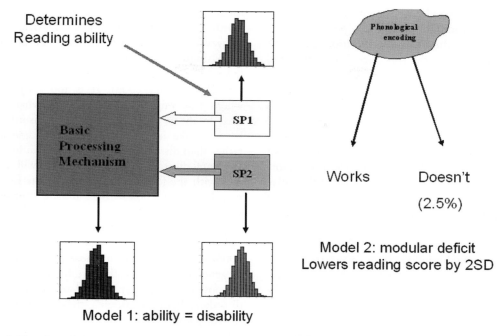

Figure 2. *Two alternative models of the relationship between intelligence and reading disorder.*

ability there are actually two independent sources of that variance. One is the latent ability of that processor and the other is the speed of processing of the basic processing mechanism that constrains the manifest ability of SP1. It would surely matter for a theory of dyslexia (even of the ability = disability variety) whether a particular child's low reading score was the result of poor latent functioning of SP1 or whether it was because of slow speed of processing. It is not hard to imagine that the cognitive profile of these two groups would be different. Even so, of course, it will be the case under this model that the majority of children diagnosed with dyslexia would have both poor speed of processing and poor latent "verbal" ability.

Model 2 (module deficit) on the other hand argues that a mechanism that functions normally in most of the population plays no role in variation in normal reading, but plays the crucial role in determining a reading deficit. An example of this would be some kind of mechanism that was a requirement for accurate phonological representations. In the theory damage to such a mechanism would seriously impair reading performance but as long as the mechanism was undamaged, variation in reading ability would be caused mainly by variation in speed of processing and in the latent power of the "verbal" processor, SP1. It is in the context of the modular deficit model that adopting an IQ-discrepancy criterion, as opposed to simply defining reading disorder by reading scores alone, is likely to have major impact. This is because if having a modular deficit is uncorrelated with intelligence, a substantial number with the deficit would still have higher reading scores than those with intact modules (because the majority of low reading scores would be caused by the combination of slow speed of processing and a poor "verbal", SP1, processor). The IQ-discrepancy criterion on the other hand would adjust for that effect and more clearly pick out those that have a modular deficit. Finally, we can see for either model that if low reading score were to be the sole criterion for diagnosing reading disorder then there would be a significant number who would be diagnosable with the "opposite" disorder caused by poor manifest functioning of the other specific processor, SP2. This is because of the influence that slow speed of processing would exert on the manifest ability of both specific processors. Thus we could anticipate that if poor manifest SP2 functioning led to a diagnosis of a spatial disorder a substantial number of those individuals would also be diagnosable with a reading disorder because of the poor manifest ability of SP1. In these cases the comorbidity would be purely a consequence of the influence of speed of processing. Another way of putting this is to say that a substantial number of comorbidities found between developmental disorders may be directly attributable to the effect of general intelligence.

Predictions such as these follow from the structure of a theory that explicitly represents the relationship between mechanisms responsible for general intelligence and mechanisms responsible for specific abilities (and disabilities). Moreover, because this theory can easily be made operational in a quantitative model (this has already been done to investigate the hypothesis of the differentiation of abilities; Anderson & Nelson, 2005) we could use the model to make more specific empirical predications about the mechanistic basis of reading disorder and the relationship with both diagnostic criteria and the genetic basis of abilities. However, this is beyond the scope of the current paper. Suffice to say for our current purpose, all that we need acknowledge is that general intelligence is likely to play an important role in the cause of reading disorder whatever model turned out to be true. Indeed, having a better understanding of this role might make it more likely that we could adequately test the veracity of each model.

Conclusions

Theories of developmental disorders in the past 20 years or so have been dominated by cognitive neuropsychological approaches to the mind (and appropriately so). This approach in turn has been dominated by the logic of dissociation and in large part by a theoretical commitment to modularity (Caramazza & Coltheart, 2006; Coltheart, 2006; Coltheart & Davies, 2003). However, a number of researchers are becoming increasingly jaundiced about what some have regarded as "single-cause" theories of disorder (see Pennington, 2006). It is too early to tell where this might lead. However, what seems clear to me is that our theories of disorder will have to take into account that it is association rather than dissociation that is the norm in developmental disorders. For example, they will have to deal with the fact that while few of the mentally retarded population have autism, autism is strongly associated with mental retardation. It may be that much of the association that we typically see and increasingly want to explain (Bishop, 2006) is a consequence of those processes related to general intelligence that are hidden from view in most contemporary models of developmental disorders. Perhaps bringing these into the light might, paradoxically, save the attempt to understand developmental disorders in terms of damage to one or some combination of the specific cognitive mechanisms that constitute the cognitive architecture of the mind.

I hope that this paper has shown that explicitly addressing the role of general intelligence in these two developmental disorders has not only illuminated the nature of the disorders (potentially at least) but made research on the disorders themselves clearly relevant to basic theories of the cognitive architecture of the mind and its development. I think this brings us back to where, for Uta Frith at least, it all started.

REFERENCES

Anderson, M. (1989). Inspection time and the relationship between stimulus encoding and response selection factors in development. In D. Vickers & P. L. Smith (Eds.), *Human information processing: Measures, mechanisms and models* (pp. 509–516). North Holland: Elsevier Science.

Anderson, M. (1992). *Intelligence and development: A cognitive theory.* Oxford, UK: Blackwell.

Anderson, M. (2000). An unassailable defense of G but a siren-song for theories of intelligence. *Psycoloquy, 11* (13). Retrieved August 31, 2007, from ftp:// ftp.princeton.edu/pub/harnad/Psycoloquy/2000. volume.11/

Anderson, M. (2001). Annotation: Conceptions of intelligence. *Journal of Child Psychology and Psychiatry, 42*, 287–298.

Anderson, M., & Nelson, J. (2005). Individual differences and cognitive models of the mind: Using the differentiation hypothesis to distinguish general and specific cognitive processes. In J. Duncan, P. McLeod, & L. Phillips (Eds.), *Measuring the mind: Speed, control and age* (pp. 89–113). Oxford, UK: Oxford University Press.

Anderson, M., Nettelbeck, T., & Barlow, J. (1997). Reaction time measures of speed of processing: Speed of response selection increases with age but speed of stimulus categorization does not. *British Journal of Developmental Psychology, 15*, 145–157.

Anderson, M., O'Connor, N., & Hermelin, B. (1998). A specific calculating ability. *Intelligence, 26*, 383–403.

Baldwin, R. S., & Vaughn, S. R. (1989). Why Siegel's arguments are irrelevant to the definition of learning disabilities. *Journal of Learning Disabilities, 22*, 513–520.

Bishop, D. V. M. (2006). Developmental cognitive genetics: How psychology can inform genetics. *Quarterly Journal of Experimental Psychology, 59*, 1153–1168.

Bishop, D. V. M. (2008). Forty Years On: Uta Frith's contribution to research on autism and dyslexia, 1966–2006. *Quarterly Journal of Experimental Psychology, 61*, 16–26.

Caramazza, A., & Coltheart, M. (2006). Cognitive neuropsychology twenty years on. *Cognitive Neuropsychology, 23*, 3–12.

Colom, R., Rebollo, I., Palacios, A., Juan-Espinosa, M., & Kyllonen, P. C. (2004). Working memory is (almost) perfectly predicted by g. *Intelligence, 32*, 277–296.

Coltheart, M. (2006). John Marshall and the cognitive neuropsychology of reading. *Cortex, 42*, 855–860.

Coltheart, M., & Davies, M. (2003). Inference and explanation in cognitive neuropsychology. *Cortex, 39*, 188–191.

Deary, I. J. (2000). *Looking down on human intelligence: From psychometrics to the brain.* Oxford, UK: Oxford University Press.

Deary, I. J., Whiteman, M. C., Starr, J. M., Whalley, L. J., & Fox, H. C. (2004). The impact of childhood intelligence on later life: Following up the Scottish Mental Surveys of 1932 and 1947. *Journal of Personality and Social Psychology, 86*, 130–147.

Duncan, J., Emslie, H., & Williams, P. (1996). Intelligence and the frontal lobes: The organization of goal-directed behavior. *Cognitive Psychology, 30*, 257–303.

Dyck, M. J., Hay, D., Anderson, M., Smith, L. M., Piek, J., & Hallmayer, J. (2004). Is the discrepancy criterion for defining developmental disorders valid? *Journal of Child Psychology and Psychiatry, 45*, 979–995.

Fodor, J. A. (1983). *The modularity of mind.* Cambridge, MA: MIT Press.

Frith, U. (1989). *Autism: Explaining the enigma.* Oxford: Blackwell.

Frith, U. (2003). *Autism: Explaining the enigma* (2nd ed.). Oxford, UK: Blackwell.

Frith, U., & Happé, F. (1998). Why specific developmental disorders are not specific: On-line and developmental effects in autism and dyslexia. *Developmental Science, 1*, 267–272.

Gardner, H. (1983). *Frames of mind: The theory of multiple intelligences.* London: Heinemann.

Gustafson, J. E. (1984). A unifying model for the structure of mental abilities. *Intelligence, 8*, 179–203.

Happé, F. (1994). Wechsler IQ profile and theory of mind in autism: A research note. *Journal of Child Psychology and Psychiatry, 35*, 1461–1471.

Hermelin, B. (2001). *Bright splinters of the mind: A personal story of research with autistic savants.* London: Jessica Kingsley.

Hermelin, B., & O'Connor, N. (1970). *Psychological experiments with autistic children.* Oxford, UK: Pergamon Press.

Jensen, A. R. (1982). Reaction time and psychometric g. In H. J. Eysenck (Ed.), *A model for intelligence.* Berlin: Springer-Verlag.

Jensen, A. R. (1998). *The g factor: The science of mental ability.* Westport, CT: Praeger.

Jensen, A. R. (2000). "The g-factor" is about variance in human abilities, not a cognitive theory of mental structure: Reply to Anderson on Jensen on Intelligence-g-Factor. *Psycoloquy, 11* (13). Retrieved August 31, 2007 from www.cogsci.ecs.soton.ac.uk/ cgi/psyc/newpsy?11.041

Morton, J. (2004). *Understanding developmental disorders: A causal modelling approach.* Oxford, UK: Blackwell.

Morton, J., & Frith, U. (1995). Causal modelling: A structural approach to developmental psychopathology. In D. Cichetti & D. J. Cohen (Eds.),

Developmental psychopathology (Vol. 1, pp. 357–390). New York: Wiley.

Nettelbeck, T. (1987). Inspection time and intelligence. In P. A. Vernon (Ed.), *Speed of information processing and intelligence*. New York: Ablex.

Norris, D. (1990). How to build a connectionist idiot (savant). *Cognition, 35,* 277–291.

O'Connor, N., & Hermelin, B. (1963). *Speech and thought in severe subnormality*. London: Pergamon Press.

Pennington, B. F. (2006). From single to multiple deficit models of developmental disorders. *Cognition, 101,* 385–413.

Plomin, R., & Kovas, Y. (2005). Generalist genes and learning disabilities. *Psychological Bulletin, 131,* 592–617.

Russell, J., & Hill, E. L. (2001). Action-monitoring and intention reporting in children with autism. *Journal of Child Psychology and Psychiatry, 42,* 317–328.

Salthouse, T. A. (2000). Aging and measures of processing speed. *Biological Psychology, 54,* 35–54.

Scheuffgen, K., Happé, F., Anderson, M., & Frith, U. (2000). High "intelligence", low "IQ"? Speed of processing and measured IQ in children with autism. *Development and Psychopathology, 12,* 83–90.

Siegel, L. S. (1989). Why we do not need intelligence test scores in the definition and analysis of learning disabilities. *Journal of Learning Disabilities, 22,* 514–518.

Spearman, C. (1904). "General intelligence", objectively determined and measured. *American Journal of Psychology, 15,* 201–293.

Stanovich, K. E. (1991). Discrepancy definitions of reading-disability—has intelligence led us astray. *Reading Research Quarterly, 26,* 7–29.

THE QUARTERLY JOURNAL OF EXPERIMENTAL PSYCHOLOGY
2008, 61 (1), 129–141

What phonological deficit?

Franck Ramus and Gayaneh Szenkovits

Laboratoire de Sciences Cognitives et Psycholinguistique (EHESS/CNRS/DEC-ENS), Paris, France

We review a series of experiments aimed at understanding the nature of the phonological deficit in developmental dyslexia. These experiments investigate input and output phonological representations, phonological grammar, foreign speech perception and production, and unconscious speech processing and lexical access. Our results converge on the observation that the phonological representations of people with dyslexia may be intact, and that the phonological deficit surfaces only as a function of certain task requirements, notably short-term memory, conscious awareness, and time constraints. In an attempt to reformulate those task requirements more economically, we propose that individuals with dyslexia have a deficit in access to phonological representations. We discuss the explanatory power of this concept and we speculate that a similar notion might also adequately describe the nature of other associated cognitive deficits when present.

How I learned to stop worrying and love the phonological deficit

Back in 1999, as I (FR) started discussing the possibility of a post-doc with Uta Frith, the target clearly was to further investigate the nature of the phonological deficit in dyslexia. This was a field where my background in psycholinguistics might conceivably be of some use. And this was indeed the topic for which I started to work in January 2000.

While thinking about new experiments tapping the phonological deficit, I embarked on a more comprehensive literature review of dyslexia. I discovered the many theories of dyslexia and the difficulties of interpreting the data relative to each theory. I was notably illuminated by Uta's "Paradoxes" paper (Frith, 1999), which, by a judicious use of the causal modelling framework (Morton & Frith, 1995), outlined particularly clearly the various possible theoretical models accounting for any set of behavioural data. One thing that particularly worried me was the presence of auditory deficits in dyslexia. If at least some individuals with dyslexia had auditory deficits, how could I expect them to perform normally in phonological tasks requiring auditory perception of the stimuli, and how would I be able to unambiguously interpret my data? I therefore felt the need to include an auditory task in my test battery, at least as a control. For that purpose I sought the collaboration of Stuart Rosen. It turned out that the choice of the relevant auditory task was not trivial, and different kinds of auditory deficits would be expected to impact on different aspects of phonology. It therefore seemed inevitable to employ a whole battery of various

Correspondence should be addressed to Franck Ramus, Laboratoire de Sciences Cognitives et Psycholinguistique, Ecole Normale Supérieure, 29 rue d'Ulm, 75230 Paris Cedex 5, France. E-mail: franck.ramus@ens.fr

We wish to thank the students and collaborators involved in some of the experiments described: Liaan Darma, Emilie Gaillard, Eva Soroli, Emmanuel Dupoux, and Sid Kouider, as well as members of LSCP for much discussion and feedback. We also thank Maggie Snowling and Peter de Jong for their critical feedback on this paper. This work was supported by grants from the Fyssen Foundation and Ville de Paris.

auditory tests. This is where the project started going seriously off-track.

The study was looking more like a test of auditory theories of dyslexia. At the same time I didn't want to reproduce the shortcomings that I found in previous studies: that is, to test the predictions of one particular theory of dyslexia and ignore the others (Ramus, 2001a). It seemed a pity to administer such a fine battery of phonological and auditory tests and not to take the opportunity to add visual magnocellular measures and motor/cerebellar tests. Quite rapidly the project got entirely out of control. With the complicity of a few more collaborators, I ended up with a 10-hour test battery. To Uta's great regret and to my great shame, out of 10 hours, less than 1 was actually dedicated to phonological tasks, and rather uninspiring ones.

Uta frequently reminded me of my culpable neglect of the phonological deficit. But she also let me entirely free to pursue my new craze, always providing as much encouragement and critical feedback as was needed. This must be a hallmark of her mentoring style, for which I am immensely grateful.

Sometimes I wonder whether she would also have encouraged me to study dyslexia in parabolic flight or under the sea. Perhaps she had somehow foreseen that the project, even if not quite the intended one, would be quite successful in the end (Ramus, Pidgeon, & Frith, 2003a; Ramus et al., 2003b; Ramus, White, & Frith, 2006; White et al., 2006a; White et al., 2006b). The present paper is, at last, about a first significant attempt to get to grips with the phonological deficit.

What we know and what we don't know about the phonological deficit

Phonologists and psycholinguists have described in great detail the structure of phonological representations, the rules (or computations) operating on them, and the various levels of representation and processing that must necessarily be involved in speech perception and production. That area has been reviewed before in relation to dyslexia (Ramus, 2001b). Here we only recall the overall cognitive architecture that we assume (Figure 1),

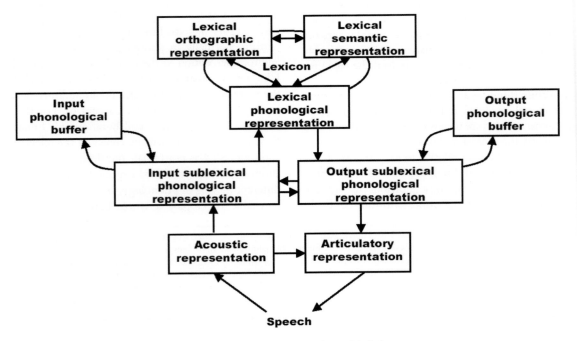

Figure 1. *An information-processing model of speech perception and production and lexical access.*

and we explain phonological and psycholinguistic concepts where they are necessary to understand our experiments.

More than 30 years of research on dyslexia have taught us that there are three main dimensions to the phonological deficit (Wagner & Torgesen, 1987):

- Poor phonological awareness (as exemplified in phoneme deletion tasks);
- Poor verbal short-term memory (as exemplified in digit span or nonword repetition tasks);
- Slow lexical retrieval (as exemplified in rapid automatic naming tasks).

The poor performance of persons with dyslexia in most (if not all) verbal tasks can be explained by one or several of these dimensions. A pertinent question therefore is why this "dyslexic triad" and why are the three dimensions affected together more often than to be expected by chance? The answer seems to be that the three dimensions have something in common: They all implicate phonological representations, each in its own way. The first dimension concerns conscious access, attention to, and manipulation of those representations and their subunits. Within Figure 1, this can be viewed as a central executive processor (not represented) accessing the contents of sublexical phonological representations. The second dimension refers to their storage for a short period of time, either briefly copied in phonological buffers (typically, holding the first words of a sentence for the very short time necessary to process the end), or actively recycling them between input and output sublexical representations (also known as the phonological loop, typically recruited in span tasks). Finally, the third member of the triad involves the retrieval of lexical phonological representations from long-term memory.

Therefore, it should come as no surprise that the most commonly accepted hypothesis regarding the nature of the phonological deficit in dyslexia is that phonological representations are degraded—that is, they are fuzzier, or noisier, or underspecified, or have a lower resolution or a larger grain size than they should, or are not sufficiently categorical and preserve too many acoustic or allophonic details (e.g., Adlard & Hazan, 1998; Elbro, 1998; Manis et al., 1997; Mody, Studdert-Kennedy, & Brady, 1997; Serniclaes, Van Heghe, Mousty, Carré, & Sprenger-Charolles, 2004; Snowling, 2000). Nevertheless, there is also much more to phonology than these three dimensions, and therefore the hypothesis of a deficit in phonological representations makes a host of additional predictions, concerning notably the early stages of phonological acquisition in the first few years of life and their consequences for on-line speech perception and production (Ramus, 2001b).

Exploring the phonological deficit

In the course of our investigations we have tested French university students with dyslexia. Self-reports of persons with dyslexia have been supplemented by data from a diagnostic battery, ensuring they met predefined inclusion criteria in terms of nonverbal IQ, reading disability, and presence of a significant phonological deficit (in the sense of the classic triad). Control students were also recruited and underwent the same tests, ensuring that they did not present any reading disability and that they were matched to the students with dyslexia in age and nonverbal IQ (Szenkovits & Ramus, 2005).

This population of university students was thought to be appropriate for testing with psycholinguistic tasks, which tend to be long, boring, and demanding. This does not excuse us from testing a more representative sample of children with age-appropriate tasks, but this was considered a second step after having delineated the most promising hypotheses to warrant confirmation in children.

In search of a locus
In a first series of experiments, we have attempted to assess specifically the most relevant levels of representations depicted in Figure 1 (Szenkovits & Ramus, 2005). Indeed, the general hypothesis of a phonological deficit does not by itself specify

which of the different levels of phonological representation is presumed to be deficient.

In order to disentangle the various levels, we adopted the following strategy: We contrasted sublexical and lexical levels of representations by comparing tasks involving words and nonwords, and we contrasted input and output pathways by comparing repetition tasks (involving both) with auditory discrimination tasks (involving only input representations). To ensure that discrimination tasks were not performed by covert use of output representations (i.e., the phonological loop), we had an additional condition where the discrimination task was performed with concurrent articulatory suppression (uttering "bababa . . . " for the whole duration of each trial, therefore keeping output representations busy). The material to be discriminated or repeated consisted of sequences of monosyllabic nonwords, of increasing length (i.e., nonword matching span). Verbal short-term memory load was an important aspect of all the experiments. In the discrimination task, two sequences were heard and compared, which either were identical or differed by one phonetic feature in one of the nonwords.

We found significant group differences in all conditions, suggesting that the phonological deficit appears no matter what levels are involved: sublexical as well as lexical, input as well as output, whether or not articulatory suppression was applied. Furthermore, participants with dyslexia were relatively more impaired in discrimination than in repetition tasks, highlighting more specifically their deficit in input representations. On the other hand, articulatory suppression slightly decreased overall performance, but did not impact differently on the two groups of participants. Thus, we are incited to take a closer look at the input pathway.

Representation versus working-memory processes

Why do persons with dyslexia fail to discriminate and repeat correctly verbal material, as soon as short-term memory load is significant? The previous series of experiments leaves open two broad classes of explanation that are not mutually exclusive. One is that phonological representations are

degraded, so some phonetic features get lost in the process and are therefore missing when they must be compared or repeated. An alternative interpretation is that phonological representations are themselves intact—that is, that all phonetic features are correctly encoded—but that short-term memory processes are limited, and that the poor performance of participants with dyslexia reflect a capacity limitation.

We have attempted to test these contrasting hypotheses using the phonological similarity effect: The more phonologically similar the words or nonwords in the sequence, the more difficult it is to recall the sequence (Baddeley, 1984). This effect shows that verbal short-term memory is limited not only by general capacity constraints but also by possible phonological confusions between the items to be remembered. Now if the phonological representations of people with dyslexia are degraded, they should have even more confusions between items and therefore show an increased phonological similarity effect. On the other hand, if their phonological representations are intact, they should show just as much phonological similarity effect as controls, not more. Yet another conceivable prediction would be that they show less similarity effect than controls, although this is predicted only in the case of known words for which conceptual or visual representations are available (McNeil & Johnston, 2004; Shankweiler, Liberman, Mark, & Fowler, 1979).

We therefore carried out a new series of experiments requiring again the discrimination of sequences of nonwords, in two different conditions (Szenkovits, Dupoux, & Ramus, 2007b). In the minimal condition, sequences were made of repetitions of two to seven nonwords that differed by just one phonetic feature ([taz]−[taʒ]). The two sequences either were identical or differed by just one of the nonwords being changed into the other (i.e., they differed by one phonetic feature). In the maximal condition the two nonwords differed maximally ([taz]−[gum]), so that different sequences differed by three phonemes and quite a few phonetic features. Furthermore, in order to ensure that sequences were encoded at the phonological (rather than acoustic) level of representation, nonwords were uttered by two different voices, which alternated constantly within a sequence, and in opposite orders between sequences. As a result, even phonologically identical sequences were different at the acoustic level.

The main results were that we found a phonological similarity effect (poorer performance in the minimal than in the maximal condition) and that participants with dyslexia performed more poorly. However, as phonological similarity decreased the performance of the dyslexic group increased by the same magnitude as that for controls. This pattern of results held under various replication variants, with concurrent articulatory suppression, with sequence repetition rather than discrimination, and whether minimal and maximal conditions were intermixed or administered in separate blocks.

Our results extend previous studies that also found no differential phonological similarity effect, during verbal recall of words or letter names (Hall, Wilson, Humphreys, Tinzmann, & Bowyer, 1983; Johnston, Rugg, & Scott, 1987; Swanson & Ramalgia, 1992), as well as during paired-associate learning (Messbauer & de Jong, 2006). Overall, these results fail to confirm the predictions of the "degraded phonological representations" hypothesis. They are more compatible with the alternative hypothesis that the deficit might lie in the short-term memory processes operating on phonological representations (i.e., in Figure 1, the input and/or output phonological buffers, or the phonological loop between input and output sublexical representations).

Universal or hypernative phonology?

A great deal of phonology is specific to each particular language. This is best illustrated by the unique phonetic repertoire of each language, but is also true at other levels of the phonological hierarchy. It is generally agreed that adequate language-specific phonological representations are acquired very early on by the child, by the end of the first year of life by some accounts and at any rate before the end of the third. Given that the phonological deficit is presumed to be congenital, it should manifest itself early on in an altered pattern of phonological acquisition. The few longitudinal studies starting at birth that have directly tested that prediction (although very succinctly) have generally supported it (Guttorm, Leppänen, Richardson, & Lyytinen, 2001; Leppänen et al., 2002; Molfese, 2000; Richardson, Leppänen, Leiwo, & Lyytinen, 2003; van Alphen et al., 2004).

Beyond the first year of life, altered phonological acquisition predicts an "atypical" structure of phonological representations. Indeed, hypotheses emphasizing poor categorical perception and/or preserved allophonic perception rest on the idea that phonological categories were not properly acquired. These hypotheses more specifically assume that phonology was incompletely acquired, so that the phonology of the child (or adult) with dyslexia is closer to the initial, universal stage of phonology: Categories are less sharply defined and less specific to any particular language, and representations still incorporate some acoustic or allophonic details that should have been eliminated through phonological acquisition (e.g., Mody et al., 1997; Serniclaes et al., 2004).

One possible further prediction of this class of hypotheses is that, as a consequence, individuals with dyslexia might retain the ability to perceive and perhaps produce foreign speech sounds. This is because people's difficulties with foreign speech sounds are a direct outcome of their phonological acquisition, which rigidifies their phonology with the categories and processes of the native language, which are often in conflict with the categories and processes of a different, later acquired language. If the phonology of a person with dyslexia is less rigidified by their native language, it might retain some plasticity for a second one. As an example, French and English both have two categories for voicing, but with a different boundary. Korean has three categories. If say, an English speaker with dyslexia has less well defined English voicing categories, she or he might be less impaired in the perception of French voicing contrasts around a different boundary. They might be even less impaired in the perception of Korean voicing contrasts, if she or he has retained in his or her phonological representation the allophonic details that are the basis for the Korean contrast (as hypothesized by Serniclaes et al., 2004).

In order to tease apart the two hypotheses, we conducted a series of experiments testing the perception and production of foreign speech contrasts by people with dyslexia (Soroli, 2005). In order to assess the role of short-term memory load, we conducted discrimination and repetition tasks using either single consonant–vowel–consonant–vowel (CVCV) nonwords, or sequences of two or three CVCV nonwords. We tested one segmental and one suprasegmental phonological contrasts. The segmental contrast was the voicing of stop consonants in Korean, which, as mentioned above, presents three categories (plain/tense/aspirated) instead of two in French (the native language of all participants). The suprasegmental contrast was lexical stress, a prosodic contrast present in many languages like Spanish or Italian, but not in French. In that condition, stress could fall either on the first or the second syllable of the nonword, and different pairs differed only by the location of the stress, phonemes being kept identical. In the repetition tasks, participants' production was recorded and coded offline by a native speaker of Korean for segmental contrasts and a native speaker of Greek (a language with lexical stress) for stress contrasts.

Overall, the results showed that when discriminating or repeating single nonwords, participants with dyslexia showed the same performance as did controls. However, group differences appeared when discriminating or repeating sequences of two or three nonwords, particularly so for the stress contrast. These results suggest that the native phonological representations of people with dyslexia are equally (un)able to represent foreign speech contrasts. Group differences appear only when short-term memory load increases. These results therefore do not support the hypothesis of a universal (initial-stage) phonology. Again, they are more compatible with the hypothesis that the phonological representations of participants with dyslexia are intact and that short-term memory processes operating on them are impaired.

From the point of view of second-language acquisition, our results suggest that the difficulties of people with dyslexia in this domain may not result from the particular format of their phonological representations, but rather from their impaired verbal short-term memory and phonological awareness, and perhaps phonological learning, as these capacities must be heavily recruited during second language acquisition (Service, 1992).

Phonological grammar
Another area of phonology that is potentially of interest with respect to dyslexia is what can be termed "phonological grammar". This refers to a whole host of rule-like processes that apply (typically probabilistically) in speech production when phonological lexical items are retrieved from the lexicon and assembled (at the sublexical level) to make phrases (Chomsky & Halle, 1968). These phenomena are mainly described in speech production but similar phenomena occur in speech perception, either as a compensation for productive processes, or simply as an adaptation to native phonological structure. Most of these phonological processes are language specific and therefore must be learnt in the course of language acquisition. Do children with dyslexia acquire them equally well as controls?

Based on a series of experiments by Darcy et al. (Darcy, Peperkamp, & Dupoux, in press-a; Darcy, Ramus, Christophe, Kinzler, & Dupoux, in press-b), we tested one particular phonological process that occurs in French: voicing assimilation. In French, the voicing feature may spread backwards from obstruents or fricatives to the preceding consonant: for instance "cape grise" [kapgriz] → [kabgriz] (grey cloak). This assimilation process is both context specific (it does not occur before nasals: "cape noire" is always [kapnwar]; black cloak) and language specific (it does not occur in English, which instead shows assimilation of place of articulation: "brown bag" [brownbag] → [browmbag]).

In the production experiment, participants saw a sentence written on the computer screen, rehearsed it as much as needed, and then were recorded as they pronounced it rapidly. Sentences were read without difficulty by participants with dyslexia, the rehearsal ensuring that each sentence could be produced accurately and rapidly (to maximize the likelihood of producing assimilations), without being hindered by reading fluency. Sentences contained either a legal context for voicing assimilation (according to French phonology), or an illegal context for voicing assimilation (to assess context specificity). Other sentences contained similar conditions for English place assimilation (to assess language specificity). The words that could be assimilated were excised from the recordings of all participants and played, one at a time, to a new set of native French listeners, together with the written version of both the assimilated and unassimilated forms. These participants judged whether the target word was assimilated or not (i.e., in the above example, whether they heard [kap] or [kab]). This yielded the probability of producing an assimilation, for each target word, in each condition, by each subject. Results showed that French persons with dyslexia, just like controls, produce voicing assimilations around 40% of the time in legal contexts, but not in illegal contexts, and do not produce place assimilations. Furthermore, voicing assimilations occur more frequently than devoicing assimilations (Snoeren, Hallé, & Segui, 2006), to the same degree in the participants with dyslexia and controls.

In the perception experiment, similar sentences were played preceded by a target word (e.g., "cape"), the task being to detect whether the target word was included and correctly pronounced in the sentence. The sentences again came in three conditions. They either contained the target word in assimilated form in a legal context ("La petite fille jette sa cab grise"; this should go unnoticed if participants compensate perceptually for voicing assimilation), or the target word in assimilated form in an illegal context ("la petite fille jette sa cab noire"; this should be noticed because no assimilation is expected in this context), or did not contain the target word. Three additional conditions tested the possibility of compensation for place

assimilation. Results showed that French participants with dyslexia compensate perceptually for voicing assimilations to the same extent as do controls (see also Blomert, Mitterer, & Paffen, 2004), but only in legal contexts (like controls), and do not compensate for place assimilation (like controls). Furthermore, an asymmetry in perceptual compensation was observed in perception as in production, to the same extent in people with dyslexia as in controls.

In another experiment, we investigated assimilations induced by phonotactic constraints. The background is that each language has its own phonotactic constraints, forbidding certain consonant clusters in certain contexts. In French, like in English, clusters like [dl] or [tl] can never occur at the beginning of a word. The consequence is that when French or English listeners hear a nonword such as [dla] or [tla], they most often assimilate it to the closest legal cluster ([gla] or [kla], respectively)—that is, they fail to hear the illegal cluster and report hearing the legal one (Hallé, Segui, Frauenfelder, & Meunier, 1998). This is also evident in discrimination tasks, where they for instance respond "same" to the "different" pair [dla]−[gla]. In such a discrimination task we found that listeners with dyslexia fall victim to this perceptual illusion just as much as controls, hearing [gla] instead of [dla]. Thus, their speech perception is constrained by the phonotactics of their native language as much as it is for controls.

In conclusion, the aspects of phonological grammar that we have investigated seem perfectly normal in people with dyslexia (Szenkovits, Darma, Darcy, & Ramus, 2007a). Our results are consistent with the hypothesis that phonological representations are intact, that grammatical processes that operate on them are intact too, and that the deficit lies somewhere else.

Unconscious speech processing and lexical access

A recurrent problem in psycholinguistics is that tasks typically require explicit instructions, attention to stimuli, and introspection, which may blur the interpretation of the effects observed, particularly so when the population tested has problems with phonological awareness. One solution to this problem is to observe indirect effects of experimental manipulations of which the subject is unaware. In the case of visual presentation of linguistic stimuli, subliminal priming has provided a particularly elegant solution. The participant performs a task (typically lexical decision) on a target word, which is preceded by a prime word. When presentation duration is sufficiently reduced, and when the prime is preceded and followed by visual masks, it is not consciously perceived, but may still be processed. One may therefore assess the effects of the prime on the recognition of the target, unbeknownst to the subject. More recently, a similar technique has been used to render auditory primes subliminal (Kouider & Dupoux, 2005). Kouider and Dupoux have used a combination of time compression, amplitude attenuation, and masking with backwards speech to achieve subliminal processing of the prime and have shown that subliminal repetition priming occurs, as evidenced by a decrease in reaction time compared to when the prime is unrelated to the target. Moreover, this priming is strictly lexical, and it operates on an abstract lexical phonological representation, because subliminal priming occurs only for words and resists large acoustic differences between prime and target (i.e., there is as much priming when prime and target are spoken by speakers of different sexes; Kouider & Dupoux, 2005).

The availability of this new method gave us the opportunity to consider new questions to ask about the phonological deficit in dyslexia—namely, how efficient are unconscious lexical access processes in people with dyslexia? What is the nature of their lexical phonological representations? The degraded phonological representations hypothesis predicts reduced subliminal repetition priming, due to the fact that phonological details might be lost and therefore distort the identity relationship between prime and target. A more specific hypothesis, according to which their phonological representations would be less abstract, and closer to acoustic representations, would predict decreased priming specifically across different speakers.

The findings from our study of control participants fully replicated those of Kouider and Dupoux (2005), and our results on dyslexia fully replicated those of controls (Gaillard, 2006). In short, participants with dyslexia show as much subliminal repetition priming as do controls, it is restricted to words like in controls, and it is of equal magnitude across as within speakers. These results do not support the predictions of the degraded phonological representations hypothesis, neither do they support the hypothesis that persons with dyslexia rely on acoustic rather than abstract phonological representations for their lexicon. Rather, they are compatible with the idea that their phonological representations and processes for lexical access are intact. Follow-up experiments manipulating the phonological relationship between prime and target will be needed to fully bolster the latter hypothesis.

A new hypothesis

The experiments that we have described were designed to test various hypotheses regarding the status of the phonological system in dyslexia. Overall, their findings converge towards one single conclusion: that the phonological representations of people with dyslexia are normal. Of course, this conclusion cannot be considered as proven. Many aspects of the phonological representations of people with dyslexia still remain to be tested. Nevertheless, let us consider for the sake of discussion that our conclusion holds. What, then, might be the nature of the phonological deficit? If phonological representations are normal, if phonological grammar is acquired normally, then what's wrong with phonology?

The first important remark to make is that our results do not challenge in any way the very existence of a phonological deficit. Indeed, our own data attest that our participants with dyslexia have a phonological deficit, as measured in the traditional sense, using for instance spoonerisms, nonword repetition, and rapid naming tasks. So it is not time to abandon the phonological deficit hypothesis, merely to rethink its precise formulation.

A comparison of phonological tasks in which participants with dyslexia show normal as opposed to poor performance provides important clues. First, task requirements, and in particular short-term memory load, seem paramount. This is obvious in span tasks where difficulties appear as sequence length increases. It is also the case in most phonological awareness tasks, which do require the subject to hold segmented phonological units in short-term memory, as well as requiring conscious access to those representations. In fact, the most difficult phonological awareness tasks for people with dyslexia turn out to be those that load most heavily on short-term memory (e.g., spoonerisms). One type of task that challenges persons with dyslexia without recruiting verbal short-term memory is rapid naming. Given that they do not always have problems with single picture naming, it seems that in this case the crucial task constraint is speed (Marshall, Tang, Rosen, Ramus, & van der Lely, 2007; McCrory, 2001; Szenkovits, Dupoux, & Ramus, 2007) (but see Snowling, van Wagtendonk, & Stafford, 1988; Swan & Goswami, 1997b).

In an attempt to provide a unifying explanation for those task constraints that seem to pose specific problems in dyslexia, we tentatively propose the concept of *phonological access*. By this, we mean all processes by which (lexical or sublexical) phonological representations are accessed for the purpose of external computations. Verbal short-term memory requires access to phonological representations for the purpose of copying them into buffers, then access to phonological buffers for retrieval (see Figure 1), as well as access to input representations to copy them into output representations, and access to output representations to recycle them into input representations (i.e., the phonological loop, Baddeley, 1984; Jacquemot & Scott, 2006). Phonological awareness tasks additionally involve a special type of access, *conscious access* to phonological representations, which may place special demands on access mechanisms. And rapid naming tasks require multiple fast access to lexical phonological representations. Therefore, it seems to us that people with dyslexia

tend to fail at tasks that are particularly demanding in terms of phonological access. A relatively similar proposal was made by Shankweiler and Crain (1986) under the name of *processing limitation hypothesis*. There are also some commonalities with Hulme and Snowling's (1992) notion of an *output deficit*.

We acknowledge that, at the present stage, our notion of phonological access needs developing and that our analysis of which tasks are demanding in terms of access is rather ad hoc. Ultimately, computational models of the phonological system would be the best way to provide an operational definition of access and to make unambiguous predictions concerning the consequences of a phonological access deficit on the performance of various tasks.

Discussion

The most striking aspect of the series of experiments that we have reported here is our consistent failure to demonstrate a deficit in the phonological representations of people with dyslexia. Could obvious reasons explain our failure? Could it be that our unrepresentative, well-compensated participants with dyslexia were not dyslexic enough, or did not present a phonological deficit at all? It should be recalled that all our participants were included on the basis of both a history of reading disability and poor performance on reading and standard phonological tasks. In fact their performance on standard phonological tasks (spoonerisms, digit span, rapid naming) did not overlap at all with that of age- and IQ- matched participants. Therefore there is good evidence that our participants with dyslexia did present a phonological deficit. But this deficit surfaces in some tasks and not in others, and the whole point of our hypothesis is to explain why.

Another potential limitation of our findings is that, in working with adults, we cannot rule out the possibility that people with dyslexia may have deficient phonological representations as children, but these representations have recovered when we test them in adulthood (e.g., Goswami, 2003). Obviously this type of critique must be taken seriously, and the only way to do so will be to replicate our main findings on children. Nevertheless, this type of hypothesis does not easily explain why performance on tasks tapping fine aspects of the phonological representation would recover, while performance on the same tasks with additional short-term memory load, or conscious awareness, or time constraints, would not. Clearly, the developmental critique is plausible to the extent that it is able to adequately explain what recovers and what does not.

Our present findings, and our conclusion that the phonological representations of people with dyslexia are normal, may seem quite provocative, but after all, are they surprising at all? In hindsight, one may consider that similar data have been around for a long time. For instance, we have always known that most children with dyslexia can repeat one- and two-syllable nonwords without much problem, and that difficulties appear only with three-, four-, and five-syllable nonwords. Such data do suggest that phonological representations are normal, and that only memory load makes a difference. In a landmark study, Swan and Goswami (1997a) tested phonological awareness in children with dyslexia while controlling for their ability to correctly retrieve the phonological form of the target words. While their findings are widely interpreted as supporting a form of the degraded phonological representations hypothesis, they have in fact shown that the phoneme awareness deficits of children with dyslexia cannot be entirely attributed to poor phonological representation of the target words. In another line of research, studies that have directly tested the quality of phonological representations in dyslexia with categorical perception experiments have often had mixed results: They sometimes found significant group differences, but often due to a subgroup of participants with dyslexia (e.g., Adlard & Hazan, 1998; Mody et al., 1997; Ramus et al., 2003b; Rosen & Manganari, 2001; White et al., 2006b). This suggests that deficits in the categories of phonological representations, just like basic auditory perception deficits, affect only a minority of persons with dyslexia and may not be part of the core phonological deficit in dyslexia.

Does our phonological access hypothesis imply a more general executive dysfunction in dyslexia? Certainly access to representations for the purpose of working memory or awareness is part of what could be termed executive function. Nevertheless, we are not proposing a general executive dysfunction in dyslexia in the same sense as executive dysfunction in autism or in frontal patients. This must be a very specific type of executive dysfunction, specific both in terms of executive processes and in terms of modality (e.g., Jeffries & Everatt, 2004). Executive function is a domain-general concept, but in practice it is plausible that the neural substrate of executive processes has central (frontal) components (which are not affected in dyslexia) and is partly distributed in each sensory modality and functional module (Carpenter, Just, & Reichle, 2000). Then it is possible to envision that, say, a left perisylvian dysfunction might disrupt executive processes only as applied to verbal (or auditory) material.

The matter of sensory deficits in dyslexia is also of interest here. Indeed, after years of investigations of auditory and visual deficits in dyslexia, some researchers have come to conclusions that are intriguingly similar to ours. Ahissar and colleagues have found that the difficulties of people with dyslexia never seem to be specific to a particular kind of stimulus, be it auditory or visual: Rather they appear or disappear depending on task requirements, being particularly prominent when the stimuli must be stored in short-term memory (Amitay, Ben-Yehudah, Banai, & Ahissar, 2002; Banai & Ahissar, 2006; Ben-Yehudah, Sackett, Malchi-Ginzberg, & Ahissar, 2001). In their interpretation, the deficit lies in the ability to "form a perceptual anchor" (Ahissar, Lubin, Putter-Katz, & Banai, 2006). Similarly, working on visual processing, Sperling and colleagues concluded that the deficit in dyslexia does not lie specifically with stimuli tapping the magnocellular system, but rather lies in the ability to perform the task when the stimuli are noisy: in their own words, a deficit in "perceptual noise exclusion" (Sperling, Lu, Manis, & Seidenberg, 2005, 2006). This is not without recalling the finding that children's difficulties with speech perception are exacerbated by presentation in noise (Brady, Shankweiler, & Mann, 1983; Cornelissen, Hansen, Bradley, & Stein, 1996; but see Snowling, Goulandris, Bowlby, & Howell, 1986) or under conditions where the stimuli are extremely minimal (Serniclaes et al., 2004). Rephrased within our framework, the interpretation of these results is that the auditory and visual representations of people with dyslexia are intact, but that they have difficulties accessing them under certain conditions involving storage in short-term memory, speeded or repeated retrievals, extraction from noise, and other task difficulty factors. Does this imply that individuals with dyslexia in fact suffer from a *general deficit* in the capacity to access sensory representations? The critique of sensory theories of dyslexia retains its force (Ramus, 2003); simply, for those who, on top of their phonological deficit, do show auditory and/or visual deficits, these may be construed in terms of access to representations, just like the phonological deficit. Therefore, individuals with dyslexia may have cognitive deficits of a single type, but expressed in several domains, with most of them having a deficit in the phonological domain (hence the link with reading disability), and some having the same kind of deficit more generally in the auditory and/or visual domains (and possibly elsewhere). The range of deficits within a particular individual would presumably depend on the spatial extent of their cortical dysfunctions (Ramus, 2004).

To summarize, a whole series of experiments conducted in our lab suggests that the phonological representations of people with dyslexia are basically intact, and that the phonological deficit surfaces only as a function of certain task requirements, notably short-term memory, conscious awareness, and time constraints. In an attempt to reformulate those task requirements more economically, we propose that they have a deficit in access to phonological representations. The same type of deficient access to representations may turn out to adequately characterize the additional sensory and cognitive deficits of the subset of individuals who have them.

REFERENCES

Adlard, A., & Hazan, V. (1998). Speech perception in children with specific reading difficulties (dyslexia). *Quarterly Journal of Experimental Psychology, 51A,* 153–177.

Ahissar, M., Lubin, Y., Putter-Katz, H., & Banai, K. (2006). Dyslexia and the failure to form a perceptual anchor. *Nature Neuroscience, 9,* 1558–1564.

Amitay, S., Ben-Yehudah, G., Banai, K., & Ahissar, M. (2002). Disabled readers suffer from visual and auditory impairments but not from a specific magnocellular deficit. *Brain, 125,* 2272–2285.

Baddeley, A. D. (1984). Exploring the articulatory loop. *Quarterly Journal of Experimental Psychology, 36,* 233–252.

Banai, K., & Ahissar, M. (2006). Auditory processing deficits in dyslexia: Task or stimulus related? *Cerebral Cortex, 16,* 1718–1728.

Ben-Yehudah, G., Sackett, E., Malchi-Ginzberg, L., & Ahissar, M. (2001). Impaired temporal contrast sensitivity in dyslexics is specific to retain-and-compare paradigms. *Brain, 124,* 1381–1395.

Blomert, L., Mitterer, H., & Paffen, C. (2004). In search of the auditory, phonetic and/or phonological problems in dyslexia: Context effects in speech perception. *Journal of Speech, Language and Hearing Research, 47,* 1030–1047.

Brady, S., Shankweiler, D., & Mann, V. (1983). Speech perception and memory coding in relation to reading ability. *Journal of Experimental Child Psychology, 35,* 345–367.

Carpenter, P. A., Just, M. A., & Reichle, E. D. (2000). Working memory and executive function: Evidence from neuroimaging. *Current Opinion in Neurobiology, 10,* 195–199.

Chomsky, N., & Halle, M. (1968). *The sound pattern of English.* New York: Harper and Row.

Cornelissen, P. L., Hansen, P. C., Bradley, L., & Stein, J. F. (1996). Analysis of perceptual confusions between nine sets of consonant–vowel sounds in normal and dyslexic adults. *Cognition, 59,* 275–306.

Darcy, I., Peperkamp, S., & Dupoux, E. (in press-a). Perceptual learning and plasticity in a second language: Building a new system for phonological processes. In J. Cole & J. I. Hualde (Eds.), *Labphon 9: Change in Phonology.* Berlin: Mouton de Gruyter.

Darcy, I., Ramus, F., Christophe, A., Kinzler, K., & Dupoux, E. (in press-b). Phonological knowledge in compensation for native and non-native assimilation. In F. Kügler, C. Féry, & R. van de Vijver (Eds),

Variation and gradience in phonetics and phonology. Berlin: Mouton De Gruyter.

Elbro, C. (1998). When reading is "readn" or somthn. Distinctness of phonological representations of lexical items in normal and disabled readers. *Scandinavian Journal of Psychology, 39,* 149–153.

Frith, U. (1999). Paradoxes in the definition of dyslexia. *Dyslexia, 5,* 192–214.

Gaillard, E. (2006). *Amorçage auditif de répétition subliminal et conscient appliqué à l'étude de la dyslexie.* [Conscious and subliminal auditory repetition priming applied to the study of dyslexia]. Unpublished MSc dissertation, ENS/EHESS/Paris V, Paris.

Goswami, U. (2003). Why theories about developmental dyslexia require developmental designs. *Trends in Cognitive Sciences, 7,* 534–540.

Guttorm, T. K., Leppänen, P. H. T., Richardson, U., & Lyytinen, H. (2001). Event-related potentials and consonant differentiation in newborns with familial risk for dyslexia. *Journal of Learning Disabilities, 34,* 534–544.

Hall, J. W., Wilson, K. P., Humphreys, M. S., Tinzmann, M. B., & Bowyer, P. M. (1983). Phonemic-similarity effects in good vs. poor readers. *Memory and Cognition, 11,* 520–527.

Hallé, P. A., Segui, J., Frauenfelder, U., & Meunier, C. (1998). Processing of illegal consonant clusters: A case of perceptual assimilation? *Journal of Experimental Psychology: Human Perception & Performance, 24,* 592–608.

Hulme, C., & Snowling, M. (1992). Deficits in output phonology: An explanation of reading failure? *Cognitive Neuropsychology, 9,* 47–72.

Jacquemot, C., & Scott, S. K. (2006). What is the relationship between phonological short-term memory and speech processing? *Trends in Cognitive Sciences, 10,* 480–486.

Jeffries, S., & Everatt, J. (2004). Working memory: Its role in dyslexia and other specific learning difficulties. *Dyslexia, 10,* 196–214.

Johnston, R. S., Rugg, M., & Scott, T. (1987). Phonological similarity effects, memory span and developmental reading disorders: The nature of the relationship. *British Journal of Psychology, 78,* 205–211.

Kouider, S., & Dupoux, E. (2005). Subliminal speech priming. *Psychological Science, 16,* 617–625.

Leppänen, P. H., Richardson, U., Pihko, E., Eklund, K. M., Guttorm, T. K., Aro, M., et al. (2002). Brain responses to changes in speech sound durations differ between infants with and without

familial risk for dyslexia. *Developmental Neuropsychology, 22,* 407–422.

Manis, F. R., McBride-Chang, C., Seidenberg, M. S., Keating, P., Doi, L. M., Munson, B., et al. (1997). Are speech perception deficits associated with developmental dyslexia? *Journal of Experimental Child Psychology, 66,* 211–235.

Marshall, C. R., Tang, S., Rosen, S., Ramus, F., & van der Lely, H. K. J. (2007). *Segmental phonological deficits in SLI and dyslexia, and their relationships with language impairments.* Manuscript submitted for publication.

McCrory, E. (2001). *A neurocognitive investigation of phonological processing in dyslexia.* Unpublished doctoral dissertation, University College London, UK.

McNeil, A. M., & Johnston, R. S. (2004). Word length, phonemic, and visual similarity effects in poor and normal readers. *Memory and Cognition, 32,* 687–695.

Messbauer, V. C. S., & de Jong, P. F. (2006). Effects of visual and phonological distinctness on visual–verbal paired associate learning in Dutch dyslexic and normal readers. *Reading and Writing, 19,* 393–426.

Mody, M., Studdert-Kennedy, M., & Brady, S. (1997). Speech perception deficits in poor readers: Auditory processing or phonological coding? *Journal of Experimental Child Psychology, 64,* 199–231.

Molfese, D. L. (2000). Predicting dyslexia at 8 years of age using neonatal brain responses. *Brain and Language, 72,* 238–245.

Morton, J., & Frith, U. (1995). Causal modeling: A structural approach to developmental psychopathology. In D. Cicchetti & D. J. Cohen (Eds), *Developmental psychopathology: Vol. 1. Theory and methods* (pp. 357–390). New York: Wiley.

Ramus, F. (2001a). Dyslexia: Talk of two theories. *Nature, 412,* 393–395.

Ramus, F. (2001b). Outstanding questions about phonological processing in dyslexia. *Dyslexia, 7,* 197–216.

Ramus, F. (2003). Developmental dyslexia: Specific phonological deficit or general sensorimotor dysfunction? *Current Opinion in Neurobiology, 13,* 212–218.

Ramus, F. (2004). Neurobiology of dyslexia: A reinterpretation of the data. *Trends in Neurosciences, 27,* 720–726.

Ramus, F., Pidgeon, E., & Frith, U. (2003a). The relationship between motor control and phonology in dyslexic children. *Journal of Child Psychology and Psychiatry, 44,* 712–722.

Ramus, F., Rosen, S., Dakin, S. C., Day, B. L., Castellote, J. M., White, S., et al. (2003b). Theories of developmental dyslexia: Insights from a multiple case study of dyslexic adults. *Brain, 126*, 841–865.

Ramus, F., White, S., & Frith, U. (2006). Weighing the evidence between competing theories of dyslexia. *Developmental Science, 9*, 265–269.

Richardson, U., Leppänen, P. H. T., Leiwo, M., & Lyytinen, H. (2003). Speech perception of infants with high familial risk for dyslexia differ at the age of six months. *Developmental Neuropsychology, 23*, 385–397.

Rosen, S., & Manganari, E. (2001). Is there a relationship between speech and nonspeech auditory processing in children with dyslexia? *Journal of Speech, Language and Hearing Research, 44*, 720–736.

Serniclaes, W., Van Heghe, S., Mousty, P., Carré, R., & Sprenger-Charolles, L. (2004). Allophonic mode of speech perception in dyslexia. *Journal of Experimental Child Psychology, 87*, 336–361.

Service, E. (1992). Phonology, working memory, and foreign-language learning. *Quarterly Journal of Experimental Psychology, 45A*, 21–50.

Shankweiler, D., & Crain, S. (1986). Language mechanisms and reading disorder: A modular approach. *Cognition, 24*, 139–168.

Shankweiler, D., Liberman, I. Y., Mark, L. S., & Fowler, C. A. (1979). The speech code and learning to read. *Journal of Experimental Psychology: Human Learning and Memory, 5*, 531–545.

Snoeren, N. D., Hallé, P. A., & Segui, J. (2006). A voice for the voiceless: Production and perception of assimilated stops in French. *Journal of Phonetics, 34*, 241–268.

Snowling, M. J. (2000). *Dyslexia* (2nd ed.). Oxford, UK: Blackwell.

Snowling, M. J., Goulandris, N., Bowlby, M., & Howell, P. (1986). Segmentation and speech perception in relation to reading skill: A developmental analysis. *Journal of Experimental Child Psychology, 41*, 489–507.

Snowling, M. J., van Wagtendonk, B., & Stafford, C. (1988). Object-naming deficits in developmental dyslexia. *Journal of Research in Reading, 11*, 67–85.

Soroli, E. G. (2005). *Perception et production des contrastes phonétiques étrangers par des sujets dyslexiques adultes* [Perception and production of foreign phonetic contrasts by adult dyslexic subjects]. Unpublished MSc dissertation, Université Paris XI, Orsay, France.

Sperling, A. J., Lu, Z. L., Manis, F. R., & Seidenberg, M. S. (2005). Deficits in perceptual noise exclusion in developmental dyslexia. *Nature Neuroscience, 8*, 862–863.

Sperling, A. J., Lu, Z. L., Manis, F. R., & Seidenberg, M. S. (2006). Motion-perception deficits and reading impairment: It's the noise, not the motion. *Psychological Science, 17*, 1047–1053.

Swan, D., & Goswami, U. (1997a). Phonological awareness deficits in developmental dyslexia and the phonological representations hypothesis. *Journal of Experimental Child Psychology, 66*, 18–41.

Swan, D., & Goswami, U. (1997b). Picture naming deficits in developmental dyslexia: The phonological representations hypothesis. *Brain and Language, 56*, 334–353.

Swanson, H. L., & Ramalgia, J. M. (1992). The relationship between phonological codes on memory and spelling tasks for students with and without learning disabilities. *Journal of Learning Disabilities, 25*, 396–407.

Szenkovits, G., Darma, Q., Darcy, I., & Ramus, F. (2007a). *Exploring dyslexics' phonological deficit II: Phonological grammar.* Manuscript in preparation.

Szenkovits, G., Dupoux, E., & Ramus, F. (2007b). *Exploring dyslexics' phonological deficit III: impaired representations or short-term memory processes?* Manuscript in preparation.

Szenkovits, G., & Ramus, F. (2005). Exploring dyslexics' phonological deficit I: Lexical vs. sub-lexical and input vs. output processes. *Dyslexia, 11*, 253–268.

Szenkovits, G., Dupoux, E., & Ramus, F. (2007). *Exploring dyslexics' phonological deficit IV: The output pathway.* Manuscript in preparation.

van Alphen, P., de Bree, E., Gerrits, E., de Jong, J., Wilsenach, C., & Wijnen, F. (2004). Early language development in children with a genetic risk of dyslexia. *Dyslexia, 10*, 265–288.

Wagner, R. K., & Torgesen, J. K. (1987). The nature of phonological processing and its causal role in the acquisition of reading skills. *Psychological Bulletin, 101*, 192–212.

White, S., Frith, U., Milne, E., Rosen, S., Swettenham, J., & Ramus, F. (2006a). A double dissociation between sensorimotor impairments and reading disability: A comparison of autistic and dyslexic children. *Cognitive Neuropsychology, 23*, 748–761.

White, S., Milne, E., Rosen, S., Hansen, P. C., Swettenham, J., Frith, U., et al. (2006b). The role of sensorimotor impairments in dyslexia: A multiple case study of dyslexic children. *Developmental Science, 9*, 237–255.

THE QUARTERLY JOURNAL OF EXPERIMENTAL PSYCHOLOGY
2008, 61 (1), 142–156

Specific disorders and broader phenotypes: The case of dyslexia

Margaret J. Snowling

University of York, York, UK

Two studies investigating the cognitive phenotype of dyslexia are described. Study 1 compared three groups of English and Italian children on speed of processing tasks: (a) children with dyslexia, (b) generally delayed poor readers and (c) CA-controls. In tests of simple and choice reaction time and two visual scanning tasks, children with dyslexia performed like controls and significantly faster than generally delayed poor readers. A second prospective longitudinal investigation of children at family risk of dyslexia showed that problems of literacy development were less circumscribed, with affected children showing phonological deficits in the context of more general oral language difficulties. An important finding was that the risk of dyslexia was continuous in this sample; among at-risk children with normal literacy development, mild impairments of phonological skills were apparent early in development, and subtle difficulties with reading fluency and spelling emerged in early adolescence. A case series extended these findings to show that phonological deficits alone are insufficient to explain literacy difficulties, and it is children with multiple deficits (including language problems) that are more likely to succumb to reading failure.

Uta Frith has contributed a remarkable number of key works spanning theory and practice to the field of dyslexia. Her defining contributions include a deceptively simple theoretical framework for literacy development within which to consider individual differences in reading and spelling disorders (Frith, 1985), her cross-linguistic studies with Heinz Wimmer and Karin Landerl showing that dyslexia is better characterized as a disorder of reading fluency in transparent languages and of reading accuracy in an opaque language like English (e.g., Frith, Wimmer, & Landerl, 1998), and her pioneering work with Eraldo Paulesu and Chris Frith examining the brain bases of dyslexia in "compensated" individuals (Paulesu et al., 1996). Fundamentally, Uta considers dyslexia to

be a specific cognitive disorder characterized by a phonological deficit (Ramus et al., 2003; White et al., 2006); furthermore, phonological deficits in dyslexia are both universal (Paulesu et al., 2001) and life-course persistent (Snowling, Nation, Moxham, Gallagher, & Frith, 1997). This paper poses the provocative question of whether this well-established theoretical position continues to be tenable.

THEORIES OF DEVELOPMENTAL COGNITIVE DISORDERS

Together Uta's theories embody a number of key concepts about developmental disorders.

Correspondence should be addressed to M. J. Snowling, Department of Psychology, University of York, York YO10 5DD, UK. E-mail: m.snowling@psych.york.ac.uk

This paper was prepared with the support of a British Academy Research Readership. I thank Uta Frith for starting me off on a fascinating search for the roots of dyslexia and for all her support during the journey thus far.

DOI:10.1080/17470210701508830

Arguably these are captured well by the title of her 1985 paper *"Beneath the surface of developmental dyslexia"*. In lay terms, and with respect to developmental disorders, we should not be tricked by what we see in surface behaviour—such behaviour cannot tell us about the causes of disorders or indeed how behaviours have been modified by experiential factors. With this in mind, John Morton and Uta Frith cleverly synthesized different strands of evidence concerning dyslexia under the rubric of "developmental contingency modelling" (Morton & Frith, 1995).

Developmental contingency modelling is a framework for considering developmental disorders at the biological, cognitive, and behavioural levels of explanation (Morton, 2004); within this framework, dyslexia is a specific cognitive disorder characterized by phonological deficits mediating brain-behaviour relationships, the effects of which can be modified by environmental experiences (Frith, 1997). An important assumption of the model is that domain-general learning disorders that affect the functioning of multiple systems should be distinguished from domain-specific disorders that are modular in nature. Moreover, speed of information processing, an index of mental efficiency (Anderson, 1992), is a useful construct for differentiating between such specific disorders and those that are domain general (Scheuffgen, Happé, Anderson, & Frith, 2000).

However, the concept of specific developmental disorders has come under scrutiny in recent times. First, from the perspective of behaviour genetics, Plomin and Kovas (2005) have argued that the genes that are associated with developmental disorders have general as well as specific effects. It follows that pure disorders should be relatively rare, and more often the effects of developmental disorders will be diffuse, commonly accompanied by effects on "g". Second, from the perspective of cognitive science, Thomas and Karmiloff-Smith (2002) have argued that rather than being viewed as circumscribed or "modular" in nature, developmental disorders should be seen as the endpoint of an aberrant developmental process, reflecting the interaction of deficient and compensatory

processes. Third, from the perspective of developmental neuropsychology, both Pennington (2006) and Bishop (2006) have argued that single-deficit accounts of developmental disorders do not explain the heterogeneity (both etiological and behavioural) observed in these conditions, and comorbidities must be explained. So how do single-deficit, modular, theories of dyslexia (e.g., Snowling, 2000) stand up to appraisal?

Dyslexia as a domain-specific disorder

The distinction between domain-specific and domain-general learning problems has been the focus of debate in the field of reading disorders, as much for practical as for theoretical reasons (Stanovich, 1994). In terms of etiology and outcome, the distinction between specific reading difficulties that are unexpected given a child's general cognitive ability (dyslexia) and general reading problems in the context of widespread learning problems has validity (Rutter & Maughan, 2005). Nonetheless, the use of IQ criteria to differentiate subgroups of failing readers (e.g., *Diagnostic and Statistical Manual of Mental Disorders—Fourth Edition*, DSM-IV, American Psychiatric Association, 1994) has declined because, at the cognitive level of description, the two groups share deficits in phonological processing (Stanovich & Siegel, 1994; Swan & Goswami, 1997), and they make equivalent response to reading intervention programmes targeting decoding skills (Hatcher & Hulme, 1999; Shaywitz, Fletcher, Holahan, & Shaywitz, 1996).

Contrary to the view that general processing resources are normal in dyslexia, some studies suggest that children with dyslexia have speed of processing impairments (Breznitz & Meyler, 2003; Nicolson & Fawcett, 1994; Sobotka & May 1977; Stringer & Stanovich, 2000); moreover, it has been proposed that such impairments play a role in the determination of reading disability (Catts, Gillespie, Leonard, Kail, & Miller, 2002; Pennington, 2006; Willcutt, Pennington, Olson, Chhabildas, & Hulslander, 2005). If this is true, then it would challenge the strong version of the hypothesis that the core deficit in dyslexia is in phonology and that *this is both necessary and sufficient to predict a reading problem* (Ramus et al., 2003). Rather, if speed of processing is an index of general cognitive capacity (Anderson, 1992; Jensen, 1998), a modified view might be that dyslexia is the outcome of resource limitations working in tandem with more specific deficits in phonological processes.

Experiment 1

The first experiment to be described was cast within the framework of Anderson's (1992) model of intelligence. It assessed the validity of the orthodox view that dyslexia is a specific cognitive disorder by contrasting speed of processing in children with specific reading difficulties with that of children who were equally poor at reading but of low IQ ("generally delayed" poor readers). A comparison group of age-matched normal readers was also included to provide a benchmark for typical performance. If it is correct to conceptualize dyslexia as a specific disorder, we predicted that speed of processing would be at the age-appropriate level among the readers with dyslexia and significantly higher than speed of processing in generally delayed poor readers. The study also incorporated a cross-linguistic comparison of English and Italian children (Bonifacci & Snowling, 2007).

Table 1 shows the mean age, IQ, and reading attainment of the children in the three groups. In the English sample, there were 20 children

with dyslexia, all with IQ scores within the normal range and 17 children whose IQ scores ranged from 70 to 85 (henceforth described as low-IQ) In the Italian sample, the poor readers were identified on the basis of reading speed not accuracy. There were 17 children with dyslexia, defined on the basis of very slow reading speed for their age and 15 children of low-IQ reading at the same level. The two chronological-age-control (CA-control) groups each comprised 21 typically developing children selected from mainstream schools and matched to the respective clinical samples for age. The pattern of scores in reading was similar across languages even though different tests were administered. In both language groups, the children with dyslexia and the low-IQ children did not differ from one another on reading tests but each did less well than controls; moreover, it is noteworthy that between-group differences in accuracy for English children were replicated by reading fluency measures.

The English and the Italian children had by necessity been given different IQ tests. However in both cases, the tasks administered comprised vocabulary (word definitions) and matrices (nonverbal reasoning) tasks. It is important to note that these IQ measures were untimed; had the IQ assessments been derived from timed tests then this would have confounded experimental findings.

We used two sets of tasks to assess speed of information processing: simple and choice

Table 1. *Experiment 1: Details of participants*

	English			Italian		
	Dyslexia (N = 20)	GPR[a] (N = 17)	CA-control (N = 21)	Dyslexia (N = 17)	GPR[a] (N = 15)	CA-control (N = 21)
Age (in months)	126.5 (22.8)	130.6 (33.4)	135.6 (29)	111.4 (21.4)	98.1 (15.2)	101.3 (18.6)
Full Scale IQ	106.9 (11.2)	77.7 (7.5)	108.8 (10.9)	102.1 (6.8)	79.3 (5.1)	104.1 (5.7)
Reading accuracy	87.2 (9.8)	84.2 (16.5)	107.2 (10.4)	—	—	—
Reading speed[b]	83.6 (10)	86.8 (22.4)	110 (9.2)	—	—	—
Reading speed[c]	—	—	—	−2.4 (0.8)	−2.5 (1.9)	−0.1 (0.7)

Note: Standard scores (mean: 100, *SD*: 15) are reported for IQ and reading scores for the English sample. Reading speed for the Italian sample is expressed in z-scores relative to age standard (mean: 0, *SD*: 1). Standard deviations are shown in parentheses.
[a]GPR = generally poor reader. [b]English test. [c]Italian test.

reaction time (RT) and visual search for digits and symbols. To measure simple reaction time, children were required to attend to the computer screen, and, whenever a "blue star" appeared, they were required to press the space bar as fast as they could. The target stimulus appeared for 1,000 ms and disappeared after a response was made. The following star appeared after a constant 1,000-ms interval. To measure choice reaction time, the icons of a hand and of a foot were presented for 1,000 ms in random sequence. Children were required to press the H key for the hand and the F key for the foot. The visual search tasks required the child to detect whether a target stimulus (the probe) appeared in a string of stimuli. After a 1-s blank screen, a probe was presented for 3 s, and then, following a 1-s delay, between 1 and 7 stimuli appeared on the screen where they remained until the child gave a response. Children were instructed to indicate whether the probe was in the sequence by responding "Yes" or "No" using two adjacent keys on the keyboard. In number scanning, the stimuli were digits, and the symbol scanning task was developed as a nonverbal analogue using letters taken from an unfamiliar alphabet and were therefore quite hard to label. In the symbol scanning task, the maximum sequence length was 5 (rather than 7 as for digits) because of the complexity of the symbols.

Preliminary analyses indicated that there was no main effect of language for any of the tasks, therefore the data from the English and Italian children were pooled within reader groups (dyslexia, generally delayed and typical). Analyses were run on mean and median RT scores and on standard deviations of RTs with age as a covariate because, although the groups were matched for age, variations in age are expected to affect speed of processing (Kail, 1991). The pattern of findings across sets of tasks was similar (see Figure 1). For simple and choice RTs, there was a significant main effect of group with generally delayed poor readers performing significantly more slowly than CA-controls, whereas the RTs of children with dyslexia were not significantly different from those of controls (and they were significantly

faster than generally delayed poor readers in choice RT). In the digit and symbol scanning tasks, generally delayed poor readers were again slower than children with dyslexia and CA-controls, who did not differ from each other on either task. In each of the four tasks, there was also a main effect of group on standard deviations with generally delayed poor readers showing more variability. Finally, a case-by-case analysis indicated that no child with dyslexia showed impairments across RT tasks, and only one was impaired in both number and symbol scanning.

The present findings fail to replicate previous studies in which slower speed of processing was observed for children with dyslexia. Although there was a trend for the children with dyslexia to be somewhat slower than CA-controls, the differences were small and not statistically significant. Indeed group differences patterned with IQ and not with reading skill, the behavioural measure on which the groups were matched. The group differences were also robust across language. Together these data offer support for the theory that dyslexia is a domain-specific cognitive deficit (Anderson, 1992). However, they do not speak either to the cognitive cause of dyslexia or to its developmental trajectory.

Dyslexia as a phonological deficit

Aside from the issue of domain specificity, the predominant theoretical account of dyslexia places its proximal cause within the phonological system of language (Morton & Frith, 1995; Pennington, 2002; Vellutino, Fletcher, Snowling, & Scanlon, 2004). Such theories have largely assumed that phonological deficits compromise the development of reading (Snowling, 2000) whereas magnocellular (Stein & Talcott, 1999) or cerebellar (Nicolson, Fawcett, & Dean, 2001) deficits are more likely to reflect associated sensory impairments that are not causally related to reading problems (Ramus, 2004; Rochelle & Talcott, 2006).

With such findings as a back-drop, in 1992 Uta and I set out to follow a cohort of children at high risk of dyslexia by virtue of the fact that they were

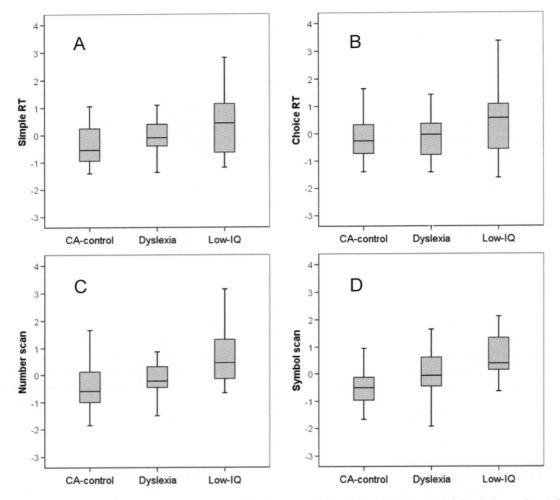

Figure 1. *Distribution of scores on speed-of-processing tasks for groups with dyslexia, borderline intellectual functioning, and controls (residualized for age): (A) simple reaction time (RT); (B) choice RT; (C) scanning numbers; (D) scanning symbols.*

born into families where there was a history of dyslexia. Scarborough (1990) had pioneered this approach by following children at family risk of dyslexia from 2 to 8 years. The findings of her study were intriguing: As well as reporting an elevated incidence of dyslexia in at-risk families (65%), Scarborough (1990, 1991) had observed that during the preschool years, these children showed expressive vocabulary and syntactic difficulties, the latter resolving by the school years, when problems of phonological awareness and

poor letter knowledge emerged as the proximal causes of "dyslexia".

Scarborough's study was small in scale and warranted replication. We proceeded to devise a battery of oral language tasks to test the prediction that the precursors of dyslexia in the preschool years would be deficits in speech and language processes tapping phonological skills—namely, articulation, nonword repetition, expressive vocabulary, and nursery rhyme knowledge. In contrast, we predicted that performance on nonphonological language tasks (e.g., narrative skills and receptive vocabulary) would be normal. Furthermore, we anticipated that children who went on to be dyslexic would show poorer letter knowledge than their peers from the outset of literacy acquisition and would have significant difficulty in acquiring the "alphabetic principle" that depends on letter knowledge and phoneme awareness (Byrne, 1998).

With Alison Gallagher, we recruited some 70 children just before their fourth birthday, all of whom were born to families with a history of dyslexia, determined initially by self-report (Gallagher, Frith, & Snowling, 2000). To provide a comparison group, we recruited 37 families in which there was no history of reading problems—the reason that we had fewer control than at-risk families was on the assumption that, if about 50% of the at-risk group became dyslexic, we would be able to compare retrospectively three approximately equal-size groups—at-risk impaired, at-risk unimpaired, and control. We went on to assess each of the parents of the children in our study on a battery of tasks comprising reading, spelling, and phonological skills. The differences between all of these measures were significant, and it was striking that, although the majority of the families comprised successful middle-class people (as typical of volunteer samples), the average standard score of the dyslexia group was 82.3 ($SD = 15.6$) for reading and 75.2 ($SD = 17.4$) for spelling, compared to 103.2 ($SD = 11.2$) and 105.6 ($SD = 13.9$), respectively, for controls.

Our study fell into two phases. In Phase 1, we assessed the children at the ages of 3;09, 6, and 8 years (Gallagher et al., 2000; Snowling, Gallagher, & Frith, 2003). In Phase 2, we followed up those that remained in the sample at 12–13 years (Snowling, Muter, & Carroll, 2007). When the children were 8 years of age we determined the number in each group who might be considered to have literacy difficulties in comparison to the mean and standard deviation of the control group on reading and spelling tests (a literacy composite). At this time, 66% of the at-risk group with scores one standard deviation below the control mean were deemed "literacy impaired" while at-risk children whose literacy scores fell within one standard deviation of the mean or above were considered "literacy unimpaired". We then went back to investigate the early development of the at-risk literacy-impaired group, comparing them with the at-risk literacy-unimpaired and the control groups.

Contrary to our predictions, the children in the at-risk group who went on to have literacy problems did not show a selective phonological deficit in the preschool years; in fact they showed a quite widespread pattern of language delay incorporating slow development of receptive and expressive language skills and vocabulary knowledge. In contrast, the at-risk unimpaired group were statistically indistinguishable from the control group on oral language tests with the exception of one task, nonword repetition, on which the two at-risk groups did not differ from each other. Turning to tests of phonological awareness: At 6 years we measured rhyme oddity (the ability to identify the odd one out from a sequence of four words, three of which rhymed) and phoneme deletion (the ability to take a phoneme away from a monosyllabic word). Not surprisingly the at-risk children who went on to have literacy difficulties were impaired on these tasks. The performance of the at-risk unimpaired group was significantly better but there was a trend for these children to perform less well than controls (with an effect size of around 0.5; see Figure 2).

Together, these findings threw doubt on the notion that dyslexia should be considered a *specific* phonological deficit. Although the data confirmed that the at-risk impaired group did indeed experience a phonological deficit, they indicated that this should be seen in the context of a broader oral language delay (though note, for the majority of children, oral language skills were within the normal range). However, an important finding was that the at-risk unimpaired group showed similarities to the at-risk impaired

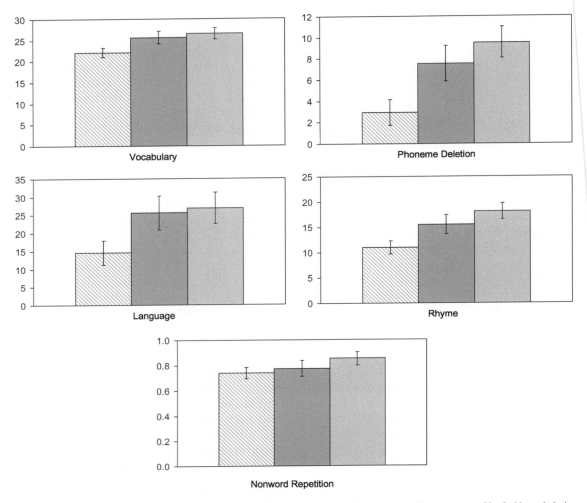

Figure 2. *Preschool language development and 6-year-old phonological awareness skills according to literacy outcome. Hatched bars: dyslexia. Dark grey: at risk normal. Light grey: CA control. Left figure: receptive vocabulary, expressive language, and nonword repetition scores at age 3;09. Right figure: phoneme deletion and rhyme tasks at age 6;00.*

group, particularly in the domain of phonological skills. Specifically, at 3;09 they were as poor at nonword repetition (and significantly less good then controls) and at 6 years, their performance on tests of phonological awareness was below what might be expected given their other oral language skills (e.g., vocabulary and grammatical abilities). A similar set of findings was reported by Pennington and Lefly (2001) from an at-risk study in which "unaffected" children from dyslexia families shared deficits in phonological awareness and verbal short-term memory with affected individuals. Together these findings suggest the simple story, "that dyslexia is a specific phonological deficit", may need to be modified. A new interpretation might be that phonological deficits represent what is described as an "endophenotype" of dyslexia—that is, a set of deficient processes, arguably closer to the genotype than the (reading) behaviour itself (Doyle et al., 2005; Skuse, 2001), shared by affected and nonaffected family members.

The development of reading and spelling in dyslexia

If it is the case that phonological deficits are an endophenotype of dyslexia, then we need to ask whether there are any subtle signs of literacy difficulty associated with this endophenotype in dyslexic families. A widely held view is that the poorly specified phonological representations that underlie phonological deficits limit a child's ability to establish mappings between phonological sequences and letter strings (Fowler, 1991; Griffiths & Snowling, 2002; Harm & Seidenberg, 1999; Swan & Goswami, 1997). Within this view, we would predict that unimpaired family members should show relatively slow development of the alphabetic principle (Byrne, 1998) when compared with children from families in which there is no history of reading impairment.

The first component of the alphabetic principle that can be measured is letter knowledge (Bowey, 2005). We measured knowledge of letter names and sounds at 3;09 and at 6 years, and at 6 years we made a more formal assessment of alphabetic competence using a test of nonword reading (of simple consonant–vowel–consonant, CVC items). Predictably, the at-risk impaired group who went on have literacy problems at 8 years performed significantly less well than controls on tests of letter knowledge at both time points. The at-risk unimpaired group did better but, in line with the view that they shared the risk of reading problems, they had poorer letter knowledge than controls, significantly poorer at 3;09 years. More striking were the data from the nonword reading task. On this test, the at-risk unimpaired group scored as poorly as the at-risk impaired group (Snowling et al., 2003). In short, they displayed one of the cardinal features of dyslexia, an impairment in grapheme–phoneme correspondence (Frith, 1997).

Within many theories, a difficulty with the acquisition of the alphabetic principle should presage a literacy impairment. However, in the present study this was not inevitably the case.

In order to explain this puzzling finding, we proposed that the children in the literacy-unimpaired group were able to circumvent reading and spelling problems by using intact oral language skills to bootstrap ineffective decoding abilities. In short, we hypothesized that they could make use of contextual cues to facilitate reading performance and thereby avoiding literacy failure (Nation & Snowling, 1998; Pring & Snowling, 1986).

Notwithstanding this, Frith and Happé (1998) have argued that, while compensation for developmental disorders is possible, it comes at a cost. Our next question was, therefore, what would be the downstream cost for the at-risk unimpaired group of relying on top-down processes to learn to read? Frith (1980) described a group of children who were good readers but had "unexpected" spelling problems (Group "B" spellers). This literacy profile highlights the fact that reading can proceed using partial cues but spelling requires access to full orthographic knowledge of the letter-by-letter sequences of words (Frith & Frith, 1980). With this in mind, we predicted that the at-risk unimpaired group who were, we presumed, reading globally, would have difficulty in developing fully specified orthographic representations. In time, such problems would affect reading fluency (Wimmer, Mayringer, & Landerl, 1998) and lead to relatively poor spelling.

To assess this hypothesis, Snowling et al. (2007) followed up the at-risk sample of children in early adolescence. Between the ages of 8 and 12 years the groups made an average rate of progress in reading and spelling, as measured by standardized tests. Encouragingly, although they remained significantly impaired relative to their peers, the at-risk impaired group showed no evidence of falling further behind (cf. Stanovich, 1986). Importantly, and in line with prediction, the at-risk "unimpaired group" were significantly slower on tests of reading fluency than were controls. In addition, they showed subtle orthographic deficits, including poor exception word reading, although their reading comprehension was comparable to that of the typically developing normal readers.

Thus, the developmental outcome for children from at-risk families is variable. Among offspring of dyslexic parents, there are children who show literacy problems in the context of poor oral language skills and others who show more subtle impairments in reading fluency and orthographic knowledge but who do not reach a threshold for "diagnosis". These "unimpaired" children constitute what might be referred to as a broader phenotype of dyslexia, and in very many respects they resemble the Group "B" spellers identified by Uta some 25 years ago. The existence of such a "broader phenotype" highlights a tension between the diagnosis of dyslexia as a categorical disorder ("dyslexic" or "not") and a dimensional view (dyslexia as a continuous trait). These individuals provide a clear demonstration that the family risk of dyslexia is continuous, and we infer that whether or not an individual eventually fulfils diagnostic criteria for reading disorder depends on the profile of cognitive skills they bring to the task of reading as well as on the environments in which they learn.

COGNITIVE DEFICITS IN CHILDREN AT FAMILY RISK OF DYSLEXIA: A CASE SERIES

Thus far, our focus has been on the average performance of groups of children, classified according to family status and literacy outcome. This approach has revealed among at-risk children differences not only in phonological abilities but also in wider language skills associated with differential outcomes. If dyslexia is to be considered a quantitative trait, it becomes important to know how well the pattern of strengths and weaknesses that we have observed at the group level holds across individuals and, hence, to what extent the group means are a true reflection of different trajectories of development. In order to elucidate this issue we turn to a case-by-case analysis of the cognitive skills of the adolescents who remained in the at-risk sample at the age of 12–13 years. Although it has been argued above that dyslexia is a dimensional disorder without clear-cut

boundaries, the objective of this analysis was to shed light on the resources available to different individuals to enable them to compensate for their phonological difficulties and also to identify any additional risk factors that may increase the probability of a child succumbing to a reading disorder.

For this analysis, individuals were classified as literacy impaired in keeping with the definition used in our previously published studies (composite based on reading and spelling skills falling one standard deviation below the control mean). Full data were available for 48 of the at-risk sample (20 "literacy impaired" and 28 unimpaired in terms of this criterion). It could be argued, however, that the criterion adopted was lenient since many of the literacy-impaired group had literacy skills that fell broadly within the average range (a composite score of >85). Two subanalyses were therefore conducted. First, within the literacy-impaired group, those whose reading as well as spelling fell below the control mean were compared with those who fulfilled the criterion for literacy impairment because they had poor spelling but normal range reading (Group B spellers). Second, the data from five individuals who gained literacy composite scores below 85 were scrutinized.

The next step was to reduce the Phase 2 data set to form composite scores reflecting performance in four domains of functioning: phonological abilities, visuo-spatial skills, attention control, and oral language. The phonology (P) composite comprised performance on a phoneme deletion task (McDougall, Hulme, Ellis, & Monk, 1994), the *Children's Nonword Repetition Test* (Gathercole, Willis, Baddeley, & Emslie, 1994), and the untimed *Graded Nonword Reading Test* (Snowling, Stothard, & McLean, 1996). The visuo-spatial composite (V) comprised performance on the *British Ability Scales* Recall of Designs task, which requires designs to be studied for 5 seconds and then reproduced from memory, and the *Wechsler Abbreviated Scale of Intelligence* (Wechsler, 1999) Block Design Task. The attention (A) composite comprised performance on two tests from the *Test of Everyday Attention for Children* (Manly, Robertson, Anderson, & Nimmo-Smith, 1998)—namely,

SCORE!, which measures sustained attention, and *Opposite Worlds*, which measures switching attention using *Same Worlds* as a baseline measure of speed of processing, and parental ratings of hyperactivity on the *Strengths and Difficulties Questionnaire* (SDQ; Goodman, 1997). The oral language composite (L) was the verbal IQ score from the *Wechsler Abbreviated Scale of Intelligence* (Wechsler, 1999) Vocabulary and Similarities subtests.

We proceeded to define a deficiency in the P, V, and A domains as a score below one standard deviation of the mean of the control group (below the 16th percentile) and below a verbal IQ of 85 for the L domain (the criterion for the L domain was more stringent than that for the other domains to avoid overestimating the overlap between dyslexia and language impairment). Table 2 provides a summary of the deficits experienced by the young people in the literacy-impaired group; those that showed reading impairments as well as spelling problems are shown in the upper part of the table, and those without reading impairments at the bottom. For purposes of comparison, Table 3 shows data from the literacy-unimpaired group who experienced deficits in any of the four key domains ($N = 14$). The remainder of the at-risk sample ($N = 14$) were free of cognitive impairments.

First, as might be expected given quantitative variation in reading and spelling skills, there was a strong inverse correlation between literacy skill and the number of cognitive deficits observed in the at-risk group as a whole ($r = -.63$). Second, it was more common for the literacy-impaired group to have multiple impairments (12 had more than one impairment) than the literacy unimpaired group (15 had one impairment and none more than one). Among the at-risk impaired group, the most common deficits were in phonology (12/20 cases) and attention (11/20 cases) but visual deficits and language impairments were also observed. In only one case was there a single deficit in phonology. Among those defined as literacy

Table 2. *Findings from case-series showing the cognitive deficits observed among at-risk children with literacy impairments*

Case No.	Phonological deficit	Visuospatial deficit	Attention deficit	Language impairment	Literacy composite	
29	✓	✓	✓	✓	67.5	RS
103	✓			✓	70.5	RS
12	✓		✓		71.5	RS
51	✓		✓		77.5	RS
36	✓	✓	✓		81.5	RS
62	✓				87	RS
44	✓	✓		✓	87	RS
15	✓	✓	✓	✓	87.5	RS
38		✓	✓		89.5	RS
106	✓				94	RS
41					86.5	S
18					88	S
24			✓		90	S
23	✓		✓		90.5	S
53					91	S
34	✓	✓			91.5	S
30			✓		93.5	S
27			✓		94	S
4	✓	✓			94.5	S
17			✓	✓	94.5	S
Total	12	7	11	5		S

Note: RS: those with reading and spelling impairments. S: spelling-only impairments.

Table 3. *Findings from case-series showing the cognitive deficits observed among at-risk children with normal literacy attainments*

Case No.	Phonological deficit	Visuospatial deficit	Attention deficit	Language impairment	Literacy composite[a]
32			✓		96
48			✓		96.5
19			✓		97
42			✓		97
31		✓			97.5
25			✓		98.5
35			✓		98.5
50		✓			100.5
84		✓			101.5
37	✓				102.5
98			✓		1.6
21			✓		107.5
59	✓				1.8
5			✓		116.5
Total	2	3	9	0	

Note: A total of 14 cases not shown here had no identifiable deficits.
[a]Standard score.

unimpaired, the most prevalent deficits were in attention control (9/28 cases) whereas neither visual nor language impairments were common. In two cases there was evidence of a phonological deficit but literacy skills were normal.

The comparison of literacy-impaired cases with and without reading problems was also instructive. Phonological deficits were pervasive in the reading (and spelling)-impaired subgroup (9/10 cases) but they also occurred in 3/10 of those with only spelling impairments. Interestingly, attention deficits were equally common in both subgroups of literacy-impaired individuals. Among the five young people with the most severe literacy impairments, three of these individuals had two impairments, one had three, and one had four; all of them had phonological impairments, and these were observed in association with language impairment in two cases.

Together these findings provide some limited support for the view that a child is more likely to reach the diagnostic threshold for dyslexia if they have a phonological deficit. However, it is more common for those with the more severe literacy problems to have deficits in more than one cognitive domain. Furthermore, some 30% of the at-risk group who experienced a significant phonological deficit had apparently normal reading even though their spelling was impaired. Together these findings challenge the notion that dyslexia is caused by a specific phonological deficit. Rather they suggest there are more diffuse difficulties in the at-risk literacy-impaired group, whereas those who show normal levels of literacy show more selectivity in impairments and hence may be more able to compensate.

These results present a complex picture but one that likely reflects the varied trajectories of development observed in any developmental disorder. Although it is possible at the group level to identify risk factors pertaining to reading difficulties (Bishop & Snowling, 2004), such an approach does not do justice to the epigenetic landscape within which development unfolds. In the case of dyslexia, there is strong evidence that the primary risk factor is poor phonology, but it is now clear that it is possible to experience a phonological processing impairment without being dyslexic. This liability was observed in a significant proportion of our at-risk sample who became normal readers and has also been reported in the case of children with speech-sound disorders who do not succumb to literacy difficulties (Nathan, Stackhouse, Goulandris, & Snowling, 2004; Raitano, Pennington, Tunick, & Boada, 2004; Stothard, Snowling, Bishop, Chipchase, & Kaplan, 1998; see also Stothard, Snowling, & Hulme, 1996, and Gathercole, Tiffany, Briscoe, Thorn, & ALSPAC Team, 2005). The present evidence suggests that a range of cognitive factors within the individual can work to modify the behavioural expression of the risk of dyslexia within high-risk families. In turn, these factors might be expected to interact with environmental experiences such as the availability of intervention.

CONCLUSIONS

This chapter has been concerned with whether dyslexia should be considered a specific, modular, developmental cognitive disorder. The first study reported showed that "dyslexia" can occur in the absence of speed-of-processing deficits and where IQ is in the normal range, suggesting a degree of modularity. However, the family study painted a different picture by revealing that phonological deficits are risk factors for dyslexia while wider language skills (including differences in verbal ability) may act as protective factors to circumvent reading failure. The corollary of this is that poor oral language is an additional risk factor for reading impairment (Snowling, Bishop, & Stothard, 2000), and the data from the current case series underline this fact. In addition, the case series also revealed a high incidence of attention problems in the family-risk sample, irrespective of whether they were literacy impaired. Thus, problems of attention control may reflect comorbid impairments rather than risk factors that are causally related to literacy impairments.

In summary, there is now a wealth of data from both behaviour and molecular genetics indicating that reading skills are highly heritable (Fisher & Francks, 2006; Pennington & Olson, 2005). Notwithstanding this, the present findings highlight the fact that further research is needed to understand how risk and protective factors interact

during development to produce different literacy outcomes (Rutter, 2005). The present data suggest that it is not appropriate to question whether a phonological deficit is necessary or sufficient to account for dyslexia—this kind of question depends upon adopting arbitrary cut-offs for defining deficits. If instead dyslexia is viewed as a continuously distributed dimension, then those who fall at the lower end of the continuum are more likely to have poor phonology. But they are also more likely to have other cognitive deficits as well. This is not to deny that specific disorders exist; indeed, individuals with pure disorders are more likely to be recruited to laboratory samples, as the findings of Study 1 make clear.

Together the present findings are compatible with the theory that the susceptibility genes associated with learning disabilities have both general and specific effects (Plomin & Kovas, 2005). The future research agenda needs to clarify the nature and severity of a phonological deficit sufficient to precipitate dyslexia both together with, and in the absence of, other adverse factors. From the practical perspective, findings from family studies suggest that children at risk of dyslexia should be carefully monitored during the early school years and are deserving of intervention to promote alphabetic competence (Snowling & Stackhouse, 2006).

REFERENCES

American Psychiatric Association. (1994). *Diagnostic and statistical manual of mental disorders* (4th ed.). Washington, DC: Author.

Anderson, M. (1992). *Intelligence and development: A cognitive theory.* Oxford, UK: Blackwell.

Bishop, D. V. M. (2006). Developmental cognitive genetics: How psychology can inform genetics and vice versa. *Quarterly Journal of Experimental Psychology, 59,* 1153–1168.

Bishop, D. V. M., & Snowling, M. J. (2004). Developmental dyslexia and specific language impairment: Same or different? *Psychological Bulletin, 130,* 858–888.

Bonifacci, P., & Snowling, M. J. (2007). *Are reading disorders domain-specific? Speed of processing in dyslexia and borderline intellectual functioning.* Manuscript submitted for publication.

Bowey, J. A. (2005). Predicting individual differences in learning to read. In M. J. Snowling & C. Hulme (Eds.), *The science of reading: A handbook* (pp. 155–172). Oxford, UK: Blackwell.

Breznitz, Z., & Meyler, A. (2003). Speed of lower-level auditory and visual processing as a basic factor in dyslexia: Electrophysiological evidence. *Brain and Language, 85,* 166–184.

Byrne, B. (1998). *The foundation of literacy: The child's acquisition of the alphabetic principle.* Hove, UK: Psychology Press.

Catts, H. W., Gillispie, M., Leonard, L. B., Kail, R. V., & Miller, C. A. (2002). The role of speed of processing, rapid naming, and phonological awareness in reading achievement. *Journal of Learning Disabilities, 35,* 510–525.

Doyle, A. E., Willcutt, E., Seidman, L., Biederman, J., Chouinard, V.-A., Silva, J., et al. (2005). Attention-deficit/hyperactivity disorder endophenotypes. *Biological Psychiatry, 57,* 1324–1335.

Fisher, S. E., & Francks, C. (2006). Genes, cognition and dyslexia: Learning to read the genome. *Trends in Cognitive Sciences, 10,* 250–257.

Fowler, A. (1991). How early phonological development might set the stage for phoneme awareness. In S. A. Brady & D. P. Shankweiler (Eds.), *Phonological processes in literacy: A tribute to Isabelle Y. Liberman* (pp. 97–117). Hillsdale: NJ: Lawrence Erlbaum Associates.

Frith, U. (1980). Unexpected spelling problems. In U. Frith (Ed.), *Cognitive processes in spelling* (pp. 495–516). London: Academic Press.

Frith, U. (1985). Beneath the surface of developmental dyslexia. In K. Patterson, M. Coltheart, & J. Marshall (Eds.), *Surface dyslexia: Neuropsychological and cognitive studies of phonological reading* (pp. 301–330). Hove, UK: Lawrence Erlbaum Associates Ltd.

Frith, U. (1997). Brain, mind and behaviour in dyslexia. In C. Hulme & M. Snowling (Eds.), *Dyslexia: Biology, cognition and intervention* (pp. 1–19). London: Whurr.

Frith, U., & Frith, C. D. (1980). Relationships between reading and spelling. In J. F. Kavanagh & R. L. Venezky (Eds.), *Orthography, reading and dyslexia.* Baltimore, MD: University Park Press.

Frith, U., & Happé, F. (1998). Why specific developmental disorders are not specific: On-line and developmental effect in autism and dyslexia. *Developmental Science, 1,* 267–272.

Frith, U., Wimmer, H., & Landerl, K. (1998). Differences in phonological recoding in German and English speaking children. *Scientific Studies of Reading, 2,* 31–54.

Gallagher, A., Frith, U., & Snowling, M. J. (2000). Precursors of literacy-delay among children at genetic risk of dyslexia. *Journal of Child Psychology & Psychiatry, 41,* 203–213.

Gathercole, S. E., Tiffany, C., Briscoe, J., Thorn, A. S. C., & ALSPAC Team. (2005). Developmental consequences of poor phonological short-term memory function in childhood: A longitudinal study. *Journal of Child Psychology and Psychiatry, 46,* 598–611.

Gathercole, S. E., Willis, C., Baddeley, A. D., & Emslie, H. (1994). The Children's Test of Nonword Repetition: A test of phonological working memory. *Memory, 2,* 103–127.

Goodman, R. (1997). The strengths and difficulties questionnaire: A research note. *Journal of Child Psychology and Psychiatry, 38,* 581–586.

Griffiths, Y. M., & Snowling, M. J. (2002). Predictors of exception word and nonword reading in dyslexic children: The severity hypothesis. *Journal of Educational Psychology, 94,* 34–43.

Harm, M. W., & Seidenberg, M. S. (1999). Phonology, reading acquisition and dyslexia: Insights from connectionist models. *Psychological Review, 106,* 491–528.

Hatcher, P. J., & Hulme, C. (1999). Phonemes, rhymes and intelligence as predictors of children's responsiveness to remedial reading instruction: Evidence from a longitudinal intervention study. *Journal of Experimental Child Psychology, 72,* 130–153.

Jensen, A. R. (1998). *The g factor.* Westport, CT: Praeger Publishers.

Kail, R. (1991). Developmental change in speed of processing during childhood and adolescence. *Psychological Bulletin, 109,* 490–501.

Manly, T., Robertson, I. H., Anderson, V., & Nimmo-Smith, I. (1998). *Test of everyday attention for children (TEA-Ch).* London: Harcourt Assessment.

McDougall, S., Hulme, C., Ellis, A. W., & Monk, A. (1994). Learning to read: The role of short-term memory and phonological skills. *Journal of Experimental Child Psychology, 58,* 112–123.

Morton, J. (2004). *Understanding developmental disorders: A cognitive modelling approach.* Oxford, UK: Blackwell.

Morton, J., & Frith, U. (1995). Causal modelling: A structural approach to developmental psychopathology. In D. Cicchetti & D. J. Cohen (Eds.), *Manual of developmental psychopathology*. New York: Wiley.

Nathan, E., Stackhouse, J., Goulandris, N., & Snowling, M. J. (2004). The Development of early literacy skills among children with speech difficulties: A test of the "critical age hypothesis". *Journal of Speech Hearing and Language Research, 47*, 377–391.

Nation, K., & Snowling, M. J. (1998). Individual differences in contextual facilitation: Evidence from dyslexia and poor reading comprehension. *Child Development, 69*, 996–1011.

Nicolson, R. I., & Fawcett, A. J. (1994). Reaction times and dyslexia. *Quarterly Journal of Experimental Psychology, 47A*, 29–48.

Nicolson, R. I., Fawcett, A. J., & Dean, P. (2001). Developmental dyslexia: The cerebellar deficit hypothesis. *Trends in Neurological Sciences, 24*, 508–511.

Paulesu, E., Demonet, J.-F., Fazio, F., McCrory, E., Chanoine, V., Brunswick, N., et al. (2001). Dyslexia: Cultural diversity and biological unity. *Science, 291*, 2165–2167.

Paulesu, E., Frith, U., Snowling, M., Gallagher, A., Morton, J., Frackowiak, F. S. J., et al. (1996). Is developmental dyslexia a disconnection syndrome? Evidence from PET scanning. *Brain, 119*, 143–157.

Pennington, B. F. (2002). *The development of psychopathology: Nature and nurture*. New York: Guilford Press.

Pennington, B. F. (2006). From single to multiple deficit models of developmental disorders. *Cognition, 101*, 385–413.

Pennington, B. F., & Lefly, D. L. (2001). Early reading development in children at family risk for dyslexia. *Child Development, 72*, 816–833.

Pennington, B. F., & Olson, R. K. (2005). Genetics of dyslexia. In M. J. Snowling & C. Hulme (Eds.), *The science of reading: A handbook* (pp. 453–472). Oxford, UK: Blackwell.

Plomin, R., & Kovas, Y. (2005). Generalist genes and learning disabilities. *Psychological Bulletin, 131*, 592–617.

Pring, L., & Snowling, M. J. (1986). Developmental changes in children's use of context in word recognition: An information processing analysis. *Quarterly Journal of Experimental Psychology, 38A*, 395–418.

Raitano, N. A., Pennington, B. F., Tunick, R. A., & Boada, R. (2004). Pre-literacy skills of subgroups of children with phonological disorder. *Journal of Child Psychology & Psychiatry, 45*, 821–835.

Ramus, F. (2004). Neurobiology of dyslexia: A reinterpretation of the data. *Trends in Neurosciences, 27*, 720–726.

Ramus, F., Rosen, S., Dakin, S. C., Day, B. L., Castellote, J. M., White, S., et al. (2003). Theories of developmental dyslexia: Insights from a multiple case study of dyslexic adults. *Brain, 126*, 1–25.

Rochelle, K., & Talcott, J. (2006). Impaired balance in developmental dyslexia? A meta-analysis of contending evidence. *Journal of Child Psychology & Psychiatry, 47*, 1159–1166.

Rutter, M. (2005). *Genes and behavior*. Oxford, UK: Blackwell.

Rutter, M., & Maughan, B. (2005). Dyslexia: 1965–2005. *Behavioural and Cognitive Psychotherapy, 33*, 389–402.

Scarborough, H. S. (1990). Very early language deficits in dyslexic children. *Child Development, 61*, 1728–1743.

Scarborough, H. S. (1991). Early syntactic development of dyslexic children. *Annals of Dyslexia, 41*, 207–220.

Scheuffgen, K., Happé, F., Anderson, M., & Frith, U. (2000). High "intelligence", low "IQ"? Speed of processing and measured IQ in children with autism. *Development and Psychopathology, 12*, 83–90.

Shaywitz, B. A., Fletcher, J. M., Holahan, J. M., & Shaywitz, S. E. (1996). Discrepancy compared to low achievement definitions of reading disability: Results from the Connecticut longitudinal study. *Journal of Learning Disabilities, 25*, 639–648.

Skuse, D. (2001). Endophenotypes and child psychiatry. *British Journal of Psychiatry, 178*, 395–396.

Snowling, M. J. (2000). *Dyslexia* (2nd ed.). Oxford, UK: Blackwell.

Snowling, M. J., Bishop, D. V. M., & Stothard, S. E. (2000). Is pre-school language impairment a risk factor for dyslexia in adolescence? *Journal of Child Psychology & Psychiatry, 41*, 587–600.

Snowling, M. J., Gallagher, A., & Frith, U. (2003). Family risk of dyslexia is continuous: Individual differences in the precursors of reading skill. *Child Development, 74*, 358–373.

Snowling, M. J., Muter, V., & Carroll, J. M. (2007). Children at family risk of dyslexia: A follow-up in adolescence. *Journal of Child Psychology & Psychiatry, 48*, 609–618.

Snowling, M. J., Nation, K., Moxham, P., Gallagher, A., & Frith, U. (1997). Phonological processing deficits in dyslexic students: A preliminary account. *Journal of Research in Reading, 20*, 31–34.

Snowling, M. J., & Stackhouse, J. (Eds). (2006). *Dyslexia, speech & language: A practitioner's handbook* (2nd ed.). London: Whurr.

Snowling, M. J., Stothard, S. E., & McLean, J. (1996). *Graded Nonword Reading Test.* Bury St. Edmunds: Thames Valley Test Co.

Sobotka, K. R., & May, J. G. (1977). Visual evoked potentials and reaction time in normal and dyslexic children. *Psychophysiology, 14*, 18–24.

Stanovich, K. E. (1986). Matthew effects in reading: Some consequences of individual differences in the acquisition of literacy. *Reading Research Quarterly, 21*, 360–364.

Stanovich, K. E. (1994). Does dyslexia exist? *Journal of Child Psychology and Psychiatry, 35*, 579–595.

Stanovich, K. E., & Siegel, L. S. (1994). The phenotypic performance profile of reading-disabled children: A regression-based test of the phonological-core variable-difference model. *Journal of Educational Psychology, 86*, 24–53.

Stein, J., & Talcott, J. (1999). Impaired neuronal timing in developmental dyslexia: The magnocellular hypothesis. *Dyslexia, 5*, 59–77.

Stothard, S. E., Snowling, M. J., & Hulme, C. (1996). Deficits in phonology but not dyslexic? *Cognitive Neuropsychology, 13*, 641–672.

Stothard, S. E., Snowling, M. J., Bishop, D. V. M., Chipchase, B., & Kaplan, C. (1998). Language impaired pre-schoolers: A follow-up in adolescence. *Journal of Speech, Language and Hearing Research, 41*, 407–418.

Stringer, R., & Stanovich, K. E. (2000). The connection between reaction time and variation in reading ability: Unraveling covariance relationships with cognitive ability and phonological sensitivity. *Scientific Studies of Reading, 4*, 41–53.

Swan, D., & Goswami, U. (1997). Phonological awareness deficits in developmental dyslexia and the phonological representations hypothesis. *Journal of Experimental Child Psychology, 60*, 334–353.

Thomas, M., & Karmiloff-Smith, A. (2002). Are developmental disorders like cases of brain damage? Implications from connectionist modelling. *Behavioral and Brain Sciences, 25*, 727–788.

Vellutino, F. R., Fletcher, J. M., Snowling, M. J., & Scanlon, D. M. (2004). Specific reading disability (dyslexia): What have we learned in the past four decades? *Journal of Child Psychology & Psychiatry, 45*, 2–40.

Wechsler, D. (1999). *Wechsler Abbreviated Scale of Intelligence*. San Antonio, TX: The Psychological Corporation.

White, S., Milne, E., Rosen, S., Hansen, P., Swettenham, J., Frith, U., et al. (2006). The role of sensorimotor impairments in dyslexia: A multiple case study of dyslexic children. *Developmental Science, 9*, 237–269.

Willcutt, E. G., Pennington, B. F., Olson, R. K., Chhabildas, N., & Hulslander, J. (2005). Neuropsychological analyses of comorbidity between reading disability and attention deficit hyperactivity disorder: In search of the common deficit. *Developmental Neuropsychology, 27*, 35–78.

Wimmer, H., Mayringer, H., & Landerl, K. (1998). Poor reading: A deficit in skill-automatization or a phonological deficit? *Scientific Studies of Reading, 2*, 321–340.

THE QUARTERLY JOURNAL OF EXPERIMENTAL PSYCHOLOGY
2008, 61 (1), 157–170

Fine cuts of empathy and the amygdala: Dissociable deficits in psychopathy and autism

R. J. R. Blair

National Institute of Mental Health, Bethesda, MD, USA

In the current paper, the "fine cuts" approach advocated by Uta Frith is applied to our understanding of empathy and amygdala dysfunction in two disorders, psychopathy and autism. A fine cut is made between cognitive (i.e., Theory of Mind) and emotional empathy. The literature with respect to psychopathy and autism and these two functions is then considered. A fine cut is also made between the amygdala's role in stimulus–reinforcement association and specific aspects of social cognition. Again the literature with respect to psychopathy and autism and these two functions of the amygdala is considered. It is concluded that while both conditions can be considered disorders of social cognition, fine cuts can be made dissociating the impairments associated with each.

One of the many important influences of Uta Frith on the child psychopathology field has been her advocacy of the "fine cuts" technique (U. Frith & Happé, 1994; Happé & Frith, 1996a, 1996b). This approach involves comparing intact and impaired abilities across tasks, which, though they might share surface similarities, can be dissociated following a deeper understanding of the neurocognitive architectures underpinning their performance. This approach is so important because of an equal and unfortunate tendency to group behaviours or phenomena together because of apparent similarities despite the empirical data. For example, references to empathy impairment in definitions of autism and psychopathy have led to claims of a common impairment despite the data (see below).

In Uta's work, the fine cuts approach was most importantly applied to the social and communication abilities in autism. In particular, the greater precision of the "Theory of Mind" (mentalizing) account of autism (U. Frith, 1989; U. Frith & Frith, 2003) made it possible to categorize behaviours according to whether they should or should not involve the ability to "mentalize" (U. Frith & Happé, 1994; Happé & Frith, 1996a, 1996b). The approach could then be used to understand why children with autism might be impaired on one task but not another despite their surface similarities. For example, the Theory of Mind account predicted impairment in children with autism on the false-belief task but not on the methodologically similar false-photograph task (e.g., Leslie & Thaiss, 1992; cf. Perner & Leekam, 2008 this issue). Similarly, it allowed the explanation for why children with autism should be unimpaired in the use of instrumental gestures but impaired in the use of

---

Correspondence should be addressed to James Blair, Mood and Anxiety Program, National Institute of Mental Health, Room 206, 15K North Drive, MSC 2670, Bethesda, MD 20892, USA. E-mail: blairj@intra.nimh.nih.gov

DOI:10.1080/17470210701508855

expressive gestures (Attwood, Frith, & Hermelin, 1988). In short, broad surface similarities may mask underlying functional differences. It is important to be aware of, and if necessary ignore, the surface similarities given that it is the functional differences that relate to the disorder. Returning to the example of empathy impairment in definitions of autism and psychopathy, there is little to be gained by referring to an ill-defined construct, empathy, when the empirical literature identifies clear impairments in specific functions that are disorder specific.

The purpose of the current chapter is to apply the "fine cuts" technique to notions of empathic and amygdala dysfunction with reference to the disorders of psychopathy and autism. As noted above, both disorders have been linked to problems in empathy and amygdala functioning. Indeed, researchers still consider that the emotional component of psychopathy might be similar to the impaired socio-emotional responsiveness seen in autism spectrum disorders (Rutter, 2005). Moreover, prominent models of both disorders consider amygdala dysfunction to be importantly involved in their development (Baron-Cohen et al., 2000; Blair, 2001; Patrick, 1994).

I first briefly describe the disorders of psychopathy and autism. I then consider "empathy" and specifically argue that a distinction must be drawn between "cognitive" and "emotional" empathy. I will suggest that while individuals with autism have clear impairment in "cognitive" empathy, it is considerably less certain whether they have impairment in "emotional" empathy. I will then contrast this with psychopathy, where individuals with the disorder can be shown to have no impairment in "cognitive" empathy but marked, and selective, impairment in "emotional" empathy. I then consider the roles of the amygdala in stimulus–reinforcement association formation and in specific aspects of social cognition. I suggest that while individuals with autism have no impairment in stimulus–reinforcement association formation, they do appear impaired in those aspects of social cognition in which the amygdala is implicated. In contrast, individuals with psychopathy have marked impairment in stimulus–reinforcement association formation but appear intact in those aspects of social cognition in which the amygdala is implicated.

The disorders

Psychopathy is a developmental disorder characterized in part by callousness, a diminished capacity for remorse, impulsivity, and poor behavioural control (Hare, 1991). It can be considered to involve two core components: emotional dysfunction and antisocial behaviour (Frick, 1995; Harpur, Hakstian, & Hare, 1988). The emotional dysfunction involves reduced guilt and empathy as well as reduced attachment to significant others. The antisocial-behaviour component involves a predisposition to antisocial behaviour from an early age. It is identified in children with the antisocial process screening device (Frick & Hare, 2001) and in adults with the revised psychopathy checklist (Hare, 1991, 2003). Importantly, this disorder is not equivalent to the psychiatric diagnoses of conduct disorder or antisocial personality disorder (American Psychiatric Association, 1994). These psychiatric diagnoses are relatively poorly specified and concentrate almost entirely on the antisocial behaviour shown by the individual rather than any form of functional impairment (see Blair, Mitchell, & Blair, 2005).

Autism is a severe developmental disorder described by the American Psychiatric Association's *Diagnostic and Statistical Manual of Mental Disorders–Fourth Edition* (DSM-IV) as "the presence of markedly abnormal or impaired development in social interaction and communication and a markedly restricted repertoire of activities and interests" (American Psychiatric Association, 1994, p. 66). The main criteria for the diagnosis in DSM-IV can be summarized as qualitative impairment in social communication and restricted and repetitive patterns of behaviour and interests. These criteria must be evident before 3 years of age.

The idea that a basic deficit in emotional responding is at the heart of the development of psychopathy has been recognized since the initial descriptions of the disorder (Cleckley, 1941).

This idea remains central to the current clinical description (Hare, 2003) as well as almost all dominant accounts of the disorder (Blair, 2004; Kiehl, 2006; Patrick, Cuthbert, & Lang, 1994; though see Newman, 1998). Similarly, the idea that the main difficulty for people with autism is an inability to enter into emotional relationships has also existed since the initial recognition of the disorder (Kanner, 1943). Following Kanner, there have been suggestions that autism is due to an innate impairment in the ability to perceive and respond to the affective expressions of others, which leads to their profound difficulties in social interaction (Hobson, 1993); however, it should be noted, other accounts of the disorder, including Uta's, do not view a problem in affect as central to the development of the disorder (Baron-Cohen, 2006; U. Frith & Happé, 2005). Given these suggestions, it has been implied that emotional detachment and disregard for the feelings of others may be common to both disorders (Rutter, 2005).

Empathic dysfunction

In a relatively recent paper, the philosopher Kennett argued that the "amoralism" of individuals with psychopathy could not be due to empathic dysfunction because individuals with autism also showed empathic dysfunction but did not show "amorality" (Kennett, 2002). The problem for this argument is the assumption that the term "empathy" has any explanatory power. Given the multitude of different definitions of empathy offered by a variety of authors, it is questionable whether it does. The problem is particularly severe since many of the definitions were made in the absence of any consideration of which neurocognitive systems might be mediating empathy and any specification of the types of processing involved. The term "empathy" has been applied to processes allowing the use by the observer of information on the internal state of the observed. However, there are two main classes of processing to which the term "empathy" can be applied and which are relevant here: "cognitive" empathy (Theory of Mind) and "emotional"

empathy. These classes of processing are at least partially separable at both the neural and cognitive levels (Blair, 2005, 2006).

Cognitive empathy (Theory of Mind)

The term cognitive empathy has been used to apply to situations where the individual represents the internal mental state of another individual. It is effectively Theory of Mind; a form of functional processing that Uta has played an integral role in understanding (C. D. Frith & Frith, 1999; U. Frith, 1989; U. Frith & Frith, 2003). In a series of neuroimaging studies, Uta and others have identified the neural systems engaged during the representation of the mental states of others. These include medial prefrontal cortex (especially anterior paracingulate cortex), the temporal-parietal junction, and the temporal poles (Castelli, Happé, Frith, & Frith, 2000; Fletcher et al., 1995; Goel, Grafman, Sadato, & Hallett, 1995; see, for a review, C. D. Frith & Frith, 2006).

Thanks to Uta's work, most autism researchers would agree that Theory of Mind impairment is at least a component of the disorder. Uta and her colleagues were the first to demonstrate this impairment (Baron-Cohen, Leslie, & Frith, 1985), and this impairment has been consistently replicated (see, for a review, Hill & Frith, 2003). Neuroimaging work by Uta and colleagues on individuals with autism spectrum disorders has examined neural responses during the performance of mentalizing (Theory of Mind) tasks. These studies have reported reduced activation in the three brain regions critical to mentalizing in normal individuals (medial prefrontal cortex, temporal-parietal junction, and the temporal poles; Castelli, Frith, Happé, & Frith, 2002; Happé et al., 1996).

In contrast to autism, the literature on psychopathy indicates no Theory of Mind impairment in this population. Four out of five studies assessing the ability of individuals with psychopathy on Theory of Mind measures have reported no impairment in the ability to represent mental states (Blair et al., 1996; Dolan & Fullam, 2004; Richell et al., 2003; Widom, 1978). Only one study reported impairment, and this used a rating scale that is not a typical measure of Theory of Mind (Widom, 1976). Even if the work is extended to the broader spectrum of antisocial individuals, there are few data suggesting any link between Theory of Mind impairment and antisocial behaviour. Hughes and colleagues have reported some indications of Theory of Mind impairment in their "hard-to-manage" preschoolers (Hughes, Dunn, & White, 1998; Hughes & Ensor, 2006). For example, Hughes et al. (1998) reported that hard-to-manage preschoolers had poorer prediction and recall of story protagonist's false beliefs than did comparison preschoolers. However, no Theory of Mind impairment has been found in children with emotional and behavioural difficulties (Happé & Frith, 1996a, 1996b), school bullies (Sutton, Smith, & Swettenham, 1999), or in adolescents with "disruptive behaviour disorder" (Sutton, Reeves, & Keogh, 2000). Indeed, Sutton et al. (1999) reported that bullying was associated with higher social cognition scores, indicating that bullies might have a superior ability to represent the mental states of others.

Emotional empathy

Emotional responding, at least basic emotional responding, can be defined as the brain's response to rewarding and punishing stimuli—that is, unconditioned and conditioned stimuli (Rolls, 1999). Emotional expressions can be considered to be reinforcers, and following this, I have argued elsewhere that facial expressions of emotion have specific communicatory functions—that they impart specific information to the observer (Blair, 2003, 2005). From this view, emotional empathy is defined as the "translation" of the communication by the observer.

Considerable work has examined the neurocognitive systems responding to emotional expressions (for reviews of this literature, see Adolphs, 2002; Blair, 2003). Two main themes of this work are: first, whether there are subcortical systems that respond to emotional expressions; and second, whether there are separable neurocognitive systems involved in the processing of different emotional expressions. With respect to the issue

of subcortical systems, it has been argued that facial expressions are processed from visual cortex to limbic areas not only via temporal cortex but also subcortically (i.e., from thalamus and onto limbic areas—in particular, the amygdala; Adolphs, 2002; Morris, Ohman, & Dolan, 1999; Pizzagalli, Regard, & Lehmann, 1999). This subcortical route transmits course-grained information expression information to the amygdala in humans very rapidly (Luo, Holroyd, Jones, Hendler, & Blair, 2007; Vuilleumier, Armony, Driver, & Dolan, 2003).

The literature on whether there are separable neurocognitive systems involved in the processing of different emotional expressions remains confused. Some data have suggested a unitary response by the brain to all emotional expressions (Fitzgerald, Angstadt, Jelsone, Nathan, & Phan, 2006; Winston, O'Doherty, & Dolan, 2003). Many other data have not supported this view (Blair, Morris, Frith, Perrett, & Dolan, 1999; LaBar, Crupain, Voyvodic, & McCarthy, 2003; Morris et al., 1996; Phillips et al., 1998). The confusion may in part be due to differences in methodology; those studies finding a unitary response have examined four or more expressions simultaneously and may not have had sufficient power to detect differences given the numbers involved ($N = 20$ and 12 in the Fitzgerald et al. and Winston et al. studies, respectively).

If, as I have argued, the facial expressions of emotion have specific communicatory functions (Blair, 2003, 2005), it is unlikely that there is a unitary system that mediates the response to the expressions of others. This is because different brain regions are involved in responding to different types of reinforcer. Thus if, as has been argued, fearful expressions are aversive unconditioned stimuli that rapidly convey information to others that a novel stimulus is aversive and should be avoided (Mineka & Cook, 1993), then it is unsurprising that fearful expressions preferentially activate the amygdala (Blair, 2003). This is because the amygdala is critical for fear-based aversive conditioning (Davis, 2000; LeDoux, 2000). Indeed, in line with this view, recent work has shown that the amygdala is more responsive to fearful expressions if they are presented in the context of trials requiring learning object–emotion associations on the basis of the expression information than if they are presented alone (Hooker, Germine, Knight, & D'Esposito, 2006). Similarly, if disgusted expressions are reinforcers that most frequently provide valence information about foods (Rozin, Haidt, & McCauley, 1993), then it is unsurprising that disgusted expressions preferentially activate the insula (Phillips et al., 1998; Sprengelmeyer, Rausch, Eysel, & Przuntek, 1998). This is because the insula is critical for taste aversion learning (e.g., Cubero, Thiele, & Bernstein, 1999); for an extended version of this argument, see Blair (2003, 2005).

With respect to the issue of emotional empathy in autism, there have been suggestions that autism is due to an innate impairment in the ability to perceive and respond to the affective expressions of others, and that this deficit leads to their profound difficulties in social interaction (Hobson, 1993). In line with this position, several studies have reported that individuals with autism have difficulty recognizing the emotional expressions of others (Bormann-Kischkel, Vilsmeier, & Baude, 1995; Hobson, 1986; Howard et al., 2000). However, many of the earlier studies did not have groups matched on mental age. When studies were conducted with groups matched for verbal mental age, individuals with autism were often found to be unimpaired in facial affect recognition (Adolphs, Sears, & Piven, 2001; Ozonoff, Pennington, & Rogers, 1990; Prior, Dahlstrom, & Squires, 1990). However, this criticism cannot be made of all the studies showing group differences. For example, a very recent study with well-matched adult groups and a well-standardized test of expression recognition found deficits for the recognition of fearful, disgusted, and happy expressions in adults with autism (Humphreys, Minshew, Leonard, & Behrmann, 2007). In short, the situation is confused.

Part of the confusion may relate to the general face-processing impairments observed in individuals with autism. For example, individuals with this disorder have impaired recognition memory for faces (Blair, Frith, Smith, Abell, & Cipolotti,

2002; Boucher & Lewis, 1992; Klin et al., 1999) and abnormal eye scan paths when viewing faces (Klin, Jones, Schultz, Volkmar, & Cohen, 2002). Such general problems with face processing may underlie any apparent impairment in the recognition of emotional expression. Moreover, it is worth noting that reductions in the recognition of facial expressions can be associated with many factors that are disturbed in individuals with autism—for example, general intelligence, age, attention, and verbal ability (Herba & Phillips, 2004; Moore, 2001). In addition, it is possible that heterogeneity in the population of individuals with autism also leads to confusion. Thus, a recent study examining a population of individuals with autism selected because of their high levels of externalizing behaviour showed that those with high teacher-assessed levels of callous and unemotional (CU) traits (the emotional component of psychopathy) showed some impairment in expression recognition relative to those with lower CU traits (Rogers, Viding, Blair, Frith, & Happé, 2006).

The literature on expression recognition in psychopathy is considerably more consistent than that in autism. Most studies of individuals with psychopathy have observed relatively selective impairments in individuals with this disorder for the recognition of fearful and sometimes sad expressions (Blair, Colledge, Murray, & Mitchell, 2001; Blair et al., 2004; Dadds et al., 2006; Dolan & Fullam, 2006; Montagne et al., 2005). However, a few have not; for example, one study reported no impairment except for disgust expressions but only when responding with the left hand (Kosson, Suchy, Mayer, & Libby, 2002). The study by Dadds et al. (2006) reported a particularly interesting result. They reported that the expression recognition deficit for fearful expressions was abolished if the participants were asked to direct their attention to the eyes of the presented stimuli. A very similar result has previously been reported in patients with amygdala lesions (Adolphs et al., 2005). Importantly, a recent meta-analytic review demonstrated a consistent and robust link between antisocial behaviour and deficits in recognizing the fear facial expression. The deficit for fear recognition was selective though it extended beyond individuals with psychopathy to other individuals defined by showing elevated levels of instrumental antisocial behaviour (Marsh & Blair, in press).

While a fine cut between autism and psychopathy cannot be made with respect to expression recognition, given the confusion in the autism literature, a fine cut can be made with respect to a major developmental consequence of empathic responding: moral development. It has long been argued that empathic responding is necessary for successful moral development (Hume, 1740/1967). I have attempted to specify more formally such an account at the cognitive and neural levels (Blair, 1995; Blair, Marsh, Finger, Blair, & Luo, 2006). Importantly children with autism show relatively preserved moral judgements as long as the judgement does not require representation of the intent of the perpetrator (Blair, 1996; Grant, Boucher, Riggs, & Grayson, 2005; Steele, Joseph, & Tager-Flusberg, 2003). In contrast, individuals with psychopathy and other instrumentally antisocial individuals do not (Arsenio & Fleiss, 1996; Blair, 1995; Nucci & Herman, 1982).

Amygdala dysfunction

With respect to functions of the amygdala, an important fine cut can be made between stimulus–reinforcement association learning and aspects of social cognition. There is a considerable animal literature (including lesion, single-cell recording, and pharmacological studies) attesting to the importance of the amygdala for stimulus–reinforcement learning (Baxter & Murray, 2002; Davis, 2000; Everitt, Cardinal, Parkinson, & Robbins, 2003; LeDoux, 1998). Neuropsychological (Bechara et al., 1995; LaBar, Gatenby, Gore, LeDoux, & Phelps, 1998) and neuroimaging (Buchel & Dolan, 2000; Buchel, Morris, Dolan, & Friston, 1998) studies have confirmed this role in humans. In short, the amygdala is necessary for the formation, though not the storage, of stimulus–reinforcement associations—that is, it is necessary

for the individual to learn whether a novel object is good or bad.

There is also considerable animal literature (predominantly involving lesion studies) attesting to the importance of the amygdala for aspects of social cognition (Bachevalier, 1994; Bauman, Lavenex, Mason, Capitanio, & Amaral, 2004; Kling & Brothers, 1992; Rosvold, Mirsky, & Pribram, 1954). For example, Rosvold et al. (1954) reported that monkeys with acquired amygdala lesions suffered profound deficits in their social behaviour, fell in the dominance hierarchy, and became extremely submissive. More recent work has shown that some of the earlier reports with respect to the role in social cognition of the amygdala (Bachevalier, 1994; Kling & Brothers, 1992; Rosvold et al., 1954) were methodologically flawed (see Amaral, 2003). The techniques adopted in these studies for making lesions damaged not only cell bodies in the amygdala but also axons travelling through the amygdala. More recent studies have used techniques that only damage cell bodies. These studies have reported that selective damage to the amygdala does not disrupt fundamental components of social behaviour—for example, the ability to produce and respond to species-typical social signals and the ability to interact in a social context (Bauman et al., 2004; Emery et al., 2001; Prather et al., 2001). However, bilateral amygdala lesions do have an impact on affiliation and aggression and disrupt appropriate formation and maintenance of a social dominance hierarchy (Bauman et al., 2004; Bauman, Toscano, Mason, Lavenex, & Amaral, 2006).

Prominent models of both autism and psychopathy relate amygdala dysfunction to their development (Baron-Cohen et al., 2000; Blair, 2001; Patrick, 1994). The autism literature has concentrated on the amygdala's role in social cognition (Baron-Cohen et al., 2000). In contrast, the psychopathy literature has concentrated on the amygdala's role in stimulus–reinforcement learning (Blair, 2001; Patrick, 1994). Indeed, fine cuts can be made with respect to these two disorders and these two aspects of amygdala functioning. Two important indices of the amygdala's ability to form and/or process stimulus–reinforcement associations are startle reflex modulation and both aversive and appetitive conditioning (Davis, 2000; Everitt et al., 2003; LeDoux, 1998). Individuals show a startle ("jump") response to unexpected threat stimuli such as a loud noise. This can be potentiated if the startle probe is preceded by a threat stimulus and suppressed if it is preceded by an appetitive stimulus (Davis, 2000; Patrick, 1994). Individuals with autism show intact modulation of the startle reflex (Bernier, Dawson, Panagiotides, & Webb, 2005). Moreover, while they show difficulty in aversive conditioning, their difficulty is in the overgeneralization of the conditioned response; they show an increased skin conductance response to both the stimulus associated with the aversive stimulus (a loud noise) as well as the stimulus not associated with the loud noise (Gaigg & Bowler, 2007). This is also seen in patients with anxiety (for a review of this literature, see Lissek et al., 2005). In short, individuals with autism are not unable to form stimulus–reinforcement associations (Bernier et al., 2005).

In contrast to individuals with autism, there appears little doubt that individuals with psychopathy are profoundly impaired in the formation and use of stimulus–reinforcement associations (Blair, 2001; Lykken, 1957; Patrick et al., 1994). An impairment in aversive conditioning was one of the earliest deficits reported in individuals with psychopathy (Lykken, 1957). This deficit has been replicated (Flor, Birbaumer, Hermann, Ziegler, & Patrick, 2002), and neuroimaging work has demonstrated that this deficit reflects reduced amygdala activity (Birbaumer et al., 2005; Veit et al., 2002). Moreover, individuals with psychopathy show notably reduced modulation of the startle reflex by threat primes (Herpertz et al., 2001; Levenston, Patrick, Bradley, & Lang, 2000; Patrick, 1994).

With respect to the amygdala's role in social cognition, it is worth noting that the earliest advocates of an amygdala dysfunction model of autism (Baron-Cohen et al., 2000) based their model at least partly on the earlier animal

amygdala lesion data that were subsequently shown to be methodologically flawed (see above; Amaral, 2003). Indeed, on the basis of the methodologically driven revision of the amygdala's role in social cognition it has been argued that it is not essential for social cognition (Amaral et al., 2003). However, neuropsychological and neuroimaging work in humans does suggest a role for the amygdala in social cognition (e.g., Adolphs, 2003); though, of course, it should be noted that the human neuropsychological work suffers the same methodological drawbacks as does the early animal work—the lesions disrupt nearby tissue and axons travelling through the amygdala.

There were various aspects of social cognition in which the amygdala may play a role. As noted above, the amygdala is thought to play a role in the response to facial expressions, particularly fearful expressions (Adolphs, 2002). Several studies have reported reduced amygdala responses in patients with autism spectrum disorders when viewing emotional expressions (Ashwin, Baron-Cohen, Wheelwright, O'Riordan, & Bullmore, 2007; Baron-Cohen et al., 1999; Critchley et al., 2000). At first glance, it might appear that the fine cut between autism and psychopathy breaks down here. Individuals with psychopathy also show reduced amygdala responses to expression information in our own and others' prior work (Gordon, Baird, & End, 2004). However, there is a big difference between the response of individuals with autism and psychopathy to face information. Individuals with autism consistently show reduced responses within fusiform gyrus to face stimuli (Critchley et al., 2000; Pierce, Muller, Ambrose, Allen, & Courchesne, 2001; Schultz et al., 2000; Wang, Dapretto, Hariri, Sigman, & Bookheimer, 2004). Individuals with psychopathy do not (Gordon et al., 2004). Given that information on facial expressions passes through fusiform gyrus to reach the amygdala (Adolphs, 2002), it is possible that any reduction in amygdala activity to faces in autism may reflect problems in the representation of these faces within fusiform gyrus.

The amygdala has also been found to play a role in affect-related judgements based on facial stimuli (Adolphs, 2003; Baron-Cohen et al., 2000). Thus, the amygdala has been implicated in the ability to make trustworthiness judgements on the basis of neuropsychological (Adolphs, Tranel, & Damasio, 1998) and neuroimaging data (Winston, Strange, O'Doherty, & Dolan, 2002). Individuals with autism may show deficits in making such judgements (Adolphs et al., 2001) though this is debated (White, Hill, Winston, & Frith, 2006). Individuals with psychopathy do not (Richell et al., 2005). The amygdala has also been implicated in the ability to judge complex social emotions based only on information from the eye region (Baron-Cohen, Wheelwright, & Joliffe, 1997) by both neuropsychological (Adolphs, Baron-Cohen, & Tranel, 2002; Stone, Baron-Cohen, Calder, Keane, & Young, 2003) and neuroimaging work (Baron-Cohen et al., 1999). Individuals with autism show deficits on this task (Baron-Cohen et al., 1997). Individuals with psychopathy do not (Richell et al., 2003).

Conclusions

The goal of this paper was to apply the "fine cuts" technique advocated by Uta (U. Frith & Happé, 1994; Happé & Frith, 1996a, 1996b) to the understanding of empathy and amygdala functioning with respect to psychopathy and autism. A summary of the application of this fine cuts technique is provided in Table 1.

I believe that the data strongly suggest that a "fine cut" can be drawn between "cognitive" empathy ("Theory of Mind") and "emotional" empathy—the response to the emotional displays of others. There is also ample evidence of a clear "fine cut" between psychopathy and autism with respect to Theory of Mind. As Uta's work has amply demonstrated, individuals with autism show Theory of Mind impairment (see, for a review, Hill & Frith, 2003). In contrast, individuals with psychopathy do not. The picture with response to emotional empathy is murkier. While it is clear that individuals with psychopathy are impaired in the processing of fearful and to a

Table 1. *Summary of the "fine cuts" technique applied to psychopathy and autism with respect to subdivisions within processes termed "empathy" and functions of the amygdala*

	Psychopathy	Autism
"Empathy"	Cognitive empathy or Theory of Mind is intact in individuals with psychopathy.	Cognitive empathy or Theory of Mind is profoundly impaired in individuals with autism.
	The representation of face information, a prerequisite for emotional responding to another's expression (emotional empathy), appears intact in individuals with psychopathy.	The representation of face information is impaired in individuals with autism.
	There is selective impairment for the processing of fearful and to a lesser extent sad expressions in individuals with psychopathy.	It is uncertain whether there is impairment in processing emotional expressions in individuals with autism. However, if there is, it does not appear to be selective for fearful expressions.
Amygdala functioning	The formation and use of stimulus–reinforcement associations is profoundly impaired in individuals with psychopathy.	The formation and use of stimulus–reinforcement associations appears intact in individuals with autism.
	Aspects of social cognition that the amygdala may be involved in (e.g., affect-related judgements based on facial stimuli) appear intact in individuals with psychopathy.	Aspects of social cognition that the amygdala may be involved in (e.g., affect-related judgements based on facial stimuli) are impaired in individuals with autism.

lesser extent sad expressions, it remains uncertain whether individuals with autism are impaired in the processing of emotional expression information and, if they are, the extent to which this is independent of their clear, more general difficulties in face processing.

The data also suggest a fine cut between functions ascribed to the amygdala. Animal and human data are clear that the amygdala plays a critical role in the formation of stimulus–reinforcement associations. There is also literature to suggest that the amygdala plays a role in some aspects of social cognition, though, it should be noted, a coherent functional account of what this role is has yet to be provided. There is evidence of a clear "fine cut" between psychopathy and autism with respect to stimulus–reinforcement association formation. Individuals with autism show no impairment in this function of the amygdala. In contrast, individuals with psychopathy show very pronounced impairment. The picture with respect to the amygdala's role in social cognition is again murkier. Both individuals with psychopathy and autism show reduced responses within the amygdala to emotional expressions. The fine cut is in the generality of this reduced response. Individuals with autism spectrum disorders show reduced amygdala activity not only to emotional expressions but also to neutral expressions. Individuals with psychopathy do not. Moreover, the reduced amygdala response in the individuals with autism spectrum disorders may reflect deficient representation of facial stimuli in fusiform gyrus.

In conclusion, the "fine cuts" approach remains important. It acts as a bulwark to the tendency to make inappropriate links due to apparent similarities driven by lay semantic definitions rather than shared genetic and neurocognitive functional properties.

REFERENCES

Adolphs, R. (2002). Neural systems for recognizing emotion. *Current Opinion in Neurobiology, 12*, 169–177.

Adolphs, R. (2003). Is the human amygdala specialized for processing social information? *Annals of the New York Academy of Sciences, 985*, 326–340.

Adolphs, R., Baron-Cohen, S., & Tranel, D. (2002). Impaired recognition of social emotions following amygdala damage. *Journal of Cognitive Neuroscience, 14*, 1264–1274.

Adolphs, R., Gosselin, F., Buchanan, T. W., Tranel, D., Schyns, P., & Damasio, A. R. (2005). A mechanism for impaired fear recognition after amygdala damage. *Nature, 433*, 68–72.

Adolphs, R., Sears, L., & Piven, J. (2001). Abnormal processing of social information from faces in autism. *Journal of Cognitive Neuroscience, 13*, 232–240.

Adolphs, R., Tranel, D., & Damasio, A. R. (1998). The human amygdala in social judgment. *Nature, 393*, 470–474.

Amaral, D. G. (2003). The amygdala, social behavior, and danger detection. *Annals of the New York Academy of Sciences, 1000*, 337–347.

Amaral, D. G., Bauman, M. D., Capitanio, J. P., Lavenex, P., Mason, W. A., Mauldin-Jourdain, M. L., et al. (2003). The amygdala: Is it an essential component of the neural network for social cognition? *Neuropsychologia, 41*, 517–522.

American Psychiatric Association. (1994). *Diagnostic and statistical manual of mental disorders* (4th ed.). Washington, DC: Author.

Arsenio, W. F., & Fleiss, K. (1996). Typical and behaviourally disruptive children's understanding of the emotion consequences of socio-moral events. *British Journal of Developmental Psychology, 14*, 173–186.

Ashwin, C., Baron-Cohen, S., Wheelwright, S., O'Riordan, M., & Bullmore, E. T. (2007). Differential activation of the amygdala and the "social brain" during fearful face-processing in Asperger syndrome. *Neuropsychologia, 45*, 2–14.

Attwood, A., Frith, U., & Hermelin, B. (1988). The understanding and use of interpersonal gestures by autistic and Down's syndrome children. *Journal of Autism and Developmental Disorders, 18*, 241–257.

Bachevalier, J. (1994). Medial temporal lobe structures and autism: A review of clinical and experimental findings. *Neuropsychologia, 32*, 627–648.

Baron-Cohen, S. (2006). The hyper-systemizing, assortative mating theory of autism. *Progress in Neuropsychopharmacology and Biological Psychiatry, 30*, 865–872.

Baron-Cohen, S., Leslie, A. M., & Frith, U. (1985). Does the autistic child have a "theory of mind"? *Cognition, 21*, 37–46.

Baron-Cohen, S., Ring, H. A., Bullmore, E. T., Wheelwright, S., Ashwin, C., & Williams, S. C. (2000). The amygdala theory of autism. *Neuroscience Biobehavior Review, 24*, 355–364.

Baron-Cohen, S., Ring, H. A., Wheelwright, S., Bullmore, E. T., Brammer, M. J., Simmons, A., et al. (1999). Social intelligence in the normal and autistic brain: An fMRI study. *European Journal of Neuroscience, 11*, 1891–1898.

Baron-Cohen, S., Wheelwright, S., & Joliffe, T. (1997). Is there a "language of the eyes"? Evidence from normal adults, and adults with autism or Asperger syndrome. *Visual Cognition, 4*, 311–331.

Bauman, M. D., Lavenex, P., Mason, W. A., Capitanio, J. P., & Amaral, D. G. (2004). The development of social behavior following neonatal amygdala lesions in rhesus monkeys. *Journal of Cognitive Neuroscience, 16*, 1388–1411.

Bauman, M. D., Toscano, J. E., Mason, W. A., Lavenex, P., & Amaral, D. G. (2006). The expression of social dominance following neonatal lesions of the amygdala or hippocampus in rhesus monkeys (Macaca mulatta). *Behavioral Neuroscience, 120*, 749–760.

Baxter, M. G., & Murray, E. A. (2002). The amygdala and reward. *Nature Reviews Neuroscience, 3*, 563–573.

Bechara, A., Tranel, D., Damasio, H., Adolphs, R., Rockland, C., & Damasio, A. R. (1995). Double dissociation of conditioning and declarative knowledge relative to the amygdala and hippocampus in humans. *Science, 269*, 1115–1118.

Bernier, R., Dawson, G., Panagiotides, H., & Webb, S. (2005). Individuals with autism spectrum disorder show normal responses to a fear potential startle paradigm. *Journal of Autism and Developmental Disorders, 35*, 1–9.

Birbaumer, N., Veit, R., Lotze, M., Erb, M., Hermann, C., Grodd, W., et al. (2005). Deficient fear conditioning in psychopathy: A functional magnetic resonance imaging study. *Archives of General Psychiatry, 62*, 799–805.

Blair, R. J. R. (1995). A cognitive developmental approach to morality: Investigating the psychopath. *Cognition, 57*, 1–29.

Blair, R. J. R. (1996). Brief report: Morality in the autistic child. *Journal of Autism and Developmental Disorders, 26*, 571–579.

Blair, R. J. R. (2001). Neuro-cognitive models of aggression, the antisocial personality disorders and psychopathy. *Journal of Neurology, Neurosurgery & Psychiatry, 71*, 727–731.

Blair, R. J. R. (2003). Facial expressions, their communicatory functions and neuro-cognitive substrates. *Philosophical Transactions of the Royal Society of London, series B, 358*, 561–572.

Blair, R. J. R. (2004). The roles of orbital frontal cortex in the modulation of antisocial behavior. *Brain and Cognition, 55*, 198–208.

Blair, R. J. R. (2005). Responding to the emotions of others: Dissociating forms of empathy through the study of typical and psychiatric populations. *Consciousness and Cognition, 14*, 698–718.

Blair, R. J. R. (2006). Dissociable systems for empathy. In G. Bock & J. Goode (Eds.), *Empathy and fairness* (pp. 134–141). Chichester, UK: John Wiley and Sons.

Blair, R. J. R., Colledge, E., Murray, L., & Mitchell, D. G. (2001). A selective impairment in the processing of sad and fearful expressions in children with psychopathic tendencies. *Journal of Abnormal Child Psychology, 29*, 491–498.

Blair, R. J. R., Frith, U., Smith, N., Abell, F., & Cipolotti, L. (2002). Fractionation of visual memory: Agency detection and its impairment in autism. *Neuropsychologia, 40*, 108–118.

Blair, R. J. R., Marsh, A. A., Finger, E., Blair, K. S., & Luo, Q. (2006). Neuro-cognitive systems involved in morality. *Philosophical Explorations, 9*, 13–27.

Blair, R. J. R., Mitchell, D. G. V., & Blair, K. S. (2005). *The psychopath: Emotion and the brain*. Oxford, UK: Blackwell.

Blair, R. J. R., Mitchell, D. G. V., Colledge, E., Leonard, R. A., Shine, J. H., Murray, L. K., et al. (2004). Reduced sensitivity to other's fearful expressions in psychopathic individuals. *Personality & Individual Differences, 37*, 1111–1121.

Blair, R. J. R., Morris, J. S., Frith, C. D., Perrett, D. I., & Dolan, R. (1999). Dissociable neural responses to facial expressions of sadness and anger. *Brain, 122*, 883–893.

Blair, R. J. R., Sellars, C., Strickland, I., Clark, F., Williams, A., Smith, M., et al. (1996). Theory of mind in the psychopath. *Journal of Forensic Psychiatry, 7*, 15–25.

Bormann-Kischkel, C., Vilsmeier, M., & Baude, B. (1995). The development of emotional concepts in autism. *Journal of Child Psychology and Psychiatry, 36*, 1243–1259.

Boucher, J., & Lewis, V. (1992). Unfamiliar face recognition in relatively able autistic children. *Journal of Child Psychology and Psychiatry, 33*, 843–859.

Buchel, C., & Dolan, R. J. (2000). Classical fear conditioning in functional neuroimaging. *Current Opinions in Neurobiology, 10*, 219–223.

Buchel, C., Morris, J., Dolan, R. J., & Friston, K. J. (1998). Brain systems mediating aversive conditioning: An event-related fMRI study. *Neuron, 20*, 947–957.

Castelli, F., Frith, C., Happé, F., & Frith, U. (2002). Autism, Asperger syndrome and brain mechanisms for the attribution of mental states to animated shapes. *Brain, 125*, 1839–1849.

Castelli, F., Happé, F., Frith, U., & Frith, C. (2000). Movement and mind: A functional imaging study of perception and interpretation of complex intentional movement patterns. *Neuroimage, 12*, 314–325.

Cleckley, H. (1941). *The mask of sanity* (1st ed.). St Louis, MO: Mosby.

Critchley, H. D., Daly, E. M., Bullmore, E. T., Williams, S. C., Van Amelsvoort, T., Robertson, D. M., et al. (2000). The functional neuroanatomy of social behaviour: Changes in cerebral blood flow when people with autistic disorder process facial expressions. *Brain, 123*, 2203–2212.

Cubero, I., Thiele, T. E., & Bernstein, I. L. (1999). Insular cortex lesions and taste aversion learning: Effects of conditioning method and timing of lesion. *Brain Research, 839*, 323–330.

Dadds, M. R., Perry, Y., Hawes, D. J., Merz, S., Riddell, A. C., Haines, D. J., et al. (2006). Attention to the eyes and fear-recognition deficits in child psychopathy. *British Journal of Psychiatry, 189*, 280–281.

Davis, M. (2000). The role of the amygdala in conditioned and unconditioned fear and anxiety. In J. P. Aggleton (Ed.), *The amygdala: A functional analysis* (pp. 289–310). Oxford, UK: Oxford University Press.

Dolan, M., & Fullam, R. (2004). Theory of mind and mentalizing ability in antisocial personality disorders with and without psychopathy. *Psychological Medicine, 34*, 1093–1102.

Dolan, M., & Fullam, R. (2006). Face affect recognition deficits in personality-disordered offenders: Association with psychopathy. *Psychological Medicine, 36*, 1563–1569.

Emery, N. J., Capitanio, J. P., Mason, W. A., Machado, C. J., Mendoza, S. P., & Amaral, D. G. (2001). The effects of bilateral lesions of the amygdala on dyadic social interactions in rhesus monkeys (Macaca mulatta). *Behavioral Neuroscience, 115*, 515–544.

Everitt, B. J., Cardinal, R. N., Parkinson, J. A., & Robbins, T. W. (2003). Appetitive behavior: Impact of amygdala-dependent mechanisms of emotional learning. *Annals of the New York Academy of Sciences, 985*, 233–250.

Fitzgerald, D. A., Angstadt, M., Jelsone, L. M., Nathan, P. J., & Phan, K. L. (2006). Beyond threat: Amygdala reactivity across multiple expressions of facial affect. *Neuroimage, 30*, 1441–1448.

Fletcher, P. C., Happé, F., Frith, U., Baker, S. C., Dolan, R. J., Frackowiak, R. S., et al. (1995). Other minds in the brain: A functional imaging study of "theory of mind" in story comprehension. *Cognition, 57*, 109–128.

Flor, H., Birbaumer, N., Hermann, C., Ziegler, S., & Patrick, C. J. (2002). Aversive Pavlovian conditioning in psychopaths: Peripheral and central correlates. *Psychophysiology, 39*, 505–518.

Frick, P. J. (1995). Callous-unemotional traits and conduct problems: A two-factor model of psychopathy in children. *Issues in Criminological and Legal Psychology, 24*, 47–51.

Frick, P. J., & Hare, R. D. (2001). *The antisocial process screening device*. Toronto, Canada: Multi-Health Systems.

Frith, C. D., & Frith, U. (1999). Interacting minds: A biological basis. *Science, 286*, 1692–1695.

Frith, C. D., & Frith, U. (2006). The neural basis of mentalizing. *Neuron, 50*, 531–534.

Frith, U. (1989). *Autism: Explaining the enigma*. Oxford, UK: Blackwell.

Frith, U., & Frith, C. D. (2003). Development and neurophysiology of mentalizing. *Philosophical Transactions of the Royal Society B: Biological Sciences, 358*, 459–473.

Frith, U., & Happé, F. (1994). Autism: Beyond "theory of mind". *Cognition, 50*, 115–132.

Frith, U., & Happé, F. (2005). Autism spectrum disorder. *Current Biology, 15*, R786–790.

Gaigg, S. B., & Bowler, D. M. (2007). Differential fear conditioning in Asperger's syndrome: Implications for an amygdala theory of autism. *Neuropsychlogia, 45*, 2125–2134.

Goel, V., Grafman, J., Sadato, N., & Hallett, M. (1995). Modeling other minds. *Neuroreport, 11*, 1741–1746.

Gordon, H. L., Baird, A. A., & End, A. (2004). Functional differences among those high and low on a trait measure of psychopathy. *Biological Psychiatry, 56*, 516–521.

Grant, C. M., Boucher, J., Riggs, K. J., & Grayson, A. (2005). Moral understanding in children with autism. *Autism*, *9*, 317–331.

Happé, F., Ehlers, S., Fletcher, P., Frith, U., Johansson, M., Gillberg, C., et al. (1996). "Theory of mind" in the brain. *Neuroreport*, *8*, 197–201.

Happé, F. G. E., & Frith, U. (1996a). The neuropsychology of autism, *Brain*, 1377–1400.

Happé, F. G. E., & Frith, U. (1996b). Theory of mind and social impairment in children with conduct disorder. *British Journal of Developmental Psychology*, *14*, 385–398.

Hare, R. D. (1991). *The Hare Psychopathy Checklist–Revised*. Toronto, Canada: Multi-Health Systems.

Hare, R. D. (2003). *Hare Psychopathy Checklist–Revised (PCL-R)* (2nd ed.). Toronto, Canada: Multi Health Systems.

Harpur, T. J., Hakstian, A. R., & Hare, R. D. (1988). The factor structure of the Psychopathy Checklist. *Journal of Consulting and Clinical Psychology*, *56*, 741–747.

Herba, C., & Phillips, M. (2004). Annotation: Development of facial expression recognition from childhood to adolescence: Behavioural and neurological perspectives. *Journal of Child Psychology and Psychiatry*, *45*, 1185–1198.

Herpertz, S. C., Werth, U., Lukas, G., Qunaibi, M., Schuerkens, A., Kunert, H. J., et al. (2001). Emotion in criminal offenders with psychopathy and borderline personality disorder. *Archives of General Psychiatry*, *58*, 737–745.

Hill, E. L., & Frith, U. (2003). Understanding autism: Insights from mind and brain. *Philosophical Transactions of the Royal Society, Series B*, *358*, 281–289.

Hobson, P. (1986). The autistic child's appraisal of expressions of emotion. *Journal of Child Psychology and Psychiatry*, *27*, 321–342.

Hobson, R. P. (1993). *Autism and the development of mind*. Hove, UK: Lawrence Erlbaum Associates.

Hooker, C. I., Germine, L. T., Knight, R. T., & D'Esposito, M. (2006). Amygdala response to facial expressions reflects emotional learning. *Journal of Neuroscience*, *26*, 8915–8922.

Howard, M. A., Cowell, P. E., Boucher, J., Broks, P., Mayes, A., Farrant, A., et al. (2000). Convergent neuroanatomical and behavioural evidence of an amygdala hypothesis of autism. *Neuroreport*, *11*, 1931–1935.

Hughes, C., Dunn, J., & White, A. (1998). Trick or treat?: Uneven understanding of mind and emotion and executive dysfunction in "hard-to-manage" preschoolers. *Journal of Child Psychology and Psychiatry*, *39*, 981–994.

Hughes, C., & Ensor, R. (2006). Behavioural problems in 2-year-olds: Links with individual differences in theory of mind, executive function and harsh parenting. *Journal of Child Psychology and Psychiatry*, *47*, 488–497.

Hume, D. (1967). *A treatise of human nature*. Oxford, UK: Oxford University Press. (Original work published 1740)

Humphreys, K., Minshew, N., Leonard, G. L., & Behrmann, M. (2007). A fine-grained analysis of facial expression processing in high-functioning adults with autism. *Neuropsychologia*, *45*, 685–695.

Kanner, L. (1943). Autistic disturbances of affective contact. *Nervous Child*, *2*, 217–250.

Kennett, J. (2002). Autism, empathy and moral agency. *The Philosophical Quarterly*, *52*, 340–357.

Kiehl, K. A. (2006). A cognitive neuroscience perspective on psychopathy: Evidence for paralimbic system dysfunction. *Psychiatry Research*, *142*, 107–128.

Klin, A., Jones, W., Schultz, R., Volkmar, F., & Cohen, D. (2002). Visual fixation patterns during viewing of naturalistic social situations as predictors of social competence in individuals with autism. *Archives of General Psychiatry*, *59*, 809–816.

Klin, A., Sparrow, S. S., de Bildt, A., Cicchetti, D. V., Cohen, D. J., & Volkmar, F. R. (1999). A normed study of face recognition in autism and related disorders. *Journal of Autism and Developmental Disabilities*, *29*, 499–508.

Kling, A. S., & Brothers, L. A. (1992). The amygdala and social behaviour. In J. P. Aggleton (Ed.), *The amygdala: Neurobiological aspects of emotion, memory, and mental dysfunction* (pp. 353–378). New York: Wiley.

Kosson, D. S., Suchy, Y., Mayer, A. R., & Libby, J. (2002). Facial affect recognition in criminal psychopaths. *Emotion*, *2*, 398–411.

LaBar, K. S., Crupain, M. J., Voyvodic, J. T., & McCarthy, G. (2003). Dynamic perception of facial affect and identity in the human brain. *Cerebral Cortex*, *13*, 1023–1033.

LaBar, K. S., Gatenby, J. C., Gore, J. C., LeDoux, J. E., & Phelps, E. A. (1998). Human amygdala activation during conditioned fear acquisition and extinction: A mixed-trial fMRI study. *Neuron*, *20*, 937–945.

LeDoux, J. (1998). *The emotional brain*. New York: Weidenfeld & Nicolson.

LeDoux, J. E. (2000). The amygdala and emotion: A view through fear. In J. P. Aggleton (Ed.), *The amygdala: A functional analysis* (pp. 289–310). Oxford, UK: Oxford University Press.

Leslie, A. M., & Thaiss, L. (1992). Domain specificity in conceptual development: Neuropsychological evidence from autism. *Cognition, 43*, 225–251.

Levenston, G. K., Patrick, C. J., Bradley, M. M., & Lang, P. J. (2000). The psychopath as observer: Emotion and attention in picture processing. *Journal of Abnormal Psychology, 109*, 373–386.

Lissek, S., Powers, A. S., McClure, E. B., Phelps, E. A., Woldehawariat, G., Grillon, C., et al. (2005). Classical fear conditioning in the anxiety disorders: A meta-analysis. *Behavior Research and Therapy, 43*, 1391–1424.

Luo, Q., Holroyd, T., Jones, M., Hendler, T., & Blair, J. (2007). Neural dynamics for facial threat processing as revealed by gamma band synchronization using MEG. *Neuroimage, 34*, 839–847.

Lykken, D. T. (1957). A study of anxiety in the sociopathic personality. *Journal of Abnormal and Social Psychology, 55*, 6–10.

Marsh, A. A., & Blair, R. J. R. (in press). *Antisocial behavior is associated with specific deficits in recognition of the fear facial expression: A meta-analysis.*

Mineka, S., & Cook, M. (1993). Mechanisms involved in the observational conditioning of fear. *Journal of Experimental Psychology: General, 122*, 23–38.

Montagne, B., van Honk, J., Kessels, R. P. C., Frigerio, E., Burt, M., van Zandvoort, M. J. E., et al. (2005). Reduced efficiency in recognising fear in subjects scoring high on psychopathic personality characteristics *Personality and Individual Differences, 38*, 5–11.

Moore, D. G. (2001). Reassessing emotion recognition performance in people with mental retardation: A review. *American Journal on Mental Retardation, 106*, 481–502.

Morris, J. S., Frith, C. D., Perrett, D. I., Rowland, D., Young, A. W., Calder, A. J., et al. (1996). A differential response in the human amygdala to fearful and happy facial expressions. *Nature, 383*, 812–815.

Morris, J. S., Ohman, A., & Dolan, R. (1999). A subcortical pathway to the right amygdala mediating "unseen" fear. *Proceedings of the National Academy of Sciences USA, 96*, 1680–1685.

Newman, J. P. (1998). Psychopathic behaviour: An information processing perspective. In D. J. Cooke, A. E. Forth, & R. D. Hare (Eds.), *Psychopathy: Theory, research and implications for society* (pp. 81–105). Dordrecht, The Netherlands: Kluwer Academic Publishers.

Nucci, L. P., & Herman, S. (1982). Behavioral disordered children's conceptions of moral, conventional, and personal issues. *Journal of Abnormal Child Psychology, 10*, 411–425.

Ozonoff, S., Pennington, B., & Rogers, S. (1990). Are there emotion perception deficits in young autistic children? *Journal of Child Psychology and Psychiatry, 31*, 343–363.

Patrick, C. J. (1994). Emotion and psychopathy: Startling new insights. *Psychophysiology, 31*, 319–330.

Patrick, C. J., Cuthbert, B. N., & Lang, P. J. (1994). Emotion in the criminal psychopath: Fear image processing. *Journal of Abnormal Psychology, 103*, 523–534.

Perner, J., & Leekam, S. (2008). The curious incident of the photo that was accused of being false: Issues of domain specificity in development, autism, and brain imaging. *Quarterly Journal of Experimental Psychology, 61*, 76–89.

Phillips, M. L., Young, A. W., Scott, S. K., Calder, A. J., Andrew, C., Giampietro, V., et al. (1998). Neural responses to facial and vocal expressions of fear and disgust. *Proceedings of the Royal Society of London, Series B, 265*, 1809–1817.

Pierce, K., Muller, R. A., Ambrose, J., Allen, G., & Courchesne, E. (2001). Face processing occurs outside the fusiform "face area" in autism: Evidence from functional MRI. *Brain, 124*, 2059–2073.

Pizzagalli, D., Regard, M., & Lehmann, D. (1999). Rapid emotional face processing in the human right and left brain hemispheres: An ERP study. *Neuroreport, 10*, 2691–2698.

Prather, M. D., Lavenex, P., Mauldin-Jourdain, M. L., Mason, W. A., Capitanio, J. P., Mendoza, S. P., et al. (2001). Increased social fear and decreased fear of objects in monkeys with neonatal amygdala lesions. *Neuroscience, 106*, 653–658.

Prior, M., Dahlstrom, B., & Squires, T. (1990). Autistic children's knowledge of thinking and feeling states in other people. *Journal of Autism and Developmental Disorders, 31*, 587–602.

Richell, R. A., Mitchell, D. G., Newman, C., Leonard, A., Baron-Cohen, S., & Blair, R. J. (2003). Theory of mind and psychopathy: Can psychopathic individuals read the "language of the eyes"? *Neuropsychologia, 41*, 523–526.

Richell, R. A., Mitchell, D. G. V., Peschardt, K. S., Winston, J. S., Leonard, A., Dolan, R. J., et al. (2005). Trust and distrust: The perception of trust-worthiness of faces in psychopathic and non-psychopathic offenders. *Personality and Individual Differences*, 38, 1735–1744.

Rogers, J., Viding, E., Blair, J. R., Frith, U., & Happé, F. (2006). Autism spectrum disorder and psychopathy: Shared cognitive underpinnings or double hit? *Psychological Medicine*, 36, 1789–1798.

Rolls, E. T. (1999). *The brain and emotion*. Oxford, UK: Oxford University Press.

Rosvold, H., Mirsky, A., & Pribram, K. (1954). Influence of amygdalectomy on social behavior in monkeys. *Journal of Comparative Physiology A*, 47, 173–178.

Rozin, P., Haidt, J., & McCauley, C. R. (1993). Disgust. In M. Lewis & J. M. Haviland (Eds.), *Handbook of emotions* (pp. 575–594). New York: The Guilford Press.

Rutter, M. (2005). Commentary: What is the meaning and utility of the psychopathy concept? *Journal of Abnormal Child Psychology*, 33, 499–503.

Schultz, R. T., Gauthier, I., Klin, A., Fulbright, R. K., Anderson, A. W., Volkmar, F., et al. (2000). Abnormal ventral temporal cortical activity during face discrimination among individuals with autism and Asperger syndrome. *Archives of General Psychiatry*, 57, 331–340.

Sprengelmeyer, R., Rausch, M., Eysel, U. T., & Przuntek, H. (1998). Neural structures associated with the recognition of facial basic emotions. *Proceedings of the Royal Society of London, Series B*, 265, 1927–1931.

Steele, S., Joseph, R. M., & Tager-Flusberg, H. (2003). Brief report: Developmental change in theory of mind abilities in children with autism. *Journal of Autism and Developmental Disorders*, 33, 461–467.

Stone, V. E., Baron-Cohen, S., Calder, A., Keane, J., & Young, A. (2003). Acquired theory of mind impairments in individuals with bilateral amygdala lesions. *Neuropsychologia*, 41, 209–220.

Sutton, J., Reeves, M., & Keogh, E. (2000). Disruptive behaviour, avoidance of responsibility and theory of mind. *British Journal of Developmental Psychology*, 18, 1–11.

Sutton, J., Smith, P. K., & Swettenham, J. (1999). Social cognition and bullying: Social inadequacy or skilled manipulation? *British Journal of Developmental Psychology*, 17, 435–450.

Veit, R., Flor, H., Erb, M., Hermann, C., Lotze, M., Grodd, W., et al. (2002). Brain circuits involved in emotional learning in antisocial behavior and social phobia in humans. *Neuroscience Letters*, 328, 233–236.

Vuilleumier, P., Armony, J. L., Driver, J., & Dolan, R. J. (2003). Distinct spatial frequency sensitivities for processing faces and emotional expressions. *Nature Neuroscience*, 6, 624–631.

Wang, A. T., Dapretto, M., Hariri, A. R., Sigman, M., & Bookheimer, S. Y. (2004). Neural correlates of facial affect processing in children and adolescents with autism spectrum disorder. *Journal of the American Academy of Child and Adolescent Psychiatry*, 43, 481–490.

White, S., Hill, E., Winston, J., & Frith, U. (2006). An islet of social ability in Asperger syndrome: Judging social attributes from faces. *Brain and Cognition*, 61, 69–77.

Widom, C. S. (1976). Interpersonal and personal construct systems in psychopaths. *Journal of Consulting and Clinical Psychology*, 44, 614–623.

Widom, C. S. (1978). An empirical classification of female offenders. *Criminal Justice and Behavior*, 5, 35–52.

Winston, J. S., O'Doherty, J., & Dolan, R. J. (2003). Common and distinct neural responses during direct and incidental processing of multiple facial emotions. *Neuroimage*, 20, 84–97.

Winston, J. S., Strange, B. A., O'Doherty, J., & Dolan, R. J. (2002). Automatic and intentional brain responses during evaluation of trustworthiness of faces. *Nature Neuroscience*, 5, 277–283.

THE QUARTERLY JOURNAL OF EXPERIMENTAL PSYCHOLOGY
2008, 61 (1), 171–181

Psychology Press
Taylor & Francis Group

Cognition to genes via the brain in the study of conduct disorder

Essi Viding

Department of Psychology and Institute of Cognitive Neuroscience, University College London, London, UK, and Social, Genetic, and Developmental Psychiatry Centre, Institute of Psychiatry, King's College London, London, UK

Alice P. Jones

Social, Genetic, and Developmental Psychiatry Centre, Institute of Psychiatry, King's College London, London, UK

Although a single diagnostic label, conduct disorder, is currently applied to children exhibiting anti-social behaviour, multiple routes to the same behavioural phenomena exist. Morton and Frith's (1995) causal modelling has been fundamentally important in influencing models of cognitive/affective and associated neural differences between callous-unemotional (CU) and reactive/threat-based antisocial behaviour. Current behavioural genetic research is still catching up with the developmental cognitive neuroscience, and very few genetically informative studies differentiate between these two subtypes of antisocial behaviour. Our own work with preadolescent twins suggests that while the CU subtype is genetically vulnerable to antisocial behaviour, the non-CU subtype manifests a primarily environmental aetiology to their antisocial behaviour. Molecular genetic work to date has not differentiated between these two subtypes, and we highlight why it might be of interest to do so. Finally, we discuss how the novel approach of imaging genetics could be harnessed to study genes to cognition pathways for different subtypes of conduct disorder. Uta Frith's contributions to articulating research strategies for developmental disorders are important in conducting and interpreting this work.

Preventing antisocial behaviour and violence is one of the most important global concerns and also features as a UK National Health Service and Government research priority (Bailey, 2002; Krug, Dahlberg, Mercy, Zwi, & Lozarno, 2002). Political, social, and economic risk factors for antisocial behaviour are well studied (Farrington, 2000). In addition a growing number of studies attest to genetically influenced individual differences in predisposition to antisocial behaviour and violence (Moffitt, 2005; Rhee & Waldman, 2002). We use the terms antisocial behaviour, conduct disorder, and conduct problems interchangeably in this paper to refer to the violation of social norms and rights of others, rather than as a clinical label.

Correspondence should be addressed to Essi Viding, Department of Psychology and Institute of Cognitive Neuroscience, University College London, Gower St., London WC1E 6BT, UK. E-mail: e.viding@ucl.ac.uk

The authors acknowledge grant support from the Medical Research Council (G0401170) and the Department of Health FMH Programme (MRD 12–37).

171

DOI:10.1080/17470210701508889

Early-onset antisocial behaviour carries a strong risk for persistent offending (Moffitt, 2003). In childhood, high levels of antisocial behaviour may be diagnosed as conduct disorder (CD). The *Diagnostic and Statistical Manual of Mental Disorders—Fourth Edition* (DSM-IV; American Psychiatric Association, 1994) defines CD as persistent antisocial behaviour, which deviates from age-appropriate social norms and violates the basic rights of others. The prevalence of CD in the UK is 2.1% for boys and 1% for girls, and the risk of being diagnosed increases with age (Maughan, Rowe, Messer, Goodman, & Meltzer, 2004).

Although a single diagnostic label, conduct disorder, is currently applied to children exhibiting antisocial behaviour, multiple routes to the same behavioural phenomena exist. This point has been illustrated several times over and with regard to various developmental disorders by Uta Frith and her colleagues (Blair & Frith, 2000; Frith & Happé, 1998; Morton & Frith, 1995). One way of subtyping conduct-disordered children is to highlight the cognitive/affective differences between callous-unemotional (CU)/premeditated and reactive/threat-based antisocial behaviour (Blair, Peschardt, Budhani, Mitchell, & Pine, 2006; Frick et al., 2003; Pardini, Lochman, & Frick, 2003). In this paper we present data that suggest that the extreme behaviour seen in CU and non-CU antisocial individuals (from now on AB/CU+ and AB/CU−, respectively) is likely to stem from different types of deficits at the cognitive-affective level, probably reflecting the operation of differentiable genetic and neural risk factors in the two subtypes.

We will trace causal models of AB/CU+ and AB/CU− starting with the behaviour and ending up with genes. Some brief examples of how AB/CU+ and AB/CU− children differ at the behavioural level are provided, followed by descriptions of the cognitive profile associated with AB/CU+ and AB/CU− subtypes. In the subsequent two sections the brain-imaging and behavioural genetic work related to AB/CU+ and AB/CU− is reviewed. The causal modelling approach advocated by Uta Frith and her

colleagues has been of extreme importance in advancing research into development of antisocial behaviour. Current behavioural genetic and brain-imaging research into childhood antisocial behaviour is still awaiting the full "Uta treatment", but new studies incorporating insights from the causal modelling tradition are on their way. These are discussed in the final section of this paper, and the promise of novel research strategies in advancing timely treatment of antisocial behaviour is emphasized.

(Mis)behaviour

In a longitudinal study conducted a few years ago, CU traits emerged alongside depression and marijuana use as the strongest predictor of later antisocial behaviour (Loeber, Burke & Lahey, 2002). The available evidence indicates that CU traits index a relatively stable characteristic that predicts future antisocial behaviour and particularly poor outcome (Forth, Kosson, & Hare, 2003; Frick & Marsee, 2006; Frick, Stickle, Dandreaux, Farrell, & Kimonis, 2005).

Frick et al. (2005) followed up a group of children from a community sample who were displaying elevated levels of antisocial behaviour with and without CU traits. At each of the four annual follow-up assessments, the AB/CU+ group showed the highest rates of conduct problems, delinquency, and police contact. In fact, this group accounted for at least half of all police contact for the sample in the last three annual assessment points. Furthermore, AB/CU+ delinquency was not limited to aggressive acts, but this group also showed the highest levels of most types of delinquent behaviour (e.g., substance misuse and property offences). In contrast the children who were initially designated to the AB/CU− group were indistinguishable from controls on the trajectory of self-reported delinquency. Although the AB/CU− group did show elevated levels of aggressive conduct problems compared with controls, they were less severe than the AB/CU+ group. AB/CU− children showed a significant increase in police contact only at the last time point of the study. It was not possible to infer a trend from this one time point, but it may indicate that AB/CU− children begin their involvement in criminal activities later than their AB/CU+ counterparts.

The presence of CU traits has also been shown to be associated with aggression and attitude to punishment. Pardini et al. (2003) demonstrated that a group of delinquent adolescents with high levels of CU traits were more likely to focus on the positive aspects of aggression (i.e., rewards, social dominance) and less likely to be concerned with the negative consequences of committing antisocial acts (i.e., subsequent punishment following the transgression) than were their antisocial peers. These findings held even after controlling for delinquency severity, cognitive ability, and demographic characteristics. In contrast, antisocial behaviour without CU traits is associated with hostile attribution biases (Frick at al., 2003), and children with AB/CU− tend to get distressed about the consequences of their antisocial behaviour (Barry et al., 2000).

Research investigating the effect of parental characteristics contrasting AB/CU+ and AB/CU− groups is scarce. However, two studies have suggested that antisocial behaviour in AB/CU+ children may be less strongly associated with negative and poor parental practices than it is for AB/CU− children (Oxford, Cavell, & Hughes, 2003; Wootton, Frick, Shelton, & Silverthorn, 1997). In addition, Hawes and Dadds (2005) have demonstrated that the use of "time-out" as a method of behaviour modification is less effective in those children with AB/CU+ than in those with AB/CU−.

In summary, CU traits can be used to distinguish two different subtypes of conduct problems at a behavioural level. AB/CU+ is associated with a poorer long-term outcome (Frick et al., 2005), increased severity of antisocial behaviour (Dadds, Fraser, Frost, & Hawes, 2005), and decreased focus on and response to punishment (Hawes & Dadds, 2005; Pardini et al., 2003). AB/CU− is associated with less severe conduct problems, a more favourable response to discipline, and distress at the consequences of one's own antisocial actions.

Cognitive profile in AB/CU+ and AB/CU−

Just as we can differentiate children with AB/CU+ and AB/CU− at the behavioural level, we can also see some differences in terms of the cognitive-affective difficulties that these children experience. As Uta Frith and her long-standing colleague John Morton have advocated time and again, to understand how behaviour comes about we need to think about cognition (Frith & Happé, 1998; Morton & Frith, 1995). With conduct disorder we are dealing with a behaviourally defined syndrome with different cognitive deficits associated with sometimes similar, but also in part distinct behaviours. In other words, there are several conduct disorders at the level of cognition. In Morton and Frith's causal modelling approach the cognitive level also includes affective processing (henceforth cognitive = cognitive-affective). An important aspect of the causal modelling approach is the maxim that any cognitive account is not merely an alternative way of describing the behaviour in question (Morton & Frith, 1995). In other words, the cognitive elements should not be mapped one for one to the behaviours they are trying to account for. Instead, a model of the underlying cognitive deficit should account for a variety of behavioural phenomena associated with a disorder.

The cognitive deficit associated with psychopathic antisocial behaviour is postulated to be related to a reduction in the salience of punishment information (see Blair, 2006, for a causal model of this subtype of antisocial behaviour). Blair's integrated emotion systems (IES) model works on the assumption that children with AB/CU+ have diminished ability to form stimulus−punishment associations. In childhood, the ability to be able to form associations between moral transgressions and the aversive outcome (e.g., others' distress) is vital for successful socialization. Individuals with psychopathic traits find the distress cues in others less aversive and therefore are less likely to learn to avoid actions that bring about a negative response. In addition socialization by punishing consequences also relies on ability to form stimulus–punishment associations. Children with AB/CU+ are poor at performing on tasks relying on stimulus–punishment learning. In contrast to AB/CU+, Blair et al. (2006) proposed that in AB/CU– there are elevated levels of anxiety, threat-related reactive aggression and hyperreactivity to threat—for example, angry faces (Dadds et al., 2006; Pardini et al., 2003; Pollak & Sinha, 2002). In line with this suggestion, Viding and Frith (2006) proposed a causal model where at the cognitive level the children with AB/CU– suffer from overreactive emotional intent encoder, which in combination with emotional memory database of maltreatment and hostility will result in a fight response bias. This fight response bias is thought to be triggered in response to acute environmental stressors and results in reactive aggression, impulsive violence, and increased propensity to make hostile attributions to ambiguous situations.

To date, there are only few direct comparisons of the cognitive profile of antisocial children with and without CU traits. Frick et al. (2003) compared groups of nonreferred AB/CU+ and AB/CU– children and found poor processing of punishment information in AB/CU+ and a hostile attribution bias in AB/CU–. Differences have also been observed in emotional reactivity: Loney, Frick, Clements, Ellis, and Kerlin (2003) demonstrated a slower recognition time for negative emotional words in AB/CU+ adolescents, compared with a faster recognition time for the same words in an AB/CU– group. Dadds et al. (2006) reported that CU traits are uniquely related to poor recognition of fearful expressions, while AB/CU– children tended to be hypersensitive to angry expressions. In addition, a large body of research by Blair and colleagues has demonstrated deficits in processing fear, sadness, and punishment in AB/CU+ individuals, as

compared with institutionalized (although not specifically AB/CU–) controls (see Blair et al., 2006, for a review).

"Antisocial" brains

Individual differences in several brain areas and cognitive functions associated with perception and regulation of emotions have been found to correlate with antisocial and violent behaviour (Davidson, Putnam, & Larson, 2000). In particular, the orbitofrontal cortex, cingulate cortex, amygdala, and interconnected regions have shown both structural and functional abnormalities in antisocial populations. Neuropsychological functions associated with these brain regions, such as perception of threat and distress as well as modulation of affective response, are compromised in antisocial individuals (Blair et al., 2006; Moffitt, 2003). Emotionally toxic environments are likely to contribute to these abnormalities in brain function in some, but not necessarily all, antisocial individuals. Unfortunately most of the sparse number of reported brain-imaging studies have not subtyped individuals according to their CU profile and as such are sometimes difficult to interpret. Given the proposed contrasting cognitive profile of AB/CU+ versus AB/CU– it would be informative to study these two subtypes separately.

The IES model proposes that for AB/CU+ individuals, various aspects of amygdala functioning are impaired (e.g., the formation of stimulus–punishment associations). Early amygdala dysfunction may also have a negative impact on the development of empathy (Blair, 2006). The IES model postulates that the cognitive and behaviour profile described above for AB/CU+ individuals is a consequence of amygdala hyporeactivity. In contrast, AB/CU– individuals are proposed to show amygdala hyperreactivity potentiated by early environmental stressors. Blair et al. (2006) suggest that this amygdala hyperreactivity leads to the fight response bias and concomitant reactive aggression but relatively unimpaired social cognition profile observed in AB/CU– individuals.

A handful of functional magnetic resonance imaging (fMRI) studies have studied brain responsivity to emotional stimuli in callous-unemotional individuals. The most conclusive study to date compared adults with psychopathy (i.e., AB/CU+) with other incarcerated individuals and demonstrated that those with psychopathy show less amygdala activation in when performing an emotional memory task (Kiehl et al., 2001). Another study compared adults with psychopathy and controls matched for age and educational level and reported deficient amygdala activation during fear conditioning (Birbaumer et al., 2005).

Only one fMRI study on children with conduct disorder has investigated brain reactivity to emotional stimuli. Sterzer, Stadler, Krebs, Kleinschmidt, and Poutska (2005) used emotionally significant stimuli and demonstrated amygdala activation in normal children and children with conduct disorder. Compared to the control children, children with conduct problems showed less amygdala activation to threat, as long as anxiety/depression was controlled for in the analyses. No fMRI studies looking at AB/CU+ and AB/CU− children separately have been published to date.

We are currently conducting a large-scale fMRI study investigating neural response to emotional stimuli in typically developing children, as well as children with AB/CU+. Given the scarcity of imaging data for typically developing children and some inconsistency in the results (Herba & Phillips, 2004), a baseline of amygdala response to emotional stimuli needed to be established as a priority. Our study thus sought to first extend the existing literature by replicating the amygdala response to nonsocial emotional pictures and fearful faces in a sample of preadolescent boys in a narrow age range. Although adult data demonstrate that both types of stimuli activate the amygdala, with left laterality for nonsocial emotional stimuli and right laterality for facial emotional stimuli (Hariri, Tessitore, Mattay, Fera, & Weinberger, 2002), to our knowledge, no study to date has provided a direct comparison of amygdala reactivity to nonsocial and social emotional stimuli in children.

Inclusion of AB/CU+ children in our study enables us to compare the strength of the amygdala response to social and nonsocial emotional stimuli in children with AB/CU+ and ability-matched typically developing (TD) children We are yet to compare AB/CU+ with AB/CU− using fMRI, but this is the natural next step in our research programme. The expectation would be for the children with AB/CU− to show greater amygdala activation than their counterparts with AB/CU+. In summary, studies looking at the specific neural profile of AB/CU+ and AB/CU− are scarce, but there is considerable research interest in this area. As we discuss later in this chapter, it will be particularly important to study how genetic vulnerabilities may manifest at the level of the brain.

In their genes?

The first step in establishing whether genetic influences are important for individual differences in any given behaviour is to conduct twin and adoption studies. As twin studies are the more common of the two, the logic of these studies is discussed briefly here, before some new data regarding heritability estimates for AB by CU subtype are reviewed.

The twin method is a natural experiment that relies on the different levels of genetic relatedness between MZ and DZ twin pairs to estimate the contribution of genetic and environmental factors to individual differences, or extreme scores in a phenotype of interest. Phenotypes include any behaviour or characteristic that is measured separately for each twin, such as twins' scores on a antisocial behaviour checklist. Statistical model fitting techniques and regression analyses methods incorporating a genetic relatedness parameter are used to investigate the aetiology of the phenotype of choice. For further details of techniques in this area see Plomin, DeFries, McClearn, and McGuffin (2000). The basic premise of the twin method is this: If identical twins, who share 100% of their genetic material, appear more similar on a trait than do fraternal twins, who share on average 50% of their genetic material (like any siblings), then we infer that there are genetic influences on a trait. Identical twins' genetic similarity is twice that of fraternal twins. If nothing apart from genes influences behaviour, then we would expect the identical twins to be twice as similar with respect to the phenotypic measure as are fraternal twins. Shared environmental influences—environmental influences that make twins similar to each other—are inferred if fraternal twins appear more similar than is expected from sharing 50% of their genes. Finally, if identical twins are not 100% similar on a trait, nonshared environmental influences are inferred—in other words, environmental influences that make twins different from each other. The nonshared environmental estimate also includes measurement error.

A wealth of twin studies confirms that individual differences in antisocial behaviour and callous-unemotional traits are heritable (Blonigen, Hicks, Krueger, Patrick, & Iacono, 2005; Larsson, Andershed, & Lichtenstein, 2006; Rhee & Waldman, 2002; Taylor, Loney, Bobadilla, Iacono, & McGue, 2003). Shared environmental influences play some role for individual differences in AB, but not CU. To our knowledge, only two twin studies to date have investigated whether the aetiology of antisocial behaviour differs as a function of CU traits. Although previous research had strongly suggested that children with early onset antisocial behaviour coupled with callous-unemotional traits form a distinct subtype (Blair et al., 2006; Frick & Marsee, 2006), possible aetiological differences between these children and others with early-onset antisocial behaviour had not been studied until recently.

To address this question we first studied teacher ratings of callous-unemotional traits and antisocial behaviour in approximately 7,500 seven-year-old twins from the Twins Early Development Study (TEDS; Viding, Blair, Moffitt, & Plomin, 2005). We separated children with elevated levels of antisocial behaviour (in the top 10% for the TEDS sample) into AB/CU + and AB/CU− groups based on their CU score (in the top 10% or not). Antisocial behaviour in children with AB/CU + was under

strong genetic influence (heritability of .81) and no influence of shared environment. In contrast, antisocial behaviour in children without elevated levels of callous-unemotional traits showed moderate genetic influence (heritability of .30) and substantial environmental influence (shared environmental influence = .34, nonshared environmental influence = .26). We have recently replicated the finding of different heritability magnitude for the AB/CU + and AB/CU− groups using the 9-year teacher data (Viding, Jones, Frick, Moffitt, & Plomin, in press). This difference in heritability magnitude holds even after hyperactivity scores of the children are controlled for, suggesting that the result is not driven by any differences in hyperactivity between the two groups. In summary, our research with preadolescent twins suggests that while the CU subtype is genetically vulnerable to antisocial behaviour, the non-CU subtype manifests a more strongly environmental aetiology to their antisocial behaviour (Viding et al., 2005; Viding et al., in press).

Common behavioural disorders are currently proposed to be the quantitative extreme of the same genetic effects that operate throughout the distribution (Plomin, Owen, & McGuffin, 1994). In this quantitative trait loci (QTL) model many genes are hypothesized to be involved in the development of any behaviour pattern, and these genes are thought to act in a probabilistic manner. There has been slow progress in identifying QTLs, as they are neither sufficient nor necessary to cause extreme behavioural outcome. They can be said to act together with other risk or protective genes to increase or reduce the risk of disorder. Furthermore, risk genes may have to be combined with environmental risk before a clinically significant outcome is produced (Moffitt, Caspi, & Rutter, 2005).

Genes regulating serotonergic neurotransmission, in particular monoamine oxidase A (MAOA), have been highlighted in the search for a genetic predisposition to antisocial behaviour (Lesch, 2003). The MAOA gene is a well-characterized functional polymorphism consisting of a variable number of tandem repeats in the promoter region, with high-activity (MAOA-H) and low-activity variants (MAOA-L). The MAOA-H variant is associated with lower concentration of intracellular serotonin, whereas the MAOA-L variant is associated with higher concentration of intracellular serotonin. Recent research suggests that genetic vulnerability to antisocial behaviour conferred by the MAOA-L may only become evident in the presence of an environmental trigger, such as maltreatment (Caspi et al., 2002; Kim-Cohen et al., 2006). This research highlights the possibility that increased serotonin availability (often associated with anxiety) in the MAOA-L carriers may serve to increase an individual's vulnerability to environmental risk. The MAOA-L findings appear to be more relevant for the AB/CU− subtype. No molecular genetic studies on CU type of antisocial behaviour exist to date.

Despite the demonstration of genetic influences on individual differences in antisocial behaviour, it is important to note that no genes *for* antisocial behaviour exist. Instead genes code for neurocognitive vulnerability that may in turn increase risk for antisocial behaviour. Thus, although genetic risk alone may be of little consequence for behaviour in favourable conditions, the genetic vulnerability may still manifest at the level of brain/cognition. Imaging genetics studies attest to genotype differences being evident in the brain structure and function in nonclinical samples (Meyer-Lindenberg & Weinberger, 2006). We can think of this as the neural fingerprint, ready to translate into disordered behaviour in the presence of unfortunate triggers. Meyer-Lindenberg and colleagues recently provided the first demonstration of the MAOA-L genotype being associated with a pattern of neural hypersensitivity to emotional stimuli (Meyer-Lindenberg et al., 2006). Specifically they reported increased amygdala activity coupled with lesser activity in the frontal regulatory regions in MAOA-L than in MAOA-H carriers. A recent paper provides further support for the view that a link between the MAOA-L allele and aggression is partly mediated by this pattern of neural hypersensitivity to emotional stimuli (Eisenberger, Way, Taylor, Welch, & Lieberman, in press).

New directions: Imaging genetics of AB/CU + and AB/CU−

Meyer-Lindenberg et al. (2006) speculate that their brain-imaging findings of poor emotion regulation in MAOA-L carriers relate to threat reactive and impulsive, rather than CU-type antisocial, behaviour. This conclusion is based on the observed amygdala hypo- rather than hyperreactivity in AB/CU+ individuals (Birbaumer et al., 2005; Kiehl et al., 2001). It is thus important to address the potential moderating role of CU on the brain reactivity associated with antisocial behaviour.

A small number of studies have reported increased vulnerability to antisocial behaviour in the presence of the MAOA-H allele (e.g., Manuck, Flory, Ferrell, Mann, & Muldoon, 2000). These may reflect false positive findings, but it is also possible to speculate that the amygdala hypo- as opposed to hyperreactivity seen in CU individuals could be influenced by MAOA-H rather than MAOA-L genotype. This suggestion remains highly speculative, and as for any behaviour, the genetic influences will not be limited to a single candidate gene.

As imaging genetic work on antisocial behaviour is currently in its infancy it has a great opportunity to incorporate lessons learned from the causal modelling tradition (Blair, 2006; Morton & Frith, 1995). We argue that it will be important to employ imaging and cognitive genomics strategies to study how genes to cognition pathways look for different subtypes of antisocial children. Currently such work is undertaken by our own group (using both twin design to measure heritability and measured genotype to estimate the contribution of individual gene effects) and others.

Practical implications

The research reviewed above suggests that there may be a particularly genetically vulnerable group of youngsters for whom early intervention is likely to be crucial to prevent life course persistent antisocial outcome. We would also like to highlight that prevention and treatment strategies should take into account the different aetiologies of subgroups of antisocial and violent children. Aetiologically heterogeneous samples may explain why intervention programmes can sometimes have mixed results on their success (Frick, 2001; Hawes & Dadds, 2005). Some children seem to respond to well-timed, early prevention and treatment while others do not. We would suggest that the root of this may lie in aetiological differences, particularly differences in cognitive profile of different conduct problem subtypes. The modest to moderate success of intervention programmes may reflect a high success rate with a particular subtype. Frick (2001) has emphasized that while there are prevention programmes available that address the needs of primarily impulsive antisocial behaviour, less is known about possible prevention and treatment of antisocial behaviour in the callous-unemotional subtype.

Research on environmental risk factors within behavioural genetic designs has highlighted a number of important issues. It is more than likely that for children with a vulnerable genotype, this genotype will react with risk environments. Furthermore, at least one of the parents will share the risk genes for antisocial behaviour and is thus more likely to either directly or indirectly contribute to a less than optimal rearing environment. As the parent or parents with the antisocial genotype are not often willing or capable of engaging in efforts for prevention and treatment, these families present a particular challenge for professionals engaged in preventing future, on-going cycle of violence. However, recent successes with nurse visit programmes in breaking the association between maltreatment and antisocial behaviour suggest that genetic risk can be effectively moderated by environmental intervention (Eckenrode et al., 2001; Olds et al., 1997). Some children may only require "milder" environmental risk factors to go down the antisocial path, perhaps due to genetic vulnerability. It is particularly challenging to map out the cognitive profile of these children and make predictions about treatment approaches that capitalize on what is known about cognitive strengths and weaknesses.

For example, children with psychopathic tendencies are strong on self-interest and get motivated by rewards, but do not characteristically process others' distress or react to punishment. These are cognitive strengths and limitations that have to be worked with to produce change in behaviour.

As a final note, behavioural genetic research should caution against entertaining ideas of gene therapy for antisocial behaviour. Genes that have variants that are common in the population are more than likely to have multiple functions, some of which are desirable, others not. Hence, a risk gene may have many functions over and above increasing risk for disorder. When this information is combined with the fact that genes interact in complex systems, as well as with environmental risk factors, it seems pertinent to conclude that removing the effects of one gene via gene therapy is unlikely to be effective (Nuffield Council on Bioethics, 2002).

This does not mean that genotype information will be irrelevant for therapeutic intervention. For example, demonstration of genetically (and consequently cognitively) heterogeneous subtypes of early-onset antisocial behaviour suggests the possibility of subtype-specific risk gene variants that index a risk for different cognitive deficits. An early knowledge of such risk genes may come to guide prevention efforts prior to the emergence of clear, overt behavioural markers for the disorder. As cognitive-behavioural approaches are likely to feature strongly in the antisocial behaviour intervention, developing better understanding of the genes–brain–cognition–behaviour pathways for particular subtypes—especially within longitudinal, developmental framework—could provide crucial insights for intervention.

Summary

One might argue that since we have behavioural tools for reliably indexing who exhibits AB/CU+ and who has an AB/CU− profile, then what do we need causal models and cognitive accounts for? One extremely useful outcome of a well-articulated model is that it enables specific, testable predictions that go beyond available data and guides further research. This notion is particularly pertinent when thinking about combining different levels of analyses to study development of antisocial behaviour. It will also be important for thinking about treatment approaches. Uta Frith's work on developmental disorders has been extremely important in guiding the current multidisciplinary work on different subtypes of antisocial behaviour. The data from genetic, brain, and cognitive studies to date suggest that AB/CU+ individuals are genetically more vulnerable to antisocial behaviour than are their AB/CU− peers. Adults with AB/CU+ show amygdala hyporeactivity to emotional stimuli, while there is some suggestion that AB/CU− may show the opposite pattern. When compared with each other, AB/CU+ children demonstrate hyposensitivity to others' distress, while AB/CU− children are hypersensitive to anger. New research combining different levels of analyses will no doubt provide further insight about the AB/CU+ versus AB/CU− distinction.

REFERENCES

American Psychiatric Association. (1994). *Diagnostic and statistical manual of mental disorders* (4th ed.). Washington, DC: Author.

Bailey, S. (2002). Violent children: A framework for assessment. *Advances in Psychiatric Treatment, 8*, 97–106.

Barry, C., Frick, P., DeShazo, T., McCoy, M., Ellis, M., & Loney, B. (2000). The importance of callous-unemotional traits for extending the concept of psychopathy to children. *Journal of Abnormal Psychology, 109*, 335–351.

Birbaumer, N., Veit, R., Lotze, M., Erb, M., Hermann, C., Grodd, W., et al. (2005). Deficient fear conditioning in psychopathy: A functional magnetic resonance imaging study. *Archives of General Psychiatry, 62*, 799–805.

Blair, R. J. R. (2006). The emergence of psychopathy: Implications for the neuropsychological approach to developmental disorders. *Cognition, 101*, 414–442.

Blair, R. J. R., & Frith, U. (2000). Neuro-cognitive explanations of the antisocial personality disorders. *Criminal Behaviour and Mental Health, 10*, S66–S82.

Blair, R. J. R., Peschardt, K. S., Budhani, S., Mitchell, D. G. V., & Pine, D. S. (2006). The development of psychopathy. *Journal of Child Psychology & Psychiatry, 47*, 262–275.

Blonigen, D. M., Hicks, B. M., Krueger, R. F., Patrick, C. J., & Iacono, W. G. (2005). Psychopathic personality traits: Heritability and genetic overlap with internalizing and externalizing psychopathology. *Psychological Medicine, 35*, 637–648.

Caspi, A., McClay, J., Moffitt, T., Mill, J., Martin, J., Craig, I. W., et al. (2002). Role of genotype in the cycle of violence in maltreated children. *Science, 297*, 851–854.

Dadds, M. R., Fraser, J., Frost, A., & Hawes, D. (2005). Disentangling the underlying dimensions of psychopathy and conduct problems in childhood: A community study. *Journal of Consulting and Clinical Psychology, 73*, 400–410.

Dadds, M. R., Perry, D. J., Hawes, D. J., Merz, S., Riddell, A. C., Haines, D. J. et al. (2006). Attention to the eyes and fear-recognition deficits in child psychopathy. *British Journal of Psychiatry, 189*, 280–281.

Davidson, R. J., Putnam, K. M., & Larson, C. L. (2000). Dysfunction in the neural circuitry of emotion regulation: A possible prelude to violence. *Science, 289*, 591–594.

Eckenrode, J., Zielinski, D., Smith, E., Marcynyszyn, L. A., Henderson, C. R., Jr., Kitzman, H., et al. (2001). Child maltreatment and the early onset of problem behaviors: Can a program of nurse home visitation break the link? *Development and Psychopathology, 13*, 873–890.

Eisenberger, N. I., Way, B. M., Taylor, S. E., Welch, W. T., & Lieberman, M. D. (in press). Understanding genetic risk for aggression: Clues from the brain's response to social exclusion. *Biological Psychiatry*.

Farrington, D. (2000). Psychosocial predictors of adult antisocial personality and adult convictions. *Behavioral Sciences & the Law, 18*, 605–622.

Forth, A. E., Kosson, D. S., & Hare, R. D. (2003). *The Psychopathy Checklist: Youth Version.* Toronto, Ontario, Canada: Multi-Health Systems.

Frick, P. J. (2001). Effective interventions for children and adolescents with conduct disorder. *Canadian Journal of Psychiatry, 46*, 597–608.

Frick, P. J., Cornell, A. H., Bodin, S. D., Dane, H. E., Barry, C. T., & Loney, B. R. (2003). Callous-unemotional traits and developmental pathways to severe conduct problems. *Developmental Psychology*, *39*, 246–260.

Frick, P. J., & Marsee, M. A. (2006). Psychopathy and developmental pathways to antisocial behavior in youth. In C. J. Patrick (Ed.), *Handbook of psychopathy*. (pp. 353–374). New York: Guilford.

Frick, P. J., Stickle, T. R., Dandreaux, D. M., Farrell, J. M., & Kimonis, E. R. (2005). Callous-unemotional traits in predicting the severity and stability of conduct problems and delinquency. *Journal of Abnormal Child Psychology*, *33*, 471–487.

Frith, U., & Happé, F. (1998). Why specific developmental disorders are not specific: On-line and developmental effect in autism and dyslexia. *Developmental Science*, *1*, 267–272.

Hariri, A., Tessitore, A., Mattay, V., Fera, F., & Weinberger, D. (2002). The amygdala response to emotional stimuli: A comparison of faces and scenes. *Neuroimage*, *17*, 317–323.

Hawes, D. J., & Dadds, M. R. (2005). The treatment of conduct problems in children with callous-unemotional traits. *Journal of Consulting & Clinical Psychology*, *73*, 737–741.

Herba, C., & Phillips, M. L. (2004). Annotation: Development of facial expression recognition from childhood to adolescence: Behavioural and neurological perspectives. *Journal of Child Psychology and Psychiatry and Allied Disciplines*, *45*, 1–14.

Kiehl, K. A., Smith, A. M., Hare, R. D., Mendrek, A., Forster, B. B., Brink, J., et al. (2001). Limbic abnormalities in affective processing by criminal psychopaths as revealed by functional magnetic resonance imaging. *Biological Psychiatry*, *50*, 677–684.

Kim-Cohen, J., Caspi, A., Taylor, A., Williams, B., Newcombe, R., Craig, I. W., et al. (2006). MAOA, maltreatment, and gene-environment interaction predicting children's mental health: New evidence and a meta-analysis. *Molecular Psychiatry*, *11*, 903–913.

Krug, E., Dahlberg, L., Mercy, J., Zwi, A., & Lozarno, R. (2002). *World report on violence and health*. Geneva, Switzerland: World Health Organization.

Larsson, H., Andershed, H., & Lichtenstein, P. (2006). A genetic factor explains most of the variation in the psychopathic personality. *Journal of Abnormal Psychology*, *115*, 221–260.

Lesch, K. P. (2003). The serotonergic dimension of aggression and violence. In M. P. Mattson (Ed.), *Neurobiology of aggression*. Totowa, NJ: Humana Press.

Loeber, R., Burke, J. D., & Lahey, B. B. (2002). What are adolescent antecedents to antisocial personality disorder? *Criminal Behaviour and Mental Health*, *12*, 24–36.

Loney, B. R., Frick, P. J., Clements, C. B., Ellis, M. L., & Kerlin, K. (2003). Callous-unemotional traits, impulsivity, and emotional processing in antisocial adolescents. *Journal of Clinical Child and Adolescent Psychology*, *32*, 66–80.

Manuck, S. B., Flory, J. D., Ferrell, R. E., Mann, J. J., & Muldoon, M. F. (2000). A regulatory polymorphism of the monoamine oxidase: A gene may be associated with variability in aggression, impulsivity, and central nervous system serotonergic responsivity. *Psychiatry Research*, *95*, 9–23.

Maughan, B., Rowe, R., Messer, J., Goodman, R., & Meltzer, H. (2004). Conduct disorder and oppositional defiant disorder in a national sample: Developmental epidemiology. *Journal of Child Psychology and Psychiatry*, *45*, 609–621.

Meyer-Lindenberg, A., Buckholtz, J. W., Kolachana, B., Hariri, A. R., Pezawas, L., Blasi, G., et al. (2006). Neural mechanisms of genetic risk for impulsivity and violence in humans. *Proceedings of the National Academy of Sciences of the United States of America*, *103*, 6269–6274.

Meyer-Lindenberg, A., & Weinberger, D. (2006). Intermediate phenotypes and genetic mechanisms of psychiatric disorders. *Nature Review Neuroscience*, *7*, 818–827.

Moffitt, T. E. (2003). Life-course-persistent and adolescence-limited antisocial behavior. In B. B. Lahey, T. E. Moffitt, & A. Caspi (Eds.), *Causes of conduct disorder and juvenile delinquency* (pp. 49–75). New York: Guilford Press.

Moffitt, T. E. (2005). Genetic and environmental influences on antisocial behaviors: Evidence from behavioral-genetic research. *Advances in Genetics*, *55*, 41–104.

Moffitt, T. E., Caspi, A., & Rutter, M. (2005). Strategy for investigating interactions between measured genes and measured environments. *Archives of General Psychiatry*, *62*, 473–481.

Morton, J., & Frith, U. (1995). Causal modeling: A structural approach to developmental psychopathology. In D. Cicchetti & D. J. Cohen (Eds.), *Developmental psychopathology: Vol. 1. Theory and methods* (pp. 357–390). Oxford, UK: John Wiley & Sons.

Nuffield Council on Bioethics. (2002). *Genetics and human behaviour: The ethical context*. London: Author.

Olds, D. L., Eckenrode, J., Henderson, C. R., Jr., Kitzman, H., Powers, J., Cole, R., et al. (1997). Long-term effects of home visitation on maternal life course and child abuse and neglect. Fifteen-year follow-up of a randomized trial. *Journal of the American Medical Academy, 278*, 637–643.

Oxford, M., Cavell, T., & Hughes, J. (2003). Callous-unemotional traits moderate the relation between ineffective parenting and child externalizing problems: A partial replication and extension. *Journal of Clinical Child & Adolescent Psychology, 32*, 577–585.

Pardini, D. A., Lochman, J. E., & Frick, P. J. (2003). Callous/unemotional traits and social-cognitive processes in adjudicated youths. *Journal of the American Academy of Child & Adolescent Psychiatry, 42*, 364–371.

Plomin, R., DeFries, J., McClearn, G., & McGuffin, P. (2000). *Behavioral genetics* (4th ed.). New York: Worth Publishers.

Plomin, R., Owen, M. J., & McGuffin, P. (1994). The genetic basis of complex human behaviors. *Science, 264*, 1733–1739.

Pollak, S. D., & Sinha, P. (2002). Effects of early experience on children's recognition of facial displays of emotion. *Developmental Psychology, 38*, 784–791.

Rhee, S. H., & Waldman, I. D. (2002). Genetic and environmental influences on antisocial behavior: A meta-analysis of twin and adoption studies. *Psychological Bulletin, 128*, 490–529.

Sterzer, P., Stadler, C., Krebs, A., Kleinschmidt, A., & Poutska, F. (2005). Abnormal neural response to emotional visual stimuli in adolescents with conduct disorder. *Biological Psychiatry, 57*, 7–15.

Taylor, J., Loney, B. R., Bobadilla, L., Iacono, W. G., & McGue, M. (2003). Genetic and environmental influences on psychopathy trait dimensions in a community sample of male twins. *Journal of Abnormal Child Psychology, 31*, 633–645.

Viding, E., Blair, R. J. R., Moffitt, T. E., & Plomin, R. (2005). Evidence for substantial genetic risk for psychopathy in 7-year-olds. *Journal of Child Psychology & Psychiatry, 46*, 592–597.

Viding, E., & Frith, U. (2006). Genes for susceptibility to violence lurk in the brain. *Proceedings of the National Academy of Sciences of the United States of America, 103*, 6085–6086.

Viding, E., Jones, A. P., Frick, P., Moffitt, T. E., & Plomin, R. (in press). Heritability of antisocial behaviour at age nine: Do callous-unemotional traits matter? *Developmental Science*.

Wootton, J. M., Frick, P. J., Shelton, K. K., & Silverthorn, P. (1997). Ineffective parenting and childhood conduct problems: The moderating role of callous-unemotional traits. *Journal of Consulting & Clinical Psychology, 65*, 301–308.

SUBJECT INDEX